MONTESQUIEU

A number of Montesquieu's lesser-known discourses, dissertations, and dialogues are made available to a wider audience, for the first time fully translated and annotated in English. The views they incorporate on politics, economics, science, and religion shed light on the overall development of his political and moral thought. They enable us better to understand not just Montesquieu's importance as a political philosopher studying forms of government, but also his stature as a moral philosopher seeking to remind us of our duties while injecting deeper moral concerns into politics and international relations. They reveal that Montesquieu's vision for the future was remarkably clear: more science and less superstition; greater understanding of our moral duties; enhanced concern for justice; increased emphasis on moral principles in the conduct of domestic and international politics; toleration of conflicting religious viewpoints; commerce over war, and liberty over despotism as the proper goals for mankind.

DAVID W. CARRITHERS is the Adolph Ochs Professor Emeritus of Government at the University of Tennessee at Chattanooga.

PHILIP STEWART is the Benjamin E. Powell Professor Emeritus of Romance Studies at Duke University.

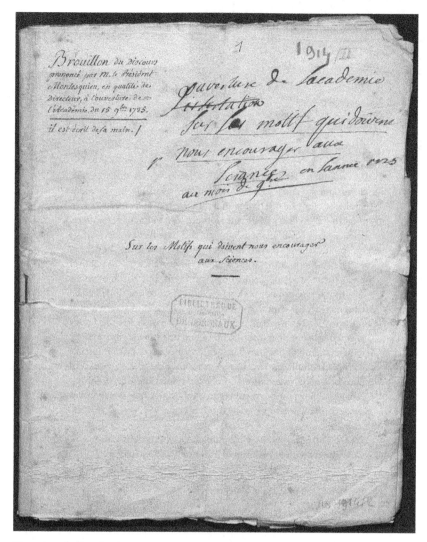

Ouverture de l'academie
Sur les mottif qui doivent nous encourager aux sciance
en lannee 1725 au mois de 9bre

Title in Montesquieu's hand of the manuscript of *On the Motives that Should Encourage Us Toward the Sciences* (Bibliothèque Municipale de Bordeaux, Ms. 1914). Other writing on the page is in the hand of François de Lamontaigne, secretary of the Bordeaux Academy where the discourse was delivered.

MONTESQUIEU

⋆

Discourses, Dissertations, and Dialogues on Politics, Science, and Religion

Edited and Translated by
DAVID W. CARRITHERS
University of Tennessee, Chattanooga
and
PHILIP STEWART
Duke University

Introduction and Notes by
DAVID W. CARRITHERS

CAMBRIDGE
UNIVERSITY PRESS

CAMBRIDGE
UNIVERSITY PRESS

University Printing House, Cambridge CB2 8BS, United Kingdom

One Liberty Plaza, 20th Floor, New York, NY 10006, USA

477 Williamstown Road, Port Melbourne, VIC 3207, Australia

314–321, 3rd Floor, Plot 3, Splendor Forum, Jasola District Centre, New Delhi – 110025, India

79 Anson Road, #06–04/06, Singapore 079906

Cambridge University Press is part of the University of Cambridge.

It furthers the University's mission by disseminating knowledge in the pursuit of education, learning, and research at the highest international levels of excellence.

www.cambridge.org
Information on this title: www.cambridge.org/9781108841467
DOI: 10.1017/9781108882521

© Cambridge University Press 2020

First published 2020

Printed in the United Kingdom by TJ Books Limited, Padstow Cornwall

A catalogue record for this publication is available from the British Library.

Library of Congress Cataloging-in-Publication Data
NAMES: Montesquieu, Charles Louis de Secondat, baron de, 1689–1755. | Carrithers, David W, 1943– editor. | Stewart, Philip, 1940– editor.
TITLE: Montesquieu : Discourses, Dissertations, and Dialogues on Politics, Science, and Religion [edited and translated by] David W. Carrithers, University of Tennessee, Chattanooga, and Philip Stewart, Duke University.
DESCRIPTION: Cambridge, United Kingdom ; New York, NY : Cambridge University Press, 2020. | Series: The Cambridge history of political thought | Includes index. | Translated from French.
IDENTIFIERS: LCCN 2020022960 (print) | LCCN 2020022961 (ebook) | ISBN 9781108841467 (hardback) | ISBN 9781108794855 (ebook)
SUBJECTS: LCSH: Political science – Philosophy. | Philosophy, French – 18th century.
CLASSIFICATION: LCC JC179 .M67513 2020 (print) | LCC JC179 (ebook) | DDC 320.01–dc23
LC record available at https://lccn.loc.gov/2020022960
LC ebook record available at https://lccn.loc.gov/2020022961

ISBN 978-1-108-84146-7 Hardback
ISBN 978-1-108-79485-5 Paperback

Contents

Contents

Abbreviations

Catalogue	*Catalogue de la bibliothèque de La Brède* and *Bibliothèque virtuelle Montesquieu*, ed. Catherine Volpilhac-Auger, 2016. Online: http://montesquieu.huma-num.fr/biblio theque/introduction
Chardin	Jean Chardin, *Voyages de Monsieur le chevalier Chardin en Perse et autres lieux de l'Orient*, 10 vols. (Amsterdam: Delorme, 1711); *Catalogue* 2739. Online: www.achemenet.com/dotAsset/ 738b64dc-7dc9-4d4b-8a8c-90adb6fd78ee.pdf
DM	*Dictionnaire Montesquieu*, ed. Catherine Volpilhac-Auger. Online: http://dictionnaire-montesquieu.ens-lyon.fr/en/ home/
Encyclopédie	*Encyclopédie ou Dictionnaire raisonné des sciences, des arts et des métiers*, ed. Denis Diderot and Jean Le Rond D'Alembert, 17 vols. plus 11 vols. plates, 1751–1765. Online: https://encyclopedie.uchicago.edu/
(M)	Text preceding this sign is a note by Montesquieu.
Mélanges inédits	*Mélanges inédits de Montesquieu*, ed. Henri Barckhausen (Bordeaux: G. Gounouilhou and Paris: J. Rouam, 1892). Online: https://archive.org/details/melangesinditoo mont/page/n21
OC	Montesquieu, *Œuvres complètes*, critical edition in progress by the Société Montesquieu (Oxford: Voltaire Foundation, 1998–2008; Lyon and Paris: ENS Éditions and Classiques Garnier, 2010–).
Pensées	Montesquieu, *Mes pensées*. *OC* xiv–xv (in preparation).[1]

---

1 There is a complete English translation by Henry C. Clark, entitled *My Thoughts* (Indianapolis: Liberty Fund, 2012). Online: https://oll.libertyfund.org/titles/montes quieu-my-thoughts-mes-pensees-1720-2012

PL	Montesquieu, *Lettres persanes*. *OC* I (2004).[2]
RM	*Revue Montesquieu*, ed. Catherine Volpilhac-Auger, 8 vols. (Lyon: Société Montesquieu and UMR Lire, 1997–2006). Online: http://montesquieu.ens-lyon.fr/spip.php?rubrique21
Romans	Montesquieu, *Considérations sur les causes de la grandeur des Romains et de leur décadence*, ed. Françoise Weil and Cecil Courtney. *OC* II (2000).[3]
SL	Montesquieu, *De l'esprit des lois*. *OC* V–VI (in preparation).[4]
Spicilège	Montesquieu, *Spicilège*, ed. Rolando Minuti and Salvatore Rotta. *OC* XIII (2002).
Trévoux	*Dictionnaire universel français et latin*, known as *Dictionnaire de Trévoux* (fourth edition, 6 vols., 1743).

---

2 The only English print edition which uses the same letter numbering as the *OC* edition (i.e., that of the original edition of 1721) is *Persian Letters*, trans. Margaret Mauldon (Oxford: Oxford World Classics, 2008). A new translation of that same version by Philip Stewart is available on the website of the Société Montesquieu: http://montesquieu.ens-lyon.fr/spip.php?rubrique245

3 There is a complete published translation: *Considerations on the Causes of the Greatness of the Romans and their Decline*, trans. David Lowenthal (Indianapolis: Hackett, 1999).

4 There are two modern translations: Anne M. Cohler, Basia C. Miller, and Harold S. Stone (trans.), *The Spirit of the Laws* (Cambridge: Cambridge University Press, 1989) and Philip Stewart (trans.), *The Spirit of Law*, online: http://montesquieu.ens-lyon.fr/spip.php?rubrique186. With respect to the serious flaws of the contemporaneous English translation (1750), see Philip Stewart, "On the Nugent Translation of *L'Esprit des lois*," *History of Political Thought* 39(1) (2018), 83–106.

A General Note on the Texts

All translations of Montesquieu are our own and are based on the definitive texts established for the ongoing French edition of the complete works (see *OC* in the List of Abbreviations), used by permission of the Société Montesquieu. We also have sometimes benefited from the annotation supplied by the various editors for those volumes.

Few of the texts presented here were published during Montesquieu's lifetime; most remained in manuscript (some autograph and some recopied by secretaries) in the safekeeping of Montesquieu's son, Jean-Baptiste de Secondat (1716–1795), at La Brède or in Bordeaux. In 1818, Joseph Cyrille de Secondat, baron de Montesquieu (1748–1829), son of Montesquieu's daughter Denise, shipped a large number of manuscripts held at La Brède to Montesquieu's other grandson, Charles Louis de Montesquieu (1749–1824), son of Jean-Baptiste, who resided in England. A Catalogue of these manuscripts was made in which the various cartons are described, often repeating notations left on them by the author himself.[5] Eight of the titles included in translation in this volume are identifiable among the manuscripts on that list. One, it is specified, *Reflections on Universal Monarchy in Europe*, is a printed book.[6] The *Treatise on Duties* is described as *mis au net*, which means it is a clean copy, doubtless made by a secretary. The *Dialogue between Xanthippus and Xenocrates* and *Reflections on the Character of Certain Princes* are stated to be autographs; so is *Considerations on the Wealth of Spain*.

Six years later many of the papers which had been sent to England were burned,[7] and in 1828 those that survived were recovered and brought back to

---

5 This document, labeled *Catalogue des manuscrits envoyés à mon cousin en Angleterre*, is reproduced in the André Masson edition of Montesquieu, *Œuvres complètes* (Paris: Nagel, 1950), III, 1575–1581.

6 A note attached, in Montesquieu's hand, asserts: "This was printed from a bad copy; I am having it reprinted from another according to the corrections I have made on it."

7 Prosper simply notes: "A part of these manuscripts were burned by my uncle, with very few exceptions."

La Brède by Joseph Cyrille's son Prosper de Secondat, baron de Montesquieu (1797–1871). He added his own summary of that shipment with, for the shorter works, descriptions so brief[8] that they cannot serve for positive identification (for example a carton labeled: "Duties, laws, reputation"), and he conflated them with other papers which he said had been willed directly to him or he had found at La Brède or in Bordeaux. Many remained there into the twentieth century.

The problems this history raises for the history of the texts is best exemplified by the fate of the *Treatise on Duties*. The catalogue of 1818 describes what can only have been a rather well fleshed-out work, the chapters of which are specifically delineated: (1) duties in general; (2) on God; (3) on our duties toward men; (4) on justice; (5) on some philosophical principles; (6) on the Stoics' principles; (7) the habit of justice; (8) imitation of the previous chapter; (9) gross ambiguity of the word justice; (10) the duties of men; (11) on some examples of the violation of man's duties; (12) what we owe to the Christian religion, for having given us equity for all men; (13) on politics; (14) on the limited utility of politics. Exactly how much of this structure survived its return to La Brède in 1828 is impossible to determine; the most evident anomaly concerns items 13 and 14, which appear to have been detached to form *On Politics*, which we include as a separate text in our volume. Certain of their titles intersect with parts of the *Pensées*, as we shall indicate below, but this is not in itself surprising, since *Mes pensées* had been a sort of repository of items to be included, if possible, in other works. But often we can no longer tell whether such a dissection and recombination was performed by Montesquieu or by someone else.

More details on individual manuscripts are provided in the headers to the separate texts.

---

8 *Œuvres complètes de Montesquieu*, ed. André Masson, 3 vols. (Paris: Nagel, 1950–1955), III, 1581–1582.

Introduction

Few *philosophes* of the Enlightenment received such accolades as Charles Louis de Secondat, Baron de Montesquieu et de la Brède (1689–1755) following publication of his *Spirit of Law* (1748),[1] the product, he said, of twenty years' study. Charles de Brosses, noted author and magistrate in Dijon, was moved to say, "What a fine work! How many ideas, what fire, what precision [. . .], what new and luminous thoughts." Across the Channel David Hume proclaimed Montesquieu an "author of great genius, as well as extensive learning" and concluded he had produced "the best system of political knowledge that, perhaps, has ever been communicated to the world." Montesquieu's work, he predicted, would be regarded as "the wonder of all centuries." Edmund Burke was similarly awed and called Montesquieu "a genius not born in every country, or every time [. . .] with an herculean robustness of mind." Charles Bonnet in Geneva wrote Montesquieu to proclaim, "Newton discovered the laws of the material world. You, Monsieur, have discovered the laws of the intelligent world."[2] In Italy, Cesare Beccaria and Gaetano Filangieri singled out Montesquieu's views on crime and punishment for praise, and Scottish theorists Lord Kames, Adam Smith, Adam Ferguson, John Millar, and William Robertson were deeply influenced by Montesquieu's economic thought and by his discussion of stages of economic growth in particular. In Russia,

---

1 Montesquieu's title *De l'esprit des lois* is often given in English as *The Spirit of the Laws*, with a second definite article, though Thomas Nugent's translation published in 1750 and often reprinted was titled *The Spirit of Laws*. The translation cited in this volume with the abbreviation *SL* (see List of Abbreviations) is rather *The Spirit of Law*.
2 Charles de Brosses to Charles Loppin de Gemeaux, 24 Feb. 1749 (Yvonne Bezard, "Le President de Brosses d'après une correspondence," *Revue d'Histoire Littéraire de la France* [1923], 349); David Hume, *An Enquiry Concerning the Principles of Morals* (London, 1751), p. 54; Edmund Burke, *An Appeal from the New to the Old Whigs* (3rd edition, London: J. Dodsley, 1791), pp. 139–140; Bonnet to Montesquieu, 14 Nov. 1753, to appear in Montesquieu, *OC* XXI.

Catherine the Great turned to Montesquieu's treatise on laws when she sought to revamp her country's legal code.

Reactions in France were similarly laudatory. By 1757 fifteen editions of *The Spirit of Law* had appeared, and that number climbed to twenty-eight by 1789.[3] Voltaire termed *The Spirit of Law* "the code of reason and liberty." Montesquieu, he asserted, "reminds men that they are free; he shows mankind the rights it has lost in most of the world, he combats superstition, he inspires good morals."[4] Rousseau termed Montesquieu "a glorious genius" and imbibed much inspiration from his discussions of republics.[5] The brilliant mathematician and *encyclopédiste* Jean Le Rond D'Alembert awarded him "the finest title which a wise man can merit, that of legislator of nations."[6] The physiocrat Victor Riqueti, marquis de Mirabeau, author of *L'Ami des hommes* (1756), found in *The Spirit of Law* a work deserving of "deep meditation," a work "where all the ideas on all the types of law are assembled, and of which we will never be more than feeble commentators."[7] For the Swiss transplant to France Benjamin Constant, whose many works displayed Montesquieu's influence, the most apt compliment was to proclaim that "everything he said, even the smallest things, is verified daily."[8]

Montesquieu's merit was also recognized in America. "He was in his particular science what Bacon was in universal science," opined James Madison. "He lifted the veil from the venerable errors which enslaved opinion, and pointed the way to those luminous truths of which he had but a glimpse himself."[9] And Madison strongly endorsed the need to separate legislative, executive, and judicial powers in order to avoid tyranny.[10] Both Thomas Jefferson and John Adams compiled detailed notes while reading *The Spirit of Law*. Jefferson remarked that whereas *The Wealth of Nations* was the "best book extant," *The Spirit of Law* was the most "recommended" book "in

---

3 See Cecil Patrick Courtney, "*L'Esprit des lois* dans la perspective de l'histoire du livre (1748–1800)," in Michel Porret and Catherine Volpilhac-Auger (eds.), *Le Temps de Montesquieu* (Geneva: Droz, 2002), pp. 65–96.
4 Voltaire, *L'ABC*, in *Philosophical Dictionary*, trans. Peter Gay (New York: Harcourt, Brace, 1962), p. 509.
5 Rousseau, *Social Contract*, Book III, chapter 4.
6 Jean Le Rond D'Alembert, *Éloge de M. de Montesquieu* (1755), in *Encyclopédie*, v (1755), p. viii.
7 *L'Ami des hommes, ou traité de la population* (Avignon, 1758), I, ch. vii, p. 153.
8 Benjamin Constant, *Œuvres*, ed. Alfred Roulin (Paris: Gallimard, 1957), p. 261.
9 Madison, "Spirit of Governments" (1792), in *Letters and Other Writings of James Madison* (New York: R. Worthington, 1884), IV, p. 474.
10 *The Federalist* 47.

the science of government,"[11] and Adams learned from Montesquieu that a nation's customs, traditions, and national character greatly affect its prospects for liberty. Alexander Hamilton welcomed Montesquieu's views on the need for strong executive power, and to bolster confidence in the future of the newly created United States of America he quoted, in *Federalist 9*, Montesquieu's discussion of how federal republics augment power and security.

The Spirit of Law was an instant classic. In the half-century after its publication anyone claiming expertise in matters of politics or economics needed to be conversant with its principal theses, including Montesquieu's classificatory scheme of governments, identifying virtue as the driving force of republics, honor of monarchies, and fear of despotisms; the role of commerce in contributing to national wealth while simultaneously fostering peace; and his contention that the laws each nation devises for itself reflect the complex interaction of both physical and moral causes that produce a unique general spirit (*esprit général*), making it unlikely that a political regime ideally suited to a particular country can be transported to another.

Montesquieu's vision for the future, as is evident in the texts translated for this volume, was remarkably clear and prescient: more science and less superstition; greater understanding of our duties as humans; enhanced concern for justice in both public and private affairs; more fairness in criminal trials; moderation in punishments; increased emphasis on moral principles in the conduct of domestic and international politics; toleration of conflicting religious viewpoints; commerce not war, and liberty not despotism as the proper goals for mankind. Far from teaching "whatever is, is right," as has sometimes been alleged, Montesquieu's writings epitomize the concerns of an enlightened moralist, economist, and political scientist to reform existing abuses. It is no wonder, then, that the lines of his influence have radiated far and wide down to the present day.

Given Montesquieu's stature, it is surprising that very few of his shorter discourses, dissertations, and dialogues have been translated into English. It is the purpose of this volume to remedy this situation and the purpose of this Introduction to suggest what can be learned from these works. In order to stress thematic linkages, the twenty-one texts translated for this volume have been arranged under the seven headings described below.

---

11 Jefferson to Thomas Mann Randolph, 30 May 1790, in *The Writings of Thomas Jefferson*, 20 vols. (Washington: Thomas Jefferson Memorial Association, 1907), VIII, p. 31.

The Uses of Science

Part I of the volume consists of two essays, *On the Motives that Should Encourage Us toward the Sciences* (1725) and *Essay on the Causes that Can Affect Minds and Characters* (1736–1738). The first of these, read to the recently founded Bordeaux Academy of Sciences, Literature, and the Arts in November 1725, advocates accelerating the pace of scientific inquiry to build on the progress made in astronomy, physics, and physiology by such luminaries of the preceding two centuries as Copernicus, Kepler, Galileo, Gassendi, Descartes, Boerhaave, Boyle, and Newton. In addition to stressing the lasting intellectual pleasures of pursuing science and the practical benefits of science to mankind, Montesquieu emphasizes the important role of scientific learning in combating superstition. Had there been a Descartes in Mexico or Peru, he asserts, the natives of the New World would not have mistaken the Spanish invaders for their own gods returning to earth; rather they would have realized that they were merely men of very different appearance subject to the same laws of mortality as everyone else, and this realization would have enabled them to mount effective resistance.

The *Essay on the Causes that Can Affect Minds and Characters* (1736–1738) reveals the depth of Montesquieu's interest in science and in physiology in particular. At the Collège de Juilly, near Paris, which he attended from 1700 until 1705 (see Chronology at end of volume), the main areas of study were Latin and Roman history, but the natural sciences were by no means neglected, and Montesquieu would eventually become an active amateur scientist. After leaving Juilly and spending three years studying law at the University of Bordeaux, followed by four years' residence in Paris to gain practical experience in the law, he returned home to southwestern France in 1713, after his father's death, to take up new responsibilities as head of family and owner of the family château at La Brède. Nearby Bordeaux provided a favorable environment for nurturing his interest in science.

In April 1716 he was voted a member of the Bordeaux Academy, and the following September he established a prize for anatomical research. He soon became an enthusiastic participant in the Academy's activities and was elected its director for 1718, a post to which he was re-elected three more times. As director, he both summarized the views of others and offered his own on such subjects as the causes of echoes, the functioning of the renal glands, the reasons for the transparency of certain bodies, and the weight of matter, and during these years he purchased microscopes to examine the papillae on the tongue of a sheep in order to observe the effects of heat and cold on nerve endings. In 1721 he read a paper to the Academy entitled *Essay on Observations on Natural History* summarizing experiments he had conducted, assisted by his secretary abbé Bottereau-Duval, on both animal and plant species.

In his *Essay on the Causes* Montesquieu demonstrates a firm grasp of the physiological science of his day. The dominant theory, entrenched since the time of Galen (130–200 CE) and reflected in the writings of René Descartes (1596–1650), was that the body's nervous system consists of hollow nerve tubes carrying invisible "animal spirits" (*esprits animaux*) which are directed by the brain to the muscles to produce movement. These same animal spirits, when flowing in the opposite direction and pressing against the fibers of the brain, were thought to convey sense impressions and affect the passions. Like Descartes, Montesquieu viewed the body as a machine, and he concluded that it is the precise array and condition of our body's parts that affects the acuity of our brains and the nature of our emotions. When brain fibers become too thick, stupidity results; when they are too flexible, mental weakness ensues. And if the animal spirits are too abundant the result will be "inconstancy, eccentricity, [and] capriciousness" (p. 35).[12] Montesquieu explains why some persons are more affected by music than others and how certain chemicals, such as "a concoction of hemp," can produce "agreeable thoughts" and "intense pleasures" followed by "total dejection and a state approaching lethargy." He also analyzes why those who drink wine need increasing quantities to experience the same effects (p. 43).

The *Essay on the Causes* is important beyond the window it provides into the depth of Montesquieu's interest in physiology and brain functions. Here, the overall purpose was to explain that there are both physical causes (*causes physiques*) and moral causes (*causes morales*) affecting human behavior, with moral causes predominating. The cumulative effect of these influences produces a nation's general character, or spirit. He was convinced that climate and topography have a strong effect on human behavior – indeed the texts on the effect of climate in Book XIV of *The Spirit of Law* were originally part of the *Essay on the Causes* – but he believed moral causes exert greater influence than physical causes. The general spirit of the ancient Romans, for example, was ferocity, as is evident in their love of gladiatorial

12 Aware that he was treading a materialist path, Montesquieu later explained (*Pensées* 2035) that physicians and moralists have different views of the passions. Physicians emphasize the body's machinery, whereas moralists consider man rather as a spirit. "But man is equally composed of the two substances," he concludes, "each of which, by an ebb and flow, dominates and is dominated."

shows. Roman brutality, however, was not the result of climate or geography but was rather nurtured by such moral causes as their love of the glory attained through conquest and the power allotted to fathers to discipline both children and slaves. The text of the *Essay* dispels any notion that Montesquieu was a climatological determinist, a conclusion some have wrongly reached after a too-hasty reading of Book xiv of *The Spirit of Law*.

The Romans

Part ii of this volume is comprised of three essays assessing aspects of Roman politics, philosophy, and religion. Relying on Cicero's *On Divination* as his guide, Montesquieu explains in his *Dissertation on Roman Politics in Religion* (1716) that the Roman republic was designed by Romulus and the early kings of Rome as a theocracy. The goal of Roman paganism was "to inspire fear of the gods in a people who feared nothing, and to make use of that fear to lead them in any way they wished." Since the magistrates could control the omens, "they had a sure way of turning the people away from a war that would have been disastrous, or of making them undertake one that might have been useful. The soothsayers who followed the armies, and who were rather the interpreters of the generals than of the gods, inspired confidence in the soldiers" (p. 64). Montesquieu emphasizes that the Roman augurs were not a separate caste of priests but were instead state officials subservient to the senate; their reading of omens was designed to assist Roman consuls in achieving state goals (p. 64). As a result, their influence was benign, unlike that of the religious priesthood in Egypt that formed a "disorderly, restless, and enterprising" caste provoking discord and civil wars (p. 69). The *Dissertation* reflects Montesquieu's familiarity with Machiavelli's analysis of Roman paganism in his *Discourses on Livy* (1518 or 1519; published 1532) and presages the strikingly utilitarian approach to religion in Book xxiv of *The Spirit of Law*, a viewpoint that was censured by both Jesuit and Jansenist critics, prompting him to compose his *Defense of The Spirit of Law* (1750; this volume, pp. 224–263).

Montesquieu's *Discourse on Cicero* (c. 1717) is so panegyrical that he later decided it should be revised to include a more balanced account of Cicero's character, though no revision was ever made. Montesquieu expresses unstinting admiration for Cicero both as a statesman and as a philosopher, remarking that there is no other ancient he would rather have resembled and praising Cicero's *De officiis* (*Treatise on Duties*) for teaching us "what is honorable and beneficial, what we owe to society, what we owe to ourselves, and what we should do as heads of families or as citizens" (p. 74). Cicero emerges from the *Discourse* as the paragon of political virtue bravely opposing the threats posed to Roman liberty not only by Caesar and Marc Antony but also by Verres, Clodius, and Catiline. Moreover, Montesquieu lauds Cicero for teaching the need for virtuous conduct without indulging in preachy moralizing (pp. 74–75). Later, when he composes *On Politics* (1725) and *Reflections on the Character of Certain Princes and on Certain Events in their Life* (c. 1731–1733), he will adopt a similarly indirect approach to teaching morality. Rather than sermonizing, he will choose to demonstrate, through concrete historical examples, that duplicitous princes fare no better than princes whose conduct is moral.

The *Dialogue between Sulla and Eucrates* (1724) was judged so important by Montesquieu's contemporaries that, beginning with the 1748 edition of his *Considerations on [. . .] the Romans* (1734), it was included in eighteenth-century editions of that work as a companion piece to the longer work. It is not hard to understand Montesquieu's fascination with the career of Lucius Cornelius Sulla (138–78 BCE). Few figures in Roman history were so controversial as this Roman general and dictator, who twice marched armies into Rome to overpower political enemies, thereby setting a precedent Julius Caesar would follow. Once Sulla had been plucked from obscurity in 107 BCE by Gaius Marius (157–86 BCE), who appointed him second in command during the war against king Jugurtha of Numidia, the two ambitious men became life-long competitors for dominance in Rome. The tangled tale of their conflict is too complex to review here; suffice it to say that Sulla finally outmaneuvered Marius and managed to have himself elected Roman dictator in 82 BCE, which enabled him to mark his political enemies for death by posting his dreaded proscription lists.

In the *Dialogue* Montesquieu has Sulla contend that none of his brutal actions was a crime since his goal had been the worthy one of restoring Roman liberty by annulling the veto power of the Roman tribunes and by restoring the senate's prerogative to approve legislation before it could be voted on in the popular assembly (p. 80). By the end of the dialogue, however, it is Sulla's interlocutor, Eucrates, who has delivered the most telling blows. Eucrates tells Sulla that he has shown how deadly heroism can be, even when based on principle. "For one man to be above humanity," he scolds Sulla, "all the others pay too dear a price" (p. 82). And Eucrates berates Sulla for marking out a path toward tyranny that others would surely follow (pp. 79, 84).

Reflections on National Character

Both Montesquieu's *Notes on England* (1729–1731) and his *Reflections on the Inhabitants of Rome* (1732) display the keen interest in national character evident in *Persian Letters* (1721), where he had juxtaposed the mores and politics of Christian France with the customs and government of Muslim Persia. The *Notes on England* are remnants of the more extensive travel notes he compiled while residing in England between 1729 and 1731. They reveal that at the same time he was composing the idealized portrait of the English constitution that became Book XI, chapter 6 of *The Spirit of Law* he was aware of shortcomings plaguing the English political system. He observes that there was widespread political corruption and remarks that "the English are no longer worthy of their freedom" because "[t]hey sell it to the king; and were the king to give it back to them they would sell it back to him again." Money, rather than honor and virtue, is what the English most prize (pp. 89–90).

Montesquieu witnessed first hand the division into warring political parties that threatened the political liberty for which the English were famous. After attending a debate in the House of Commons in January 1730 where he heard the English king, George II, called a "tyrant" and "usurper" scheming to raise a standing army in peacetime (p. 90), he remarked that the English king and queen are subject to much stronger criticism than any French king would tolerate. He concludes, however, that this was a sign of the English genius for checking power, which had made England "at present the freest country in the world." Neither the House of Commons nor the king wields unlimited and dangerous power because neither possesses both legislative and executive authority (p. 94).

Montesquieu finds much to admire about English politics and culture, including strong support for freedom of the press. The people of England, he remarks, are allowed to write what in other countries one can only think (p. 89). He sums up English national character by wryly observing that what the typical Englishman wants most is "a good dinner, a prostitute, and comfort." If denied these things, he may resort to thievery or even commit suicide (p. 88). Montesquieu was aware that many travelers to England had found the English unfriendly; his own view was that it is best to take people as they are and accept the great diversity of character and lifestyle one encounters from place to place. "[W]hen I visit a country," he writes, "I do not examine whether there are good laws, but whether the ones they have are enforced, for there are good laws everywhere" (p. 90).

In *Reflections on the Inhabitants of Rome* (1732) Montesquieu explores several causes, some physical and others moral, for the striking contrasts between ancient and modern Romans. The ancient Romans, he observes, were much more robust and needed less sleep, even following gluttonous consumption of food. They consumed five meals a day, whereas modern Romans consume only one (p. 95). To explain the difference he emphasizes, as he had in his *Essay on the Causes*, the effect of the air one breathes on human behavior and notes that air quality had greatly deteriorated since ancient times. He also observes that Romans no longer take baths prior to eating or use emetics to increase appetite. And he points to moral causes at work in modern times very different from those that formerly shaped Roman character. Political life in the ancient Roman republic had been agitated; fierce politicking had formed the backdrop to daily life. Modern Rome, by way of contrast, is "the most tranquil city in the world" (p. 96).

Politics and Morality

The texts in Part IV of the volume reveal Montesquieu's moral idealism and life-long concern with ethics. He was clearly a moral theorist as well as a political philosopher. In his essay entitled *In Praise of Sincerity* (c. 1717) he stresses the importance of providing moral guidance to one's friends by speaking to them sincerely, that is, with complete candor regarding their shortcomings. Blunt talk can be reformative of character, and when we do not summon the courage to speak the truth to our friends, choosing instead to purposefully ignore their flaws, truth becomes buried "under maxims of false civility" (p. 100). And yet, too often, our friends flatter our vices instead of becoming our tutors in virtue. Montesquieu also emphasizes how crucial it is to speak truth to power since those who flatter princes "plunge their state into an abyss of disasters" (p. 103).

Another text displaying Montesquieu's prowess as a moral philosopher is the partially reconstituted *Treatise on Duties* (1725) whose contents we know from a summary prepared by Montesquieu's friend Jean-Jacques Bel, published in the March 1726 edition of the *Bibliothèque Française* (this volume, pp. 106–109), from the still extant two final chapters entitled *On Politics* (this volume) and from lengthy fragments preserved in Montesquieu's notebooks (*Mes pensées*, also this volume). Inspired by Cicero's *De officiis*, and also drawing insights from Samuel Pufendorf's *On the Duties of Man and Citizen* (1673), Montesquieu stresses the importance of duties rather than rights, laying the ground for his later assertion, in his preface to *The Spirit of Law*, that he would be "the happiest of mortals" if after reading his work "everyone had new reasons for loving his duties, his prince, his homeland, and his laws."

Following Cicero's lead, Montesquieu explains that we have duties to God, family, country, our fellow human beings, and ourselves. Our duties stemming from our ontological condition as human beings have a higher priority than our duties associated with being a citizen of a particular country. Hence we should prioritize our obligations to mankind ahead of our more parochial attachments. Our highest duty, just as the ancient Stoic philosophers had taught, is not owed to ourselves, to our family, or even to our country, but rather to humankind as a whole (p. 107). Although love of country "can do honor to an entire nation," Montesquieu writes, it too often grows extreme and becomes "the source of the greatest crimes," as the examples of Roman and Spanish excesses in conquest reveal. "Civic spirit," he pronounces, "is not seeing one's own country devour all the others" (p. 126).

Montesquieu expresses the conviction that cultivating virtue is essential to human flourishing and should be "the constant object of our pursuits" (p. 116).[13] Yet, regrettably, virtue "has almost always been allowed to go unrewarded." Too often we are ruled by "a base self-interest which is properly nothing more than the animal instinct of all men" (p. 113). The most "felicitous" country, he notes, would be the one where "ranks, positions, and pardons were granted only for virtue, [and] intrigues and shady means were unknown" (p. 132). In reviewing the history of French morals and manners, Montesquieu at times channels the elder Cato, so distressed is he over moral decline in France, which he traces back to the reign of Francis I in the sixteenth century (p. 128). Ever-increasing levels of moral laxness, he laments, had been accompanied by a loss of stabilizing respect for parents and for those of high rank (pp. 129–130).

In several fragments of the *Treatise on Duties* preserved in *Mes pensées* Montesquieu asserts, just as he will later emphasize in Book 1, chapter 1 of *The Spirit of Law*, that there are absolutes of justice traceable to nature and applicable to all societies. Justice, he contends, ranks as the highest virtue and is "not dependent on human laws" (p. 107). Justice is a "general relation" whereas other virtues, such as friendship, love of country, and compassion, involve only "particular relations"; moreover "any virtue that destroys this

---

13 *Virtue*, an important word in Montesquieu's vocabulary, is strongly conditioned by its Latin connotations of manhood, courage, and valor. *Trévoux* defines the word first in terms of strength and vigor and secondarily in "moral" terms such as uprightness, probity, disposition to do good, and so on. Montesquieu later clarified his intent in *The Spirit of Law* by saying that his man of virtue was "not the righteous man of Christianity" but one imbued with "political virtue" such as love of country (*SL*, preface to the 1758 edition).

general relation is not a virtue" (p. 110). Thus Hobbes was wrong to believe that justice "is nothing more than what the laws of empires command or forbid" (p. 122).

Some of the most impassioned lines in the *Treatise on Duties* are those attacking the atheistic propositions of Thomas Hobbes and Baruch Spinoza.[14] Whatever his eventual views on the Christian God – a much debated topic – Montesquieu asserts that God "must fill all our desires and occupy all our thoughts." "[W]e owe everything to God," he proclaims, and he ridicules Spinoza as "a great genius" who "has promised me that I shall die like an insect," as if there were no immortal soul (pp. 107, 121). It is God, not blind fate, that created us and all of creation, as he will again assert in the first chapter of *The Spirit of Law* (p. 121).

On Consideration and Reputation (1725) is a brief essay influenced by Madame de Lambert (1647–1733) and her circle, who gathered weekly in her Paris apartments to discuss moral and political subjects. Here Montesquieu dwells on our eagerness to gain the esteem of our friends. We crave being "well considered" even more than we desire birth, wealth, positions, and honors," and yet, regrettably, this causes us to neglect the virtues of "probity, good faith, modesty" – traits that are undervalued by our friends. In order to gain attention in the immediate present, we too often "utter a witticism that will dishonor us tomorrow" (p. 134). Reputation, Montesquieu asserts, is something altogether different from the consideration we seek from our friends; reputation is gained by means of accomplishments known to the general public and confers less happiness than consideration because those who enjoy it take it for granted until it is lost. And reputation is difficult to sustain because most people believe they can best display intelligence by deflating the reputations of the great (pp. 134, 135).

In his *Discourse on the Equity that Must Determine Judgments and the Execution of Laws* (1725), read at the opening session of the parlement of Bordeaux in 1725, Montesquieu asserts that the "essential virtue" for a magistrate is "justice, a quality without which he is but a monster in society" (p. 139). Should a judge become aware of his incapacity to rule justly, he should resign his post. Moreover, since judges are "always dealing with unfortunate persons," they must be "attentive to their slightest concerns" (p. 142). Montesquieu dares to criticize his fellow magistrates and other officials of the parlement for failing to exemplify justice in all their public and private

---

14 The nearly uniformly held opinion was that Spinoza's pantheistic equation of God with nature and his denial of Creation was tantamount to atheism, no matter how often he spoke of God in his works.

affairs, and he ends the *Discourse* with a stirring encomium on the young king Louis XV, expressing hope and optimism that he will rule justly and wisely. May the new king seek, Montesquieu asserts, to "cultivate in peace virtues which are not less royal than the military ones" and understand that he does not need war to achieve greatness (p. 144).

Two other treatises revealing Montesquieu's prowess as a moral philosopher are set in ancient times. In his *Dialogue between Xanthippus and Xenocrates* (1727) he faults the Romans for their ruthless treatment of defeated foes. The hero of the dialogue is the Spartan mercenary Xanthippus, who came to the aid of the Carthaginians in 255 BCE after they had lost an epic battle with the Romans near Tunis. Montesquieu suggests that the Romans should have negotiated peace after defeating the Carthaginians, but instead they offered terms so harsh they were certain to be rejected. The result was that Carthage fought on, and with the assistance of Xanthippus defeated the Romans in several battles during what is now called the First Punic War. The duty we owe to our fellow human beings emerges as one of the key themes in this dialogue. Xanthippus responds to Xenocrates' praise of his selfless valor by remarking it is duty that "binds me to all humans," adding that, like other Spartans, he had been taught by the legendary lawgiver Lycurgus to watch over the interests of all humans (p. 148).

In *Lysimachus* (1751) Montesquieu recounts the story of Callisthenes of Olynthus (c. 360–327 BCE), grandnephew of Aristotle and chronicler of Alexander the Great's Asian expedition. Unlike others in Alexander's retinue, Callisthenes refused to bow down before Alexander in the Persian manner after Alexander proclaimed himself divine and began to dress like a Persian. In Montesquieu's version of the tale, an angry Alexander cuts off Callisthenes' feet, nose, and ears and imprisons him in an iron cage (p. 152). Subsequently, Callisthenes is befriended by Lysimachus (c. 360–281 BCE), one of Alexander's generals and bodyguards. When Lysimachus marvels that he could endure such harsh punishment, Callisthenes responds that he has little regard for living "an easy and sensuous life" since he greatly prizes virtue, strength, and courage. He recounts a dream in which Lysimachus becomes a king and rules justly. After learning of these friendly conversations, Alexander casts Lysimachus into an arena with a lion; against all odds, Lysimachus survives by ripping the lion's tongue from its mouth, an act of courage so impressive that Alexander forgives him for befriending Callisthenes. Montesquieu ends the saga by having Lysimachus become king of Asia, ruling with Callisthenes as his counselor (p. 154).

Statecraft

Part v of the volume contains five essays exploring the politics and practice of statecraft. In *Letters from Xenocrates to Pheres* (1724), Montesquieu assesses the character of Alcmenes, a stand-in for Philip, Duke of Orléans, who served as regent of France from 1715 until Louis XV came of age in 1723. Xenocrates praises Alcmenes for ruling with an ease of command that made people eager to obey and love him and for displaying a preference for clemency over vengeance (p. 156). He also remarks that, although Alcmenes lacks principles, he has a good heart, and while prone to making mistakes, knows how to remedy them quickly. Too often, however, Alcmenes tries to correct things best left alone,[15] and he errs in valuing men of talent rather than virtue, the result being that "he is wholly unaware of the infinite distance that exists between the honest and the wicked man, and all the different degrees between these two extremes" (p. 156).

Major events occurred during Philip's regency, and Montesquieu includes in Xenocrates' letters criticism of him for accepting disastrous advice to establish a national bank and a mercantile company with monopoly powers (p. 158). He is referring to the schemes of the Scotsman John Law who brought the already insolvent French state to the brink of ruin. The sale of shares in Law's Mississippi company, as Montesquieu had previously explained in *Persian Letters* 138, created an insatiable desire for wealth and caused the French to seek to suddenly acquire riches not through hard work but by ruining the prince and state and one's fellow citizens. Law's "System" caused widespread bankruptcy when prices of Mississippi stock plummeted, and the whole debacle proved so disastrous that, as Montesquieu has Rica explain in *Persian Letter* 132, Law's policies turned the state inside out the way a secondhand clothes dealer turns a coat.[16] The letters end with Xenocrates asserting that the new king replacing the deceased Alcmenes (i.e., Louis XV whose coming of age in 1723 ended the regency) "likes to do good, to correct evil, and finally truth pleases him." Only good princes, he observes, can bestow a "calm of the spirit," "security," and "inner peace" as well as "riches and abundance" on their subjects (p. 160).

15 Cf. *SL*, Preface: "In a time of ignorance no one has any doubt, even while doing the greatest harm; in an enlightened time, we tremble even while doing the finest of deeds. We realize the former abuses, and see how to correct them; but in addition we see the abuses of the correction itself. We leave the harm alone if we fear the worst; we leave the good alone if we are unsure about what is better."

16 This numbering follows the 1721 edition. In the revised 1758 edition letter 132 is number 138 and letter 138 is number 146.

In *On Politics* (1725), which originally formed the concluding chapters of the *Treatise on Duties* (1725), Montesquieu counsels princes to employ strategies at once straightforward and moral rather than resorting to the ruthless tactics Machiavelli recommended in *The Prince* (1516), though some, including Bacon, Spinoza, Diderot, and Rousseau, chose to read that work as a warning rather than an approval of the ruthlessness of princes.[17] Rather than attacking the doctrine of reason of state on abstract moral grounds, Montesquieu explains how actual historical events demonstrate the futility of immoral statecraft. He identifies two reasons why princes modeling their conduct on Machiavelli's prince are not likely to succeed. First, no prince can foresee the precipices along his path since "[m]ost effects occur via such circuitous paths or depend on causes so imperceptible and remote that they defy prediction" (p. 161). Moreover, every prince will be constrained by a "tone," or general spirit of the times, that may assist him in governing but often will not (p. 165). Montesquieu concludes that princes are foolish if they think they can subdue Fortune by resorting to immorality. Thus, *On Politics* is a veritable *anti-Machiavel*, a plea for simple, straightforward, and honest statecraft that does not violate fundamental principles of justice.[18]

Montesquieu's *Reflections on Universal Monarchy in Europe* (1734) reinforces his conviction of the need to inject morality into international relations, a central theme in his writing from his youth to maturity. Passing in review the behavior of many modern princes, he sees heads of state just as addicted to the pursuit of glory as Roman generals had been. Very little, he concludes, had been learned from what he regarded as the lessons of Roman history: expansion does not pay, empire is not sustainable, and conquest in unjust wars violates what should be regarded as binding international law based on respect for the rights of other peoples. Nations, he observes, are now roughly equivalent in size and power, making success in war much more difficult than in ancient times. Yet each state maintains "an inordinate number of

17 We know from *Spicilège* 529 (*OC* XIII, 468) that Montesquieu was familiar with the argument of William Cleland (1674–1741), whom he met in England, that "Machiavelli spoke of princes only as Samuel did, without approbation. He was a great republican." (The allusion to the prophet Samuel is apparently to his objections to kingship in I Kings [I Samuel], chapters VIII and IX.)
18 Cf. *SL* XXIX, 19, where Montesquieu berates Machiavelli for praising the tactics of the ruthless *condottiero* and son of Pope Alexander VI, Cesare Borgia (1475–1507), and *SL* XXI, 20, where he remarks: "We have begun to be cured of Machiavellianism and will continue to be so every day. There must be more moderation in councils. [. . .] It is fortunate for men to be in a situation where, while their passions inspire in them the thought of being wicked, it is nevertheless not in their interest to be so."

troops," as if "threatened with extermination." Such is the "malady of our times" (pp. 185–186).[19]

Modern nations should understand, Montesquieu counsels, that warfare no longer bestows the same benefits as in Roman times. Standing armies and modern wars are so expensive that they take states to the brink of bankruptcy. Moreover, a balance of power in modern times makes lasting superiority unachievable. All European states are of roughly equivalent size and are similarly committed to the "spirit of liberty"; besides, any new military tactic will be duplicated quickly by other heads of state (p. 174). Montesquieu expresses the fervent hope that new standards of international law, influenced by Christian principles, will lead to the introduction of more humane rules of warfare (p. 171).[20] Montesquieu had originally planned to publish *Reflections on Universal Monarchy* along with his history of Rome; but realizing at the last moment that few readers, including government censors, would fail to see that the essay targeted the war-mongering of Louis XIV, he withdrew the work after only one copy of the book had been printed.

Reflections on the Character of Certain Princes and on Certain Events in their Lives (c. 1731–1733), originally conceived as part of a larger work, never completed, tentatively entitled *The Prince* or *The Princes*, chronicles the exploits of various secular and ecclesiastical rulers active during the fifteenth through the seventeenth centuries. Its overall teaching is the need for morality in politics, particularly on the part of those wielding power. Employing Plutarch's method of parallel lives, Montesquieu points out the strengths and weaknesses of assorted leaders, while emphasizing the role general causes play in shaping history and reducing the influence of princes, no matter how clever or devious they may be. "There are circumstances," he explains, "where men of the least ability can govern well enough; there are others where the greatest minds are taken aback; the art of ruling is sometimes the easiest art in the world, and sometimes the most difficult" (p. 194). Often, the failures of princes to achieve their goals result from overly

19 Cf. *SL* xiii, 17: "A new disease has spread through Europe; it has seized upon our princes and made them maintain an inordinate number of troops. It redoubles in strength, and it necessarily becomes contagious. For as soon as one state increases what it calls its troops, the others suddenly increase theirs, so nothing is gained thereby except their common ruin. Each monarch keeps ready all the armies he would have if his peoples were in danger of extermination, and this state of all against all is called peace."

20 Cf. *SL* x, 2: "The right of war therefore derives from necessity and strict justice. If those who direct the conscience or the counsels of princes do not limit themselves to that, all is lost; and when they base themselves on arbitrary principles of glory, advantage, or utility, rivers of blood will inundate the earth."

complex and devious conduct. Some princes succeed, however, owing to sheer genius. Montesquieu compares the success of Cromwell, whose genius, he believes, was on a par with Caesar's, with the hapless Duke of Mayenne (1554–1611), who went from mistake to mistake during the French Wars of Religion, owing to constant miscalculations (pp. 193–194). Similarly, both Philip II (1527–1598) of Spain and Louis XI (1423–1483) of France are written off as failures. Each acted duplicitously without good result and made mistakes that could have been avoided: Philip unwisely chose to simultaneously attack France, England, and the Low Countries, and Louis XI foolishly walked into a trap and became the prisoner of Charles, Duke of Burgundy (1433–1477; pp. 163–164).

In his *Memorandum on the Silence to Impose on the Constitution* (1754), Montesquieu offers Louis XIV advice on how best to deal with the crisis created by the persistence of Jansenism in France. Originating in the views of Cornelius Jansen (1585–1638) as outlined in his *Augustinus* (1640), Jansenism was an austere Catholic movement represented to the public by the abbey of Port Royal and a number of prominent figures attached to it, including Antoine Arnauld, Pierre Nicole, Jean Racine, and Blaise Pascal. Essentially the court and the Jesuits were aligned against the Jansenists and the parlements, but to the king what was most intolerable was the very existence of such a deep division within the Church at a time when his priority was to suppress Protestantism and thereby unite the kingdom in a single faith. Louis XIV had prevailed upon pope Clement XI to issue the bull *Unigenitus* (1713), which declared numerous Jansenist propositions[21] either heretical or false, but the promulgation of the bull only spawned a further battle over whether it was law in France, and if so, how it could or should be enforced. The quarrel festered for decades.

In the early 1750s, Christophe de Beaumont, the stern archbishop of Paris, instructed the priests in his diocese to refuse last rites to anyone who had not confessed to a pro-*Unigenitus* priest. The Parlement of Paris, after reacting to protect the rights of all believers, was sternly reproached by Louis XV for meddling in purely spiritual affairs and sent into exile in April 1753. In June, Montesquieu, known to all by this time as the author of *The Spirit of Law*, was among those called to a royal audience to discuss the situation, and he may have been invited to submit his proposal that the king impose silence on the doctrinal disputes that had set Jesuits and Jansenists against one another.

---

21 As represented in Pasquier Quesnel's *Le Nouveau Testament en français avec des réflexions morale* of 1692.

Though it is not known whether the king ever read it, a royal declaration to the same effect was issued in September 1754.[22]

Montesquieu recommended, in sum, that the bull continue to be recognized, but at the same time that it should be ignored. Priests should be forbidden to inquire of parishioners whether they were Jansenists, who in turn should not identify themselves as such. Convinced that such a religious debate could not be settled, insofar as it is in the nature of doctrinal controversies to be irresolvable, "the salvation of the state" required the king to impose silence on all and adopt a policy of "outward" rather than "inner" toleration of unorthodox convictions (pp. 201–202). Montesquieu makes no declaration in his *Memorandum* of religious freedom as a natural right, but instead treats toleration as a practical necessity. He links toleration to the king's foremost political responsibilities, and his central point is that laws must conform not to religious but to political principle.[23]

Economics and Fiscal Policy

In 1715 the regent Philip, Duke of Orléans, issued an open invitation to his French subjects to offer plans for resolving the calamitous debt problem, which the wars of Louis XIV had bequeathed to France. Montesquieu responded with his *Memorandum on the Debts of State* (1715). Rather than recommending a state bankruptcy, as Saint-Simon and others suggested, Montesquieu proposed a gradual reduction of the debt by means of a partial repudiation. Every purchaser of the annuities which the crown had offered for sale since 1522 would lose a portion of his investment; similarly, those who owned a venal office, or were royal employees, would be subjected to a reduction in the amount of interest, wages, or salary received. The core principle of Montesquieu's debt-curbing proposal involved shared sacrifice. The greater the proportion of one's overall wealth invested in the crown's debt, the less the reduction would be, since such individuals would have few other investments (pp. 207–208).

Montesquieu was so confident that his debt reduction plan would succeed that he predicted the crown would be able to reduce taxes: what would be required was an exchange of depreciated annuities on which the king would no

22 Previous decrees of silence had been issued in 1717, 1719, 1730, and 1752.
23 Cf. *SL* XXVI, 9: "The laws of perfection drawn from religion have as their object more the goodness of the man who observes them than of the society in which they are observed; civil laws, on the contrary, have as their object more the moral goodness of men in general than of individuals. ¶Thus, however respectable the thoughts that arise directly from religion, they should not always serve as the principle of civil laws, because these have a different principle, which is the general welfare of society."

longer need to pay interest in return for equivalent amounts of tax immunity. His plan included the buyback of the salt taxes and ending two new progressive taxes, to which the nobility had been subjected by Louis XIV late in his reign (pp. 208, 210). In truth, it is doubtful that Montesquieu's plan could have retired the debt, which was much greater than he or any others, including the government's own financiers, had any way of calculating. The salt taxes which he was proposing to end were one of the main sources of badly needed French revenues. Whatever its shortcomings, Montesquieu's essay displays a surprising level of knowledge regarding French finance for a twenty-six-year-old whose studies had primarily focused on law and Roman history. It also provides notice of what would become his long-term interest in fiscal and economic policy developed in Books XIII and XXII of *The Spirit of Law*.

As a writer of history Montesquieu is best known for his treatise on the decline of Rome, but he was also intrigued by the collapse of Spain as a powerhouse in modern Europe. Spain had long been considered the sick sister of Europe, and many theorists had pondered the paradoxical reasons for her impoverishment. It seemed puzzling that such a great power, having gained enormous wealth in the sixteenth century by importing gold and silver from the Americas, could end up powerless to fulfill the grandiose ambitions for European empire that had motivated Charles V (reigned 1516–1556) and his son Philip II (reigned 1581–1598). As Montesquieu explains in his *Considerations on the Wealth of Spain* (c. 1727), later incorporated in Book XXI, chapter 21 of *The Spirit of Law*, the Spanish became the victims of inflation. The more bullion Spain brought to her shores, the less valuable it became, with more and more specie chasing roughly the same amount of goods. At the same time, owing to a lagging economy at home, Spain had to import basic goods from other countries, which caused a steady outflow of bullion toward other countries (pp. 216–217).

It was sheer folly, Montesquieu concludes, for Spain to have mistaken symbolic wealth, in the form of bullion, for real wealth (p. 216). Even as Spanish mines poured forth their riches, the Spanish people remained mired in poverty, deriving no benefit from the revenues acquired by Spanish monarchs from their colonies. As a result, the Spanish king became only "a very rich individual" in an impoverished state (pp. 182, 221). The ancient Egyptians, Athenians, Macedonians, and Carthaginians, Montesquieu observes, had derived much more profit from their mines than Spain, since they were located either within their domains, or, in the case of the Carthaginians, within her "sphere of power" (p. 221). Spanish mines, on the other hand, were distant, and Spain needed to expend great sums in what proved to be a futile attempt to ward off European competition in trade with her colonies (p. 214). Montesquieu ends his essay by remarking that France had not been mistaken in the decision, unlike that of Ferdinand and Isabella of Spain, to decline to sponsor the voyages of the Italian explorer Christopher Columbus.

Defense of The Spirit of Law

Although *The Spirit of Law* (1748) was greeted very favorably in many quarters, ecclesiastical critics found much to censure, and in the 9 and 16 October 1749 issues of the Jansenist broadsheet *Nouvelles ecclésiastiques*, abbé Jean-Baptiste Gaultier (1685–1755) unleashed a stinging attack on Montesquieu for irreligion.[24] Gaultier was scandalized by the depiction in Book I, chapter I of man as "having been created unknowing, concupiscent, subject to sickness and death" without any mention of original sin, or man having been created "to know and love God." Compounding this blasphemy, Montesquieu had substituted "natural religion for the noble ideas that revelation gives us of our origin, destination and duties," had wrongly identified peace rather than love of God as "the first law of nature," and had denigrated God's Providential powers by asserting that the intelligent world is not as well governed as the physical world. And he had affronted all of Christian France by making virtue the activating principle only of republican governments while asserting that monarchies are held together by "false honor" rather than virtue.

Throughout the book, the abbé asserted, Montesquieu had treated numerous immoralities, such as polygamy, not as a Christian author would, but rather with a non-judgmental attitude. The chapter entitled "That the Law of Polygamy Is a Matter of Calculation,"[25] for example, suggested that where women greatly outnumber men, husbands should be permitted to have several wives, and where the numbers are reversed, women may take several husbands. Moreover, Montesquieu had erred in locating the origin of marriage in "the natural obligation that the father has to nourish his children" rather than in God's creating a companion for Adam. And he had erred grievously in praising the Stoics for making "good citizens" and "great men."[26] "A Christian," said the abbé, "does not speak of an impious sect."[27]

---

24 For the text of Gaultier's two attacks, see *OC* VII, 23–37.   25 *SL* XVI, 4.
26 *SL* XXIV, 10: "The various ancient schools of philosophy were sorts of religions. There never was one which had principles worthier of man, and better at forming persons of good will, than the Stoics; and if I could for a moment cease to think that I am a Christian, I would have to list the destruction of the school of Zeno among the misfortunes of humanity. [. . .] It alone was able to make citizens; it alone made great men; it alone made great emperors."
27 Gaultier, in *OC* VII, 30, 31, 34.

Montesquieu was clearly stung by the level of vitriol in Gaultier's criticisms and spent the closing months of 1749 composing a spirited rebuttal that was widely read and praised by many, including Voltaire.[28] Posing as a third-party observer of the conflict rather than writing under his own name, Montesquieu says his critic has completely failed to understand the nature of his project. His work, he says, was not that of a theologian but rather of a "jurisconsult" (a legal scholar) exploring what laws are most suitable for a given people considering their character and situation (p. 257). Montesquieu also asserts that the author of *The Spirit of Law* "is a Christian, but not an imbecile," and "that he worships these [Christian] truths, but does not want to broadcast at random all the truths he believes" (p. 249). Montesquieu complains that his "critic never wants the author to treat his subject; he constantly wants him to treat his own, and because he is always the theologian, he does not want anyone to be a jurisconsult, even in a book of law." "It is a sad thing," he continues, "to have to deal with a man who censures every paragraph in a book and has only one prevailing thought. It's the tale of that village curate to whom astronomers show the moon in a telescope, and who sees nothing but his steeple" (p. 235).

Montesquieu yields no ground to his Jansenist critic, stating that *The Spirit of Law* has shown he "not only believes the Christian religion, but loves it." He asks how the critic could "have so far missed the subject and the purpose of a work he had before his eyes?" – a work which "[t]he most sensible persons of various countries in Europe, the most enlightened men and the wisest, have regarded [. . .] as a useful work" whose "morality is pure and its principles just" and "proper for the instruction of good men" (p. 238). The author's "object," he explains, had been to explore "the laws, customs, and various ways of all the people of the earth" to determine which "are best suited to society and to each society" while at the same time he "seeks their origin, discovers their physical and moral causes, examines those which have a degree of goodness in themselves and those that have none." This "research" is "useful," he continues, "because good sense consists largely in knowing the nuances of things" (pp. 238–239).

In writing the *Defense*, Montesquieu acknowledges that *The Spirit of Law* discusses many non-Christian customs, such as polygamy, but he explains that the author was "not justifying the customs but giving the reasons for them." As for his frequent discussion of non-Christian religions, he explains

---

28 *Remerciement sincère à un homme charitable* ("Sincere thanks to a charitable man," 1750), in Voltaire, *Œuvres complètes* (Oxford: Voltaire Foundation, 32A, 2006), pp. 195–208.

he had spoken of them "only with respect to the good derived from them in the civil state, whether [. . .] speak[ing] of the one that has its root in heaven, or of those that have theirs on earth" (pp. 228, 239). He had labeled many religions "false," he reminds his critic, since they were "human institutions," and had been "spawned on earth," while he treated Christianity as the "one true religion." And everywhere he spoke of Christianity, "he has done so in such a manner as to make one sense its full grandeur, and while it has not been his purpose to try to make people believe in it, he has thought to make it cherished" (p. 224).

Gaultier censured Montesquieu for calling Pierre Bayle (1647–1716) "a great man,"[29] and his rebuttal was that it was far more important that he had rebutted Bayle's opinions (p. 231). Bayle had asserted that "a society of true Christians could not survive" owing to "the Gospels' command to turn the other cheek when we are slapped; to renounce the world; to withdraw into the deserts, etc."[30] Montesquieu explained that his belief, to the contrary, was that "true Christians" can "form a state capable of lasting. [. . .] They would be citizens infinitely enlightened about their duties, and would have very great zeal for fulfilling them; they would be quite conscious of the rights of natural defense. The more they believed they owed to religion, the more they would think they owed to their homeland. The principles of Christianity, deeply engraved in their hearts, would be infinitely more powerful than the false honor of monarchies, the human virtues of republics, and the servile fear of despotic states." Bayle's error, Montesquieu explains, had been failing to recognize the difference between mere precepts, which are "no more than words of counsel," and hard and fast rules that Christians are obligated to obey (p. 241).[31]

The charge that most upset Montesquieu was the accusation that he was a follower of Spinoza, whose pantheism and denial of the creation had become the scandal of Europe, giving rise to the nearly uniform opinion that he was an atheist. Montesquieu a Spinozist? Not so, he protests vigorously. Had he not said in Book I, chapter I that "God has a relationship with the universe as creator and as preserver; the laws by which he created are those by which he preserves"? And had he not demolished Spinoza's fatalism

---

29 See *SL* xxiv, 6.
30 In 1682 Bayle published his controversial assertions in *Pensées diverses écrites à un docteur de Sorbonne sur l'occasion de la comète qui parut au mois de décembre 1680* ("Various thoughts written to a doctor of the Sorbonne on the occasion of the comet that appeared in the month of December 1680"; *Catalogue* 1521).
31 See *SL* xxiv, 6.

by asserting that "[t]hose who have said that a blind fate has produced all the effects that we see in the world have uttered a great absurdity"? Moreover, had he not refuted Spinoza's pantheism by stating that "spiritual intelligences" are distinct from the material world (p. 225)? As for his praise of the Stoics, he pointed out that although he had lauded their moral teachings, he had condemned their "physics and metaphysics" for positing a "blind fatality, a necessary chain of events" tantamount to fatalism (p. 231). As for the charge that he was an adherent of natural religion, Montesquieu's rebuttal was that natural religion had always been a source for religious belief, and acceptance of its design argument as proof of a creator God did not preclude believing in revelation. Natural religion, he affirmed, is the perfect weapon to prove not only the existence of God but the truth of revelation. Indeed Christianity is "the perfection of natural religion" (p. 237).

Conceived as it was in a thoroughly defensive mode, the *Defense* concentrates on those aspects of *The Spirit of Law* that abbé Gaultier had assaulted, in the hope of heading off more threatening condemnations from ecclesiastical authorities in France and in the Vatican that might risk stifling the work altogether. All the same, the *Defense* is the most revelatory of all Montesquieu's writings regarding his understanding of his method as a political philosopher in *The Spirit of Law*, and of the space within which he meant to work. He repeatedly protests that he is not a theologian viewing all matters through the Church's lens. He affirms that he is a political writer and that whatever he said about religion, polygamy, climate, toleration, celibacy, or usury – remarks his ecclesiastical critics uniformly excoriated as irreligious – was not written from the perspective of a theologian. Montesquieu explains that he could have kept his focus much more on "human virtues and Christian virtues, but it is not with these questions that one makes books of physics, politics and jurisprudence" (p. 245).

David W. Carrithers

I

The Uses of Science

On the Motives that Should Encourage Us toward the Sciences

(1725)

Sur les motifs qui doivent nous encourager aux sciences, text by Sheila Mason
(*OC* VIII, 495–502). On 28 August 1725 Montesquieu was for the second
time elected director of the Academy of Bordeaux, and on 15 November
he delivered this discourse extolling the value of scientific inquiry. The
autograph manuscript of the text was housed in the Academy collection
until being transported, during the French Revolution, to the Bordeaux
museum and later to the municipal library of Bordeaux, established in
1803. It remains part of the Montesquieu collection of the municipal
library in Bordeaux (MS 1914/11). This manuscript serves here as base
text, following the text edited in *OC* VIII.

* * *

The difference between great nations and savage peoples is that the former
have applied themselves to the arts and sciences and the others have totally
neglected them.

It is perhaps to the knowledge they impart that most nations owe their
existence.

If we behaved like the savages of America, two or three European nations
would soon have devoured[1] all the others.

And perhaps some conquering nation of our world would claim, like the
Iroquois, to have devoured seventy nations.

---

1 An allusion to the reputed cannibalism of the Iroquois. Cf. *Pensées* 1263.

But without bringing up savage peoples, if a Descartes had come to Mexico or Peru a hundred years before Cortés[2] and Pizarro[3] and had taught those peoples that men made like them cannot be immortal, that the springs of their machine wear out like those of all machines, that the effects of nature are but a consequence of the laws and the transmissions of movements,[4] Cortés would never have destroyed the Mexican empire with a handful of men, nor Pizarro that of Peru.[5]

Who would have said that this destruction, the greatest history has ever recorded, had been merely a simple effect of the ignorance of a principle of philosophy? Yet that is the truth, as I am going to demonstrate.

The Mexicans had no firearms, but they had bows and arrows, which is to say that they had the weapons of the Greeks and the Romans.

They had no iron, but they had flints that cut like iron with which they tipped their weapons; they even had an excellent thing for military art, which is that they kept their ranks closed, and as soon as one soldier was killed he was instantly replaced by another.

They had a valiant and intrepid nobility raised on the principles of the European nobility which envies the fate of those who die for glory.

Moreover, the vast expanse of the empire gave the Mexicans a thousand ways of destroying foreigners if they were unable to defeat them.

The Peruvians had the same advantages, and besides, everywhere they defended themselves and everywhere they fought, they did so with success; the Spaniards even thought they were going to be exterminated by small populations who were determined to defend themselves.

So how does it happen that they were so easily destroyed? It was because everything that seemed new to them, whether a bearded man, a horse, a firearm, was to them the effect of an invisible power which they thought they were unable to resist.

The Americans never lacked courage, but only the expectation of succeeding.

Thus a bad principle of philosophy, the ignorance of a physical cause, paralyzed in an instant all the might of two great empires.

---

2 Hernán Cortés (1485–1547), the Spanish conquistador who arrived in Mexico in 1519, was taken for a god by the Aztec emperor Moctezuma II (1466–1520) and was therefore welcomed to his palace, where he made his host his hostage as a buffer against Aztec attacks.
3 Francisco Pizarro (1471–1541), the Spanish conquistador who captured and executed the Incan emperor Atahualpa (c. 1502–1533).
4 Montesquieu owned an edition (Paris, 1659) of Descartes's *Principes de la philosophie* (*Catalogue 1438*).
5 Montesquieu's main source of information for the indigenous people of Mexico and Peru was the 3rd edition (Barcelona, 1691) of José d'Acosta, *Historia natural y moral de las Indias* (1591; *Catalogue 3162*).

In Europe, the invention of powder[6] gave such a slim advantage to the nation that first used it that it is still unclear which one first took advantage of it.

The invention of spyglasses[7] served the Dutch only once.

We have learned to consider in all these effects only a pure mechanism, and through it there is no contrivance that we are not in a position to elude with another contrivance.

The sciences are therefore useful insofar as they cure peoples of destructive prejudices, but since we can hope that a nation that has once cultivated them will always cultivate them enough not to fall to the degree of crudeness and ignorance that can cause its ruin, we are going to address other motives that should persuade us to apply ourselves to them.

The first is the inner satisfaction we experience when we see a gain in the excellence of our being and render an intelligent being more intelligent.

The second is a certain curiosity that all men have and which has never been so reasonable as in our time. We hear it said every day that the boundaries of human knowledge have just been infinitely extended, that the learned are surprised to find themselves so knowledgeable, and that their achievements are so great that they have sometimes made them doubt that these achievements are real. Will we claim no share of this good news? We know that the human mind has gone very far; shall we not see just how far it has traveled, the distance it has covered, the distance that remains to be covered, the knowledge it claims, that it strives for, that it despairs of acquiring?

A third motive which should encourage us toward the sciences is the well-founded expectation of success. What makes the discoveries of our time so admirable is not the simple truths we have discovered but methods for discovering them; it is not a stone in the edifice but the instruments and machines for building the whole thing.

One man boasts of possessing gold, another boasts of knowing how to make some.[8] Certainly, the genuinely rich man would be the one who knew how to make gold.

A fourth motive is our own happiness. The love of learning is almost the only eternal passion in us; all the others leave us as this miserable machine[9] that procures them for us approaches its demise.

Ardent and impetuous youth, which flits from pleasure to pleasure, can sometimes give them to us in a pure form, because before we have had time

---

6 I.e., gunpowder.   7 I.e., the hand-held telescope.
8 An allusion to the "Great Work" of alchemy.   9 A Cartesian term for the body.

to feel the pains of one, it makes us enjoy the next. But in the age that follows it, the senses may offer us sensual delights but almost never pleasures.

That is when we realize that our soul is our principal part and, as if the chain that attaches it to the senses were broken, it alone has all the pleasures, but all independent.[10]

And if at that time we do not give our soul occupations appropriate to it, that soul which is made to be active, and is not, falls into a languor that seems to lead us to oblivion. And if, in a revolt against nature, we insist on seeking pleasures not made for us, they seem to flee us as we approach them.

Exuberant youth triumphs in its happiness and endlessly offends us; as it feels all its advantages, it makes us feel them; in the liveliest gatherings all the joy is for youth, and the regrets for us.

Learning cures us of these drawbacks, and the pleasures it gives us do not call attention to our increasing years.

We need to find a happiness which stays with us at all ages. Life is so short that we must count as nothing a felicity that does not last as long as we do.

The only old age that is a burden is an idle one; it is not a burden in itself, for if it degrades us in a certain world, it gives us standing in another.

It is not the old man who is unbearable, it is man; it is man who has put himself under the necessity of perishing from tedium or going from one gathering to the next drawing out all the pleasures.

Another motive that should encourage us to apply ourselves to learning is the utility which the society to which we belong may derive from it. To the many conveniences we have we can add many conveniences we do not yet have. Trade, navigation, astronomy, geography, medicine, and physics have received a thousand advantages from the labors of those who have gone before us. Is it not a fine objective to contribute to leaving behind men happier than we have been?

We shall not complain, as did one of Nero's courtiers, of the injustice of all the ages toward those who have made the sciences and arts flourish. *Miron qui fere hominum animas foerarumque ære deprehenderat non invoenit heredem.*[11] Our time is perhaps as thankless as another but posterity will be fair to us and pay the debts of the present generation.

---

10 Cf. Descartes's *Passions de l'âme* ("Passions of the soul"), ¶46.

11 "And Miro, who had almost enclosed in bronze the soul of men and beasts, found no one to succeed him." The quotation is from *Satirycon liber* ("The book of Satyrlike adventures"), a work of satirical fiction by Gaius Petronius Arbiter (27–66 CE), Roman courtier, voluptuary, and fashion advisor to Nero. Petronius served as suffect consul in 62 CE.

We forgive the merchant made rich by the return of his ships for laughing at the uselessness of the man who led him as if by the hand through the vast seas. We allow an arrogant warrior laden with honors and titles to look down on the Archimedes's of our day who have put his courage to work. Men who have set out to be useful to society, men who love it, are willing to be treated as if they were a burden to society.

After speaking of the sciences, we will say a word about literature.

Purely mental books[12] like books of poetry and eloquence at least have general uses, and these sorts of advantages are often greater than individual advantages.

In purely mental books we learn the art of writing, in other words the art of capturing our thoughts and expressing them nobly, intensely, with force, grace, and order and with the variety that refreshes the mind.

There is no one who has not in his lifetime seen people who, applied to their art, could have taken it very far, but who for want of education, equally incapable of capturing a thought and of staying with it, lost all the advantage of their labors and talents.

The sciences are all interconnected; the most abstract border on those that are the least abstract, and the whole body of the sciences is allied with literature.[13]

For the sciences greatly benefit from being treated in an ingenious and delicate manner; that is how one can counter their aridness, avoid tiresomeness, and put them within reach of every mind.[14]

If Father Malebranche had been less enchanting, his philosophy would have stayed buried in some school as in a sort of subterranean world.[15]

---

12 *Livres de pur esprit*. Montesquieu shifts from the empirical work of science to other aspects of the Academy's purview recognized in its formal name, Académie Royale des Sciences, Belles-Lettres, et Arts.

13 The interrelatedness of the sciences and the humanities was a main theme for Bernard Le Bovier, sieur de Fontenelle (1657–1757), friend of Montesquieu and Secretary of the French Academy of Sciences from 1697. Fontenelle's published eulogies of the Academy's members did much to popularize scientific achievements and enhance scientists' prestige.

14 This is precisely what Fontenelle had done in his eulogies of members of the science academy.

15 Nicolas Malebranche (1638–1715), prominent theologian, metaphysician, and member of the Congregation of the Oratory, a clerical body much influenced by the writings of René Descartes (1596–1650). Montesquieu had attended the Oratorian Collège de Juilly and, following Malebranche's death in 1715, he purchased twenty-four books to assist him in studying his works. In November 1716 he read a paper to the Academy of Bordeaux explaining that Malebranche's system of ideas had ancient roots. Subsequently, he termed Malebranche a "religious visionary" possessing "more common sense" than other visionaries (*Pensées* 305).

There are Cartesians who have never read anything but the *Worlds* of M. de Fontenelle:[16] that work is more useful than a stiffer work because it is the most serious book which most people are capable of reading. The usefulness of a book must not be judged by the style which the author has chosen. Often puerile thoughts have been uttered solemnly; very serious truths have often been uttered in jest.

But independently of these considerations, books that refresh the mind of educated persons are not without their uses; such readings are the most innocent entertainment of the worldly because they almost always complement gambling, debauchery, gossipy conversations, and the projects and actions of ambition.

Essay on the Causes that Can Affect Minds and Characters

(1736–1738)

Essai sur les causes qui peuvent affecter les esprits et les caractères, text by Pierre Rétat (*OC* IX, 219–269). This is an uncompleted work, though one Montesquieu frequently revisited, adding footnotes and also marginal notations regarding contemplated revisions; sometimes he also pillaged it for passages used in other writings. We have translated all of the substantive notes, but have chosen not to include others. The title was added by the editors when the manuscript was first printed in *Mélanges inédits* (1892). Portions of the text that were moved to Book XIV of *SL* on climate have been placed within square brackets.

* * *

[Part One: Physical Causes that Can Affect Minds and Characters][17]
These causes become less arbitrary as they have a more generalized effect. Thus we know better what gives a certain character to a nation than what gives a particular mentality to an individual, what modifies one sex than what affects a man, what makes up the genius of societies that have embraced a way of life than that of a single person.[18]

16 *Entretiens sur la pluralité des mondes* ("Conversations on the plurality of worlds," 1686), a work that did much to popularize and gain acceptance of the Copernican system while also suggesting the possibility of extraterrestrial life.
17 Added by the editors in 1892. Montesquieu gave a title to the second part of the manuscript, but not to the first.
18 The next seven paragraphs, which we have placed within square brackets, following modification, were integrated into *SL* XIV, 2.

[Cold air shrinks the extremities of the exterior fibers of our bodies, which increases their compression and favors the return of blood from the extremities toward the heart. It decreases the length[19] of these same fibers, thereby further increasing their strength. Warm air on the contrary relaxes the extremities of the fibers and lengthens them; it thus reduces their strength and compression.

People therefore have more vigor in cold climates. The action of the heart and the reaction of the extremities of the fibers work better; the fluids are in better balance; there is more blood in the heart, or at least the blood is more strongly propelled toward the heart, and reciprocally the heart has more strength.[20] This greater force must produce many effects: for example, more confidence in oneself, in other words more courage; more awareness of one's superiority, in other words less desire for vengeance; more sense of security, in other words more candor, fewer suspicions, less maneuvering and guile. In short, it must make for entirely different geniuses and characters. Put a man in a warm, closed space: he will suffer, for the reasons I have just stated, considerable heart failure. If in this circumstance a strenuous act is proposed to him, I think he will be found quite indisposed; his present weakness will plant discouragement in his soul; he will fear everything because he will feel he can do nothing. The peoples of warm countries are timid, as are the aged; those of cold countries are courageous, as are the young. If we pay close attention to the last wars,[21] which are the ones we have most readily in view, and in which we can more easily see certain slight effects imperceptible from afar, we will be quite aware that peoples of the north transported into southern countries have not performed such great feats there as their compatriots who, fighting in their own climate, were in full possession of their courage there.

Because of the strength of the fibers of peoples of the north, the coarser juices are extracted from food. Two things result from this: first, the parts of the chyle or lymph[22] can with their large surface be more easily applied to the fibers and nourish them; the other is that they are less able with their coarseness to enter into the composition of the animal spirits.[23] These peoples will therefore have large bodies and limited energy.

19 We know that it shrinks iron. (M)
20 Ext. univ. hist. (M) Refers to reading notes entitled "Universal History," no longer extant. Extract from Herodotus, p. 424 (*Catalogue* 2781).
21 The War of the Spanish Succession (1701–1714), fought both in Flanders and in Spain.
22 Galen of Pergamum (130–200 CE) believed that chyle (from *chylos*, the Greek word for juice), was the fluid produced when food is digested and transported from the intestine to the liver by the portal vein.
23 Animal spirits, since the time of Galen, were thought to be produced in the brain and sent by the soul through a system of hollow nerve tubes, producing contraction when entering muscle fibers. Flowing in the other direction back to the brain, they carried

Each of the nerves which come from every direction into the tissue of our skin makes a bundle of nerves; they terminate in a sort of papilla. Ordinarily it is not the entire nerve which is stimulated, but only an infinitely small part of it. In warm countries, where the skin tissue is slack, the nerve endings are expanded and exposed to the smallest movement of the slightest objects. In cold countries, the skin tissue is tight and the papillæ compressed, the small tufts are more or less paralyzed, and sensation can scarcely reach the brain except when it is extremely strong and comes from the entire nerve. But it is on an infinite number of small sensations that imagination, taste, sensitivity, and energy depend.

I have observed the outer tissue of a sheep's tongue, in the spot where it appears to the naked eye covered with papillæ. With a microscope I have seen small hairs, or a sort of down, on these papillæ; between the papillæ were pyramids that were shaped at their ends into something like small paintbrushes. It seems quite likely that these pyramids are the principal organ of taste.[24]

I had half of this tongue frozen and found the papillæ considerably reduced to the naked eye; several rows of papillæ had even withdrawn into their sheaths. I examined its tissue with the microscope and no longer saw any pyramids. As the tongue thawed, the papillæ seemed to the naked eye to rise up again, and in the microscope the small pyramids began to reappear.

This observation confirms what I have said. In cold countries the nerve tufts are less expanded; they withdraw into their sheaths, where they are shielded from the action of exterior objects. The sensations are therefore les vivid.]

Several effects must follow from this physical constitution. The peoples of the North will not have the immediate insight, the conceptual quickness, the facility of receiving and communicating all sorts of impressions that people in other climates have. But if they do not have the advantage of quickness, they will have that of detachment; they will have more constancy in their resolutions and make fewer mistakes when they carry them out.

The Dutch are famous for the deliberation with which they absorb ideas. It is to this that they owe the consistency of their political principles and the constancy in their passions that has enabled them to accomplish such great things.

sensations to the brain. Albrecht von Haller (1708–1777), however, discovered that muscles possess an inherent ability for contraction following stimulus (*Elements of the Physiology of the Human Body*, 8 vols., Lausanne and Bern, 1759–1766).

24 Marcello Malpighi (1628–1694) discovered the nerve endings forming the taste buds by dissecting a calf's tongue (*Catalogue* 1151, 1254, 1381).

Accordingly, the imagination of northern peoples will be more tranquil; they will be less capable of accomplishing what are called creative works than works of compilation, and for the same reason they will be more adept than other peoples at making discoveries in the arts that require assiduous effort and sustained experimentation.[25]

[In cold countries people will be largely insensitive to pleasures; they will be more sensitive in temperate countries and extremely so in warm countries. As we distinguish climates by degrees of latitude, they could be distinguished, so to speak, by degrees of sensitivity. One has only to observe what happens in the operas of Italy and England; they are the same plays and the same actors, but the same music produces such different effects on the two nations, one being so calm and the other so exalted, that it seems inconceivable.

Pain is provoked in us by the rending of some fiber in our body. The way the author of nature has made things, this pain is sharper as the disturbance is greater; now it is evident that the large bodies and coarse fibers of the peoples of the North are less susceptible to disturbance than the delicate fibers of the peoples of warm countries; the soul is thus less sensitive to pain. You have to flay a Muscovite to make him feel anything.

With this delicacy of people's organs in warm countries, the mind is supremely moved by anything related to the union of the two sexes; everything leads to this objective.

In northern climates, even physical love has scarcely the power to make itself strongly felt; in temperate climates love, accompanied by a thousand accessories, becomes agreeable through things which seem to be the thing itself, and are not yet; in warmer climates love is loved for itself, it is the sole cause of happiness: it is life.]

It is this difference in the constitution of the machine that gives rise to different strengths of the passions. In a country where love is the primary interest, jealousy is the greatest passion.[26]

[In warm climates, a delicate and feeble yet sensitive machine finds its delights in the repose of a seraglio and in the arms of an odalisque. In northern countries a healthy and well-constituted but heavy machine finds its pleasures in whatever can quicken the spirits: hunting, travel, war, wine.

---

25 The next four paragraphs, which we have placed within square brackets, became part of SL xiv, 2.
26 The next seven paragraphs, placed within square brackets, following modification, were integrated into SL xiv, 2 and SL xiv, 10.

With regard to morals, you will find in Northern climates peoples who have few vices, virtues enough, and much sincerity and candor. Moving in a southerly direction, it is like leaving morality itself behind; more intense passions will multiply crimes; everyone will seek to seize the advantages over others that can favor those same passions. In temperate countries you will see people inconsistent in their manners, and even in their vices and their virtues: the climate there is not of sufficiently determinate quality to fix them.

We must note that the heat of the climate can be so excessive that the body will utterly lack strength. At that point, exhaustion will even affect the wits: no curiosity, no noble enterprise, no generous feeling; all inclinations will be passive, indolence will make for happiness; punishments will be less difficult to bear than action of the mind, and servitude less unbearable than the strength of mind required for governing oneself.

In warm climates, the slackness of the fibers produces a great loss of fluids, but the solid parts dissipate less. The fibers which have only a very weak activity and little force do not wear out; little nutritive juice is needed to restore them; thus people eat very little.

Water is an ideal drink in warm countries; the aqueous part of the blood is largely dissipated by perspiration and thus must be replaced by such a liquid. Strong liquids would coagulate the globules of the blood[27] that remain after the dissipation of the aqueous part.

In cold countries, little of the aqueous part of the blood is exhaled through perspiration; it remains in great abundance. Spirituous liquids can therefore be used without the blood coagulating. The body has no want of humors;[28] there strong liquids that give movement to the blood can be appropriate.

From these different needs that people have in these different climates must follow the different manners of living that we encounter and, consequently, sharply contrasting behavior and very divergent characters.]

The peoples of hot countries, as we have said, need to eat watery foods, and these are the lightest. Besides, they must also have delicate things to eat because their fibers are fragile, and their fibers become fragile because they eat delicate foods.

---

27 In the blood there are red globules, fibrous parts, white globules, and water in which all those things swim. (M)

28 See blood mixed with water or blood which you infuse with spirits of wine. (M)

The peoples of cold countries need coarse food to sustain themselves. The attrition that takes place in their organs needs to be compensated for.[29] Their food also must be coarse because their fibers are strong, and their fibers are strong because their food is coarse.

Those who were responsible for training the athletes and young men who exercised in the palestra found that their strength depended entirely on the coarseness of the food they gave them; it was pork seasoned with dill and a sort of very heavy bread kneaded with cheese. If they gave them a lighter diet, regardless of the quantity they gave, the strength of their pupils was immediately observed to diminish. The coarse food must therefore have thickened their fibers and given them a sturdier contexture. When the thickening and toughness of the fibers reaches a point of excess, the brain is perpetually sluggish. The fibers and spirits prove incapable of receiving the infinite number of varied, sudden, and distinct movements they need. The athletes of whom we have been speaking are proof of this;[30] all the writers agree on the dullness of their wits.[31]

Although it would appear that impressions are communicated to the soul by means of a spirit or a fluid contained in the nerves,[32] the fibers must still be flexible and possess a certain capability of moving and being moved. These things are reciprocal; the nerve fluid cannot be transported without some tension of fibers, nor can the fibers be made taut, or be moved unless the nervous fluid reaches them.[33]

29 The wearing away of the solid parts of the body by friction or by the action of the body's fluids was termed *anachoresis* and *pleurosis* by Plato, consumption and repletion by Hippocrates, depredation and reparation by Bacon, and decrement and increment by Herman Boerhaave (1668–1738) in his *Institutiones medicae* (Leiden, 1708; *Catalogue* 1050). See Thomas S. Hall, "Life as Opposed Transformation," *Journal of the History of Medicine and Allied Sciences* 20 (1965), 262–275.

30 Polybius cites Gorgus Messenius as an exception to this stupidity characteristic of athletes (Excerpta ex Polybio. Libro vii). (M) *Polybii, Diodori Siculi, Nicolai Damasceni [. . .] Excerpta ex collectaneius Constantini Augusti Porphyrogenetae* ("Excerpts from the collection of Constantine August Porphyrogenitus") (Paris, 1634).

31 When the nerve diameters are larger, there is a broader column of liquid contained between the extremity of the nerve and its inner part, and the impressions could be weaker. It appears that the neural ganglia, attached in various places along the pathways of the nerves, contradict the vibration theory. (M) See also *Pensées* 1191 and 1192 for the effects of food on mental acuity. Montesquieu's source for his comments on the dullness of athletes was very likely *Lives and Opinions of Eminent Philosophers* (*Catalogue* 1442), by Diogenes Laertius, a third-century CE writer about whom little is known.

32 Marcello Malpighi (1628–1694; *Catalogue* 1151, 1254, 1381) was the source of Montesquieu's discussion of this nerve fluid (*OC* ix, 228, note 40).

33 Monsieur Bertin reports having made a fine experiment. Tying the diaphragmatic nerve of a dog, he squeezed it above the ligature and found that movement was restored as if he had squeezed it below the ligature. Thus the experiment that was cited against vibrations supports vibrations. (M) Experiments with ligatures were quite

The mind will be able to renew thoughts when it can reproduce in the brain the movements the brain has received and make the nerve fluid flow to the brain. The flexibility of the fibers can therefore give it the capacity for creating thoughts.

The thinner the string of a musical instrument, the better able it is to make a high note; that is, it makes more vibrations in the same lapse of time than a string whose sound is pitched lower; and contrariwise, the thicker the string, the lower the note, which is to say, it makes fewer vibrations in the same lapse of time than another with a higher pitch. So when the fibers that the mind moves are thick, their vibrations are less frequent and slower.[34]

External objects give the mind sensations. It cannot re-experience them, but it can recall that it has had them. When it has felt a pain, it does not repeat that pain to itself, but it feels that it has had it, which is to say that it places itself again, insofar as possible, in the state of the sensation. In order actually to experience that sensation, it would have to come to it along the path by which it had previously come. A thought is thus simply a feeling experienced as a result of a sensation one has had, a present situation occasioned by a past situation.[35] When, by means of the senses, the mind has felt a pain, the irritation of that part has pressed on the nerve's origin[36] and excited a movement as perceptible as the irritation was strong; now the mind, which has the ability to make the spirits go wherever it wants, as the experience of all voluntary movements shows, can make the spirits take once more the paths where they had been when they were stimulated by an external cause.[37] They there-fore pass again into the brain, or press on it, which is the same thing.[38] Now,

common and were generally thought to prove the existence of animal spirits, since the lack of sensation beyond the ligature could be attributed to the blocked flow of the nerve fluid. Experiment by Exupère Joseph Bertin (1712–1781), however, supported the contrary theory of transmission by vibrations continuing their course beyond a ligature.

34 Our brain fibers, incessantly in motion, must be like those fibers in a harpsichord player's fingers, which appear, by force of habit, to move completely unaided, that is, without dependence on the will. (M).

35 Cf. John Locke on sensation as the first step toward thought, or reflection (*Essay concerning Human Understanding*, 1690; *Catalogue* 1489).

36 I.e., in the brain.

37 The mind can do three things: (1) hold back the animal spirits and use them to renew its sensations; (2) use the animal spirits to bring about the various movements that it wishes to give to the body; and finally, allow them to flow through the cerebellum for vital movements. (M)

38 Monsieur Sénac [Jean-Baptiste Sénac, 1693–1770, physician to Louis XIV] says that the reverse action of the animal spirits is inexplicable. Why is this so? I am well aware that they do not circulate from the outer parts to the brain, and that they appear to continue their course. But why can't they exert pressure from the extremities of the body toward the brain since they are inside completely filled tubes? From this I conclude by

this new feeling is only a thought or representation, since the soul is quite aware that this is not the sensation itself and that this movement, unlike the other, does not come to it from the whole length of the nerve nor from an external action, but by means of its own will. Nothing more is required to explain feeling. Perception, thoughts, memory are all the same operation, which comes from nothing but the mind's ability to feel; but it is clear how necessary it is that the fibers of the brain be flexible.

Too much rigidity or coarseness of the fibers can render the wits sluggish, but their excessive flexibility, when it is accompanied by slackening, can produce its weakness; and when this delicacy and this slackening are accompanied by a great abundance of animal spirits, then inconstancy, eccentricity, and capriciousness naturally result. The brain is briskly moved by the present object and ceases to be moved by others.

We are not too sure what particular disposition of the brain is requisite for mental alertness, but we can conjecture something on the subject. For instance, we know that liveliness of the eyes often indicates an alert wit. Now the peoples of cold countries rarely have lively eyes. Since they have superfluous humidity in the brain, what are called motor nerves, being perpetually moistened, slacken and become incapable of producing the quick and lively vibrations in the eyes that make them sparkle. So, as I have just said that the liveliness of the wit and of the eyes generally go together, it seems to follow from this that excess humidity which is adverse to the one is almost as adverse to the other. Thus, the Ancients were right, albeit without knowing what they were saying, when they regarded wit as a moderate dryness of the brain.[39]

It has been observed in England that the bones of a thoroughbred, that is, one born of a Barbary stallion and an English mare, of equal size, weigh more by half than those of an ordinary English horse. The bones of the former have less marrow and their fibers are more

---

functional analogy that the mind receives sensations through the ministry of the nerves only by means of pressure, and that a canal full of liquid, pressed at one end, affects the other end and must, likewise, when pressed at the opposite end, have a similar effect. If, then, the mind, by pressing the fibers in the region of the medulla oblongata, sends animal spirits toward the legs, the nerves that extend from the brain to the legs when pressed in the area of the legs must likewise exert pressure in the brain. (M) Montesquieu owned Sénac's *Anatomie avec les essais de physique sur l'usage des parties du corps humain et sur le mécanisme de leur mouvement* (1724; *Catalogue* 1249), but favored the views of Alfonso Borelli, *De motu animalium* (1710; *Catalogue* 1411) over the conclusions of Sénac, who adopted the position of Descartes and rejected the possibility of reverse action of the animal spirits (*OC* IX, 231, note 50).

39 In his *Parts of Animals*, 652a35, Aristotle had asserted that the brain is "the driest" of all the "moist parts of the body."

compact, and their consistency is more dense. I would like to do the same experiment with the bones of a Dutchman and a man from the Pyrenees. If the difference was similar, we could surmise that the fibers, more or less dry, or more or less compact, would contribute to making up the differences between their characters.

Air entering our lungs inflates the vesicles[40] over which teem the small branches of the pulmonary artery and pulmonary vein, which ceasing to be collapsed, allow the blood to fill the whole substance of the lungs. When the air is very elastic, there occur an infinite number of small impacts on the walls of the vesicles, and consequently on the sheaths of the blood vessels spread out over them. These are degrees of movement continually added. The blood is more readily thinned out and becomes better adapted to an abundant secretion of spirits.

The wit of the Athenians was attributed to the subtlety of the air in Athens,[41] and it would appear that it was indeed one of the major causes, since today when the Athenians, uneducated slaves, have nothing but the air in their favor under the empire of the Turk,[42] their genius still attracts notice.

We often hear about the wit of the Canarians,[43] peoples who inhabit the territory of Goa: they have so many advantages over the Portuguese that they make more progress in the schools in six months, regardless of the subject, than the Europeans do in a year, and this superiority is so pronounced that it gives umbrage to the dominant nation. The Portuguese forbid the Canarians to fit out ships; they weaken them in heart and mind by a kind of slavery; they allow them no profession other than that of trial lawyer, where they exercise such a shrewd ability at dispute that they exceed the litigants' expectation.

And from this we can conclude two things: first, that the climate contributes immeasurably to modifying the mind; and second, that the

---

40 I.e., the *vesiculae pulmonales*, or Malpighi's vesicles, now called alveoli. Malpighi had discovered that pulmonary arterial blood is oxygenated in these air sacs prior to flowing into the atrium on the left side of the heart. Montesquieu's chief interest in them was the effect of the air they contain on the blood's secretion of animal spirits in the cortex of the brain.

41 Cicero had discussed the influence of air quality in *On Fate* (*De fato*), IV, 7 (*Catalogue* 1841), as had Malebranche (*Catalogue* 1495). On air quality and mental acumen, see also Montesquieu's *Reflections on the Inhabitants of Rome*.

42 The Greeks were ruled by the Ottoman Turks from the late Middle Ages until 1830.

43 The Canarians were a people of Goa in western India. Pierre du Jarric's account of Portuguese activities in India (*Catalogue* 3159) was the likely source of Montesquieu's information for this paragraph.

effect is not immediate, and it takes a long sequence of generations to produce it, for the Portuguese since the conquest are still much as they were before.[44]

In every country the foods consumed have a quality analogous to the nature of the soil. We find iron in honey; the particles of this metal must therefore have been absorbed by the plants and the flowers from which the bees extract it. We find it in the blood. Therefore the plants and animals which men consume contain it.[45] The same can be said of the other metals and other minerals.[46] There we see minds and characters veritably subjected to differences of soils.[47]

[The air is laden, as are plants, with particles of the soil of each country, and there can be no doubt that these enter our body since we find them even in the metals that we smelt.

All this acts so greatly on us that our temperament is fixed by it. When we go from one country to another, we usually become sick. Our fluids have taken on a certain consistency and a certain movement through a particular mixture of parts, and our solids, accustomed to a certain disposition, are no longer able to bear another and resist adopting a new manner.]

If the air in every country acts on minds, the winds, which are movements of air, affect them no less. There is very notable evidence of this throughout the world. The peoples who live along the Pyrenees, on this side, are quite different from those who live along them on the other side; the peoples who have the Apennines to the north are very different from those who have them to the south, and so forth.

Winds act either by moving air that is heavier or thinner, drier or more humid, than that of a particular climate, or bearing more of the particles peculiar to the country through which they have passed, or finally by giving greater buoyancy to the air; but the force of their action is much increased by its quickness, for winds catch us unawares and change us in a moment.

---

44 Simon de La Loubère in *The Kingdom of Siam* (*Du royaume de Siam*, 1691; *Catalogue* 2747) observed, to the contrary, in a text which one of Montesquieu's secretaries copied, that the Indian climate produced immediate changes in the Portuguese colonizers.

45 Cf. John Arbuthnot's *An Essay on the Effects of Air on Human Bodies* (1733) and Descartes's *Traité de l'homme* ("Treatise on Man," 1648, in *Œuvres de Descartes*, Paris: Cerf, 1897–1913, IX, 169; *OC* IX, 234, note 60).

46 Enough of them enter to influence the body but not enough to harm it. (M)

47 Montesquieu placed a longer discussion of trace elements and their effect on national character in *De la différence des génies* ("On the difference of intellects," 1717), which is no longer extant. See *Pensées* 2265 for more on the influence of soil on minds and character.

There is in Italy a southerly wind[48] called the Sirocco,[49] which has passed over the sands of Africa. It dominates Italy. It exerts its power over all minds; it produces lethargy and general unease. A man can feel in his bed that the Sirocco is blowing; he behaves differently than he did the day before. In short, the Sirocco is the intelligence that rules over every Italian, and I would be tempted to believe that the difference existing between the mentality and character of the inhabitants of Lombardy[50] and that of other Italians comes from Lombardy having the Apennines to shield her, protecting her from the ravages of the Sirocco.

The English also have their easterly wind, but the difference is that whereas the maladies that attack Italian minds strongly incline them to self-preservation, those that attack the English mind incline them to self-destruction; the English malady is not simply the effect of a passing cause, but of several other, long-standing causes.[51] [It is a flaw in the filtration of the nerve juice, which stems, no doubt, from the thickening of the blood. The machine, whose motor forces are fatigued, is weary of itself; the mind is aware of no pain, but of a certain difficulty of existing. Pain is a local affliction that makes us desire to see that pain cease; the weight of life is an affliction that has no particular locus and makes us desire to see this life end.[52]]

The difference of the sexes ought also to diversify minds. The periodic change that occurs in women has very extensive effects; it must attack the mind itself. We know that its cause lies in an abundance that increases steadily over approximately a month, whereupon the blood which is present in too great quantity forces its way out. Now, with this quantity changing daily in them, their mood and personality must similarly change.[53]

Women's fibers are softer, slacker, more flexible, and more delicate than men's. This is because a portion of their vessels are less pressed, since the

---

48 It is actually southeastern. According to Father Ansleb's account of Egypt, that country is subject to the ravages of the same southerly wind. (M) See Johann Wansleben's *Relation of Egypt* (Paris, 1698; *Catalogue* 2757).

49 Originating in the Arabian or the Sahara deserts, the Sirocco is a counter-clockwise wind that carries red sand and at times reaches hurricane force in North Africa and southern Europe.

50 Lombardy is a triangle, the apex of which is in Piedmont, the base on the Adriatic, and the sides formed by the Alps and the Apennines. (M)

51 The remainder of this paragraph became, with modifications, the second paragraph of *SL* xiv, 12.

52 Montesquieu's physical explanation of the English penchant for suicide was censured by his Jansenist critic Jean-Baptiste Gaultier (see *Defense of The Spirit of Law*), by the Jesuit *Journal de Trévoux*, and also by the faculty of theology at the Sorbonne for seeming to excuse suicide. Montesquieu added this footnote to Book xiv, chapter 12 of the 1757 edition of *SL*: "Suicide is contrary to the law of nature and to revealed religion."

53 Cf. *Spicilège* 249.

cavity formed by the sacrum, the coccyx, and the pubic and innominate bones[54] is larger in them. Just as veins have a weaker composition than the arteries because they can dilate more, it will be the same with these vessels. Moreover, as the excess of blood can force open passages, the vessels will not require such strong contraction to propel it from the extremities toward its center.[55]

Furthermore, men have an organ which, through a function it assumes in them at the age of puberty, in very short order changes the consistency of their fibers, which were previously as delicate as those of women. We do not know how to explain in what way this liquid, separated, filtered, and stored in these organs produces these effects, but we see it, and we see that it occurs neither in women nor in eunuchs.[56] We know, moreover, that this liquid is so active that the females of animals we consume change in taste once they have conceived, which supposes, given the manner in which our sense of taste comes about, an extraordinary disturbance in their fibers. All these things make us quite aware of the physical difference in the character of the two sexes.

Anatomical observations make visible to us a prodigious variety from one subject to another, such that there have perhaps never been two men whose organic parts have been arranged alike in all respects. If we look at works on anatomy and take the veins, for example, we will see that there are few that intertwine in one subject as in another. One person will have only one vein of a certain name, whereas another will have two. What we find with regard to veins will also be found with regard to arteries, nerves, and lymphatic vessels.[57] I will not go into details: they would be endless, and even the observations which we have made are nothing compared with those that are not within our purview.

These variations which our eyes show us in the parts we can distinguish in the human body are not fewer in the imperceptible vessels in the brain.

54 I.e., bones in the hips that had not yet been named.
55 It was generally thought that the uterine vessels bleed easily because the fibers of women are softer, the descending trunk of the aorta is larger in women, and the vessels of the womb are not surrounded by muscles or fat.
56 It was believed that semen is derived from the blood by a process of filtration in the testes, and stored in the seminal vesicles (Boerhaave, *Institutiones medicae*, v, 649). The secretion of androgen in the testes, creating secondary sexual characteristics at puberty, was not yet understood, and such bodily changes, experienced neither in women nor in eunuchs, were commonly attributed to the reabsorption by the blood of a portion of the semen (*ibid.*, v, 647).
57 The German chemist Georg Ernst Stahl (1659–1734), in his *Opuscula chimico phisoco medica* (Halle, 1715; *Catalogue* 1351), reported that blood vessels also vary considerably from individual to individual.

If with the onset of circulation,[58] it happened that the blood for some reason found more resistance in passing[59] through the descending aorta than through the branches of the thoracic aorta, it would rise in greater quantity to the brain; there is no doubt that the filtration of the spirits would be very different from what it would be in the opposite case; and this effect would be permanent because the vessels, having to contain more liquid, would increase in diameter.[60]

The parts do not properly fulfill their intended functions unless their size is proportionate to what the mechanics of the body requires. The head must accommodate six lobes of the brain and two of the cerebellum; its shape must therefore correspond to this purpose. If we do not see that this is so, there must be some irregularity in that of the brain.[61]

Although, when we think, we can tell that the action is taking place in the head and not in the feet and the hands, it is nevertheless not only the fibers of the brain that relate to the mind. An example will illustrate this.

The portio dura of the auditory nerve[62] forms what is called the *chorda tympani* of the ear, which ends in the lingual nerve of the third branch of the fifth pair. The hard portion is divided into three branches: the lower, the middle, and the upper. These communicate with the three branches[63] of the

---

58 I.e., in the fetus.

59 There are persons in whom two external jugular veins are found on each side. The blood empties more easily from the brain, and, as a result, rises to the brain more easily. (M)

60 The function of the vasomotor nerves in effecting or inhibiting the contraction of blood vessels was explained by Claude Bernard (1813–1878).

61 We must note that the more necessary the sensation, the more it is clear, strong, and common to all. Thus the senses of sight, hearing and touch are very clear. The nerves that occasion them are as alert and sensitive in one climate as in another. It is the milder sensations, unessential to the well-being of the machine, that are not given to everyone and occur only in refined persons. It is necessary that everyone hear sounds but not that everyone be sensitive to the beauties of music. In a word, the strong and unrefined sense operations are bestowed on all men. The delicate ones are bestowed on only a few. (M) Montesquieu's interest in brain functions, already pronounced, partly as a result of his reading of Nicolas Malebranche's *The Search after Truth* (1674–1675), was likely increased in 1738 when his friend Martin Folkes, secretary of the English Royal Society, sent him Henry Ridley's *The Anatomy of the Brain containing its Mechanism and Physiology* (London, 1695; *Catalogue* 1260; *OC* IX, 238, note 72).

62 The auditory nerve has both a hard portion (*portio dura*), or vestibular nerve, and a soft portion (*portio mollis*), or cochlear nerve. The *portio dura* to which Montesquieu refers controls balance rather than hearing. He draws here on works on anatomy by Bartolomeo Eustachi (*Catalogue* 1242) and Raymond Vieussens (*Catalogue* 1274).

63 The upper branch of the trunk of the *portio dura* is connected to the first branch of the fifth pair, called the ophthalmic nerve; the middle branch joins the second branch of the fifth pair, or the upper maxillary nerve, and the lower branch is connected to the third branch of the fifth pair, or the lower maxillary nerve. (M)

fifth pair, which send two branches to the intercostal.[64] Furthermore, this hard portion joins the cervical nerves which themselves communicate with the intercostal nerve; this intercostal is the great instrument of the movements not produced by our will because it goes to the heart and to the lungs and into all the parts contained in the chest and the lower abdomen. Whence I conclude that when we hear singing or declamation, two equally mechanical things occur: the first, that we hear the sounds clearly; the other, that we are moved by these sounds. And it is a daily occurrence that of two persons, the one who hears better is the less moved. To hear well, it suffices that the ear organ be well formed; to be moved when we hear, there must be good communication between the nerves of the ear and the nerves which go to other parts of the body to produce involuntary movements: for then the heart is stirred, as are most of the internal parts, and the emotion, which it seemed should come to the brain solely from the ear, comes to it from almost every part of the body.

But since the feeling of the mind is almost always a result of all the various movements produced in the different organs of our body, men in whom the communication of these movements occurs easily may have more delicacy of feeling and more refinement of mind than those in whom it is difficult.

The mind is in our bodies like a spider in its web, which cannot move without setting in motion one of the threads which extend away from it, and likewise none of these threads can be moved without affecting the spider. Nor can any of the threads be touched without making another that corresponds with it move as well. The more taut the threads, the better the spider is alerted; if some of them are slack, then communication will be lessened from that thread to the spider or from that thread to another thread, and the fate of the spider will be dependent on how it is positioned in its own web.

Just as those who play some musical instrument are careful to install on it strings free of knots and places thicker or thinner, tighter or looser than others, so to insure that no interruption occurs, it is likewise essential in our machine for the easy communication of movements that all the nerve parts be uniform and smooth, that there be no spot tighter, drier, or less able to receive the enabling fluid,[65] that each part correspond to the whole, that the whole be an entity, and that there be no break in the contexture.

---

64 Sometimes the seven cervical nerves are connected to the intercostal. (M) Raymond Vieussens, in his *Neurographia universalis* (1716), had catalogued eight cervical nerves (*OC* IX, 240, note 76).

65 I.e., the animal spirits that he sometimes terms nerve juice (*suc nerveux*).

Nothing that exists in nature has complete uniformity, but each thing has more or less of it, and this greater or lesser uniformity in each fiber causes great differences in movements.

The number of things on which the state of our minds depends is beyond belief; it is not just the disposition of the brain that modifies it; the whole machine together and almost all the parts of the machine contribute to it, and often those one would not suspect. There is a certain type of men who are usually sad, angry, capricious, weak, spiteful, eccentric, and timid: and that is eunuchs. Whether the semen reenters the blood or fails to separate from it, it is certain that they become different from other men; this failure of separation, which applies also to women,[66] makes for at least one similarity between their bodies. For example, the temperament of eunuchs becomes weak like that of women, and they have no more beard than women do.[67]

Perpetual continence can place those who, without the permission of nature or a true vocation from above, have committed themselves to celibacy in about the same situation as eunuchs. They indeed have the capacity,[68] but being separated from the use of that capacity can contribute to distressing them further. The liquid separates in the seminal vesicles; it remains there too long, it irritates them, and signals to the mind to dispatch spirits, and the mind dares not obey.[69]

Passions act greatly on us. Life is just a succession of passions, which are sometimes stronger, sometimes weaker, now of one kind, now of another. It cannot be doubted that the combination of these passions over a whole lifetime, a different combination in each individual, introduces a great variety of minds.

There are passions that add resilience to the fibers, others that relax them. This is proved, on the one hand, by the strength and power of anger, and on the other by the effects of fear: the arms drop, the legs bend, the voice fails, the muscles relax.[70] Thus a life that is long timid or long courageous will stay that way forever.

---

66 The presence of semen in women, to which Montesquieu here attests, had been debated since antiquity and was discussed in the article "Semen" (*Semence*) in the *Encyclopédie* (OC IX, 242, note 82).

67 The role of hormones was not discovered until the early twentieth century.

68 *Propriété*.

69 The seminal vesicles were thought to store the semen prior to venery; they are now known to contribute the bulk of the seminal plasma. For a contemporary analysis of their functioning, see Albrecht von Haller (1708–1777), *First Lines of Physiology*, translated from a Latin edition of 1775 (London, 1786).

70 Cf. *Pensées* 182, ¶3, originally part of *De la différence des génies* (see p. 37, note 42).

We must make extremely careful use of our brain fibers. As moderate movements promise us endless others, the violent ones take a toll of those that are to follow. The Orientals cheer themselves up with a concoction of hemp that gives them such agreeable thoughts and such intense pleasures that for a few hours they are completely transported. It is followed by total dejection and a state approaching lethargy. The effect of this liquor[71] is to tug[72] at the fibers, which become unresponsive to lesser stimulation. One dose stupefies only for a while; extensive use stupefies permanently. Great joy is a state as far removed from good health as is great sorrow. The pleasure of being is the pleasure only of a person presently in good health.

The immoderate use of wine stupefies progressively. The fibers are stimulated, but only for a time; they relax and it soon takes more wine to affect them. The same dose will not suffice and to produce the same effect a stronger effect will be necessary every day.

Great nobles who exhaust themselves with pleasures sink into dejection, boredom, and feeble-mindedness, and these are afflictions which they communicate to their children. They grow dull because they can no longer receive new impressions; they are overwhelmed because they are no longer capable of quick movements; they are sometimes feeble-minded because, receiving nothing but the impressions of present objects, they are necessarily controlled by the passing and momentary movement they are given.[73]

Too much sleep is extremely stupefying.[74] The fibers remain too long unmoved; the spirits thicken and remain in their reservoirs. Athletes[75] were the greatest sleepers, and the stupidest of all men.

Long waking periods produce not stupidity, but imbecility and even madness,[76] especially if they are accompanied by prolonged fasting: the spirits become excited and run impetuously through the brain as in a frenzy and leave deep traces there.

71 It produces heat, strengthens the heart, and increases the movement of the blood. The lightened liquids move forcibly through the vessels of the brain where they should move only weakly. (M)
72 This tightening is the cause of the loss of ideas that takes place in certain illnesses. (M)
73 See also *Pensées* 408.
74 According to Aulus Gellius, it has been noticed that children who sleep too long become slow-witted. See my extract. (M)
75 Plato, *Republic* Book I. (M) (*Republic* Book III, 404a.)
76 Read [the chapter on] wakefulness [*vigilia*] in Boerhaave's *Institutiones medicae* and in addition his pathology; it is the same theme. (M) Note 93 in *OC* IX, 244, identifies this work on pathology as *Aphorisms on Ways of Recognizing and Curing Illnesses* (*Aphorismi de cognoscendis et curandis morbis*, Paris, 1728; *Catalogue* 1048).

No one could suspect the ancient Fathers of the Desert[77] of having been feeble of mind. The great reputation they enjoyed in their time and the homage which worldly people paid their insight by coming from all over to consult them show that independently of their holiness they were not disreputable; yet these fathers, by their fasts and nightly vigils carried too far, pitifully wrecked their minds, and the ceaseless combats they imagined themselves having with the demons were one of the weaknesses that seemed attached to their way of life.

Prolonged chanting, especially yelling, further stupefies. We see in Livy[78] that the debauched sect who celebrated the Bacchanalia and gathered in secret places, where amid the mysteries of the most impious superstition they depraved or slaughtered young persons to the sound of voices and of musical instruments, were entirely stultified by their vigils and their continual yelling.

We know that the Mohammedans who enter tombs where they stay awake and scream unceasingly to induce trances, always emerge with weaker minds. Mahmut,[79] one of the conquerors of Persia, experiencing some sort of disgrace, wanted to consult Heaven in this way and lapsed into a kind of madness which never left him.

Screaming benumbs a person and gives irregular movements to the fibers; the spirits carom here and there without order; all the traces run together; some are imprinted more vividly, others fade away, and confusion prevails in the brain.

The effects of solitude on the mind are no less dangerous than those of fasts, vigils, and cries: the repose in which it leaves the fibers of the brain makes them almost incapable of movement. We observe that the Indian quietists who spend their lives contemplating the void become veritable animals. There is no part of our body which can be preserved without exercising its functions; teeth not used for chewing decay, and if a person uses only one eye, the other goes blind.

I believe that, in a subject as complicated as this, it is better not to go into too much detail. Huarte,[80] a Spanish writer who has treated this subject before me, tells us that Francis I, disappointed in his Christian doctors and the

---

77 Christian monks of the third through fifth centuries CE, the first of whom was St. Anthony (c. 251–356), who gave up worldly possessions to live in the mountains of Egypt where he believed he was tempted many times by the devil in various guises.

78 *Fourth Decade*, Book 9. (M) (XXIX, 8.)

79 *History of the Most Recent Revolution in Persia* (Paris, 1728), II, p. 295. (M) By Jean Antoine du Cerceau (1670–1730). Mirr-Mahmoud, alternatively spelled Myrr-Magmud, was an Afghan leader whose forces occupied a portion of Persia between 1722 and 1730. Cf. *Pensées* 295 and *Spicilège* 302.

80 I.e., Juan Huarte de San Juan (c. 1529–1588), a medical doctor trained at the University of Alcalá and author of *The Examination of Men's Wits*. Montesquieu owned a French edition: *Examen des esprits pour les sciences* (Catalogue 1474).

impotence of their remedies, sent to Charles V for a Jewish doctor. The good fellow tries to discover why the Jews have more aptitude for medicine than Christians, and he finds it is because of the excessive quantity of manna which the Israelites ate in the desert.[81]

Part Two: Moral Causes that Can Affect Minds and Characters

Those who begin to make use of their reason either find themselves among a barbarous people where there is no education at all, or else among a civilized people where one receives a general education in society.

Those who are born among a barbarous[82] people appropriately possess only ideas that have some connection with self-preservation; they live in eternal darkness with regard to all the rest. There, differences from one man to another, from one mind to another, are less great; primitiveness and the paucity of ideas somehow equalize them.

One proof that they are short of ideas is that the languages they use are all very sparse: not only do they have few words, since they have few things to express, but they also have few ways of conceptualizing and of feeling.[83]

Their brain fibers, little accustomed to being flexed, have become rigid. Men who live among these peoples should be compared to the old folks among us who have never learned anything; their brains have not, if I dare say, done any work, and their fibers are not trained in the required movements. They are incapable of adding new ideas to the few they have, and this weakness is not restricted to their brains. It would also be found in their throats if we tried to make them sing and in their fingers if we tried to have them play a musical instrument.

It has been discovered that the savages of America are immune to discipline, incorrigible, and incapable of any insight or instruction.[84] Indeed, to try to teach them something, to try to flex their brain fibers, is like undertaking to make people walk who suffer from paraplegia.

Coarseness can reach a point among such nations that men will be little different from beasts: witness the slaves whom the Turks take from Circassia

---

81 *Pensées* 1191, a fragment of *De la différence des génies* (1717), also mentions Huarte's book.
82 It seems to me matters of education are overlooked; for who doubts that education is very useful. (M)
83 Cf. Descartes, *Discourse on Method*, v; and Locke, *Essay concerning Human Understanding*, Book III (*OC* IX, 247, note 105).
84 Let. Edif. (M) I.e., *Edifying and Curious Letters of Some Missionaries of the Society of Jesus from Foreign Missions* (1717–1776).

and Mingrelia,[85] who spend the whole day with their heads bent toward their stomachs, saying nothing and doing nothing, oblivious to anything going on about them.

Brains thus abandoned lose their functions; they have almost no appreciation of their soul, nor the soul of its union with the body.

It is education that makes this union perfect; we find it among civilized nations. There, as I have said, we receive a particular education in our family and a general one in society.

Individual education consists of (1) acquiring ideas and (2) apportioning them to the correct value of things. Now, more or less ideas, more or less correctness in establishing their relation, must greatly diversify minds.

Those who raise us are, in a manner of speaking, makers of ideas: they multiply them, they teach us to combine them, to make abstractions; at every moment they are giving us new ways of being and perceiving.[86]

The elderly, on the other hand, lapse gradually into feeble-mindedness through their daily loss of their ideas: they return to childhood by losing them just as children outgrow it by acquiring them.

Men who have few ideas are bound to err in almost all their judgments. Ideas are related to each other; the principal faculty of the mind is comparison, and it cannot exercise it in such a vacuum.[87]

Education does not multiply our ideas without also multiplying our ways of feeling. It heightens the mind's awareness, refines its faculties, and causes us to perceive the slight and delicate differences that are imperceptible to people disadvantaged by their birth or upbringing.

It is not sufficient to have many ideas and many ways of feeling; there must also be harmony between them and things: it is foolish to be too much affected by an object: it is foolish to be too little affected by it.

But it is rare for men to receive the impressions of objects in a manner commensurate with their value. The first impression we receive almost always strikes us with indelible force, and this is quite understandable; the first ideas are always accepted by the mind because, being unable to compare them with others, it has no reason for rejecting them. Now the second idea can scarcely make it get over the first, nor the third the second, for it is only

---

85 Circassia, in the Greater Caucasus Mountains, was overrun by the Crimean Tatars in 1725. Mingrelia, the Black Sea region known as Colchis in ancient times, became independent in 1557 but was absorbed by Imperial Russia in 1803.

86 See the difference between a language in which there have been no writers at all, and another in which great geniuses have written. (M)

87 Cf. Locke, *Essay concerning Human Understanding*, Book II, chs. 11, 25–28 (*OC* IX, 249, note 114).

by the first that it judges the second, and by the second that it judges the third. Thus, the first things that have struck it, regardless of their value, seem somehow destined to be indestructible.[88]

It has been observed that old people who forget what they have done the day before remember very well what happened to them thirty years earlier. The strength of impressions thus depends more on the time of the action than on the action itself, more on the circumstances in which we are affected than on the significance of the thing that affects us.

After the impressions we have received in childhood, our mind successively receives a great number of others, which are stored along with the earlier ones, but in an order that might have taken shape in a thousand and one different ways.

Do we have great confidence in a man who is speaking to us, or in a philosopher who has written? We create for ourselves an order of things that are true, good, or appropriate; they are the things that the latter has written or the former has told us: we take from an outside source the grounds for our opinions.

When we are very fond of someone, there is yet another source of things true, good or appropriate, which are those that person has approved, advised, prescribed, or done, things that will immediately assume a privileged position in our thinking.

To sense better how greatly our mind is being affected differently by the same objects on different occasions, we need only picture to ourselves the times when we are enraptured by love and those when our passion subsides. How changed is our entire soul; how unaffected it now is by everything that affected it; how everything that no longer affected it begins to affect it once more! Our soul is very limited and it cannot respond to several emotions at the same time; when it has several, the least must follow the strongest and be pulled in its direction.

As if by a common movement, in the fury of love, all other ideas take on the hue of that love to which alone the mind is attuned. Hatred, jealousy, fear, and expectation are all like glasses of different colors through which we see an object that always appears to us equally red, or green, differing only in shade.

Moreover, our machine is unlikely to be constituted in such a way that our brain is not physically disposed to receive rather the impression of one order of things than of another.

---

88 See also *Pensées* 1187 and 1341.

A man who has imagination and another who has none see things as differently as two romantic heroes of whom one would be enchanted and the other not. The first would see walls of crystal, roofs of rubies, streams of silver, and tables of diamonds; the other would see in them only dreadful mountains and arid lands.

Such is the physical constitution of our machine that we are too greatly struck or too little by the things that reach us through the senses or through a certain sense, or by mathematical or moral relationships, or by general or individual conceptions of facts or rationales. One person will be convinced by rhetoric, another only by simple logic; one will be impressed by words and the other only by manifest fact; one will never see the thing without the difficulty and will remain uncertain; the other will see the thing better than the difficulty and will believe everything; another, finally, will see the difficulty better than the thing itself and will believe nothing. One will be sensitive to the things and not to the connections and will have no order, or he will think he sees connections in everything and will be confused. Here the impulse is always to create, there always to destroy.[89] Ideas that merely skim one man's brain will pierce another's, so to speak, to the point of madness.

But when, besides the particular disposition of the brain, rarely constructed so as to receive ideas in proper proportion, education too is inadequate, all is lost; our masters give us impressions only as they themselves have received them, and if they are not commensurate with the objects, they spoil in us the ability to compare, which is the mind's great faculty.

Education, as I have said, consists in giving us ideas, and a good education in putting them in proper perspective. A dearth of ideas results in stupidity, lack of harmony among ideas foolishness, and extreme disharmony madness.

With a man of wit[90] things make on him the impression they should, whether putting him in a position to judge, or in a position to please. Hence two kinds of education: one we receive from our masters and one we receive from worldly society.[91] We must receive both because all things have two values, an intrinsic value and a value based on opinion: these two educations give us an accurate understanding of these two values, and wit enables us to

89 One person will have activity in his mind, another will merely take things in like a purse that will give back only the money one puts in it. (M)
90 *Homme d'esprit.*
91 Cf. *SL* IV, 2, 4. Montesquieu's discussions likely draw on the Spanish Jesuit Baltasar Gracián y Morales, *L'Homme de cour* ("The courtier," *Catalogue* 2388) and *L'Homme universel* ("The complete gentleman," *Catalogue* 2389).

put one or the other to use, depending upon the time, the persons, and the place.

A man of wit perceives and acts instantly as he should perceive and act: he creates himself, so to speak, in each moment according to the present need; he knows and senses the proper relationship between things and himself. A man of wit senses what others can only know. All that is mute for most people speaks to him and informs him. Some people read men's faces, others physiognomies; still others see right into the mind. One could say that while a fool communes only with bodies, people of wit commune with intellects.

A man of wit is not a man who always has quips to make, because three-fourths of the time they are out of place; nor does wit always consist in being on target because that too is often out of place, as for example, in bantering conversations that are but a web of false reasoning that engage by their very falseness and singularity. For if one sought nothing but truth in conversations, they would not be varied and would no longer be entertaining.[92]

A man of wit is thus more versatile, but, in the strict sense, this type of man is quite rare. He must combine two qualities almost physically incompatible, for there is genuinely as much difference between what is called a man of wit in society and a man of wit among philosophers as there is between a man of wit and a stupid one.[93] Wit according to the worldly consists in combining the most unrelated ideas; wit among philosophers is distinguishing between them. Among the first, all ideas that have some connection, however distant, are conjured up; among the others, they cannot be conflated.

Here is a song of the Greeks:[94] The foremost of all goods is health; the second, beauty; the third, wealth honestly accumulated; the fourth, youth spent with friends. There is no mention there of wit, which is the principal quality of our times.

We have just mentioned the particular education that shapes each character, but there is also a general education that we receive in the society where we live. For every nation has a general character which that of each individual more or less assumes. It is produced in two ways: by physical

92 See *Pensées* 107, 1682, and 1971.

93 Among the Greeks the very idea of a man of wit was scarcely known. See the song at the end of the ex. from the Journ. of Scav. [*Journal des Savants*]. (M)

94 See this song in l'hist. de l'ac des Inscript. Vols. IX and X. (M) I.e., *Histoire de l'Académie royale des inscriptions et belles-lettres depuis l'année 1731*, quoted in the August 1736 edition of the *Journal des Savants*, as Montesquieu indicates in *Pensées* 1354.

causes that are relative to climate, of which I will say no more, and by moral causes which are a combination of laws, religion, customs, manners, and that sort of emanation of the way of thinking and of the manner and foolishness of the court and the capital whose influence spreads.[95]

The laws that mandate ignorance to Mohammedans and the customs that prevent them from communicating with one another, leave their minds lethargic. The works of Confucius, which combine an immense detail of civil ceremonies with moral precepts, putting the most puerile things on the same plane as the most essential, greatly affect the minds of the Chinese. Scholastic logic greatly modifies the minds of the nations that apply themselves to it. The great freedom in some countries to say anything and write anything makes for countless unique minds. The extraordinary writ small, which is the character of the Talmud, like the extraordinary writ large, which is that of the Holy Scriptures, has very much shrunk the heads of Jewish scholars.

The complexity of the causes that shape the general character of a people is indeed great. If a man in Constantinople enters the house of a Turk, he will hear from him only the words that must be spoken. If he enters the house of a Greek, he will find a whole family talking incessantly. The Turkish nation is solemn because it knows that it rules. The nation that obeys has no pronounced character; moreover, the house of a Turk is a monarchy, whereas the Greek's is a popular state. Having only one wife, the Greek savors the joy which always accompanies things in moderation; the Turk, with many wives, falls into an habitual sadness and lives crushed by his pleasures.

When one sees some of our young men[96] go about bantering, laughing, eager to do all the foolish things they have seen others do, compensating for their lack of reflection by their flashes of wit, who would not say that they are very clever people? Most of the time that is not so, but their machine is trained for that exercise, either by the penchant we have for imitating what we see, or by the prejudice for what is stylish, or by a desire to please women, or seem to; for while in the countries where they are restrained success with them comes with a reserved demeanor, in those where they are free you appeal to them with a frivolous demeanor, whether because reflection is in itself unappealing or because impetuosity better suits the nature of passion.

The capital importance attached by the Spanish to the honor of ladies has established there a grave and respectful chivalry. Their constant adoration for

---

95 See *Pensées* 1903.
96 Do not state this absolutely, but only that their vivacity is aided. (M)

them has banished the gaiety that comes from familiarity. Moreover, as the code of honor has permeated all ranks, every individual in the nation desires to be honored by all the others, and gravity has been universally adopted, all the more so because it is easier to acquire than genuine merit, and because ordinary people can more readily assess the dignity of a man than his mind and his talents. Finally, so many petty officials, sent into all four corners of the world where they are like Chinese mandarins, having lived in positions of authority, have returned to Spain with more solemnity than when they left.[97]

Thus, independently of the climate, which has great impact in this respect on the Spaniards,[98] they could have been trained in the phlegmatic manner as we French have been in vivacity. A Spaniard born vivacious could halt the movement of his machine and a Frenchman born listless could arouse his.

It is a commonplace that Spartans spoke very little. It had to have been so: on the one hand, respect for the elderly must have imposed silence on the young, and gravitas must likewise have imposed it on the elderly.

Moral causes more substantially shape the general character of a nation and influence minds more than physical causes. A major proof of this is to be found among the Jews who, dispersed throughout the earth, born in all times and every country, have had many authors, of whom one could barely cite two who possess any common sense.

One could surmise, however, that rabbis had some intellectual advantage, over the rest of their people as reasonably as one could assume that those who enjoy the reputation of men of letters in Europe have some intellectual advantage over other Europeans. Yet among that plethora of rabbis who have written, there is not a single one whose talent was not minimal. The reason for this is natural. The Jews returning from Assyria were very much like the captives delivered from Algiers who are paraded in the streets, but they were more uncouth because they and their fathers had been born into slavery. Although they had an unbounded respect for their sacred books, they had little familiarity with them; they no longer understood much of the language in which they were written; they had only traditional accounts of the great marvels that God had performed in favor of their fathers. Ignorance, which is the mother of traditions, which is to say of marvels accepted by the people, created new ones, but these were born with the quality of the spirit that produced them and further took on the hue of all the minds through

97 They were already solemn before. (M) For Montesquieu's views on gravitas as the central feature of Spanish national character, see also *PL* 75 and *SL* xix, 8, 9.
98 See Strabo. (M) (See Strabo's *Geographica* [*Catalogue* 2646] iii, 13 for his characterization of the wildness of the Iberians.)

which they passed. Learned men, that is, men whose heads were filled with these primitive traditions, collected them, and since the earliest writers of all nations, whether good or bad, have always had an inflated reputation because they have always been, for a time, superior to all those who read them, it happened that these earliest, wretched works were regarded by the Jews as perfect models on which they formed and have ever since formed their taste and their genius.[99]

I am not referring to sacred books[100] written since the captivity.[101] They embody a very different taste than the rabbinical works. They are divinely inspired, and, even had they not been, in purely historical works the author would scarcely have been able to express anything on his own.

Here is another example that shows clearly the extent to which the moral cause overrides the physical cause. The people who live farther south, like the Asians, have a certain timidity, which inclines them naturally to obey, and the peoples who live farther north, like the Europeans, have a boldness that inclines them to risk life and wealth in order to command others. Now this timidity which in the South inclines everyone to obey renders authority tyrannical, and that boldness that makes everyone want to command in colder countries renders authority moderate. For those who exercise power always continue on until they are checked; they do not check themselves where reason would prescribe, but where patience runs out.[102] Yet we must admit that these timid people who shun death to enjoy real benefits, such as life, tranquility, and pleasures, are born with brains of better temper than the madmen of the North who sacrifice their lives for vainglory, that is, who choose to live for posterity rather than the present. But since it turns out that the good minds of the former result in servitude, and the poor temper of the others' minds results in liberty, what happens is that slavery debases, oppresses, and destroys the mind, whereas liberty shapes, elevates, and fortifies it. The moral cause destroys the physical cause, and nature is so greatly deceived that the people whom she created to have better minds have less sense, and those to whom she had given less sense have better minds.

Here in Europe there are two kinds of religions: the Catholic, which asks for submission, and the Protestant, which desires independence.[103] From the

99 Most likely an allusion to the Talmud, including the Mishna and the Gemara.
100 I.e., the books of the Hebrew Bible, which are maintained in the Christian Bible.
101 I.e., the Babylonian captivity or period of the exile of the Jews of Palestine to Babylonia after Nebuchadnezzar conquered the kingdom of Judah, first in 598–597 BCE and again in 587–586 BCE.
102 Cf. *SL* XI, 4.   103 I.e., independence from the pope.

start, peoples of the North embraced Protestantism; those of the South kept Catholicism.[104] Now this independence of Protestant peoples insures that they are perfectly instructed in human knowledge, and because of this submission of Catholic peoples, in itself very reasonable and almost essential to a religion founded on mysteries, these people who know precisely what is necessary for salvation are in the dark about everything unrelated to it. And so it is that the southern peoples, with sounder notions of the great truths and even naturally better minds, nonetheless have a very great disadvantage compared to the peoples of the North.

When we have received an education, there are many causes, some deriving from certain physical circumstances, others from certain practices or certain professions, or types of life we embrace, which can greatly modify our minds. We must enter a bit into the details.

Our genius is largely shaped by that of the people whose company we keep. Association with people of wit provides us a perpetual education; a different association makes us lose the education we already have. We are enriched by some, and we are impoverished by others. We likewise share our character; human machines are invisibly linked; the springs that propel one lift the others; moderate people train us to be gentle, impetuous people to be vivacious.

Books are a kind of society that one provides oneself, but each person chooses them after his own fashion. Those who read good books are analogous to those who keep good company; those who read bad ones are like those who keep bad company and who at the very least waste their time.

Knowledge greatly expands the mind. The ancient philosophers lacked knowledge: they had good minds; they made little use of them; they were never well informed on questions; they wanted to explain what was inexplicable and spent their time explaining false facts with principles just as false.[105]

Traveling also very greatly expands the mind. You get outside the narrow circle of the prejudices of your country, and you are hardly likely to take on those of foreigners.

Certain fortunate circumstances when we enter society give us a useful boldness for the rest of our lives. Reputation has two good effects: it accredits,

---

104 Cf. *SL* xxiv, 5.

105 Cf. *Pensées* 1605 where Montesquieu asserts that the ancient philosophers "reasoned on such vague and general things" as "the sovereign good," "the principle of things" in "either fire or water," "whether the soul is immortal," and "whether the gods govern the world." He concluded that "[w]hoever had figured out one of these questions was instantly a philosopher, however little beard he wore."

and it encourages. But the dejection that follows contempt suspends all the functions of the soul.

The common people claim to have observed that hunchbacks are ordinarily clever. One might say that if deformed people lack bodily graces, they also lack the insipidness and foolishness of those who think they are pleasing. Their minds are thus not so easily spoiled; moreover, the good opinion they assume of their mind is still less ridiculous than that which one conceives on the basis of one's face. Besides, they are generally doomed to a condition that leaves them no pursuit other than cultivating their mind and developing their talents.

There is another popular observation, in which there may be some truth, that most deformed people have a malicious turn of mind. The reason is natural enough: having a defect which they know everybody sees, they at every moment have petty insults to avenge, and when they are clever they feel their power and make merciless use of it.

Certain habits can affect our minds. Just as engravers see on the walls figures which are not there, because their brains have received the impression of the ones they have engraved, and just as those who have been struck by the idea of a phantom continue to be haunted by it because the same movement is repeated in their brain, in like fashion we can say that people who have accustomed their minds to seeing numerical relationships or geometrical figures see and find relationships everywhere and measure and calculate everything. One who is used to the problematic style accustoms his mind to receiving always two equally strong impressions simultaneously. Another who has always adopted a decisive tone has trained himself to accept the first idea that comes to him. He who has familiarized himself with scholastic terms at first feels no ideas awaken in him, but by dint of repeating them succeeds in gradually attaching a vague idea to them. And, finally, a man who has long told himself, or has long been told, that metaphysical concepts are solid, but not the principles of physics, that Greek histories are true but not modern ones, will in the end be convinced of it: we create for ourselves the mind we want, and we are its true makers.

It is not the mind that makes opinions, it is the heart: and of this, religious orders offer a striking proof. Each has its particular philosophy that is embraced in its totality by all the members of the order. If you see a man's habit, you see his mind itself. If that habit is gray, you can count on the wearer having his head full of entities. Do not imagine that you will find the same brain when the habit is white and black, but it will be something else again if the habit is black.[106]

All our ideas are intertwined among themselves and with us. If we knew in how many ways an opinion is sustained in a man's brain, we would no longer be surprised by his obstinacy in defending it.

Why are all authors so enamored of their writings? It is because they are vain, you will say: I agree. But why is such vanity always uniformly misplaced? The reason is that what we have put into our books is bound up with all our other ideas and relates to things that we have liked, since we have learned them. Our masterpieces charm us less after a certain time because, on account of changes that have occurred in our brains, they are no longer so closely linked to our way of thinking.

Differing professions can greatly affect our minds. For instance, a man who teaches can easily become obstinate because he exercises the profession of a man who is never wrong; a philosopher can easily lose his agreeable temperament because he becomes used to viewing and judging everything with considerable precision and exactness; a ladies' man can become very foolishly vain because he makes too much of women's liking for him. Yet this liking proves their weakness and not his merit, being a reflexive consent and not a mental judgment. Men of the robe[107] can become extremely vain because, dealing only with people who need them, they imagine that their prudence rules all. A soldier can become a boring storyteller because he is struck with all the little things that have happened to him by the way he relates them to the most important events, and besides, a certain boldness makes him readily undertake to make others listen to him. Finally, as big talkers are people whose minds are struck by many things, and so forcefully that they believe them all to be equally important, a learned man can manage to become a very great talker, for he constantly brings to mind an infinite number of ideas, and he can even believe they are all important; he has taken great pains to acquire them, and we judge the value of things by the effort their acquisition has cost us.

The Persians call brokers *dellal*, big talkers,[108] and, generally, all people whose business it is to persuade others talk a great deal because it is in their

---

106 The order in gray is Franciscan, the one in white and black Dominican, and the one in all black is Benedictine.

107 Members of the legal profession, often those of the robe nobility (*noblesse de robe*).

108 This observation is borrowed from Jean Chardin's *Voyages en Perse*: "They are called *delal*, as if to say great talkers, a term which is the opposite of *lal*, which means mute" (Chardin, IV, 267).

interest to prevent others from thinking and to fill minds with their own reasoning. That is not true of people who seek to persuade themselves.

Those who have little business are very big talkers; the less one has to reflect, the more one talks. To think is to talk to oneself, and when we speak to ourselves we hardly intend to speak to others.

Generally, all professions destroy the harmony of ideas. We are inclined to regard as very important the things that constitute our worth and that people like us do every day. Our vanity bestows on these things a very eminent rank among all those that are done on earth. There is the story of a master of ceremonies in Rome who wept with grief because the cardinal[109] he served had bowed at the wrong time. In this man's brain a bow was a greater matter than a battle in the brain of Prince Eugene.[110]

Fragments[111]

Whether the causes that contribute to its preservation are stronger than those that contribute to its destruction. Histories teach us that all the princes of the *maison carlienne*[112] were feeble of mind. There is scarcely any country where the hereditary stupidity of some house is not notorious. It is obvious that such remarks could hardly be made except about families in the public eye.

From conception to birth and from birth to the time when the child ceases to grow, the brain develops gradually, and nature is so wise that the termination of its growth is ordinarily the point of the greatest perfection it can attain for receiving ideas. But if it should chance to happen that it was perfectly formed before the whole had ceased to grow, you can see that, with its fibers thickening, it would lose the disposition of perfection which it had already

---

109 The Cardinal d'Estrées. (M, manuscript note.) (César d'Estrées, 1628–1714, French diplomat and cardinal.)

110 Prince François Eugène of Savoy (1663–1736), commander of the imperial armies of Austria in the War of the Spanish Succession. See *On Consideration and Reputation*, p. 135.

111 This segment consists of pages 9–10, 37–44, and 49–50 of what the first two editors of this text concluded was an early draft of the *Essay on the Causes* (*Mélanges inédits*, p. 267; Masson edition of Montesquieu, Paris: Nagel, 1950, III, 427). *Pensées* 1191, 1192, 2035, and 2265 show that these fragments are remnants of *De la différence des génies* (1717). Just prior to the beginning of the first fragment (page 9) Montesquieu discusses the respective influence of ovum and spermatozoa in producing traits in offspring, stating that certain features "will remind us of the face of the father or the mother, that is to say, will look like them. The qualities of the child being thus relative to those of the father and of the mother, they derive from both and there results a third sort of character that will pass down from generation to generation, if the causes," etc.

112 The Spanish line of kings descending from Charles V.

acquired. Thus one can say that there is no surer prejudice of future stupidity in children than early signs they are smart.[113]

The fibers of our brain, constantly stirred, must be like those of the hands of a harpsichord player which seem by force of habit to work by themselves and no longer depend on will.

* * *

The fibers thicken and strengthen through work. At rest, the branched and oleaginous parts of the blood accumulate in the fatty cells, which are always open to receive them; but in motion, the nutritive parts are attracted to the extremities of the fibers. The force of circulation deposits and inserts them into the fibers and into the interstices of these fibers. The fiber must therefore become thicker, more solid, and more compact.[114]

We notice that, of two parts of the body that have the same functions, those which are used more are better nourished and stronger. We have also observed that working people are more difficult to purge and that other medical remedies have less effect on them. Their fibers are therefore firmer, more massive, and tougher; they are more resistant to remedies that irritate or sting them.

In addition to thickening fibers, work also gradually hardens them. Here is how I conceive of this happening. Muscular action is a movement of contraction. The nerve fluid entering the muscular vesicles renders them firmer and more taut; the fleshy fibers are pressed and the blood they contain is expelled and no new blood can enter. Soon the blood, after filling the neighboring vessels, presses the muscular vesicles more strongly than the nerve fluid itself, forces a passage, and enters with all the more force the longer it has been held back. A kind of struggle[115] therefore ensues between the blood which abounds in the muscle and presses the nerves, and the nerve fluid in the same muscular fibers; or rather two struggles ensue, one for the inflow of spirits and by the blocking of the inflow of blood, and the other for the inflow of spirits and the blocking of the inflow of blood.[116]

---

113 We do not know all that much about what particular disposition of the brain is required for perfection. (M)

114 Guillaume Barrera suggests (*OC* IX, 265, note 171) the influence of Stephen Hales's *Haemastaticks* (1733). Montesquieu owned Hales's earlier *Vegetable Statics* (1728; *Catalogue* 1471), and he may also have had access to *Haemastaticks* in other libraries.

115 Struggle for intromission of spirits and refusal of intromission of blood and struggle for intromission of blood and refusal of intromission of the spirits. (M)

116 There is some confusion in the syntax arising from the heavy overwriting of the manuscript

Thus, in addition to the action and reaction of the two fluids, there is also the action and reaction of the solid parts, which is proportionate to it.[117]

What happens next is that the fluids forcefully beat against the walls of the solids, and that the solids, whose fibers are thickened by a heavy fluid, rub against each other and toughen, much as a worker's hand toughens when it has rubbed for a long time against a wooden handle.[118]

A certain humidity of the air, certain foods, or the use of certain drinks thickens the fibers of some peoples [*two illegible words*] thick. [*One illegible line.*] This results, in part, in their having, as I have said, less vivacity. If they do not have the advantage of [*illegible*], they have more constancy in their resolutions and make fewer mistakes in carrying them out.

The Dutch are famous for the deliberation with which they absorb ideas. It is to this that they owe the consistency in their political principles and the constancy in their passions that has enabled them to accomplish such great things. Thickness of fibers produces stupidity, their too great flexibility when it is accompanied by relaxation [*illegible words*] which is mental weakness; and when this delicacy and this relaxation of the fibers happen to be joined to a great abundance of animal spirits, inconstancy, whimsicalness, capriciousness are the natural effects that result, for the brain is briskly moved by the object presently affecting it and loses the trace of all the others.

Much more blood rises to the brain through the carotid and vertebral arteries than the ratio between the size of the head and the rest of the body seems to require. It is therefore borne there for a particular use. It is to filter or separate a fluid or nerve spirit.[119] It is in the cortical substance of the brain that this separation takes place; from there the nerve spirit can pass into the medullary substance,[120] and thence into the nerves.

This must be a major reason for the variety that will be found in the characters and minds of people in various climates, and which will follow the greater or lesser disposition of the blood for the filtration of the nervous fluid.

---

117 Muscular "irritability" was explained by Albrecht von Haller in 1739; prior to that, the nervous system was thought to be involved in muscular contractions (see p. 30, note 23).

118 As the *OC* editor observes, John Arbuthnot discussed interactions of solids and fluids in *An Essay on the Effects of Air on Human Bodies* (1733).

119 *Esprit nerveux.* Montesquieu is referring to the animal spirits and is discussing their filtration, as Descartes had done.

120 The medulla oblongata.

The quickness of our minds, our inconstancy, the buoyancy of our character, and the joy which reigns among us, can lead us to believe that we are as well supplied in animal spirits as any nation in the world.[121]

The things which provide our nourishment do not affect us only by their coarseness or their delicacy but also by a certain quality they have in each country which stems from the nature of the soil. An observation that has recently been made clearly proves this; one finds iron in honey, which substantiates this.

Yet we must admit that little of these metals or minerals enters the bloodstream.[122] They would work too much havoc there, and the illnesses of so many artisans, as we can see in the treatise of Bernardo Ramazzini.[123] In mining countries, only as much must enter the blood as is needed to affect the bodies, and not enough to damage them to any degree.

It is true that when one has often changed climates, one can subsequently do so without danger, for the solids have never assumed an absolutely fixed habit, and they lend themselves to whatever change happens either to them or to the blood.[124]

The air, charged with particles of earth, has in each climate specific qualities analogous to the remedies of medicine that make use of metals, minerals, and plant secretions. Thus it is only seldom that a change of air does not have on us the effect of some remedy. But the trouble is that the remedy provided by chance, is almost always taken in the wrong situation.

---

121 Cf. *SL* XIX, 5.
122 Besides that, the juice of the plants of each country, in particular the ones that nourish us, can cause even greater changes. (M)
123 Bernardo Ramazzini (1633–1714), author of *De morbis artigicum diatriba* ("Diseases of workers," Modenas, 1701). Montesquieu owned a 1717 Latin edition of his complete medical and physiological works (*Catalogue* 1184).
124 Besides, the blood is not composed of the juices of the plants from a single country. The change is therefore not so great. (M)

II

The Romans

Dissertation on Roman Politics in Religion

(1716)

Dissertation sur la politique des Romains dans la religion, text by Lorenzo Bianchi (*OC* viii, 83–99). Montesquieu became a member of the Academy of Bordeaux in May 1716, and this paper, read on 18 June of that same year, was his first composition shared with that body, not counting his reception oration. It was first published in 1796 in the Plassan edition of Montesquieu's works (*Œuvres*, Paris: Plassan *et al.*, 1797, iv, pp. 193–207). Our base text, as in *OC* viii, is the manuscript (in the hand of a copyist) which is part of the Montesquieu collection in the municipal library of Bordeaux (MS 828/vi, no 6).

* * *

It was neither fear nor piety that established religion among the Romans, but rather the necessity in all societies to have one. The first kings were no less attentive to regulating worship and ceremonies than to making laws and building walls. I find this difference between Roman lawmakers and those of other peoples: that the former made the religion for the state, the latter the state for the religion. Romulus,[1] Titus,[2] and Numa[3] subordinated the gods to politics: the worship and ceremonies they instituted were found to be so wise that when the kings were expelled the yoke of religion was the only one from which this people, in clamoring for freedom, dared not emancipate itself.

---

1 According to legend, Rome's first king, Romulus (reigned 753–716 bce), consulted the gods before laying out the sacred boundaries of Rome in 753 bce, dedicated a temple to Jupiter, and established religious festivals and rites.
2 Titus Tatius, king of the Sabines, was for a brief time the co-ruler with Romulus of a combined Roman and Sabine kingdom.
3 Rome's legendary second king, Numa Pompilius (reigned 715–673 bce), called "the founder of divine law" by Livy, established the *flamines*, priests of Roman religion, and also the *pontifices* and the Vestal Virgins (Livy 1.20).

When the Roman lawmakers established religion, they were not thinking of reforming morals, nor of laying down moral principles; they did not mean to constrain people who were not yet acquainted with the obligations of a society into which they had just entered.

Accordingly, they had at first only a general intention, which was to inspire fear of the gods in a people who feared nothing, and to make use of that fear to lead them in any way they wished.

Numa's successors did not dare to do what that prince had not done. The people, which had lost much of its fierceness and roughness, had become capable of greater discipline. It would have been easy to add to the religious ceremonies principles and rules of morality which it lacked, but the Romans were too shrewd not to realize how dangerous such a reform would have been. It would have meant acknowledging that their religion was imperfect; it would have given it a history and weakened its authority by attempting to strengthen it. The Romans' wisdom led them to choose a better course by establishing new laws. Human institutions may well change, but divine ones must be immutable like the gods themselves.

Thus the Roman senate, having charged the praetor Petillius[4] with examining the writings of king Numa which had been found in a stone chest four hundred years after that king's death, resolved to have them burned on receiving that praetor's report that the ceremonies which were prescribed in those writings differed greatly from the ones that were then being practiced, which could raise doubts in the minds of simple people and show them that the prescribed cult was not the same as the one which had been instituted by the original legislators and inspired by the nymph Egeria.[5]

They carried prudence further. No one could read the Sibylline books without the permission of the senate, which granted it only on great occasions and when the purpose was to console the people. All interpretations were prohibited. The books themselves were always kept locked up, and, by a very wise precaution, fanatical and seditious persons were disarmed.[6]

---

4 Quintus Petillius Cerialis (c. 30–c. 83 CE), Roman general, governor of Britain, and son-in-law of the emperor Vespasian.

5 According to Livy (1.21.3), Numa claimed that the spring-goddess Egeria, who had a grove outside the Porta Capena where the Vestal Virgins came to draw water, advised him on religious matters.

6 During times of crisis or unrest and following inexplicable portents and prodigies, the senate could order the *quindecimviri* to consult the Sibylline books containing the utterances of Sibyl of Cumae, brought to Rome by Tarquin Superbus, fifth king of Rome. The books contained information about rituals and sacrifices to be performed to placate the gods and avert calamities.

Soothsayers could make no pronouncements on public affairs without permission of the magistrates. Their art was absolutely subordinated to the will of the senate as had been ordered by the books of the pontiffs,[7] some fragments of which Cicero has preserved for us:[8] "Let them be the arbiters of war; let wonders and extraordinary events be deferred, if the senate so orders by the Etruscan haruspices."[9] And in another place: "There are two kinds of priests: one to preside over ceremonies and sacrifices, the other to interpret the mysterious words of those who tell destinies and of soothsayers, when the senate and the people call for them."[10]

Polybius included superstition among the advantages the Roman people had over other peoples:[11] what appears ridiculous to the wise is necessary for the fools; and this people, which is so easily moved to anger, needs to be checked by an invisible power.

The augurs[12] and haruspices[13] were the genuine grotesques of paganism, but they will not be thought ridiculous if one reflects that in a wholly popular religion like that one, there was nothing extravagant. The credulity of the people made amends for everything among the Romans; the more contrary a thing was to human reason, the more it seemed to them divine. A simple truth would not have affected them deeply: they had to have causes for wonderment; they needed signs from the deity, and they found them only in the supernatural or the ridiculous.

In truth, it was a very extravagant thing to make the welfare of the republic depend on the sacred appetite of a chicken[14] and on the disposition of the

---

7 I.e., the *Commentarii pontificum*, containing the so-called "Laws of Numa," manuals to guide the pontiffs (*pontifices*), who were the ultimate authority on all religious questions, in the proper performance of religious observances.

8 Book II, *De Legibus*. (M) (II, 20–21.)

9 In Latin in Montesquieu's text: *Bella disceptanto: prodigia, portenta ad Etruscos et aruspices si senatus jusserit deferunto.*

10 In Latin: *Sacerdotum genera duo sunto: unum quod praesit ceremoniis et sacriis, alterum quod interpretetur fatidicorum et vatum fata incognita cum senatus populusque ads[c]iverit.*

11 See Polybius, *Histories*, 6, ch. 56, 6–12.

12 Augurs interpreted the will of the gods from the flight of birds, and their art was called *augurium*, or *auspicium*. Roman magistrates would scan the skies prior to meetings of the Roman assembly, and the augurs interpreted what they had seen. Being an augur was considered one of the highest dignities in the state, and Cicero was proud of being one, though by his time educated Romans no longer believed in the science of divination.

13 The haruspices were Etruscan soothsayers who divined the will of the gods by inspecting the entrails of animals sacrificed to honor the gods, or by interpreting natural phenomena such as lightning or earthquakes.

14 The "sacred chickens" were kept by the Roman augurs. If they eagerly consumed grain when it was offered to them, this was regarded as a good omen for conducting senate business, or for commencing a military expedition.

victims' entrails.[15] But those who introduced these ceremonies were well aware of their strength and weakness, and it was only for good reasons that they sinned against reason itself.

If this rite had been more reasonable, clever people would have been fooled by it as well as the commoners, and in that way all the advantage which could be expected from it would have been lost. Ceremonies were therefore required which could sustain the superstition of some and enter into the politics of others; that is what divinations provided. There the decrees of heaven were placed in the mouths of the leading senators, enlightened men who knew equally well the foolishness and the utility of the divinations.

Cicero[16] says that Fabius[17] when he was an augur held as a rule that what was advantageous to the republic was always done under good auspices: "What is done under the best auspices is what is done for the welfare of the republic; what is done against the republic is done against the auspices."[18] The same author[19] says he agrees with Marcellus[20] that although the credulity of the common folk had originally established the auguries, the practice had been retained for the benefit of the republic; and he makes this distinction between Romans and foreign nations, that the latter invoked it indiscriminately on all occasions, and the former only in matters which involved the public interest. Cicero[21] informs us that a thunderbolt striking on the left was a good omen, except in assemblies of the people, *praeterquam ad comitia*: the rules of the art ceased on that occasion; the magistrates judged the favorability of the auspices as they saw fit, and these auspices were a bridle with which they led the people. Cicero adds: "It was settled for the good of the republic that the leading citizens be the judges either for the holding of assemblies, or for voting on laws, or for judgments of the people or the

---

15 All the sacrificial victims referred to by Montesquieu in this essay are animals. The Romans considered the sacrifice of humans emblematic of foreign, barbarian customs, though there were occasional human sacrifices in Rome. In the fourth century CE, the emperor Theodosius banned the sacrifice of animals, labeling the practice *superstitio*.

16 *On Old Age*. (M) (IV, II.)

17 Quintus Fabius Maximus Verrucosus (280–203 BCE), Roman statesman, general, dictator, and augur.

18 In Latin: *optimis auspiciis geri quae pro salute reipublicae gererentur; quae contra repulicam gererentur contra auspicia fieri.*

19 *On Divination*. (M) (II, 35–36.)

20 Marcus Claudius Marcellus (268–208 BCE), the Roman general renowned for numerous military feats in both the Gallic War of 225 BCE and the Second Punic War (218–201 BCE).

21 *On Divination*. (M) (II, 35.)

election of magistrates."[22] He had previously stated that one read in the holy books "when Jupiter thunders and casts bolts of lightning, it is forbidden to hold assemblies of the people."[23] That had been introduced, he said, to provide the magistrates with a pretext for breaking off assemblies of the people: "That had been instituted in the public interest; indeed the intent was to have a reason for not convening the assemblies."[24]

Moreover, it was immaterial whether the victim that was sacrificed was found to be a good or a bad omen, for when they were not happy with the first, they sacrificed a second, a third, a fourth which were called *hostiae succedaneae*. Aemilius Paullus,[25] wishing to sacrifice, was obliged to slay twenty victims; the gods were appeased only with the last one in which were found signs that promised victory. That is why it was customary to say that in sacrifices the last victims were always more valuable than the first.

Caesar was not as patient as Aemilius Paullus. "After sacrificing several victims without obtaining good omens, he went into the curia, scorning all religion."[26]

As the magistrates found themselves the masters of omens, they had a sure way of turning the people away from a war that would have been disastrous, or of making them undertake one that might have been useful. The soothsayers who always followed the armies, and who were rather the interpreters of the generals than of the gods, inspired confidence in the soldiers. If by chance some ill omen had terrified the army, a shrewd general converted its meaning and made it favorable to himself. In such a way Scipio,[27] who fell while jumping from his vessel onto the African shore, took some earth in his hands: "I hold you," he said, "O land of Africa!" and with these words rendered favorable an omen which had seemed so dire.[28] The Sicilians,

---

22 In Latin: *hoc institutum reipublicae causa est, ut comitiorum, vel in jure legume, vel in judiciis populi, vel in creandis magistratibus principes civitatis essent interpretes* (Cicero, *On Divination*, II, 35).

23 In Latin: *Jove tonante et fulgurante comitia populi habere nefas esse* (Cicero, *On Divination*, II, 18).

24 In Latin: *hoc reipublicae causa constitutum, comitiorum enim non habendorum, causas esse voluerunt.*

25 Lucius Aemilius Paullus (229–160 BCE), twice consul of Rome (182, 168 BC) and victor in 168 over king Perseus at the Battle of Pydna ending the Third Macedonian War (171–168 BCE).

26 In Latin: *pluribus hostiis caesis, cum litare non posset introiit curiam spreta religione.* See Suetonius, *De vita Caesarum* ("Lives of the Caesars"), Caesar, LXXXI).

27 Publius Cornelius Scipio (236–183 BCE), the Roman general whose victory over Hannibal at the Battle of Zama in 202 BCE ended the Second Punic War and earned him the cognomen Africanus.

28 Actually it was Caesar, not Scipio, who said this: see Suetonius, *De vita Caesarum* ("Lives of the Caesars"), Caesar, LIX).

having embarked on some expedition to Africa, were so terrified by a solar eclipse that they were ready to abandon their mission; but the general explained to them that in truth this eclipse would have been a bad sign if it had appeared before their embarkation, but that, since it had appeared only afterwards, it could threaten only the Africans: in that way he put an end to their fright and found in a cause for fear a means of bolstering their courage.

Caesar was warned several times by the soothsayers not to go to Africa before winter; he did not listen to them, and thus got the jump on his enemies who, without this advance, would have had time to unite their forces.[29]

When Crassus[30] during a sacrifice allowed his knife to slip from his hands, it was taken as a bad omen, but he reassured the people by saying: "Bon courage: at least my sword has never fallen from my hands."[31] When Lucullus[32] was ready to do battle with Tigranes,[33] they came to tell him it was an inauspicious day: "Then let us [. . .] strive with might and main," he said, "to make this, instead of an ill-omened and gloomy day, a glad and welcome day to the Romans."[34] Tarquin the Proud,[35] meaning to establish games in honor of the goddess Mania,[36] consulted the oracle of Apollo, which answered obscurely and said they had to sacrifice heads for heads: *capitibus pro capitibus supplicandum*. The prince, even more cruel than superstitious, had some children sacrificed. But Junius Brutus[37] changed this horrible sacrifice, for he had it carried out with garlic and poppy heads, and thereby fulfilled or evaded the oracle.[38]

They cut the Gordian knot when they could not untie it. Thus Clodius Pulcher, wanting to begin a naval battle, had the sacred chickens thrown into the sea, to make them drink, he said, since they refused to eat.[39]

---

29 See Caesar, *Bellum Africum* 3.1, a work which is not actually by Caesar but by one of his officers. See also Suetonius, *De vita Caesarum* ("Lives of the Caesars"), Caesar, LIX.

30 Marcus Licinius Crassus (115–53 BCE), an extremely wealthy supporter of Sulla in the Civil War between Sulla and Marius (83–82 BCE). He was praetor in 73 BCE, consul in 70 BCE, and censor in 65 BCE prior to forming the First Triumvirate with Caesar and Pompey in 60 BCE; he was killed in battle in 54 BCE during an invasion of Parthia.

31 See Plutarch, *Life of Crassus*, XIX.

32 Lucius Licinius Lucullus (118–57/56 BCE), skilled general and victor in the third Mithridatic War (73–63 BCE).

33 Tigranes II, king of Armenia from 95 to 55 BCE.

34 Plutarch, *Sayings of the Romans* (*Moralia*, trans. Frank Cole Babbitt, Cambridge, MA: Harvard University Press, 1931, III, 205) and *Life of Lucullus*, I.

35 Tarquin Superbus (d. 495 BCE), who according to legend was the last king of Rome.

36 Mania was the goddess of the dead who ruled the underworld along with Mantus.

37 Lucius Junius Brutus, the legendary founder of the Roman republic (509 BCE) who overthrew Rome's last king after the rape of Lucretia by Tarquin's son Sextus Tarquinius.

38 Macrobius, Book I. (M) *Saturnalia* vii.

39 Valerius Maximus, Book I. (M) (*Nine Books of Memorable Deeds and Sayings*, I, 4.) Publius Claudius Pulcher (died c. 249–247 BCE), consul and commander of the Roman fleet in

It is true that they sometimes punished a general for failure to follow the omens, and even that was a new effect of the Roman policy: they wanted the people to see that defeats, cities captured, and battles lost were not the result of a bad constitution of the state or of the weakness of the republic, but of the impiety of a citizen who had angered the gods. With this conviction, it was not difficult to restore their confidence to the people: all it took for that was a few ceremonies and sacrifices.

Thus, when the city was threatened or afflicted by some misfortune, they did not fail to look for the cause, which was always the anger of some god they had neglected to worship; it was enough, to avoid that happening, to make sacrifices and processions and to purify the city with torches, sulfur, and salt water. The victim was led around the ramparts before being slaughtered, which was called "sacrificium amburbium, et amburbiale."[40] They even went so far sometimes as to purify the armies and the fleets, after which everyone again renewed his courage.

Scævola,[41] a high priest, and Varro,[42] one of their great theologians, said that the people had to be kept in the dark about many true things, and believe many false ones. St. Augustine[43] says that Varro had thereby revealed the entire secret of politicians and ministers of state. "He made known the true means of the wise by which kingdoms and people would be governed."[44]

The same Scævola, according to St. Augustine,[45] divided the gods into three classes: those who had been established by the poets, those who had been established by the philosophers, and those who had been established by the magistrates, *a principibus civitatis*.

Those who read Roman history and are a bit discerning find at every turn aspects of this policy we have just pointed out. Thus we see Cicero, who in private and among his friends repeatedly confesses his unbelief: "Do you think me mad enough to believe these things?"[46] And we see the same Cicero speaking in public with extraordinary zeal against the impiety of

---

249 BCE during the First Punic War, was fined for incompetence and impiety after ignoring the omen of the sacred chickens refusing to eat.

40 "Sacrifice led around the city."
41 Publius Mucius Scævola (died c. 115 BCE) was tribune of the plebs in 141, praetor in 136, consul in 133 and *pontifex maximus* from 130 to 115.
42 Marcus Terentius Varro (116–27 BCE), author of *Antiquitates rerum humanarum et divinarum* ("Of antiquities human and divine"), dividing Roman religion into mythical, natural, and civil theology.
43 *De civitate Dei* ["On the city of God"], I.4 c. 31. (M)
44 In Latin: *Totum consilium prodidit sapientum per quod civitates et populi regerentur.*
45 *The City of God*, Book IV, chapter xxxi [IV, 27].
46 In Latin: *adeone me delirare censes ista ut credam* (Cicero, *Tusculan Disputations*, I, vi, 10).

Verres.[47] We see a Clodius,[48] who had insolently profaned the mysteries of the good goddess, and whose impiety had been marked by twenty decrees of the senate, himself delivering an oration full of zeal, to that senate which had denounced him, against the disrespect of ancient practices and religion. We see a Sallust,[49] the most corrupt of all the citizens, placing at the head of his works a preface worthy of the gravity and austerity of Cato. I would never finish, if I wanted to exhaust all the examples.

Although the magistrates did not subscribe to the religion of the people, one must not imagine that they had none at all. Mr. Cudworth[50] has very ably proven that those among the pagans who were enlightened adored a supreme deity of whom the gods of the multitude were only an element. Pagans, who were not scrupulous about rites, believed that it did not matter whether one worshiped the divinity itself or the divinity's manifestations: to worship, for example, in Venus the passive power of nature, or the supreme divinity insofar as it can subsume all generation, or to worship the sun or the supreme being insofar as it gives life to plants and makes the earth fertile with its warmth. Thus the Stoic Balbus[51] says in Cicero that God participates by his nature in all things here below; that he is Ceres on earth, Neptune on the seas: "They could discern a god who participates in the essence of each thing, Ceres on earth, Neptune on the sea, other divinities in other places. We must venerate and worship these gods, whatever their nature may be and by whatever name we are accustomed to calling them."[52] We would know more about this if we had the book that Asclepiades[53] composed, entitled *The Harmony of All Theologies*.

47 Gaius Verres (115–43 BCE), proconsul of Sicily forced into exile in 69 BCE following Cicero's successful prosecution of him for corruption.
48 In 62 BCE Publius Clodius Pulcher (93–52 BCE) profaned the rites of *bona dea* ("the good goddess"), reserved for women, by disguising himself as a woman to gain entry to Caesar's house where he hoped to seduce Caesar's second wife, Pompeia. Cicero, facing a bribed jury, unsuccessfully prosecuted Clodius for his violation of religious protocol, and they became bitter enemies as a result. See also note 98 on p. 75.
49 Gaius Sallustius Crispus (86–35 BCE), author of *The Conspiracy of Cataline*, *The Jugurthine War*, and the *Histories*.
50 Ralph Cudworth (1617–1688), author of *The True Intellectual System of the Universe* (London, 1678).
51 Quintus Lucilius Balbus was a Stoic philosopher from Cadiz and a pupil of Panaetius; in *On the Nature of the Gods* (2.71) Cicero makes Balbus the spokesman of Stoic views.
52 In Latin: *deus pertinens per naturum cujusque rei, per terras Ceres, per mare Neptunus alia per alia poterunt intelligi qui qualescunque sint quoque eos nomine consuetudo mencupaverit, hos deos et venerari et colere debemus.* (Montesquieu slightly misquotes Cicero's text, which is *De natura deorum*, II, 28.)
53 Asclepiades of Phlius (c. 350–c. 270 BCE), Greek philosopher in the Eretrian school of philosophy.

As the dogma of the world-soul was almost universally accepted, and as each part of the universe was considered a living member in which this soul was diffused, it seemed permissible to worship all those parts indiscriminately and that the ritual should be arbitrary, as was the dogma.

Such was the source of that spirit of tolerance and kindness that prevailed in the pagan world. There was no thought of persecuting and mangling one another; all religions and all theologies were equally good; heresies, wars, and religious quarrels were unknown; provided everyone went to the temple to worship, every citizen was high priest in his family.

The Romans were even more tolerant than the Greeks, who always spoiled everything. Everyone knows the unhappy fate of Socrates.

It is true that the Egyptian religion was always proscribed in Rome, because it was intolerant, and wanted to reign alone, and to establish itself on the ruins of the others. So the spirit of kindness and peace that prevailed among the Romans was the real cause of the war they relentlessly waged against it.

Valerius Maximus[54] reports the action of Aemilius Paullus who, following a report of the senate ordering the destruction of the temples of the Egyptian deities, himself took an ax and struck the first blows so as to encourage by his example the workers stricken by a superstitious fear.

But the priests of Isis and Serapis had even more zeal for establishing these ceremonies than Rome had for prohibiting them. Although Augustus, according to Dio,[55] had forbidden their practice in Rome, Agrippa,[56] who governed the city in his absence, was obliged to forbid it a second time. One can see in Tacitus and in Suetonius[57] the frequent edicts that the senate was obliged to issue in order to banish this cult from Rome.

We must note that the Romans confused the Jews with the Egyptians, as we know they confused the Christians with the Jews:[58] these two religions were long regarded as two branches of the first, and shared with it the hatred, contempt, and persecution of the Romans. The same edicts that abolished the Egyptian ceremonies in Rome always included the Jewish ceremonies

54 Book I, ch. iii. (M): see p. 65, note 39.
55 Book 34. (M) (Book 54, 6.) Dio Cassius (c. 150–235 CE) was a Roman senator, consul, and proconsul of Africa, who wrote a history of Rome (in Greek) that is a key source for the last years of the republic and the early empire.
56 Marcus Vipsanius Agrippa (64/62–12 BCE), son-in-law of Augustus, played a key role in the Battle of Actium in 31 BCE, Augustus' victory over Marc Antony and Cleopatra.
57 [Tacitus, *Annals*], I, 2. (M) Suetonius, *De vita Caesarum* ("Lives of the Caesars"), Augustus, XXXI and XCIII.
58 Cf. *PL* 83 and *Pensées* 167 and 232.

with them, as we see in Tacitus[59] and Suetonius in the lives of Tiberius and Claudius.[60] It is even more clear that historians have never distinguished the Christians' rite from the others. They had not even corrected this error in Hadrian's time, as we see from a letter which the emperor wrote from Egypt to the consul Servianus: "All who in Egypt worship Serapis[61] are Christians, and even those who are called bishops, are attached to the cult of Serapis; there is no Jew, no prince of a synagogue, no Samaritan, no Christian priest, no mathematician, no soothsayer, and no baptizer who does not worship Serapis; even the patriarch of the Jews indiscriminately worships Serapis and Christ. These people have no god but Serapis: he is the god of the Christians, of the Jews, and of all peoples": *illi qui Serapium colunt, christiani sunt; et devoti sunt Serapi, qui se Christi episcopos dicunt. Nemo hic archisynagoga Judaeorum, nemo Samarites, nemo christianorum presbyter, non mathematicus, non aruspex, non aliptes, qui non Serapium colat; Ipse ille patriarcha judeorum scilicet, cum Aegyptum venerit, ab aliis Serapidam adorare, ab aliis cogitur Christum ... viris illis deus est Serapia: hunc Judei, hunc christiani, hunc omnes et gentes.*[62] Is it possible to have more confused notions of these three religions, and to conflate them more crudely?

Among the Egyptians, the priests formed a separate caste,[63] which was maintained at public expense. Whence arose several drawbacks. All the wealth of the state was being sunk into a society of men who, always receiving and never giving back, imperceptibly were taking everything. The priests of Egypt, thus paid wages for doing nothing, were all languishing in an idleness from which they emerged only with the vices it produces; they were disorderly, restless, and enterprising, and these qualities made them extremely dangerous. In short, a body whose interests had been violently separated from those of the state was a monster, and those who had established it had sown in the society seeds of discord and of civil wars. Such was not the case in Rome, where the priesthood had been made a civil function: the ranks of augur and of head pontiff were magistracies; those who were invested with them were members of the senate, and consequently did not have interests different from those of that body. "Far from using superstition to oppress the republic, they employ it usefully to sustain it. In our

59 Book ii. (M) (Tacitus, *Annals*.)
60 Suetonius, *De vita Caesarum* ("Lives of the Caesars"), Tiberius, xxvi and Claudius, xxii and xxv.
61 Serapis was a Graeco-Egyptian god whose worship was introduced by Ptolemy I Soter of Egypt (366–282 BCE).
62 Flavius Vopiscus, *Vita Saturnini*. (M) (See *Histoire Augustae scriptores*, 1620.)
63 Cf. *Romans*, chapter 22.

city," says Cicero,[64] "the kings and the magistrates who have succeeded them have always had a double character, and have governed the state under the auspices of religion": "In ancient times those who held power also possessed knowledge of augury, witness our city, where both the kings and augurs, and later private citizens invested with the same priesthood, governed the republic by the authority of religion."[65]

The *duumviri*[66] were in charge of sacred matters; the *quindecimviri* attended to the religious ceremonies and kept the books of the Sibyls which the *decemviri* and the *duumviri* had done formerly. They consulted the oracles when the senate had so ordained and reported back, adding their opinion. They were also assigned to execute all that was prescribed in the books of the Sibyls, and to arrange for the celebration of secular games. In this way all religious ceremonies passed through the hands of the magistrates.

The kings of Rome had a kind of priesthood; there were certain ceremonies which only they could perform. When the Tarquins[67] were expelled, it was feared the people would perceive some change in the religion, for which reason a magistrate was established called *rex sacrorum*, and whose wife was called *regina sacrorum*,[68] who in the sacrifices fulfilled the functions of the former kings. This was the only vestige of royalty that the Romans retained at home.

The Romans enjoyed the advantage of having as legislator the wisest prince of which secular history has ever spoken:[69] that great man sought throughout his reign only to make justice and equity flourish, and his neighbors benefited no less from moderation than did his subjects. He established the *fetiales*,[70] who were priests without whose ministry neither peace nor war could be decided. We still have formularies of oaths taken by

64 Book I, *On Divination.* (M) (I, 40.)
65 In Latin: *apud veteres qui rerum potiebantur iidem augiria tenebant, ut testis est nostra civitas, in qua et reges et augures, et postea privati eodem sacerdotio praediti rempublicam religionum autoritate vexerunt* (Cicero, *De divinatione*, I, 40; Cicero is slightly misquoted).
66 "Kings of sacred things" or *duumviri sacrorum*, allegedly created by Tarquin Superbus. The *duumviri* performed sacrifices and kept the Sibylline Books. They served life terms and were chosen from the nobility. Their numbers were increased to ten (*decemviri sacris faciundis*) and then to fifteen (*quindecimviri sacris faciundis*) by Sulla.
67 The Tarquins were the legendary first five kings of Rome, expelled, according to tradition, in 509 BCE.
68 "King of sacred things" and "queen of sacred things."
69 Likely a reference to Numa Pompilius, although both Plutarch and Livy attributed the establishment of the *fetiales* to Tullus Hostilius (673–642 BCE), or to Ancus Marties (677–617 BCE), the legendary fourth king of Rome.
70 The *fetiales* were priests devoted to the worship of Jupiter. They served as ambassadors, advised the senate on foreign affairs, proclaimed war and peace, and confirmed treaties.

these *fetiales* when peace was concluded with some people. In the one that Rome concluded with Alba, a *fetial* says in Livy: "if the Roman people is the first to violate it, *publico consilio dolove malo*,[71] may he pray that Jupiter will strike them as he is about to strike the pig which he was holding in his hands": and immediately he struck it dead with a stone.

Before starting a war, one of these *fetiales* was sent to express grievances to the people which had caused some harm to the republic: he gave them a certain time to confer and seek means of re-establishing good relations; but if they neglected to come to a settlement, the fetial took leave and left the territory of that unjust people, after invoking against them the gods of both heaven and hell. Thereupon the senate decreed what it deemed just and pious; thus wars were never undertaken in haste, and they could only be the result of lengthy and mature deliberation.[72]

The policy that held sway in the Romans' religion developed even more in their victories. If superstition had been heeded, the gods of the conquerors would have been introduced among the vanquished; their temples would have been destroyed, and the establishment of a new rite would have imposed on them a servitude more severe than the first. They did something better. Rome herself submitted to the foreign divinities; she took them to her bosom, and through this bond, the strongest there is among men, she attached to herself peoples who regarded her more as a sanctuary of religion than as ruler of the world. But, so as not to make too many of them, the Romans, following the Greek example, skillfully conflated the foreign divinities with their own. If they found in their conquests a god similar to one of those who were worshipped in Rome, they adopted him, that is what it must be called, giving him the name of the Roman divinity, and bestowed upon him, if I dare use this expression, the right of citizenship in their city. Similarly, whenever they found some famous hero who had rid the earth of some monster, or subdued some barbarous people, they at once named him Hercules.

"We have advanced as far as the Ocean," says Tacitus,[73] "and we found there the columns of Hercules, either because Hercules has been there, or because we have attributed to that hero all the deeds worthy of his glory": *Ipsum quim etiam Oceanum illa tentavimus et superesse adhuc Herculis columnas fama vulgavit, sive adiit Hercules, sive quidquid ubique magnificum est in claritatem eius referre consuevimus.*

---

71 "Through public deliberation or fraudulently."   72 See Plutarch, *Life of Numa*, xii, 7–8.
73 Book v, ch. xxxiv. (M) (*On the Origins and Situation of the Germans*.)

Varro counted forty-four of these subduers of monsters. Cicero[74] counted only six, twenty-two Muses, five Suns, four Vulcans, five Mercuries, four Apollos, and three Jupiters.

Eusebius[75] goes much further, counting almost as many Jupiters as peoples.

The Romans, who actually had no divinity other than the genius of the republic, paid no attention to the disorder and confusion into which they threw mythology. The credulity of peoples, which always surpasses foolishness and extravagance, made up for everything.

Discourse on Cicero

(c. 1717)

Discours sur Cicéron, text by Pierre Rétat (*OC* VIII, 125–135). Montesquieu added this note at an indeterminate date: "I wrote this essay in my youth. It could be made good, if made into less of a panegyric. It also needs more detail on Cicero's works, especially his letters, and more development on the causes of the downfall of the republic and the character of Caesar, Pompey, and Antony." The text was first published in *Mélanges inédits* (1892), after which the manuscript disappeared. It resurfaced and was acquired in 1957 by the municipal library of Bordeaux (MS 2099; another partial copy with some variants is catalogued as MS 2538).

* * *

It is Cicero who of all the ancients had the most personal merit, and whom I would most like to resemble; there was none who sustained finer or greater roles, or loved glory more, or established his own more firmly, or who achieved it by less frequented paths.

Reading his works elevates the heart no less than the mind: his eloquence is always great, always majestic, and always heroic: one must picture him triumphing over Catiline,[76] one must picture him rising up against Antony,[77]

---

74 Book III, *On the Nature of the Gods*. (M) (III, 16, 21–23, 34.) Eusebius, bishop of Caesarea (c. 260–c. 340 CE), was a noted historian of Christianity and expositor of its doctrines.

75 *Praeparatio evangelica* [*Preparation for the Gospel*], Book III. (M)

76 Lucius Sergius Catilina (108–62 BCE), experienced Roman politician and senator, having run unsuccessfully against Cicero for consul in 64, laid plans to seize control of the Roman government. After Cicero discovered the plot and denounced the conspirators in October 63, they were put to death without trial by vote of the senate, though Catiline fled and was killed in battle along with most of his army in January 62.

77 Marc Antony (83–30 BCE), co-consul with Caesar in 44 and leader with Octavian and Lepidus of the Second Triumvirate (43–33), was killed at the Battle of Actium in 31, after Octavian, Caesar's great-nephew and adopted son, convinced the senate to declare war on Cleopatra and declare Antony a traitor.

and finally one must picture him mourning the pitiful remains of a dying liberty. Whether he is reporting his own actions or reporting those of the great men who have fought for the republic, he is exhilarated by his glory and theirs; the boldness of his expressions makes us feel the intensity of his sentiments. I can feel him sweeping me up in his enthusiasm and enthralling me with his raptures. What portraits he draws of the likes of Brutus,[78] of Cassius,[79] and of Cato![80] What ardor, what vivacity, what rapidity, what a torrent of eloquence. I know not whether I would rather be like the hero or the panegyrist.

If he sometimes draws attention too ostensibly to his own talents, he does no more than express to me what he had already made me feel; he anticipates the praise that is due him; I do not resent having it pointed out to me that it is not a mere orator who is speaking, but the liberator of his fatherland and the defender of liberty.

He merits the title of philosopher no less than that of Roman orator; it can even be said that he stood out more in the Lyceum than on the rostrum: he is original in his philosophical works, but he has had several rivals for his eloquence.

He is the first of the Romans to rescue philosophy from the hands of the learned and free it from the impediments of a foreign tongue. He made it common to all men, like reason, and in the plaudits he received for this, men of letters found themselves in agreement with the people.

I cannot admire enough the depth of his reasoning at a time when sages distinguished themselves only by the oddity of their garb.[81] I could only wish that he had been born in a more enlightened century and had been able to utilize for the discovery of truths those auspicious talents, which served only to destroy errors. It must be admitted that he left a frightful void in philosophy; he destroyed everything that had been conceived until then, and everything had to be conceived all over again; the human race re-entered infancy, so to speak, and was set back to where it started from.[82]

What a pleasure to see him in his book on the nature of the gods[83] examine all the sects, confound all the philosophers, and brand each prejudice with some stigma! Sometimes he combats against these monsters, sometimes he

---

78 Marcus Junius Brutus (c. 85–42 BCE), co-conspirator in the assassination of Caesar in 44.
79 Gaius Cassius Longinus (c. 87–42 BCE), co-conspirator in the assassination of Caesar.
80 Marcus Porcius Cato Uticensis (95–46 BCE), called Cato the Younger.
81 Cato, for example, is said to have worn little clothing in order to learn how to endure cold and rain.
82 In his presentations of Greek philosophy in dialogue form, Cicero pointed out the flaws in various philosophical schools, leaving few received opinions unscathed.
83 *On the Nature of the Gods* (*De natura deorum*), 45 BCE, in which Cicero critiques first Epicurean and then Stoic views on the gods.

makes light of philosophy; the champions he introduces destroy themselves; one is confounded by the next, who is beaten in his turn; all these systems fade away in the presence of the others, and there remains in the reader's mind only scorn for the philosophers and admiration for the critic.

With what satisfaction one sees him, in his book on divination[84] free the Romans' spirit from the ludicrous yoke of soothsayers[85] and the rules of that art which was the shame of pagan theology, which was established at the outset by the cunning[86] of magistrates among crude peoples and weakened by that same cunning when they became more enlightened.

Sometimes he discloses to us the charms of friendship and makes us feel all its delights;[87] sometimes he makes us see the advantages of an age that reason illuminates, and that saves us from the violence of passions.[88]

Sometimes shaping our conduct[89] and showing us the scope of our duties, he teaches what is honorable and beneficial, what we owe to society, what we owe to ourselves, and what we should do as heads of families or as citizens.[90]

His conduct was more austere than his spirit. In his government of Cicilia[91] he behaved with the disinterest of the likes of Cincinnatus,[92] of Camillus,[93] of Cato; but his virtue, which was by no means austere, did not prevent him from enjoying the civility of his times. Notable in his moral writings are an air of gaiety and a certain contentment of spirit unknown to lesser philosophers. He never enunciates precepts, but he makes us aware of them. He does not incite to virtue but attracts us to it: it is enough to read his works to be turned away forever from Seneca[94] and others like him, men sicker than those they

84 *On Divination (De divinatione,* 44 BCE), in which Cicero refutes Roman beliefs in divination.
85 Haruspices (*aruspices*) were Etruscans with no official role in Roman religion. See p. 62, note 13.
86 *Politique.*   87 *On Friendship (De amicitia),* 44 BCE.
88 *De senectute* ("On old age"), 44 BCE.   89 *Mœurs.*
90 *De officiis* ("On duties"), 44 BCE.
91 Cicero's record as governor of the province of Cilicia from May 51 to November 50 was unblemished. A previous governor, Gnaeus Cornelius Dolabella, had been convicted in 80 BCE of illegally plundering the province.
92 Lucius Quinctius Cincinnatus (c. 519–430 BCE), Roman statesman and military leader of the early republic who, according to legend, was appointed dictator in 458 or 457 following an invasion of Rome by the people of Æqui and promptly returned to his farm once victory had been won.
93 Marcus Furius Camillus (446–365 BCE), military hero and five times Roman dictator, who according to legend was the victor in the long and costly wars against the Etruscan peoples of Veii, Falerii, and Capena; he was later dubbed the second Romulus after defeating the invading Gauls in 390.
94 Lucius Annæus Seneca (1 BCE–65 CE), tutor and advisor to Nero, and author of letters and essays on the healing powers of philosophy.

wish to cure, more desperate than those they console, and more tyrannized by their passions than those they wish to free from them.

Some individuals accustomed to measuring all heroes by Quintius Curtius[95] have formed a very false notion of Cicero: they have seen him as a weak and timid man and have reproached him for something which Antony, his greatest enemy, never did. He avoided danger because he recognized it, but he no longer recognized it when he was no longer able to avoid it. This great man always subordinated all his passions, his fear, and his courage to wisdom and reason. I even dare say that there are perhaps none among the Romans who gave greater examples of strength and courage.

Is it not true that to declaim the Second Philippic[96] before Antony was to court certain death, to make a courageous sacrifice of his life for the sake of his offended glory? Let us, then, admire the orator's courage and daring even more than his eloquence. Let us picture Antony the most powerful of men, Antony the master of the world, Antony who dared all and could do anything he dared, in a senate which was surrounded by his soldiers and where he was more king than consul; picture him, I say, covered with humiliation and ignominy, overwhelmed, crushed, forced to listen to the most humiliating words from the mouth of a man whose life he could have taken a thousand times.

It was moreover not only at the head of an army that he required steadiness and courage: the setbacks he had to suffer in times so difficult for men of good will made death ever present. All the enemies of the republic were his as well, the likes of Verres,[97] Clodius,[98] Catiline,[99] Caesar,[100] Antony;[101] indeed all the villains of Rome declared war on him.

95 Quintus Curtius Rufus (first century CE), whose *Histories of Alexander the Great* (*Historiae Alexandri Magni*) is only partially extant.
96 Cicero delivered twelve orations in the senate against Marc Antony in 44–43 BCE, the second of which catalogued atrocities committed by Antony; they are called the Philippics because they were modeled on Demosthenes' speeches denouncing Philip of Macedon, father of Alexander the Great.
97 I.e., Gaius Verres (115–43 BCE), the proconsul prosecuted by Cicero in 70 BCE for his corrupt governance of Sicily.
98 I.e., Publius Clodius Pulcher (93–52 BCE), the Roman senator prosecuted by Cicero for unlawfully gaining entry to the ceremony of the *bona dea* in December 62 BCE. A bribed jury acquitted him, and Clodius took revenge on Cicero by securing passage of a law punishing with exile consuls who executed Roman citizens without trial. Since Cicero, with senatorial support, had done just that to end the Catilinarian conspiracy in 63 BCE, he found it necessary to flee Rome; he was granted the right to return in 57 BCE.
99 See p. 72, note 76.
100 Gaius Julius Caesar (100–44 BCE), conqueror of Gaul (58–50), co-leader with Pompey and Crassus of the First Triumvirate (59–53), victor in the civil war against Pompey (49–48 BCE), dictator for life (46–44), and victim of assassination in March 44 BCE.
101 See p. 72, note 77.

It is true that there were times when his strength of spirit seemed to abandon him. When he saw Rome torn apart by so many factions, he gave in to sorrow; he allowed himself to be disheartened, and his philosophy was less strong than his love of the republic.

In that famous war that settled the destiny of the universe[102] he trembled for his fatherland. He saw Caesar approaching with an army which had won more battles than it had legions; but what was his sorrow when he saw that Pompey was abandoning Italy and leaving Rome exposed to the fury of the rebels? After such cowardliness, he said, I can no longer respect that man, who rather than choosing exile from his fatherland, as he did, should have perished on the walls of Rome and buried himself under her ruins.

Cicero, who had long been studying Caesar's projects, would have subjected this ambitious man to the fate of Catiline if his prudence had been heeded. "If my advice had been followed," the orator said to Antony, "the republic would be flourishing today, and you would be nothing. It was my opinion that Caesar should not have been allowed to remain governor of Gaul beyond the five-year term; it was also my opinion that during his absence he should not have been allowed to seek the consulate. If I had been fortunate enough to prevail in either case, we would never have fallen into the abyss we are in today. But when I saw," he continues, "that Pompey had handed the republic to Caesar, when I could see that he was beginning too late to perceive the evils that I had for so long foreseen, then I spoke constantly of an accommodation, and spared nothing to bring the factions together."[103]

Since Pompey had abandoned Italy, Cicero, as he himself says, knew very well that he should flee but he did not know whom he should follow and remained there for a while. Caesar conferred with him and hoped to convince him with entreaties and threats to side with his party; but this republican rejected his propositions with as much contempt as pride. Once the party of liberty had been destroyed, he submitted to him along with everyone else; he made no futile resistance; he did not, like Cato, shamefully abandon the republic along with his life;[104] he waited for a more auspicious time and sought in philosophy consolations which others had found only in death.

---

102 I.e., the civil war that raged between the forces of Caesar and Marc Antony and Pompey and his son (Pompey the Younger), from 49 to 44 BCE.

103 This text is modeled on Cicero's *Second Philippic*, x, 24.

104 Cato the Younger (95–46 BCE), choosing not to live in a Rome ruled by Caesar, committed suicide after Caesar's victory in the Battle of Thapsus in North Africa.

He withdrew to Tusculum in search of the liberty which his fatherland had lost. Those fields were never so gloriously fertile: we owe to them those lovely works which will be admired by every school and through all the transformations of philosophy.[105]

But when the conspirators had committed that great deed which still today astonishes tyrants, Cicero emerged as if from the tomb, and that sun which the star of Julius had eclipsed took on a new light. Brutus, all covered in blood and glory, showing the people the dagger and liberty, cried out: "Cicero." And, whether he was calling for his assistance, or wished to congratulate him for the liberty that he had just restored, or whether, finally, this new liberator of his fatherland was declaring himself his rival, he gave him in a single word the most magnificent praise a mortal has ever received.

Cicero immediately sided with Brutus; the dangers did not surprise him. Caesar lived on in the hearts of his soldiers; Antony, who inherited his ambition, held the consular authority in his hands: all this did not prevent him from speaking out, and by his authority and his example he determined whether a still uncertain world should regard Brutus as a parricide or as the liberator of his fatherland.

But the liberalities Caesar had shown the Romans in his testament[106] were new bonds for them. Antony harangued that greedy people, and, showing them Caesar's bloody robe, so greatly moved them that they went and set fire to the houses of the conspirators. Brutus and Cassius, forced to abandon their thankless fatherland, had only that means of escaping the affronts of a populace as angry as it was blind.

Antony, emboldened, usurped more authority in Rome than even Caesar had done: he seized the public purse, sold provinces and magistracies, and waged war on Roman colonies; in short, he broke every law. Proud of the effects of his eloquence, he no longer feared Cicero's. He declaimed against him even in the senate, but was quite taken aback to find still one Roman in Rome.

Soon after, Octavian made the infamous agreement by which Antony, for the price of his friendship, demanded Cicero's head: never was a war more fatal to the republic than this scandalous reconciliation where the only victims sacrificed were those who had so gloriously defended it.

---

105 The years 45 and 44 BCE were enormously productive for Cicero. Having withdrawn from politics after Caesar's victory in the Civil War, and while mourning the death of his daughter Tullia in February 45, he wrote, in rapid succession, thirteen works, including most of those alluded to in this essay.

106 In his will Caesar bequeathed his gardens bordering the Tiber to Rome and 300 sesterces to every Roman citizen.

This is how the detestable Popilius[107] is cleared by Seneca for Cicero's death: this odious crime was the crime of Antony who had commanded it, not of Popilius, who had obeyed; it had been Cicero's proscription to die, and Popilius' to take his life; it was no marvel that he had been compelled to kill him since Cicero, the first of all the Romans, had been forced to lose his head.[108]

Dialogue between Sulla and Eucrates

(1724)

Dialogue de Sylla et d'Eucrate, text by Pierre Rétat (*OC* VIII, 315–322). This is a fictional dialogue between the Roman general and dictator Lucius Cornelius Sulla (138–78 BCE) and an interlocutor he names Eucrates. Montesquieu explained the genesis of this work as follows: "Some scenes from Corneille gave me the idea for this dialogue. I was young, and you had to be very young to be incited to write by reading the great Corneille" (*Pensées* 1948). The essay was first published in February 1745 in the *Mercure de France* and was included three years later in the second edition of *Romans*. The manuscript was among those sent to England in 1818 (see "A General Note on the Texts"), and now belongs to the Académie de Bordeaux (828/III, no. 5).

* * *

A few days after Sulla had resigned the dictatorship, I learned that my reputation among philosophers made him wish to see me. He was at his villa in Tibur, where, for the first time in his life, he was enjoying a peaceful existence. I did not experience in seeing him the panic one usually feels in the presence of great men. And as soon as we were alone, I said to him: "Sulla, is it true that you put yourself voluntarily into a state of mediocrity, a cause of affliction for most men? That you have willingly renounced the influence which your glory and your virtues gave you over all men? Fortune seems embarrassed at no longer elevating you to positions of honor."[109]

---

107 Popilius Laenas was a military tribune sent by Marc Antony in December 43 BCE to kill Cicero, whose name had been placed on a list of the proscribed. Cicero was murdered on 7 December, during his attempted escape to Macedonia.
108 See Seneca the Elder, *Controversiae* ("Controversies," or "Declamations"), VII, 2.
109 Sulla voluntarily relinquished the dictatorship in 79 BCE and "walked up and down the forum like a private man, exposing his person freely to all who wished to call him to account" (Plutarch, *Life of Sulla*, XXIV).

"Eucrates," he replied, "if I am no longer on view to the whole world, this is not my fault but the fault of human affairs, which have limits. I believed I had fulfilled my destiny as soon as there were no longer any great deeds I needed to perform. I was not made to rule peacefully over a people of slaves. I like to win victories, to found or destroy states, to make alliances, to punish a usurper, but as for the petty details of government where modest talents have so many advantages, the slow execution of the laws, the discipline of an inactive militia, my soul cannot concern itself with these things."

"It is surprising," I said to him, "that you have brought such scruples to ambition. We have indeed seen great men who are unaffected by the vain celebrity and the pomp which surrounds those who govern; but there are very few of them who have been untouched by the pleasure of governing, and of molding to their whim the respect which is due only to the laws."

"Eucrates, as far as I am concerned," he replied, "I have never been so unhappy as when I found myself absolute master in Rome, as when, looking around me, I found neither rivals nor enemies.

"I thought that one day people would say that I had punished only slaves.[110] Do you desire, I said to myself, there to be no one left in your fatherland who can be stirred by your glory? And since you are establishing tyranny, do you not see that, after you, there will be no prince so weak that flattery will not place him on the same level as you and confer on him your name, your titles and even your virtues?"

"My Lord, you are changing all my ideas by the manner in which I see you act. I thought you had ambition, but no love of glory; I saw clearly that you had a lofty soul, but I did not suspect that it was great; everything in your life seemed to me to reveal a man consumed by the desire to command and who, filled with the most fatal passions, was willing to assume with pleasure the shame, the remorse and even the baseness associated with tyranny. After all, you have sacrificed everything to your power; you had made yourself formidable to every Roman; you had showed no mercy in exercising the functions of the most terrifying magistracy there ever was. The senate quaked to find itself with such a pitiless defender.[111] Someone said to you: 'Sulla, how much Roman blood will you shed? Do you wish to rule over

---

110 I.e., by means of Sulla's proscriptions, posted lists of individuals marked for execution as punishment for their support for the anti-Sullan regime established by Gaius Marius and Lucius Cornelius Cinna while Sulla was away (87–82 BCE) commanding Roman legions engaged against Mithridates VI Eupator (132–63 BCE), king of Pontus.
111 Sulla pushed through the popular assembly a repeal of the Hortensian Law of 287 BCE that had authorized the popular assembly, the *comitia tributa*, to pass legislation without prior senate approval.

nothing but walls?' At that point, you published those tables which determined the life or death of every citizen."[112]

"And it is all the blood that I have shed, which has enabled me to perform the greatest of all my actions. If I had governed Rome with leniency, how surprising would it have been that boredom, loathing or caprice had prompted me to abandon government! But I have given up the dictatorship at a time when there was not a man alive who did not believe the dictatorship was my only asylum. I stood before the Romans, a citizen among citizens, and I dared say to them: 'I am ready to account for all the blood I have spilled for the republic; I shall answer to all who come asking for their father, their son, or their brother. Every Roman fell silent before me.'"

"This noble act of which you speak strikes me as highly imprudent. It is true that you had in your favor the astonishment you had just produced among the Romans. But how did you dare speak to them of justifying your actions and taking as your judges persons who had so many reasons for taking vengeance on you?

"Had all your actions been judged merely severe when you were the master, they became frightful crimes as soon as you no longer were."

"Are you calling crimes," he said, "things that have saved the republic? Would you have wished that I should stand by idly while senators betrayed the senate to aid the people who, imagining that liberty must be as extreme as slavery can be, wished to abolish the magistracy itself?

"The people, constrained by the laws and by the gravity of the senate, have always striven to overthrow both. But any man who is ambitious enough to aid the people against the senate and the laws, was always also ambitious enough to become its master. That is why we have seen so many republics fail in Greece and in Italy.

"To prevent such a disaster, the senate has always been obliged to keep this unruly people occupied with war. It has been compelled, in spite of itself, to ravage the earth and to conquer so many nations whose obedience is a burden to us. Now that the universe has no more enemies with which to confront us, what would be the fate of the republic? And, without me, could the senate have prevented the people, caught in its blind frenzy for liberty,

112 Plutarch says that Sulla, after his return to Rome in 82 BCE, "now busied himself with slaughter, and murders without number or limit filled the city. [. . .] At last one of the younger men, Caius Metellus, made bold to ask Sulla in the senate what end there was to be of these evils." Sulla declined to say who would be spared, but agreed to name those who would be punished. Bounties were paid to those who brought in the severed heads of the condemned (*Life of Sulla*, IV, XXX–XXXI).

from subjecting itself to Marius or to the first tyrant who offered some hope for independence?

"The gods, who have given to most men a kind of cowardly ambition, have attached to liberty almost as many misfortunes as to servitude. But whatever must be the price of this noble liberty, we must necessarily pay it to the gods.

"The sea swallows up ships, it submerges whole countries; and yet it is useful to mankind.

"Posterity will judge what Rome has not yet dared to examine; it will find, perhaps, that I did not shed enough blood, and that not all the followers of Marius were proscribed."

"Sulla," I replied, "I have to say that you astonish me. What! It was for the good of your country that you spilled so much blood, and you have felt devotion to her?"

"Eucrates," he replied, "I never had that dominant love of country which we find so often exemplified in the early times of the republic, and I admire Coriolanus who carried the flame and sword to the walls of his ungrateful city, who made each citizen repent for the affront that each citizen had made to him,[113] quite as much as the man who drove the Gauls from the Capitol.[114] I have never prided myself on being either the slave or the worshiper of the society of my peers; and this much-vaunted love [of country] is too vulgar a passion to be compatible with the loftiness of my soul. I have conducted myself solely by my thoughts and especially by the contempt I have had for mankind. You can judge from the manner in which I have treated the world's only great people how great is my contempt for all the others.

"I have believed that, being on this earth, I must be free. If I had been born among the barbarians, I would have sought to usurp the throne less in order to command than to avoid having to obey. Born in a republic, I have obtained the glory of conquerors simply by seeking the glory of free men.

"When I entered Rome with my soldiers,[115] I was breathing neither fury nor revenge. I judged the astonished Romans without hatred, but also

---

113 According to legend, Gaius Marcius was called "Coriolanus" after he defeated the Volscians in a pitched battle in the city of Corioli in 493 BCE. Later, threatened with prosecution, he fled Rome and led the Volscians in war against his native land; only the tearful pleas of his mother and his wife finally persuaded him to lay down his arms. See Livy 2.34–35 and 2.40–41.

114 Marcus Furius Camillus (446–365 BCE), five times dictator of Rome, roused the Romans to drive the Gauls out of Rome in 390 BCE. See Livy 5.47–55.

115 I.e., Sulla's march on Rome in 82 BCE after signing a peace treaty with Mithridates, enabling him to return to Italy; he defeated supporters of the Roman consul Cinna at the Battle of the Colline Gate.

without pity. You were once free, I said, and you wanted to live as slaves. No. But die now, and you will have the advantage of dying as citizens of a free city.

"I believed that to take away the liberty of a city of which I was a citizen was the greatest of crimes. I have punished that crime, and I have not worried about whether I was to be the good or the evil genius of the republic. In the meantime, the government of our fathers has been re-established; the people have atoned for all the affronts they had inflicted on the nobles; fear has suspended jealousies, and Rome has never been so tranquil.

"Now you know what made me determined to commit all the bloody tragedies you have witnessed. If I had lived during those happy days of the republic when the citizens, tranquil in their houses, committed to the gods a free soul,[116] you would have seen me spend my life in this retreat that I have obtained only with so much blood and sweat."

"My Lord," I said, "it is fortunate that Heaven has spared the human race many men like yourself. Born for mediocrity, we are overwhelmed by sublime spirits. For one man to be above humanity, all the others pay too dear a price.

"You have regarded the ambition of heroes as a common passion, and you have esteemed only rational ambition. The insatiable desire to dominate, which you have found in the hearts of a few citizens, made you resolve to be an extraordinary man; love of your liberty made you resolve to be formidable and cruel. Who would have said that a heroism of principle could be more deadly than a heroism of impetuosity? But if, to avoid being a slave, you had to usurp the dictatorship, how did you dare to give it up? The Roman people, you say, has seen you unarmed and made no attempt on your life. You have escaped that danger; perhaps a greater danger awaits you. Some day you may see a great criminal taking advantage of your moderation[117] and consider you merely part of the crowd of subjugated people."

"I have a name," he said, "and it is sufficient to ensure my safety and that of the Roman people. This name halts any attempt; and there is no ambition that is not terrified by it. Sulla breathes, and his genius is more powerful than that of all the Romans. Sulla is surrounded by Chaeronea, Orchomenus, and Signia;[118] Sulla has given to every Roman family a dreadful example and one close to home; every Roman will always have me before his eyes, and even in his dreams I shall appear to him covered in blood; he will see the deadly

116 I.e., they died free men, a paraphrase of the expression *rendre l'âme à Dieu*.
117 I.e., Sulla's voluntary relinquishment of the dictatorship.
118 These were the three major battles Sulla fought against the forces of Mithridates.

Tables, and see his name first among the proscribed. People mutter in secret about my laws, but they will not be effaced even by waves of Roman blood. Am I not in the very heart of Rome? In my villa you will still find the javelin that I used at Orchomenus and the shield I carried on the walls of Athens. Am I any less Sulla because I have no more lictors? I have on my side the senate, together with justice and the laws; the senate has on its side my genius, my luck[119] and my glory."

"I recognize," I said, "that once you have made someone tremble, you almost always retain some of the advantage you have seized."

"No doubt," he said. "I have astounded men, and that is an accomplishment. Review the story of my life in your mind: you will realize that I have derived everything from that principle, and it has been the soul of all my actions. Remember my quarrels with Marius.[120] I was indignant to see a man with no name, proud of his lowly birth, undertaking to drag the first families of Rome down to the level of the populace; and in this situation I bore all the burden of a great soul. I was young, and I resolved to put myself in a position to force Marius to answer for his contempt. To that end, I attacked him with his own weapons, that is to say with victories against the enemies of the republic.

"When the caprice of fate obliged me to leave Rome, I continued to act in the same way; I set out to make war on Mithridates, believing that I would destroy Marius by vanquishing the enemy of Marius. While I was allowing this Roman to enjoy his power over the populace, I was multiplying his mortifications and forcing him to go to the Capitol every day to give thanks to the gods for victories with which I was driving him to despair. I was waging a war of reputation against him, a hundred times more unrelenting than the war my legions were waging against the barbarian king. Not a single word left my mouth that did not signal my audacity; and the least of my actions, always magnificent, were for Marius deadly presages. Mithridates eventually sued for peace. The conditions he was offering were reasonable, and if Rome had been tranquil, or if my fortune had not been uncertain, I would have accepted them.

119 Sulla attributed his military successes to good fortune rather than skill, and, once made dictator of Rome, he asked to be given the title of "Fortunate," thus becoming Lucius Cornelius Sulla Felix. See Plutarch, *Life of Sulla*, XXIV.
120 Gaius Marius (157–86 BCE) launched Sulla's military career in 107 by appointing him quaestor during the war against the North African king Jugurtha of Numidia. It was Sulla, however, not Marius, who skillfully negotiated the surrender of Jugurtha by his father-in-law, Bochus I, and this launched a personal rivalry that continued up until the death of Marius in 86.

But the poor state of my affairs obliged me to make the conditions more onerous. I demanded that he should destroy his fleet and restore to the neighboring kings all the kingdoms he had taken from them.[121] 'I will leave you,' I told him, 'the kingdom of your fathers. You should thank me for allowing you to keep the hand with which you signed the order to put to death a hundred thousand Romans in one day.'[122] Mithridates was stopped in his tracks, and Marius, back in Rome, trembled at the news.

"This same audacity which served me so well against Mithridates, against Marius, against his son, against Telesinus[123] and against the people, and which made my whole dictatorship tenable, also defended my life on the day I gave it up, and that day ensures my liberty forever."

"My Lord," I said, "Marius reasoned as you do when, covered with the blood of his enemies and that of the Romans, he displayed the audacity that you have punished. It is true that you have in your favor a few more victories and greater excesses. But, in assuming the dictatorship, you exemplified the crime you have punished. That is the example which will be followed, and not that of moderation, which will only be admired.

"When the gods allowed Sulla to make himself dictator of Rome with impunity, they proscribed liberty there forever. They would have to perform too many miracles now to tear the ambition to rule from the hearts of all the Roman captains. You have taught them that there is a much surer path to move toward tyranny and keep it without danger. You have divulged this fatal secret, and taken away the single factor that makes people into good citizens in an overly rich and overly large republic: futility of hoping to oppress it."

His expression changed, and he remained silent for a moment. "I fear only one man," he said with emotion, "in whom I see many Mariuses.[124] Chance,

---

121 Sulla did not in fact drive a hard bargain with Mithridates, who only handed over seventy ships and five hundred archers and sailed away to Pontus (Plutarch, *Life of Sulla*, XXIV). Mithridates, however, was required to relinquish all territory outside Pontus and return his Roman prisoners. The lenient terms enabled Mithridates to become Rome's long-term nemesis until his final defeat by Pompey in 66 BCE.

122 Plutarch reports that Mithridates, prior to the Roman senate's declaration of war on him, had massacred, on a single day, 150,000 Romans in Asia (*ibid.*).

123 Pontius Telesinus, the Samnite leader allied with Cinna's regime, defeated by Sulla at the Battle of the Colline Gate in 82 BCE.

124 The reference is to Caesar, I. The "many Mariuses" comment, now thought to be apocryphal, is recorded in Plutarch's *Life of Caesar* and also in Suetonius' *De vita Caesarum* ("Lives of the Caesars"), Caesar, I.

or perhaps a more powerful fate, has led me to spare him.[125] I watch him incessantly; I study his soul: in it he is hiding deep designs. But if he ever dares form the plan of commanding men whom I have made my equals, I swear by the gods that I will punish his insolence."

125 Sulla did not proscribe Caesar, even though he was the son-in-law of Cinna and the nephew of Marius. He did tell Caesar, however, that he would have to divorce his wife as the price for his safety. Instead, Caesar left Rome and did not return until Sulla died in 78 BCE.

III

Reflections on National Character

Notes on England

(1729–1731)

Notes sur l'Angleterre, text by Cecil Patrick Courtney (*OC* x, 495–506). The text of this work is probably a portion of Montesquieu's travel notes, entitled "Trip to England," which was shipped to England in 1818 (see "A General Note on the Texts") and has since been lost. It was first published in 1818 in the Lefèvre edition of Montesquieu's complete works and is the base text for *OC* x and for our translation. The title was added by Lefèvre.

* * *

I left The Hague on the last day of October 1729. I made the crossing with Lord Chesterfield,[1] who was so kind as to offer me passage on his yacht.

The common people of London eat a lot of meat;[2] this makes them very robust, but at the age of forty or forty-five, they croak.

There is nothing as frightful as the streets of London. They are very dirty, and the cobble stones are so poorly maintained that it is almost impossible to travel on them by carriage, and one must make one's will when taking a hackney coach, which are conveyances as high as a stage, with the driver even higher, his seat being on a level with the canopy. These coaches are jolted by potholes that seem to shake your head loose.[3]

Young English noblemen are of two sorts; the first are very knowledgeable because they have spent a long time in universities, which gives them an awkward look and a sheepish appearance. The second know nothing at all,

1 Philip Dormer Stanhope, 4th Earl of Chesterfield (1694–1773), English ambassador to The Hague between February 1728 and February 1732.
2 Editor Cecil P. Courtney notes (*OC* x, 495) that this observation seems to be frequent in travels to England: cf. César François de Saussure (1705–1783), *Lettres et voyages en Allemagne, en Hollande et en Angleterre, 1725–1729* (Lausanne: G. Bridel, 1903), p. 226.
3 Cf. *ibid.*, pp. 171–172.

and they are anything but ashamed; they are the nation's fops. Generally speaking, the English are humble.

On 5 October 1730 (n.s.),[4] I was presented to the prince,[5] the king,[6] and the queen[7] at Kensington. After speaking to me about my travels, the queen spoke of the English theater; she asked Lord Chesterfield why it was that Shakespeare, who lived in the time of Queen Elizabeth, had made women speak so poorly and made them so silly. Lord Chesterfield made an excellent reply, saying that in those times women did not appear on stage, and that it was bad actors who played those roles, which is why Shakespeare took less trouble to make them speak well. I would give another reason, which is that making women speak requires familiarity with high society and decorum. To make heroes speak well requires only familiarity with books. The queen asked me if it were not true that, in France, Corneille was more admired than Racine. I replied that generally Corneille was regarded as the greater mind, and Racine as the greater author.

It seems to me that Paris is a beautiful city where there are some uglier things, London an unsightly city where there are some very beautiful things.

In London, liberty and equality. The liberty of London is the liberty of proper folk, and as such it differs from that of Venice, which is the liberty to live in obscurity and with whores, and to marry them; the equality of London also is the equality of proper folk, and as such it differs from the liberty of Holland, which is the liberty of the rabble.

The *Craftsman*[8] is written by Bolingbroke[9] and by Mr. Pulteney.[10] They have it checked by three barristers before printing it, lest it contain anything that infringes the law.

The complaints voiced by foreigners in London, especially by the French, are lamentable. They say that they are unable to make a single friend there; that the longer they stay, the fewer they have; and that their gestures of politeness are taken as insults. Kinski,[11] the Broglies,[12] Madame

---

4 New style, in other words the European date: Britain did not adopt the Gregorian calendar until 1752 and was therefore eleven days behind the European calendar.

5 Frederick Louis, Prince of Wales (1707–1751).

6 George II (1683–1760), monarch from 1727.

7 Caroline of Brandenburg-Ansbach (1683–1737), who had married George in 1705.

8 Tory opposition journal, published from 1726 until 1736.

9 Henry St. John, 1st Viscount Bolingbroke (1678–1751), Tory politician and Secretary of State under Queen Anne (reigned 1702–1707).

10 William Pulteney, 1st Earl of Bath (1682–1764), member of parliament from 1705 until 1734 and Secretary of War from 1714 until 1717.

11 Count Philip Kinsky (1700–1749), Austrian envoy to London between 1728 and 1736.

12 François Marie, comte de Broglie (1671–1745), French ambassador to London from 1724 to 1729; Charles Guillaume, marquis de Broglie (1669–1751); Victor Maurice, comte de Broglie (1647–1727).

Villette,[13] who when in Paris called Lord Essex[14] her son, offered little remedies to all and sundry, and asked all the women for news of their health: those people want the English to be like them. How could the English like foreigners? They do not even like themselves. How would they invite us to dinner? They don't offer dinner to each other. "But you visit a country in order to be liked and honored." That is not essential. Thus we should act like them, live only for ourselves, and, like them, care for nobody, love nobody, and rely on nobody. In short, one must take countries as they are; when I am in France, I am friendly with everyone, in England with no one; in Italy, I pay everyone compliments; in Germany, I drink with everyone.

People say, "In England no one is friendly to me." Do people have to be friendly to you?

The Englishman wants a good dinner, a prostitute, and comfort. Because he does not get around much, and is limited to that, once his fortune falls apart and he can no longer have that, he kills himself or turns to thievery.

15 March (o.s.).[15] Scarcely a day goes by that someone does not treat the king of England with disrespect. A few days ago, Lady Bell Molineux, acting on her own,[16] had some trees cut down on a small plot of land the queen had bought[17] for Kensington,[18] and sued her, without ever desiring, under some pretext, to come to terms with her. She kept the queen's secretary waiting for three hours when he came to tell her that the queen did not believe she had a seigniorial right to that plot since the queen held it for three lives,[19] but with the stipulation that she not sell it.

It seems to me that most princes are better people than we are, since, being in the public eye, they have more to lose with regard to their reputation.

Corruption has invaded all social strata. Thirty years ago no one ever heard any talk of a thief in London; today nothing is more common. Whiston's

---

13 Bolingbroke's wife, whom he calls *la Villette*, was Marie-Claire Deschamps de Marcilly (1675–1751), marquise de Villette by her first marriage.

14 William Capel, third Earl of Essex (1697–1743), gentleman of the bedchamber to George II, close friend of Bolingbroke, and ambassador to Turin from 1731 until 1738.

15 Old style, in other words by the Julian calendar; outside Great Britain the date would be 26 March (cf. note 4 above).

16 The somewhat puzzling (and perhaps sarcastic) expression used here (*maîtresse fille*) may refer to the fact that Lady Elizabeth or Beth (not Bell), sister of William Capel, had become an autonomous agent by the death of her husband, Samuel Molyneux, on 13 April 1728.

17 I.e., from her.

18 Montesquieu may be confusing Kensington with Kew, where the Molyneux had significant property; the queen was invested in the development of both gardens.

19 In other words, she held a ninety-nine-year lease.

book against the Savior's miracles,[20] which is read by the common people, will not reform morality. But since people want ministers of state to be criticized, they want freedom of the press to be allowed.

As for the ministers, they have no fixed project. Sufficient unto the day is the work thereof.[21] They govern day by day.

Moreover, there is great outward freedom. Lady Denham,[22] being masked, said to the king: "By the way, when will the Prince of Wales be coming? Are you afraid to show him? Could he be as much of a fool as his father and grandfather?" The king learned her identity because he made inquiries among his household. From that day on, every time she came to court she was pale as death.

Here money is sovereignly esteemed, honor and virtue not much.

People of high intelligence should be sent here. Otherwise, they will deceive themselves regarding the English people and never come to know them. Here, if you commit yourself to a faction, you hold to it. Now, there are a hundred million little factions, as there are passions. D'Hiberville,[23] who saw nothing but Jacobites about him, was induced to try to convince the French court that it could make a Tory parliament. The Whigs won, after a great deal of money was wasted, and that was, they say, the cause of his fall. In my time, French ministers knew no more about England than a babe of six months. Kinski was forever fooled by Tory pamphlets. Since frightening things are reported in the weekly press, it is easy to believe the people are going to rebel tomorrow, but one must merely realize that in England, as elsewhere, the people are dissatisfied with the ministers, and here they write what people elsewhere only think.[24]

I see the king of England as a man who has a lovely wife, a hundred servants, fine coaches and horses, and excellent fare; people believe he is happy. All that is on the surface. When everyone has withdrawn, when the door is closed, he cannot help quarreling with his wife and his servants and swearing at his butler; he is no longer so happy.

---

20 It was Thomas Woolston (1670–1773) who wrote *Discourses on the Miracles of our Savior* (London, 1727–1729) and was imprisoned for blasphemy. William Whiston (1667–1752) was the author of *A New Theory of the Earth* (1696).
21 Matthew 6:34.
22 Likely Jane Steuart-Denham, wife of Sir Archibald Steuart-Denham, or Anne Denham, wife of Dr. William Denham (1657–1735).
23 Charles François de La Bonde d'Iberville (1653–1723), French envoy to London between 1713 and 1717.
24 Cf. *Pensées* 814.

When I visit a country, I do not examine whether there are good laws, but whether the ones they have are enforced, for there are good laws everywhere.

Since the English are clever, whenever a minister from abroad is less so they scorn him from the start; and suddenly he is finished, since they never get over their scorn.

The king gets a tax from the papers,[25] which number about fifty: thus the king is paid for the insults they pay him.

Since people here do not like one another very much for fear of being duped, they become hardened.

A slater used to have the gazette brought to him to read on the roof.[26]

Yesterday, 28 January 1730 (o.s.), Mr. Chipin spoke in the House of Commons about the national troops; he said that only a tyrant or a usurper needs troops to maintain his position, and therefore they were means which H. M.'s indubitable prerogatives could not require.[27] At the words "tyrant" and "usurper" the whole chamber was shocked, and he repeated them a second time; then he said that he did not like Hanoverian maxims... All this was so passionate that the chamber feared a debate, so everyone cried: "Divide, divide!"[28] in order to close off debate.

When the king of Prussia[29] decided to wage war on Hanover, he was asked why he had suddenly assembled his troops before he had sought reparation. The king of Prussia replied that he had twice or thrice done so, but that Sir Reichtembach,[30] his minister, had always been rebuffed and paid no heed by the prime minister Debouche, who had an aversion for the color blue. Now as it happened the most elegant suit I have seen on Reichtembach was blue, and for that reason said minister could not obtain a minute's audience.

There are certain Scottish members who get only two hundred pounds for their vote, and who sell it at that price.

The English are no longer worthy of their freedom. They sell it to the king; and were the king to give it back to them, they would sell it back to him again.[31]

---

25 Beginning in 1712, Parliament imposed a stamp duty on periodicals, which remained on the books until 1855.

26 See Saussure, *Lettres et voyages*, p. 167 for a similar remark.

27 William Shippen (1673–1743), English Tory MP and critic of the Hanoverians and of a standing army. After the debate, the House of Commons voted to fund a standing army of 18,000 soldiers.

28 I.e., a call for a division of the house.

29 Frederick William I (1688–1740), king of Prussia and Elector of Brandenburg from 1713.

30 Benjamin Friedrich von Reichenbach, later Prussian envoy to London from 1726 to 1730.

31 For Montesquieu on English corruption, see his letter to William Domville in *Pensées* 1960.

A minister thinks only of triumphing over his adversary in the lower house, and provided he achieves that, he would sell England and all the powers in the world.

A nobleman named. . ., who has an income of fifteen crowns sterling, had repeatedly wagered a hundred guineas at ten to one that he would perform on the stage. Perform a play to collect a thousand guineas, and this scandalous act is not viewed with horror! It seems to me that many extraordinary acts occur in England, but they are all done to get money. Not only is there no honor and virtue here, but there is not even the notion of them. Extraordinary acts in France serve to spend money; here, to obtain it.

I do not judge England by these men, but I do judge England by the approval she gives to them. And if these men were regarded as they would be in France, they would never have dared to do it.

I have heard it said by knowledgeable persons that England, in times when she is making an effort, is capable of yielding only five million pounds sterling in taxes without bankrupting herself; but presently, in peacetime, she is paying six million.

The day before yesterday I went to the lower house of Parliament; they were debating the Dunkirk business.[32] Never have I seen such fireworks. The session lasted from one o'clock in the afternoon until three o'clock in the morning. The French came in for rough handling; I noted how far the terrible jealousy between the two nations goes. Mr. Walpole[33] attacked Bolingbroke in the cruelest manner, and said that it was he who had led the whole plot. The chevalier Wyndham[34] defended him. Walpole related in Bolingbroke's favor the story of a peasant who, passing under a tree with his wife, found that a man who had been hanged was still breathing. He untied him and took him to his home; the man recovered. They discovered the next day that the man had stolen their forks; they said: "It is wrong to interfere with the course of justice: we must take him back where we got him."

It had always been the custom for the Commons to send two bills to Lords: one against mutineers and deserters, which the Lords always passed, the other against corruption, which they always rejected. In the last session, Lord

---

32 I.e., the allegation that Walpole's government had allowed France, contrary to the terms of the Treaty of Utrecht (1713) and the Treaty of Hague (1717), to rebuild the harbor of Dunkirk.

33 Robert Walpole (1676–1745), Whig leader of the House of Commons, and First Lord of the Treasury from 1721 to 1742.

34 Sir William Wyndham (1687–1740), leader of the Tories in the House of Commons.

Thousand[35] said: "Why do we always draw on ourselves the public's wrath by always rejecting the bill? We should increase the penalties and word the bill in such a way that the Commons itself would reject it." And so, in keeping with these excellent ideas, the Lords increased the penalty against the corrupter as well as the corrupted from ten to five hundred pounds, and stipulated that ordinary judges and not the chamber would judge elections, and that each court would always follow the most recent precedent. But the Commons, who perhaps sensed the ruse or wished to take advantage of it, also passed it, and the court was forced to do the same. Since that time, in the new elections which have been held, the court has lost several members, who were chosen from among the great landowners, and it will be difficult to constitute a new Parliament to the court's liking: and so it is that the most corrupt of parliaments is the one which has done most to secure public liberty.

This bill is miraculous, for it was passed against the will of the Commons, the Lords, and the king.[36]

In times past the king held a quarter of England's property, the nobles another quarter, and the clergy another; so that, with the nobles and clergy joining together, the king was always defeated. Henry VII allowed the lords to sell, and commoners acquired, which raised up the Commons.[37] It appears to me that under Henry VII[38] the commoners got the property of the nobility, and under Henry VIII[39] the nobles got the property of the clergy. Under the ministry of Queen Anne,[40] the clergy regained some strength and got considerably more wealthy by the year. The English ministry, which wished to win over the clergy, prevailed on Queen Anne's piety to leave to them certain royal assets, such as the first year's revenue from each bishopric, and something more, amounting to fourteen thousand pounds sterling per year, to supplement the poorer livings, on the condition, which the churchmen had added, that each parson who asked for a share of this sum would be obliged to pay a corresponding amount of his own so as to increase the income which the living provided. Moreover, it allowed anyone to give to the Church, even by testament, which abrogated the former law, causing the clergy to continue getting richer, despite the English

35 I.e., Charles, Viscount Townshend (1674–1738), Robert Walpole's brother-in-law and Secretary of State for the Northern Department from 1714 to 1717 and 1721 to 1730.
36 The bill was the Bribery at Elections Act, passed in 1729.
37 In *Spicilège* 533 Montesquieu records the following sentence from the 21 November 1730 edition of *The Craftsman*: "In the queen's Mary [*sic*] time the effect of the causes laid in the reign of Henry began to appear[.] [T]he king the lords and the church had now in hand little [more] than one third of the whole." (*OC* XIII, 469.)
38 King of England from 1485 to 1509.   39 King of England from 1509 to 1547.
40 Queen of England from 1702 to 1707 and of Great Britain (England and Scotland) from 1707 to 1714.

indifference to religion. The Whig ministry would not have done that, but it has not dared to change it, for it still needs the clergy.[41]

I believe it is in France's interest to maintain the king in England, for a republic would be much more ominous: she would act with all her strength, whereas with a king, she acts with divided strength. However, this state of affairs cannot last for long.

The power is where the property is. The nobility and the clergy used to have the property; they have lost it in two ways: first, by increasing the pounds to a marc (the marc of three pounds under St. Louis[42] having gradually reached forty-nine, its present value); second, by the discovery of the Indies, which made silver very common, and consequently the nobility's incomes, being almost all in silver, have been lost. The king has surtaxed the commons heavily in proportion to what the nobility has lost with respect to them, and the king has succeeded in becoming a prince feared by his neighbors, with a nobility which had no resources other than to serve, and with commoners he has had paid however much he likes: the English are the cause of our servitude.

There is in this work[43] a flaw which seems to me to be that of the genius of the nation for which it has been created, which is less concerned with her prosperity than with her envy of others' prosperity, which is her prevailing spirit, as all of England's laws bearing on commerce and shipping make clear enough.

I do not know what will come of sending so many inhabitants of Europe and Africa to the West Indies, but I think that if any nation is abandoned by her colonies, it will begin with the English nation.

There is no English word for *valet de chambre*, because they have none, and no difference between masculine and feminine.[44] Whereas in France we say "to eat up one's property," in England the common people say "to eat and drink up one's property."

The English don't show many courtesies, but never discourtesies.

Women are reserved there because Englishmen see little of them; they imagine that a foreigner who speaks to them wants to mount them. "I don't want to give him any encouragement," they say.

No religion in England; four or five members of the Commons go to mass or to the house sermon, except on important occasions, when they arrive

---

41 The bill, known as Queen Anne's Bounty (February 1704), was designed to increase the revenues of the poorer clergy.

42 Louis IX, king of France from 1226 until 1270, canonized in 1297.

43 *Ouvrage.* Montesquieu is here referring to a political work in progress, namely the evolution of the British system of government.

44 I.e., between men and women equally called *valets.*

early. If someone brings up religion, everyone begins to laugh. When someone said, during my stay: "I believe that as an article of faith," everyone began to laugh. There is a committee to inquire into the state of religion; that is seen as ridiculous.[45]

England is at present the freest country in the world; I except no republic. I call her free because the prince has no power to do any imaginable harm to anyone at all, for the reason that his power is regulated and limited by law. But if the lower house were to become dominant, its power would be unlimited and dangerous because it would at the same time have executive authority, whereas at present unlimited power lies with the parliament and the king, and executive authority with the king, whose power is limited.

A good Englishman must then seek to defend freedom both against the encroachments of the crown and those of the chamber.

Even if an Englishman had as many enemies as hairs on his head, he would come to no harm for it. That is important, for the health of the soul is as important as that of the body.

When M. de Broglie's blue sash was seized,[46] someone said: "What a nation: they have driven out the Father,[47] denied the Son[48] and confiscated the Holy Spirit."

Reflections on the Inhabitants of Rome

(1732)

Réflexions sur les habitants de Rome, text by Sheila Mason (*OC* IX, 77–82). The manuscript of this text remained at La Brède until 1939 when it was purchased by Robert Schuman. It was sold to the municipal library of Bordeaux in 1965 (MS 2133/VI). It was first published in volume II of *Voyages de Montesquieu, publiés par le baron Albert de Montesquieu*, 2 vols. (Bordeaux: Gounouilhou, 1894–1896).

* * *

45 An Anglican ecclesiastical committee met in 1711 and issued a report entitled "A representation of the present state of religion, with regard to the late excessive growth of infidelity, heresy, and profaneness." The House of Lords took no action.

46 The *cordon bleu*, designating the Order of the Holy Spirit, was the highest honor awarded in France under the Ancien Régime. Since the incident alluded to seems to have occurred in England, the victim of the seizure must have been François Marie II, comte de Broglie (1671–1745), ambassador of France from 1724 to 1729.

47 I.e., James II (1633–1701), king of England from 1685 until the Glorious Revolution of 1688.

48 I.e., James III (1688–1766), son of James II, known as the "Old Pretender" around whom rallied Jacobites seeking the restoration of the Stuarts.

Those who see Rome and remember what they have read about the prodigious gluttony of the ancient Romans must be struck by the surprising sobriety of the Romans of today.

If formerly in Rome gastronomic debauchery was carried to a point of ridiculousness, today it can be said that the excess of frugality is no less so.

The ancient Romans ate five meals;[49] the last one, called *comissatio*, lasted well into the night.[50] Nowadays in Rome it is impossible to eat more than once.

I can think of several reasons for this change, some physical and others moral. Modern Rome is built in a low-lying area which was formerly not inhabited, and one no longer breathes there the subtle air by the City of the Seven Hills.[51]

When the popes returned to Rome, which had been made empty by their absence, they took up residence near the church of St. Peter and the tomb of Hadrian, which is the Castel San Angelo; that was hardly surprising because that church was the object of the whole world's devotion, and Hadrian's tomb was the city's best fortification. Rome was rebuilt round the papal palace, that is to say in the Campus Martius and on the plain alongside the Tiber, a low-lying area where the air is foul; this area was almost uninhabitable in former times, on account of the terrible flooding of the river, but its frequent overflowing and the various demolitions in the city somewhat raised the land level.

The air has changed even in the parts of the town which were previously well populated: this is proven by new diseases and can easily be explained: the constructions made over such a long expanse of time by a huge population are mostly buried underground; water stagnates in them and the air is trapped.

The manner of living, moreover, has completely changed.

The ancient Romans had techniques for eating to excess; they always took a bath before a meal in order to prepare their stomachs. Artemidorus[52] said that in his day baths were merely a preparation for meals. This custom was so ingrained that physicians could not be obeyed when they forbade it.[53]

In the eleventh volume of the *Lettres édifiantes*, Father Antoine Seep writes to Father Guillaume Slinchaim that rivers are essential to Indian settlements:

49 Not everyone ate five meals a day, but women, children, the elderly, people with a weak stomach, and the debauched. (M)

50 Cf. *Pensées* 682. The late night *comissatio* was a drunken revelry at first involving only men, but later women could also be present.

51 Abbé Jean-Baptiste Dubos included similar observations in his *Critical Reflections on Poetry and Painting* (1719), II, p. 264.

52 Artemidorus of Ephesus, a Greek writer of the second century CE, whose discussion of baths prior to meals was cited by Justus Lipsius (1547–1606) in his *Fax historica* (1671; *Catalogue* 2847).

53 The doctors of Antiquity used to complain of this. (M)

these people who live by hunting are prone to severe indigestion which only bathing can cure.[54]

The ancient Romans also used emetics[55] in order to eat more. I am not referring to the debaucheries of Vitellius[56] and those who were like him; I am talking of average daily life.

Life in Rome was extremely agitated: the constitution of the government, the great number of duties and civil affairs, the intrigues of elections, required a man to know a great many people and to be known by them made the same demands. Nowadays, Rome is the most tranquil city in the world. For the ambitious all the agitation is in the mind, and the body rests.

Today, because of special circumstances, poor people put all the money they have into outward pomp and sacrifice even their sensual pleasures to their vanity; it used to be that a huge number of wealthy people, none of whom stood out because of his opulence, devoted their wealth almost entirely to their pleasures.

The ambition for one of the highest offices, which can be obtained only by age, by a disciplined life and upright behavior, inspires general sobriety in everyone today; everyone safeguards their expectations by always looking after their health; thus Rome is a city of convalescents.

Owing to a quiet lifestyle which the constitution of the state makes necessary, people do not dine in company: that factor alone favors sobriety; for at banquets the variety of dishes stimulates the appetite, and every guest prods the others to excesses.

The stomach gets used to all the work one chooses to give it. Athletes, whose profession required them to eat a lot, and who did so, are the authentic proof of that.

54 "Letter of Father Antoine Sepp, Missionary of the Company of Jesus, to Father Guillaume Stinglhaim [...]" in *Lettres édifiantes et curieuses* ("Edifying and curious letters"), II (Paris, 1715), pp. 414–415. Cf. *Pensées* 665, where Montesquieu quotes part of Sepp's letter about the Indians of Paraguay and concludes with: "The Romans always bathed before dinner. This appears in Plutarch, I think in the *Life of Cato*. See my Plutarch extract, where I think I put down some passages on this." The note referred to is apparently lost; all that is found in the life of Cato (the Younger) is a mention of a bath before dinner (LXVII).

55 Cicero, in a letter to Atticus, Book XIII, describing the way Caesar lived in his home says: "ἐμετικὴν agebat; itaque edit et bibit et ἀδεῶς et jucunde. Qui mane vomuit, says Celsius, *ungi debet deinde cœnare?*" (M) ("He sat down to dinner. As he had made himself copiously vomit, he ate and drank much, and was in very good humor.")

56 Suetonius, *De vita Caesarum* ("Lives of the Caesars"), Vitellius, XIII, writes: "But his principal vices were gluttony and cruelty; he always ate three meals, sometimes four: breakfast, lunch, dinner and orgy, and his stomach was easily up to all of them, thanks to his habit of making himself vomit."

It could be objected to what I have said above that the Turks bathe frequently and eat very little.

But they wash more than they bathe, and the coffee they are forever drinking and the smoking of tobacco prevent hunger, and besides they are weakened by a more indolent life and a continually immoderate enjoyment of women.[57]

Today it is absolutely essential in Rome to sleep after dinner.[58] The Ancients make no mention of any such need.

Toward midday one becomes incapable of applying oneself; one is unable to stay awake; the organs seem to fall in on one other.

I come to believe that the ancient inhabitants, *patiens pulveris atque solis*,[59] were much more robust than today's: institutions, habit and custom all easily allow one to overcome the force of the climate.

Furthermore, excessive heat brings about sleep just because it increases the expansion of the fluids and the distension of the fibers, and the brain more easily relaxes; but the bathing which the Ancients practiced continually brought a certain coolness to the members, restored body to the fluids and activity to the fibers.

---

57 Similar comments were made by Jean Chardin in his *Voyages* (Chardin, IV, 166); by Jean-Baptiste Tavernier, in his *Six Voyages [. . .] en Turquie, en Perse, et aux Indes* (Paris, 1676), Book V, chs. 14 and 17; and by Joseph Pitton de Tournefort, in his *Relation d'un voyage au Levant* (Lyon, 1717), II, 360.

58 By dinner was meant the midday meal.

59 From Horace (*Odes*, I, 8, v. 4): it applies to Sybaris, "who could bear the dust and sun."

IV

Politics and Morality

In Praise of Sincerity

(c. 1717)

Éloge de la sincérité, text by Sheila Mason (*OC* VIII, 137–145). The text of this manuscript is in the hand of a secretary who worked for Montesquieu and for the Academy of Bordeaux between 1715 and 1718. It is listed on the 1818 manifest of papers sent to England (see "A General Note on the Texts"). Subsequently preserved at La Brède until its first sale in 1939, it was sold again in 1957, this time to the municipal library of Bordeaux (MS 2100). It was first published in *Mélanges inédits* (1892).

* * *

To the Stoics almost all of philosophy consisted in knowing oneself; life, they said, was not too long for such a study. This precept had gone from the schools to the friezes of temples, but it was not very difficult to see that those who advised their disciples to work at knowing themselves did not know themselves.

The means they gave for succeeding made the precept useless: they would have you examine yourself endlessly, as if you could know yourself by examining yourself.

Men study themselves at too close range to see themselves as they are; as they perceive their virtues and vices only through the pride that embellishes everything, they are always unreliable witnesses and corrupt judges of themselves.

Thus, those were very wise men who, knowing how naturally far men are from truth, had all their wisdom consist in telling them what it is. A fine philosophy, which did not limit itself to speculative knowledge, but to the exercise of sincerity! Finer yet if some skewed minds[1] who pushed it too far had not exaggerated reason itself, and by a refinement of liberty had not in every way breached decorum.

In the design I have undertaken, I cannot help making a sort of reflection on myself; I feel a hidden satisfaction at being obliged to sing the praise of a virtue which I cherish, to find a resource in my own heart to make up for the insufficiency of my mind, to be the painter after working all my life being the portrait, and finally to discuss a virtue that defines the man of breeding in private life and the hero in the company of the great.

Part One: On Sincerity in Relation to Private Life

Men living in society have not had this advantage over animals just to procure ways of living more delectably. God wanted them to live in common to serve as guides for each other so they might see through others' eyes what their narcissism hides from them and so that, in short, by a sacred communication of trust they should be able to tell each other and give themselves the truth.

Men therefore all owe it to each other; those who neglect to tell us the truth take from us something that is ours; they nullify the intentions God had for them and for us; they resist him in his designs and oppose him in his providence; they behave like the evil principle of the magi[2] who spread darkness in the world in place of the light which the good principle had created.

We ordinarily imagine it is only in youth that men need education; you would say they all leave their masters' hands either perfect or incorrigible.

Thus, as if we had too good or too bad an opinion of them, we also neglect to be sincere and believe there would be something inhuman about tormenting them either over flaws they do not have or which they will always have.

But happily or unhappily, men are neither so good nor so bad as they are made out to be, and there is none who could not become virtuous, even if very few of them are.

There is no one who, if he were apprised of his flaws, could maintain a constant contradiction; he would become virtuous if only out of weariness.

---

1 The Cynics. (M) The Cynics took to the extreme the ideal of an ascetic, self-sufficient life according to nature, as exemplified by Diogenes (412–324 BCE) who often slept in a large ceramic jar in the market of Athens and begged for food.
2 Either followers of the sixth-century BCE prophet Zoroaster or those of Mani, a Persian religious prophet of the third century CE. In both cases, believers posited good and evil as eternal, warring principles.

We would be impelled to do good not only by the inner satisfaction of the conscience that sustains the wise, but even by fear of scorn that exercises them.

Vice would be reduced to the sorry and deplorable condition in which virtue languishes, and it would take as much strength and courage to be wicked as it does in these corrupt times to be a person of good will.

Were sincerity to cure us only of arrogance, it would be a great virtue which would protect us from the worst of all vices.

There are only too many Narcissuses in the world, those people in love with themselves; they are devastated if they find any condescension in their friends; prepossessed of their own merit, full of a thought they cherish, they spend their lives in self-admiration. What would it take to cure them of a folly that seems untreatable? It would take no more than making them notice how few rivals they have, make them aware of their own weaknesses, put their vices in the necessary perspective so they will perceive them, join with them against themselves, and speak to them in the simplicity of truth.

Shall we instead live compelled at all times to disguise all our opinions? Must we forever praise, and forever approve? Shall tyranny control even our thoughts? Who is entitled to demand of us that sort of idolization? Surely man is very weak to render such homages and very unjust to require them.

Yet as if all merit consisted in serving, we parade a base subservience: this is the virtue of our times, what everyone strives for today; those who still have some nobility in their hearts do everything they can to shed it; they adopt the soul of the base courtier so as not to pass for eccentrics not made like other men.

The truth remains buried under maxims of a false civility; we call good etiquette the art of living ignobly; we do not distinguish between knowing people and deceiving them, and ceremony that ought to be entirely limited to our external conduct slips into our behavior.

We leave bluntness to petty minds as a sign of their imbecility; candor is regarded as a vice in our education; we do not ask that the heart be in the right place, only that ours be like everyone else's, as in portraits where all we require is that they be a good likeness.

We think that with the sweetness of flattery we have found the way to make life delightful. A simple man who has only truth to tell is considered a disturber of public pleasure; we flee him because he is disagreeable; we flee the truth he speaks because it is bitter; we flee the sincerity which he professes because it bears only wild fruits.

We fear truth because it humiliates, because it revolts pride, which is the dearest of passions, because it is a faithful portrayer that depicts us as deformed as we are.

We must therefore not be surprised if it is so rare, if it is dismissed, if it is everywhere banned; strange to say, it can scarcely find a haven in the bosom of friendship.

Ever seduced by the same mistake, we form friendships only to have people particularly designated to please us; our esteem goes no farther than their indulgence; the end of friendship is the end of gratifications. And what are these gratifications? What pleases us most in our friends? It is the continual compliments that we raise from them like tribute.

Indeed, to take sincerity out of friendship is to make a stage virtue of it, to disfigure that queen of hearts, to make the union of souls an illusion, to insert artifice into what is most sacred and constraint into what is most free. Such a friendship, furthermore, is friendship only in name, and Diogenes[3] was right to compare it to the inscriptions we put on tombs, which are but vain signs of something nonexistent.

The Ancients who left us such magnificent eulogies of Cato[4] depicted him to us as if his heart were sincerity itself; that liberty which he so greatly cherished never appeared better than in his words; it seemed he could give his friendship only with his virtue; it was rather a bond of probity than of affection, and he found fault with his friends both because they were his friends and because they were men.

It is doubtless a sincere friend whom the fable hides in its shadows when it depicts for us a favorable divinity, wisdom herself,[5] who takes care to guide Ulysses, turns him toward virtue, spares him a thousand dangers, and makes him enjoy heaven even in her anger.

If we really knew the value of a true friend, we would spend our lives looking for him; it would be the greatest of blessings we would entreat heaven for, and should it fulfill our wishes we would deem ourselves as happy as if it had created us with several souls to keep watch over our feeble, pathetic machine.

---

3 *In assentatione velut in sepulchra quædam solum amicitiæ nomen insculptum est.* (M) "With adulation, as on those tombs where the name of friendship alone is engraved." The quotation is in Conrad Gessner's Latin translation (*Catalogue* 2532) of the *Florilegium* of Joannes Stobaeus, a Greek writer of the fifth century CE.

4 A reference either to Cato the Elder (234–149 BCE), or to his great-grandson Marcus Porcius Cato Uticensis (85–46 BCE), Cato the Younger.

5 I.e., Athena, the Greek goddess of wisdom and war, said to have sprung from the head of Zeus.

Most people, seduced by appearances, are fooled by the deceptive attractions of base and servile indulgence; they take it as a sign of a genuine friendship and confuse, as Pythagoras used to say, the song of the Sirens with that of the Muses.[6] They believe, I say, that it produces friendship, as simple folk think that the earth has made the gods, instead of saying that it is sincerity that breeds friendship, as the gods have created signs and the celestial powers.

It is, in truth, from such a pure source that friendship must arise, and it is a fine origin it gets from a virtue which is the source of so many others.

The great virtues arise, if I dare say, in the most lofty and divine part of the soul and seem to be linked to each other. When a man has the strength to be sincere, you will see a certain courage spread throughout his character, a general independence, a self-control equal to his control over others, a soul exempt from the clouds of fear and terror, a love of virtue, a hatred of vice, a disdain for those who abandon themselves to it; from so noble and fine a stalk can spring only golden branches.[7]

And if in private life where languishing virtues suffer from the mediocrity of conditions, where they ordinarily lack force because they almost always lack action, where for want of being practiced they go out like a fire lacking fuel; if, I say, in private life sincerity produces such effects, what will it be in the courts of the great?

Part Two: On Sincerity in Relation to the Company of the Great

People whose heart is corrupt discount sincere men because they rarely attain to honors and high rank, as if there were a finer occupation than telling the truth; as if what enables a good use to be made of rank were not above those very ranks.

Indeed, sincerity never shines so brightly as when it is brought into the courts of princes, the center of honors and glory. We can say it is the crown of Ariadne[8] which is placed in the heavens; it is there that this virtue shines with the names of magnanimity, firmness, and courage; and as plants are stronger

---

6 The Sirens of Greek mythology used their beguiling voices to lure Greek sailors to the waters around small islands, the Sirenum Scopuli, where they were shipwrecked. The Muses were Greek goddesses, nine in number in Hesiod's *Theogony*, who imparted inspiration to artists and writers.

7 *Aureus arbore ramus.* (M) (Vergil, *Aeneid*, I, VI, 187.)

8 *Sumptam de fronte coronam immisit cœlo.* (M) (Ovid, *Metamorphoses*, VIII, 178.) In Greek mythology, Ariadne, daughter of king Minos of Crete, was the wife of Dionysius, god of wine. Hesiod and Ovid, among others, credited the myth that Dionysius gave Ariadne a crown upon marrying her and then placed it among the stars where its nine jewels form the constellation Corona.

when they grow in fertile ground, so is sincerity more admirable when addressed to the great, where the very majesty of the prince who dims everything around him makes it shine brighter.

A sincere man at a prince's court is a free man among slaves; although he respects the sovereign, the truth that he speaks is always sovereign; and while a crowd of courtiers is the plaything of the prevailing winds and the tempests that rumble about the throne, he is firm and unshakeable because he attests the truth, which is by its nature immortal and by its essence incorruptible.

He is, so to speak, the peoples' guarantor of the prince's acts; he seeks to destroy with his wise counsel the vice of their court, like those peoples who tried by the strength of their voice to frighten the dragon who, they said, was eclipsing the sun;[9] and as they once adored the hand of Praxiteles[10] in his statues, they cherish a sincere man for the felicity of peoples which he procures and for the virtuous acts of princes which he incites.

When God in his anger wants to chastise peoples, he allows flatterers to capture the confidence of the princes who soon plunge their state into an abyss of disasters; but when he wants to rain blessings on them, he allows sincere men to possess the heart of their kings and show them the truth they need, as those who are in a tempest need a lucky star to guide them.

So we see in Daniel how God, irritated at his people, includes among the misfortunes he means to inflict on them that truth will no longer be heard, that it will lie prostrate on the ground in a state of contempt and humiliation: *et prosternetur veritas in terra.*[11]

While the men of God were announcing heaven's decrees to his people, a thousand false prophets were rising up against them. The people, uncertain which path they should take, suspended between God and Baal,[12] knew not which way to turn. In vain did they seek clear signs to resolve their uncertainty; did they not know that Pharaoh's magicians, filled with the strength of their art, had tested the power of Moses, and had, so to speak, tired him?[13] By what trait might they then recognize the ministers of the true god? It is this: it is the sincerity with which they spoke to princes, the freedom with which

---

9 In ancient China and India, eclipses were sometimes said to be caused by dragons eating the sun.

10 The fourth-century BCE Greek sculptor who was the first to sculpt lifesize nude female forms.

11 Daniel 8:12. (M) ("and truth will be prostrated on the ground.")

12 In Canaanite mythology, Baal was the god of the sun, storms, and fertility. In Deuteronomy 6:14–15, God warns the Hebrews not to worship the false god Baal, but after his warning is ignored, he sends the prophet Elijah to demonstrate that only the true god could control drought and direct lightning strikes.

13 The miracles performed by Pharaoh's magicians are described in Exodus chs. 7 and 8.

they announced the most unpleasant truths and tried to recapture minds seduced by flattering and deceitful priests.

The historians of China attribute the long duration, and if I dare say, the immortality of that empire to the rights held by all who approach the prince, and especially a principal officer named Kotaöu, to alert him to anything that might be irregular about his conduct.[14] The emperor Tkiou, who can justly be called the Chinese Nero, in one day had twenty-two mandarins who had succeeded one another in this dangerous duty of Kotaöu attached to a red-hot column of bronze; the tyrant, weary of hearing himself forever reproached for new crimes, yielded to men who were endlessly coming forth. He was astonished by the firmness of these courageous souls, and at the futility of the punishments: and cruelty finally had limits, because virtue did not.

In such a harsh and perilous trial, they did not hesitate a moment between silence and death: the laws always found mouths that spoke for them, virtue was not shaken, nor truth betrayed, nor constancy fatigued. Heaven produced more wonders than the earth did crimes, and the tyrant was finally given over to remorse.

Would you see, on the other hand, a detestable effect of cowardly and base subservience, how it poisons the heart of princes and makes them incapable of distinguishing virtues from vices? You will find it in Lampridius,[15] who says that Commodus, having designated his mother's adulterer as consul, was given the epithet Pious, and that after having Perennis[16] put to death he was surnamed Fortunate: *Cum adulterum matris consulem designasset Commodus, vocatus est pius, cum occidisset Perennem vocatus est felix.*

Will no one be found who will overturn these pompous titles, who will teach this emperor that he is a monster, and render to virtue titles usurped by vice?

---

14 See Montesquieu's "Some remarks on China which I have drawn from the conversations I have had with M. Ouanges," in *Geographica*, OC xvi, 114. There is compelling evidence that this paragraph, which is based on conversations with Arcadio Hoange or Hoam-gé, a Chinese Christian who visited Paris at the age of twenty-three, was drafted by Nicolas Fréret, and not by Montesquieu: see Catherine Volpilhac-Auger, "Un texte en quête d'auteur: les 'Quelques remarques sur la Chine que j'ay tirées des conversations que j'ay eües avec Mr Ouanges'," online: http://montesquieu.ens-lyon.fr/spip.php?article3274

15 Aelius Lampridius, a Roman author who composed a life of the emperor Commodus (161–192 CE).

16 Sextus Tigidius Perennis, a member of the Praetorian Guard and advisor to Commodus executed in 185 CE for plotting against the emperor.

No, to the shame of the men of that time, no one spoke for the truth; the emperor was allowed to enjoy his felicity and criminal piety. What more could be done to favor crime than to spare it even shame and remorse?

Wealth and rank, said Plato,[17] engender nothing more corrupt than flattery; we can compare it to rocks hidden between two waters that are the cause of so many shipwrecks. A flatterer, according to Homer,[18] is as fearsome as the gates of hell; it is flattery, we read in Euripides,[19] that destroys the most populous cities and makes so many wastelands.

Happy the prince who lives among sincere people who care about his reputation and his virtue; but how unhappy is he who lives among flatterers, to spend his life thus surrounded by his enemies.

Yes, in the midst of his enemies: and we must regard as such all who do not speak to us with an open heart, who, like that Janus of the fable, always show themselves to us with two faces, which make us live forever in the dark and cover us with a thick cloud to prevent us from seeing the truth that turns up.

Let us detest flattery; let sincerity reign in its place; let us bring it down from heaven if it has left the earth. It will be our tutelary virtue; it will bring back the golden age and the age of innocence, while untruth and artifice will go back into Pandora's baleful box.

The more flourishing earth will be an abode of felicity. We will see the same change as the one which the poets describe when Apollo, driven from Olympus, came amongst the mortals, having himself become a mortal, to make faith, justice, and sincerity prosper, and soon made the gods envy the happiness of men, and men, in their happiness, even rivals of the gods.[20]

Treatise on Duties

(1725)

Traité des devoirs, text by Sheila Mason (*OC* VIII, 437–439). This treatise, inspired by Cicero's *De officiis* (*On Duties*) and also displaying the influence

---

17 In *Epistola ad Dion.* (M) (Plato's third letter to Dionysius I, tyrant of Syracuse, 432–367 BCE.) Montesquieu's source is the Latin translation, by Conrad Gessner (*Catalogue* 2532), of the *Florilegium* of Joannes Stobaeus (see p. 101, note 3).
18 *Iliad*, Book IX, in Stobaeus, p. 236.
19 In *Hyppolito.* (M) (Euripides, v, 486–487.) See *Catalogue* 2039 for Montesquieu's source for Euripides.
20 Montesquieu's likely source for this observation regarding Apollo was Fénelon's *Aventures de Telemaque fils d'Ulisse* ("Adventures of Telemachus son of Ulysses") (*Catalogue* 650).

of Samuel Pufendorf's *De officio hominis* ("On the Duty of Man," 1673) was left unfinished. Montesquieu read portions of it to the Academy of Bordeaux on 1 May 1725, and his friend Jean-Jacques Bel, having assumed the editorship of the *Bibliothèque Française*, published extracts from it in March 1726. The manuscript remained among Montesquieu's papers at La Brède prior to being sent to England in 1818 (see "A General Note on the Texts") where it may have been burned; in any case, it has not been seen since. Significant fragments, as indicated by Montesquieu's own notations, preserved in portions of *Mes pensées*, are published here immediately following the text of Bel's summary, which was first printed in the Édouard Laboulaye edition of Montesquieu's complete works (Paris: Garnier Frères, 1875–1879, VII, 68).

* * *

Letter to the authors of the March journal[21]

Sirs,

The public, which is expecting a complete relation of what took place in the public assembly of the Bordeaux Academy, would no doubt see with regret that all they did was announce the work of the president Montesquieu on the duties of man. It is to fill in for this omission that I send you the extract of his dissertation.

The author stresses, in his preface, how much more difficult it is for a Christian philosopher to discuss duties than for a pagan philosopher. He says that it is useful for morality to be treated at the same time by Christians and philosophers, so attentive minds can see in the relationship between what the two groups teach how short a path it is from philosophy to Christianity.

The first chapter is on duties in general. God is their universal object, in the sense that he must fill all our desires and occupy all our thoughts; he is also their particular object, in the sense that we owe him worship. The author adds: "Those who have said that a blind fate has produced all the effects we see in the world have uttered a great absurdity: for what greater absurdity is there than a blind fate which has produced creatures which are not blind?"[22]

"If God is more powerful than us, we must fear him; if he is a beneficent being, we must love him; and as he has not made himself visible, to love him

---

21 I.e., the March 1726 edition of the *Bibliothèque Française*.   22 Cf. *SL* I, I.

is to serve him with the inner satisfaction one feels from giving signs to someone of one's gratitude. Finally," the author continues, "our duties toward God are all the more indispensable for not being reciprocal as are the duties men render to each other, for we owe everything to God, and God owes us nothing."

Chapter III deals with our duties toward men. These duties are of two kinds, says the author: those that relate more to other men than to us, and those that relate more to us than to other men. He includes among the duties of the first kind all those that originate in justice.

In chapters IV and V, the author shows that justice is not dependent on human laws, that it is based on the existence and the sociability of reasonable beings, and not on dispositions or particular desires of those beings.

This question leads the author to refute the principles of Hobbes on morality. He then surveys the principal philosophical schools which have striven to fashion or regulate man, and of all of them he prefers the Stoics. "If I could for a moment cease to think that I am a Christian," says the author, "I would not be able to keep from putting the destruction of the school of Zeno among the misfortunes of humankind:[23] the things on which it went too far were things in which there is only greatness: the disdain of pleasure and of pain."

After several acute remarks on the great men who followed Zeno's school, the author ends by saying that "the Stoics, made for society, all believed that their destiny was to work for that society, all the less burdensome since their rewards were intrinsic, and being happy through their philosophy alone, they seemed to believe that only the happiness of others could increase their own."[24]

The author, still considering justice which he regards as the foundation of society, speaks of making a habit of that virtue and the ways to acquire it to the highest degree. "Most virtues," he then adds, "are only particular relations, but justice is a general relation: it concerns man as man, it concerns man in relation to all men."

The author draws from this principle the general maxim that "all particular duties cease when one can no longer fulfill them without going against the duties of man. Should we think, for example, of the good of the fatherland, when the good of humankind is at issue? No, the duty of the citizen is a crime when it makes us neglect the duty of man. The impossibility of including the whole globe in a single society has made men strangers to men, but this arrangement prescribed nothing against the first duties,

23 Cf. *SL* XXIV, 10. 24 Cf. *SL* XXIV, 10.

and man, everywhere possessing reason, is neither a Roman nor a barbarian."

The author then chose some historical facts, and particularly the conquest of the Indies by the Spanish, to offer examples of the violation of the duties of man.[25]

In chapter XII the author shows that we are indebted to the Christian religion for having given us equity for all men.

As nothing offends justice more than what is ordinarily called politics, that science of ruse and artifice, in chapter XIII the author decries it in a more useful manner than if he were proving its injustice: he shows its needlessness. First, by reason. Most effects, according to him, arrive along such singular paths and depend on such imperceptible or such distant causes, that we cannot foresee them. Politics consequently is without purchase with respect to this sort of event. It is also useless with respect to foreseen events, because any revolution that is foreseen almost never occurs.

The author then surveys the greatest events in history. He proves that they could not have been either prepared or avoided. "Who would have told the Huguenots, for example, who came with an army to conduct Henry IV[26] to the throne, that their religion would be oppressed by his son[27] and crushed by his grandson?[28] Their total ruin was linked to accidents that they could not predict. The reason why politics has so little success," says the author, "is that its partisans never know men. Since they are clever, able thinkers, they think all men are the same; but it is far from the case that all men are shrewd. On the contrary, they almost always act out of caprice or passion, or they act only to be acting, and so that it cannot be said that they are doing nothing.

But what ruins the greatest politicians is that their reputation of excelling in their art discourages almost everyone from dealing with them, and they are thereby deprived of all the advantages of agreements."

The author next relates the example of several princes who have succeeded in their designs without finesse and by the simplest of means.

President Montesquieu's work was in our hands so briefly that I was unable to make a more extensive extract from it. I foresee that the public will not accept this excuse, and will regret even more what I have omitted than it will thank me for what I am providing him; that is precisely what I myself have felt. This work is filled with such a great number of acute and sensible remarks

25 Cf. *SL* x, 4 and *On the Motives that Should Encourage Us toward the Sciences* (1725).
26 Henry IV (1553–1610), nominally French king from 1589 but crowned only in 1594 after converting to Catholicism.
27 Louis XIII (1601–1643), king from 1610.   28 Louis XIV (1638–1715), king from 1643.

that it seemed to me I had no choice and that it was a sort of duty for me to copy it all.

I am, sir, etc.

Bordeaux, 7 July 1725

Fragments of *Treatise on Duties* preserved in *Mes pensées*

Pensées 220

Human actions are the subject of duties. It is reason which is their principle and which makes us able to fulfill them. It would diminish that reason to say that it was given to us only for the preservation of our being, for animals preserve theirs just as we do. Often, they preserve it even better: the instinct that leaves them all the passions necessary for the preservation of their life almost always depriving them of the ones that could destroy it, whereas our reason not only gives us destructive passions, but often even has us make very poor use of those that preserve us.

As there are principles that obliterate the civic spirit in us, by urging us to do wrong, there are also some which diminish it by diverting us from doing good. Such are those that inspire a sort of quietism that take a man from his family and his country.

The way to acquire perfect justice is to make such a habit of it that we observe it in the smallest things and conform even our manner of thinking to it. Here is a single example of this: it makes no difference to the society in which we live whether a man living in Stockholm or Leipzig writes good or bad epigrams or is a good or bad physicist; yet if we judged them we must try to get it right, so as to prepare ourselves to do likewise on a more important occasion.

We all have machines that subject us continually to the laws of habit. Our machine accustoms our soul to thinking in a certain way; or it accustoms it to thinking in another way. This is where physics could find a place in morality by making us see how dispositions for vices and human virtues are dependent on our mechanism.

Pensées 221

It is love of country which has given the Greek and Roman histories that nobility which ours do not have. In them it is what continually drives all acts, and there is pleasure in encountering everywhere that virtue that is dear to all who have a heart.

When one thinks of the pettiness of our motives, the baseness of our methods, the avarice with which we pursue miserable rewards, that ambition so different from the love of glory, one is taken aback by the difference between these spectacles, and it is as if, since these two great peoples disappeared, men have shrunk by a cubit.[29]

Pensées 222

Of all utterances of the Ancients, I know of none that better characterizes barbarity than one of Sulla's.[30] He was introduced to a fisherman of the city of ★★★ who was bringing him a fish. "After all I have done," he said, "is there still a man in ★★★?" This sinister man was taken aback to learn that his cruelty had known some bounds.

Pensées 223

If physics had invented nothing other than powder[31] and Greek fire, we would do well to banish it, like magic.

Pensées 224

It is a very false principle of Hobbes that when the people have authorized a prince, the prince's actions are those of the people, and consequently the people cannot complain about the prince, nor call him to any account for his acts, because the people cannot complain about the people. Thus Hobbes has forgotten his principle of natural law: *pacta esse servanda*.[32] The people have authorized the prince conditionally; they have installed him under a covenant: he must observe it, and the prince represents the people only as they have wished or are supposed to have wished him to represent them. Moreover, it is false that one who is delegated has as much power as those who delegate and that he no longer depends on them.

Pensées 1008

Nearly all virtues are a particular relation of a certain man to another. For example, friendship, love of country, mercy are particular relations. But justice is a general relation. So any virtue that destroys this general relation is not a virtue.

---

29 Cf. *Pensées* 1268.
30 Lucius Cornelius Sulla (138–78 BCE), the Roman general and dictator whose troops decimated the Boetian city of Halææ during his lengthy eastern campaigns against the Pontic ruler Mithridates.
31 I.e., gunpowder.   32 "The covenants must be respected."

Pensées 1251
On Oaths

Oaths are used in lieu of the token one is naturally inclined to give for a promise, for there has always been a need to obtain the confidence of others. Thus the following covenants have often been made: "if I do not do what I promise, I am willing to forfeit the token which I place in your hands; if I do not do what I promise, I am willing for my friend to take offense and be constrained to repair the wrong I have done you; if I do not do what I promise, I submit to the greatest of misfortunes, in other words, to God's vengeance. And in that case, if I do not believe in him I would be giving you a false token and would be deceiving you in two ways: for you have neither the thing I have promised you, nor the collateral you think you have.

Those who say that an oath adds nothing to a promise are gravely mistaken, for your promise binds you only because it persuades me to believe you. The bond thus increases on account of trust. I have counted on what you were saying to me not only because you were saying it but also because I believed that you had some religion and that you have given me no cause for thinking you were an atheist.

If it is false that the oath is a new bond, it is also false that one's word is a bond: for one's word binds only by the degree of credibility it gives to the person to whom it was given.

Pensées 1252
On the Government of England

The English can ask, on the question of whether it is permissible to resist tyranny: "Which opinion is it more useful to mankind to have established, that of blind obedience or that which limits power when it becomes destructive?"

Was it better for flourishing cities to be bathed in blood than to have exiled Pisistratus,[33] driven out Dionysius,[34] and stripped Phalaris[35] of his power?

Let us suppose for a moment that a cruel and destructive government were established throughout the world and that it subsisted not by the force of tyrants, but because of a certain credulity and popular superstition. If someone came to disabuse men of that superstition and teach them invariable and fundamental laws, would he not be in fact the benefactor of humankind, and what hero would more rightly deserve altars?[36]

---

33 Peisistratos, tyrant of Athens (c. 600–c. 527 BCE).
34 Dionysius I (c. 432–c. 367 BCE), tyrant of Syracuse.
35 Phalaris (c. 570–c. 554 BCE), tyrant of Acragas, Sicily.   36 I.e., divinization.

It makes no good sense to want the prince's authority to be sacred and not that of the law.

Civil war occurs when subjects resist the prince; civil war occurs when the prince inflicts violence on his subjects: both kinds of violence are exterior.[37]

But, it will be said, we are not disputing the rights of peoples; but the calamities of civil war are so great that it is more useful never to put it into play. How can one say that? Princes are mortal, the republic is eternal; their dominance is temporary, obedience to the republic never ends. There is therefore no greater evil, and none which has such dreadful consequences, than tolerating a tyranny which perpetuates itself into the future.

Pensées 1253[38]

On Friendship

The Stoics said that the wise man loved no one. They took their reasoning too far; yet I believe it is true that if men were perfectly virtuous they would have no friends.

We cannot attach ourselves to all our fellow citizens. We choose a small number of them to whom we limit ourselves. We agree to a sort of contract for our common utility which is but a retrenchment of the one we have agreed to with society as a whole, and it seems even in a certain sense to prejudice it.

Indeed, a genuinely virtuous man ought to be impelled to aid a man utterly unknown as if he were his own friend. He has in his heart a commitment that need not be confirmed by words, oaths, nor external witnesses, and need not limit him to a certain number of friends: that would be to turn his heart away from all other men and separate it from the trunk to attach it to the branches.

If that is so, what can be said about those craven souls who betray even that commitment which was established only to rescue the imperfection of our nature?

Friendship was the signal virtue of the Romans: see how far Lucilius took friendship for Brutus and Antony (Saint-Réal).[39] Instances can be found in the

---

37 I.e., involve not conflict among the people themselves, but rather between the people and the government.

38 What follows up to page 134 [i.e., *Pensées* 1280] are fragments which remain from what I have done on duties. I made a beginning of it, which I gave as a paper to the Bordeaux Academy. Since I will not continue it by all appearances, I think I must break it off and add it here. (M)

39 César de Saint-Réal, author of "Considérations sur Antoine" in *Œuvres* (The Hague, 1722, II, pp. 290–291), recounts how Lucilius, to save Brutus, assumed his identity and came before Antony, only to learn of Brutus' death.

history of their most corrupt centuries: never more heroes than when they were friends.

The constitution of the state was such that everyone was motivated to make some friends. The constant need they had of friendship established its rights; a man was powerful in the senate and the populace only through his friends; he achieved public office only through his friends, and when his administrative term was over, faced with all the accusations, he had even more need of his friends. Citizens were linked to other citizens by all sorts of bonds: a man was tied to his friends, his freedmen, his slaves, and his children; today all that is abolished, even the power of a father; every man is isolated. It seems that the natural effect of arbitrary power is to particularize all interests.

Yet these ties that detached man from himself to attach him to his neighbor made men do great things; without that, everything is common, and there remains nothing but a base self-interest which is properly nothing more than the animal instinct of all men.

Among us, those who are able to help others are precisely those who do not have and cannot have friends. I am speaking of princes and of a third sort of men who are midway between the sovereign and his subjects: I refer to ministers, men who enjoy only the misfortunes of the condition of princes and possess neither the advantages of private life nor those of sovereignty.[40]

Pensées 1254

The custom of women of the court arranging things has produced many evils. (1) It fills all sorts of positions with men of no merit. (2) It has banished generosity, good nature, candor, and nobility of soul. (3) It has ruined those who did not engage in this shameful traffic by obliging them to promote themselves at the expense of others. (4) Women being more adept at such dealings than men, they made their own private fortune, which is the one thing that contributes the most to the ruin of morals and to their luxury and licentiousness.

Pensées 1255

The love of money so degrades a prince that one can no longer see any virtues in him. That is what made the father of the great Condé[41] the talk of

---

40 What I am saying about ministers I have put in my treatise on the Prince. (M) Cf. *Reflections on the Character of Certain Princes.*

41 The father of the "Grand Condé" (Louis II, prince de Condé, 1621–1686) was Henry II de Bourbon, also prince de Condé (1588–1646).

Europe. The father's avarice was as often celebrated as the heroic acts of the son.

Pensées 1256

We are attracted to a noble pride arising from that inner satisfaction with which virtue imbues us; it becomes the great and enhances rank. A great soul cannot fail to manifest itself completely; it feels the dignity of its existence. And how could it not be aware of its superiority over so many other souls that are degraded in nature?

Those proud men are the least arrogant. For they are not the ones we see cowering before the great, low as the grass under their equals, or raised like cedars over their inferiors.

A base, arrogant soul has lowered itself to the only point of servility to which it could descend. A great soul that humbles itself is at the height of its grandeur.

One of the causes of the infirmity of our courage is our education in which we have not sufficiently distinguished greatness of soul from arrogance and from that vanity, unsuited to any good use, which has no supporting motive: this means that we have weakened the principle of actions, and the more we have removed motives from men, the more we have demanded of them.

Pensées 1257

One's manner of dressing and of lodging are two things which call for neither too much affectation nor too much negligence.

The table contributes not a little to providing us with the gaiety which, combined with a certain modest familiarity, is called *politeness*.

We avoid the two extremes which are indulged by the nations of the south and of the north: we often eat together, and we do not drink to excess.

Pensées 1258

We have not failed in France to produce some of those rare men whom the Romans would have claimed. Faith, justice, and greatness of soul mounted the throne with Saint Louis.[42] Thanneguy du Châtel[43] abandoned his functions as soon as the public voice was raised against him; he left his country without complaint to spare it his grumbling. Chancellor Olivier[44] introduced justice even into the kings' council, and once there politics yielded to it. France has

---

42 Louis IX (1214–1270), king of France from 1226. 43 Viscount of La Bellière (d. 1477).
44 François Olivier, chancellor of France (1487–1560).

never had a better citizen than Louis XII.[45] Cardinal d'Amboise[46] identified the interests of the people with those of the king and the interests of the king with those of the people. Even in his youth Charles VIII understood all the vanities of his youth. Chancellor de l'Hôpital,[47] like the laws, was wise in a court which was calmed only by the most profound dissimulations or agitated only by the most violent passions. We saw in La Noue[48] a great citizen in the midst of civil discords. The admiral[49] was assassinated with only the glory of the state in his heart, and his fate was such that after so many rebellions he could be punished only by a great crime. The Guises[50] were extreme in the good and evil they did to the state; how fortunate France would have been if they had not felt the blood of Charlemagne flowing through their veins. It seemed that the soul of Miron,[51] provost of the merchants, was the soul of all the people. About Henry IV I shall have nothing to say; it is the French I am addressing.[52] Molé[53] showed some heroism in a profession that ordinarily depends only on other virtues. Caesar would have been compared to Monsieur le Prince[54] had he come after him. M. de Turenne[55] had no vices, and if he had, he might have taken certain virtues farther; his life is a hymn in praise of humanity. The character of M. de Montausier[56] has something of the character of the ancient philosophers, and of their excess of reason. Marshall de Catinat[57] bore victory with modesty and

45 Louis XII (1462–1515), king of France from 1498.
46 Georges I d'Amboise (1460–1510), archbishop of Rouen (1493) and cardinal (1498).
47 Michel de l'Hôpital (1507–1573), counsellor to the Parlement of Paris (1537–1547) and chancellor of France from 1560.
48 François de La Noue (1531–1591), celebrated Huguenot warrior.
49 Gaspard II de Coligny (1519–1572), admiral of France and proponent of toleration for French Protestants; he was one of the first victims of the St. Bartholomew's Day massacre on 24 August 1572.
50 The ultra-Catholic House of Guise claimed descent from Charlemagne and harbored designs to rule France. In spite of aid from Philip II of Spain (1527–1598), they failed in their attempt to eradicate the House of Bourbon during the Wars of Religion of the sixteenth century. For commentary on various members of the Guise family, see Montesquieu's *Reflections on the Character of Certain Princes* (c. 1731–1733).
51 A reference to either François III Miron (1560–1609) or Robert Miron (1570–1641) his brother, both *prévôt des marchands*, an important administrative position in the city.
52 Henry IV was among the best known and most studied of all French kings. Montesquieu analyzed his career in his *Reflections on the Character of Certain Princes*.
53 Mathieu Molé (1584–1656), first president of the Paris Parlement from 1641 and later keeper of the seals, displayed bravery on the Day of the Barricades (26 August 1648), choosing to defend and demand release of several members of the parlement imprisoned after the scuffle that presaged the revolt known as the Fronde (1648–1653).
54 Henri Jules de Bourbon (1643–1709), son of the Grand Condé (see p. 113, note 41) and prince de Condé after his father's death in 1686.
55 Henri de La Tour d'Auvergne, viscount of Turenne, Marshal of France (1611–1675).
56 Charles de Sainte-Maure, marquis of Salles, and later Duke of Montausier (1610–1690), tutor of Louis XIV's eldest son, Louis of France (1661–1711).
57 Nicolas Catinat (1637–1712), Marshal of France.

failure with majesty, still great even after the loss of his reputation. M. de Vendôme[58] has never had anything that belonged just to him except his glory.

Pensées 1259
On Rewards

It is not my intention to speak of the descendants of those six bourgeois of Calais who offered to face death in order to save their homeland, and whom M. de Sacy has rescued from oblivion.[59] I do not know what has become of the offspring of the woman who saved Amiens in the time of Charles VIII.[60] Those bourgeois are still bourgeois, but if in our France there has been some notable knave, you can surely count on his descendants being among the honored.

But virtue should nonetheless be the constant object of our pursuits. It has almost always been allowed to go unrewarded. It has been fled from, feared, and persecuted; never yet has it been scorned.

Pensées 1260
On History

It is appropriate that every person read history, especially that of his or her own country. We owe this to the memory of those who have served their homeland, and in that way we continue to give to virtuous people the reward they deserve, which has often encouraged them.

The feeling of admiration which their fine acts inspire in us is a sort of justice which we render them, and the horror we have for the wicked is another. To allow the wicked to have their names and crimes forgotten is not just; to allow great men to be forgotten in the way that the wicked seemed to hope for is not just.

Historians are stern examiners of the acts of those who have appeared on earth, and they are an image of those magistrates of Egypt who called up the souls of all the dead to judge them.[61]

---

58 Louis Joseph, duc de Vendôme (1654–1712), Marshal of France.

59 Louis Silvestre de Sacy, in his *Traité de l'amitié* (Paris: Jean Moreau, 1703, pp. 171–173), cites as a modern-day example of Greek and Roman ideals of love of country the six burgers of Calais who offered themselves up as sacrificial victims to save Calais from England's Edward III during the Hundred Years' War.

60 According to Scipion Dupleix, *Histoire générale de France* (Paris: Denys Béchet and Louis Billaine, 1658, III, p. 156; *Catalogue* 2936–2937), Catherine de Lice alerted the defenders of the city to the approach of the enemy in 1493 during the war-filled reign of Charles VIII (1483–1498).

61 According to ancient Egyptian religious beliefs, the souls of the dead had to be judged by Osiris, god of the underworld, before they could pass to the afterlife.

Pensées 1261

It is not only serious reading that is useful but also enjoyable reading, there being a time when a person just needs relaxation. Even scholars must be paid for their exertions with pleasure; even the sciences gain by being treated in a refined and tasteful manner. It is therefore good for us to write on all subjects and in all styles. Philosophy ought not to be isolated: it is related to everything.

Pensées 1262

What still slows our progress is that knowledge attracts mockery and ignorance passes for style.

The talent for mockery is so common in our nation that you will more easily find people who have some degree of it than people who lack it entirely.

This taste for derision is a good demonstration of this; it is the sort of product which even a modest wit cannot botch.

In a nation one must be wary of the penchant people can have for mocking things that are good; it must be kept in reserve as a weapon against things that are not good. Thus fanaticism, in England, was destroyed by this means. Thus it can be at most for people's good that we can call upon human malice.

This way of demonstrating something or opposing it determines nothing because making fun of something is not reasoning.

Pensées 1263

Cicero divides those things that are praiseworthy into four headings: attachment to the sciences and the search for truth, the maintenance of civil society, greatness of soul, and a certain appropriateness of actions, *secundum ordinem et modum.*[62]

He believes that a good citizen ought to work on his country's behalf rather than striving to acquire knowledge, but he fails to note that scholars are very useful to their country and all the more estimable because they almost always serve it without self-interest, not being compensated for their pains either with pecuniary rewards or with distinction.

The only difference there is between civilized peoples and barbarous ones is that the former have applied themselves to the sciences while the latter have utterly neglected them.

62 "In keeping with the order and means."

It is perhaps to this knowledge we possess and that savage peoples do not have that most nations owe their existence.[63]

If we behaved like the peoples of America, two or three nations of Europe would soon have exterminated or eaten all the others.

Pensées 1264

There is a body in a neighboring state[64] which examines the state of the nation every year. Let us examine here the current state of the republic of letters.

Pensées 1265

Particular Instances of Spanish Conquests in the Indies

If we want to know how useful philosophy is, we have only to read the history of the conquest of two great empires in Mexico and Peru.

If a Descartes had come to Mexico a hundred years before Cortés, you may be sure that he would have taught the Mexicans that, given the way men are made, they cannot be immortal; he would have made them understand that all the effects of nature are a series of laws and communications of movements, and he would have made them recognize, in all the effects of nature, the collision of bodies, rather than the invisible power of spirits. Cortés with a handful of men would never have destroyed the vast empire of Mexico, and Pizarro that of Peru.

When the Romans for the first time saw elephants in combat against them, they were amazed but did not lose their wits as the Mexicans did at the sight of horses.

Elephants appeared, in the eyes of the Romans, only as larger beasts than any they had seen. The impression those beasts made on their minds was simply the one they were naturally bound to make: they realized they needed greater courage because their enemy had greater forces. Attacked in a new way, they sought new ways to defend themselves.

The invention of powder in Europe gave to the nation that first used it such a modest advantage that it is yet to be decided which nation had that first advantage.

The discovery of the spyglass was only useful a single time to the Dutch.[65]

We find in all effects only one pure mechanism, and for that reason there is no invention which we are not in a position to counteract with another invention.

---

63 Cf. *On the Motives that Should Encourage Us toward the Sciences.*   64 I.e., England.
65 Descartes in his *Dioptrique* mentions the invention of "Dutch glasses" in Amsterdam. It is unclear in which battle they might first have been used.

Those effects which through ignorance of philosophy get attributed to invisible powers are pernicious not because they cause fear, but because they make one despair of overcoming and do not allow those who are impressed by them to utilize their strengths, causing them to judge them futile.

Therefore nothing is so dangerous as to fill the minds of the people with miracles and wonders. Nothing is more likely than superstition to give rise to destructive prejudices, and if it sometimes happens that wise legislators have made good use of it, mankind in general has a thousand

It is true that the earliest kings of Peru found a great advantage in passing themselves off as sons of the Sun and that they thereby made themselves absolute over their subjects and respectable to strangers who flocked to become their subjects; but these advantages which the monarchs of Peru had drawn from superstition, superstition made them lose. The mere arrival of the Spanish intimidated the subjects of Atahualpa[66] and him as well because it seemed to him a sign of the Sun's wrath and its abandonment of the nation.

The Spanish took advantage, against the emperors of Mexico and Peru, of the veneration, or rather the inner reverence, which their peoples had for them, since once they had taken them prisoner by the most shameful tricks, the entire nation was intimidated and made little attempt thereafter to defend itself, concluding it was futile to fight against angry gods.

Moctezuma,[67] who could have exterminated the Spanish on their arrival had he been courageous in the use of force, or who, without risk, could even starve them to death, attacked them only with nothing more than sacrifices and prayers which he proceeded to make in all the temples. He sent them all sorts of provisions and allowed them to form leagues and subjugate all his vassals at their leisure.

In truth, the Mexicans had no firearms, but they had bows and arrows, which were the strongest weapons of the Greeks and Romans. They had no iron, but they had flint which cut and pierced like iron, and which they attached to the ends of their weapons; they even had something which was

---

66 Atahualpa (many spellings, 1502–1533) was an Inca emperor ruling over territory encompassing modern-day Peru, Chile, Ecuador, Bolivia, and Columbia. Francisco Pizarro captured him through trickery in 1532 and had him executed following a trial in 1533 where the charges against him were polygamy, incestuous marriage, and idolatry. Cf. *SL* XXVI, 22.

67 Moctezuma II (1466–1520), ninth ruler of Tenochtitlan. Montesquieu's source was Antonio de Solis y Ribadeneyra (trans.), *Histoire de la conquête du Mexique par Fernand Cortez* (Paris, 1714, I, Book II, III, p. 154 and Book III, VIII, p. 401; *Catalogue* 3175).

good for military strategy, which is that they fought in closed ranks, and when one man was killed, he was immediately replaced by another so as to hide their loss from the enemy.

The proof of what I am advancing is that the Spanish who ventured out to conquer Peru were very nearly exterminated by the small barbarian peoples on whom they descended and were saved only by a prompt retreat, after being badly beaten;[68] whereas they encountered no resistance in Peru, and little in Mexico, where superstition deprived those empires of all the strength they could have drawn from their size and structure. In order to be worshipped as gods, the princes had made their peoples as stupid as animals, and they perished by that same superstition which they had built up to their advantage.[69] In almost every case where the Peruvians defended themselves they had the advantage over the Spaniards. All they were missing, therefore, was the expectation of success and delivery from the evils of weakness of spirit.

Pensées 1266

Continuation of Some Thoughts that Did Not Make It Into the
Treatise on Duties

Let us make an effort to strip the concept of God from our heart; let us shake off once and for all this yoke which error and prejudice have placed on mankind; let us strengthen ourselves in the idea that we are no longer in that dependency and see what will become of us. From that moment, we will lose all our resources in adversity, in our maladies, our old age, and what is still more, in our death. We are going to die, and there is no God! Perhaps we will enter into the void, but what a frightful thought! And if our soul survives, isolated, without support and helpless in nature, what a sorry state it will be in! By losing its body, it will have lost all the pleasures of the senses which made this life delectable; and all it will have left is what is more proper to it: that irritating desire for happiness and the impossibility of attaining it; that anguishing view of itself which reveals only its own meanness; that emptiness, that

---

68 Spanish forces suffered a defeat in January 1525 at the Battle of Punta Quemada on the coast of Columbia where Francisco Pizarro (1471–1541) suffered multiple wounds. This initial defeat delayed by several years Pizarro's invasion of Peru and the eventual capture and trial of Atahualpa.

69 The Aztecs of Mexico mistook the Spaniards for envoys of the god Quetzalcatl, prophesied to return from the east in a "One Reed" year, which was 1519. The Incas of Peru, according to some accounts, thought the Spaniards were gods (*viracocha cuna*) who might benefit them. They came too late to the realization that they were just men.

disappointment, that void which it finds in itself; that impossibility of being satisfied inwardly and by the sole strength of its being. What wretched immortality! If it is not quite certain that there is no God, if our philosophy could have left us the least doubt about that, we must hope that there is one.

We are a great proof that this God we long for is a beneficent being, for he has given us life: in other words, a thing none among us would be willing to give up; he gave us existence, and what is much more, the awareness of our existence.

If God is a beneficent being, we must love him, and as he has not rendered himself visible, to love him is to serve him with the inner satisfaction one feels for having given someone signs of one's recognition.

That being would be far from perfect if he had not created, or if you wish, only set in motion or arranged the universe with some purpose, and if, acting without design, or disappointed in his handiwork, he abandoned us as we left his hands.

That providence that watches over us is extremely powerful, for as it required infinite strength to put the universe in the state it is in, we cannot conceive how God, having once exercised such a power, could have since lost it, or how, still possessing it in the universe, he could not have it over us.

Above all, God was able to make us happy; for as there have been moments when we have experienced feeling happy in this life, we can hardly conceive that God should have been able to make us happy once, and not always to have been able to do so.

If he was able to, he desired to, for our happiness does not at all detract from his own; if he did not desire to, he would be more imperfect than even men.

Yet a great genius[70] has promised me that I shall die like an insect; he seeks to flatter me that I am nothing more than a modification of matter; he marshals geometrical reasoning and arguments said to be very strong, and which I have found very obscure, to raise my soul to the level of my body, and instead of that immense space which my mind embraces he restricts me to my own matter and to a space of four or five feet in the universe.

According to him, I am not a being distinct from another being; he takes away everything I thought was most particularly mine. I no longer know where to locate that self in which I was so invested; I am more lost in extension[71] than a particle of water is lost in the sea. Why the glory? Why

70 Baruch Spinoza (1632–1677).
71 In Cartesian physics extension is the defining attribute of matter.

the shame? Why this pretended modification? Does it intend, in a manner of speaking, to constitute a body apart from the universe? It is not this one, nor that one; it is nothing distinct from being; and in the universality of substance, the lion and the insect, Charlemagne and Chilperic,[72] have existed and passed on indistinguishably.

That same philosopher is kind enough to assist me by destroying my freedom. Every act in my life is merely like the action of aqua regia, which dissolves gold; like that of the magnet, which sometimes attracts and sometimes repels iron; or like that of heat which softens or hardens mud. He suppresses the motive of my every act and relieves me of all morality; he honors me to the point of wanting to make me a very great knave but free of crime, and no one should be entitled to object. I have many thanks to give to that philosopher.

Another, much less extreme and consequently much more dangerous than the first (this is Hobbes) warns me to be generally wary of all men and not only of all men but of all beings that are superior to me, for he tells me that justice is nothing in itself, that it is nothing more than what the laws of empires command or forbid. I am displeased at that, for being obliged to live with men, I would have been most gratified if there were some inner principle in their heart that could reassure me against them. And not being sure that there are not in nature other beings more powerful than I, I should have wished them to have a rule of justice that would keep them from harming me.

Hobbes says that since natural right is just the freedom we have to do whatever serves our preservation, the natural state of man is the war of all against all. But besides the falsehood that defense necessarily entails the necessity of attacking, we must not imagine, as he does, that men have fallen from the sky, or emerged from the earth fully armed, somewhat like the soldiers of Cadmus:[73] that is not the condition of men.

The first and only man fears no one; that lone man who found a woman who was herself alone would not make war on her; all the others would be born into a family and soon into a society. There is no war; on the contrary: love, education, respect, gratitude; everything is redolent of peace.[74]

It is not even true that two men fallen from the skies into an unoccupied land would seek out of fear to attack and subjugate each other. A hundred

72 Chilperic I (c. 539–584), king of Neustria (now Soissons) from 561.
73 According to Greek mythology, Cadmus was the Greek hero who founded Thebes. His soldiers were said to have sprung from the teeth of a dragon sown on the ground at Athena's behest.
74 Cf. *SL* I, 2.

circumstances, combined with the particular character of each man, could cause them to act differently: the appearance, gesture, demeanor, and individual way of thinking would result in differences. In the first place, fear would cause them not to attack but to flee; the mutual signs of fear would soon make them approach; the tedium of being alone and the pleasure that any animal feels at the approach of an animal of the same species would incline them to join together, and the more miserable they were, the more determined they would be to do so. So far, we see no preemptive aggression: it would be as with other animals, who war with their own kind only in particular cases even though they encounter each other in the forests every day, more or less like Hobbes's men. The first feelings would be for the true needs they would have and not for the benefits of domination. It is only when society is formed that individuals, amidst abundance and peace, having at every moment reason to feel the superiority of their mind or their talents, seek to turn the principal advantages of that society to their benefit. Hobbes wants to make men do what lions themselves do not do. It is only through the establishment of societies that they take advantage of each other and become the strongest; before that they are all equal.

If they establish societies, it is through a principle of justice. Therefore they possessed one.

Pensées 1267

Considering men before the establishment of societies,[75] we find that they were subject to a power that nature had established; for infancy being the state of greatest weakness that we can conceive, children had to be dependent on their fathers who had given them life and were still giving them the means of preserving it.

What is said about the unlimited power of fathers is not correct: it is not unlimited, and there is no such power. Fathers have preservation as their object like other powers, and even more than other powers.

This dependency having been established by the natural law that subjects infancy to every imaginable need, children could never come out from under it. For such an authority, having preceded all covenants, had no limits at its origin; and if age had imperceptibly diminished the power of fathers, that could only have come about by a progression of disobedience. Now the father who commanded and the son who obeyed

75 This is good for book on *Law*. (M) (See *SL* I, 2.)

would never have been able to agree on the time when blind obedience was to cease, nor on the way in which it was to diminish.

Children have therefore never been able to limit that power. Paternal power is self-limiting because, as children emerge from youth, fathers are entering into old age, and the strength of the children increases as that of the father weakens. It is only the fathers' reasoning that has limited it when, in establishing societies, they have modified it by the civil laws, and the modifications have sometimes gone so far that the laws are almost entirely abolished, as if they had wished to foster the ingratitude of the children.

Nature herself has limited paternal power by increasing, on one side, the children's reason and on the other the weakness of the fathers, by diminishing on one side the needs of the children and increasing the needs of the fathers on the other.

Families split up; the fathers, having died, left the collaterals[76] independent; it was necessary to come together by covenants and bring about by means of civil laws what natural law had originally done.

Chance and the turn of mind of those who have covenanted have established as many different forms of governments as there have been peoples, all good since they were willed by the contracting parties.

What was arbitrary became necessity: it was no longer possible, except through tyranny or violence, to change a form of government even for the sake of a better one because, as all the members could not change their manner of thinking at the same time, there would have been a period of time between the establishment of the new laws and the abolition of the old ones fatal to the common cause.

All the changes that took place in the laws had to result from those established laws; whoever abolished old laws could do so only by the force of the laws, and even the people were able to recapture their authority only when they were allowed to by civil or natural law.

What was only a covenant became as strong as natural law: it was necessary to love one's country as one loved one's family; it was necessary to cherish the laws as one cherished the will of one's fathers.

But as the love of one's family did not entail hating others, so love of one's country should not have inspired hatred of other societies.

---

76 *Collatéraux*: an archaic legal term for relatives outside the immediate family: uncles and aunts, nephews and nieces, cousins.

Pensées 1268

The Spaniards overlooked the duties of man at each step they took in their conquest of the Indies, and the pope who put the sword in their hands, who gave them the blood of so many nations, forgot them even more.

I would willingly see this whole conquest expunged; I could not bear to read these histories stained with blood. The story of the greatest marvels in them always leaves something dark and sad in the mind.[77]

I like to see a few Greeks destroy the innumerable armies of the Persians at Thermopylae, at Plataea and at Marathon:[78] those are heroes who sacrifice themselves for their homeland and defend it against usurpers; here it is brigands who, burning with the avarice that drives them, exterminate a prodigious number of peaceful nations in order to satisfy it. The victories of the Spaniards do not exalt man, and his defeats of the Indians demean him pathetically.

The Spanish conquered the two empires of Mexico and Peru through the same treachery: they have themselves brought before the kings as ambassadors only to take them captive.

We are indignant to see Cortés[79] forever talking about his equity and moderation to peoples against whom he is committing a thousand barbarities.

In an extravagant act previously unheard of, he takes as the object of his mission the abolition of the dominant religion. While endlessly repeating that he seeks peace, what is his intent other than a conquest made without resistance?

The fate of Moctezuma is deplorable. The Spanish keep him alive only to help them become the masters of his empire.

They burn his successor, Cuauhtémoc,[80] to force him to reveal his treasures.

But what are we to say of the Inca Athualpa? He comes before the Spaniards with a numerous retinue; a Dominican priest subjects him to a harangue which he finds impertinent because the interpreter is unable to

---

77 Cf. *Pensées* 207, where Montesquieu berates the Spanish for their cruel treatment of the natives and blames them for using conversion to Christianity as the pretext for their actions.

78 At Marathon (490 BCE) Athenian forces defeated Persian invaders; at Thermopylae (480 BCE), the Persians were victorious; at Plataea (479 BCE) Greek warriors defeated the Persian army of Xerxes I (ruled 486–465 BCE).

79 Hernán Cortés (1485–1547), Spanish conqueror of the Aztec empire.

80 Cuauhtémoc, successor to Moctezuma as the Aztec ruler, was captured by Cortés in August 1521 and subjected to torture in a vain attempt to discover the whereabouts of hidden booty. He was allowed to keep his position and title, but Cortés executed him in 1525 for allegedly plotting to kill him and other Spaniards.

explain it to him properly and which he would have found even more impertinent if it had been explained well to him. This angry monk races off and incites the Spaniards, who take Athualpa prisoner, with horrible carnage among his men, who never defended themselves; yet this monk was shouting with all his strength for them to run through these infidels instead of striking with the flat of their swords.

The unhappy prince agreed to his ransom, which was as much gold as he could fit into a large room to a height which he indicated. Despite this agreement he was condemned to die.

This sentence, handed down deliberately to lend formality to injustice, is to me a sordid murder.

But the charges are bizarre: they tell him he is an idolater, that he has waged unjust wars, that he keeps several concubines, that he has diverted tributes from the empire while he has been in prison. He is threatened with being burned if he does not have himself baptised, and as a reward for his baptism they strangle him.

But what is revolting in these histories is the constant contrast of devotions and cruelties, of crimes and miracles. The way they have it, heaven by a particular favor guides these villains who preached the gospel only after dishonoring it.

But if it is true that love of country has always been the source of the greatest crimes, because to this particular virtue more general virtues have been sacrificed, it is no less true that, once properly corrected, it can do honor to an entire nation.

It is this virtue which, when less extreme, gives the Greek and Roman histories that nobility which ours do not have. In them it is what continually drives all acts, and there is pleasure in encountering everywhere that virtue that is dear to all who have a heart.

When I think of the pettiness of our motives, the baseness of our methods, the avarice with which we pursue miserable rewards, that ambition so different from the love of glory, I am taken aback by the difference between the spectacles, and it is as if, since these two great peoples are no more, men have shrunk by a cubit.

Pensées 1269

Civic spirit is not seeing one's own country devour all the others. The desire to see one's city ingest all the wealth of nations, constantly to feast one's eyes on the triumphs of captains and the wrath of kings – all of that is not what makes for civic spirit. Civic spirit is the desire to see order in the state, to feel joy in public tranquility, in the strict administration of justice, in the security of the magistrates, in the prosperity of those who govern, in the respect paid to the laws, in the stability of the monarchy or the republic.

Civic spirit is loving the laws even when they include provisions that harm us, and considering the general good which they always do us rather than the individual harm they sometimes cause us.

Civic spirit is performing with zeal, with pleasure, and with satisfaction the sort of magistracy which in the body politic is entrusted to each person; for there is no one who does not participate in the government either through his employment, or his family, or the management of his property.

A good citizen never thinks about making his individual fortune except by the same means that produce the public fortune; he regards the man who acts otherwise as a cowardly knave who, having a pirated key to a common treasury, filches a part of it, and refuses to share legitimately what he would rather make off with entirely.

Pensées 1270

Next I discussed duties founded on charity and which are useful in making society more pleasant.

We can judge what our fellow citizens can be expected to demand of us by what we ourselves demand of those among whom we wish to live in a fairly close relationship, and whom we choose for this purpose from the society as a whole. We do not only want them to be just, opposed to fraud and deceit, at least with respect to us; for unfortunately we are much less concerned about whether they are the same with respect to others: we also want them to be attentive, helpful, tender, affectionate, and sensitive, and we would consider as a dishonest man a friend who was content to observe, with respect to us, the rules of strict justice. Thus there are certain duties different from those that come directly from justice, and those duties are based on propriety and derive from justice only in the sense that it is generally just that men should show consideration for each other, not only in the things that can make society more useful, but also in those that can make it more agreeable to them.

To achieve that, we must seek to approach all men with respect, all the men among whom we live: for ordinarily, as we have no more right to demand kindness from others than they from us, if we all waited for each other, neither of the two parties would have consideration for the other, which would make society harsh and make a people barbarous.

Hence a society gives rise to that gentleness and easiness of manner that makes it pleasant and makes everyone living there content with himself and with others.

The principal rule is to seek to please as much as one can without affecting one's integrity because it serves the public for men to have credit and influence on each other's minds, something which will never be achieved with a stern and fierce temperament; and such is the disposition of things and minds in a polite nation that a man, however virtuous he may be, if he had nothing but sternness in his mind, would be almost incapable of doing anything good and could only in very few situations put his virtue into practice.

Pensées 1271

On Politeness

That inner disposition has produced among all peoples an outward ceremonial we call politeness and civility, which is a kind of code of unwritten laws that men have promised to observe among themselves; and they have agreed that they would consider their application to themselves a sign of esteem and that they would be offended if they were not observed.

Barbarian peoples have few such laws, but there have been certain nations among whom they are so numerous that they become almost tyrannical and tend to suppress freedom, as among the Chinese.

In France we have greatly reduced our ceremonial, and today all politeness consists, on the one hand, in demanding little of people, and on the other in giving nothing beyond what is demanded.

The change has come from women, who regarded themselves as the dupes of a ceremonial that made them respected.

Pensées 1272

On the Change of Behavior that Has Occurred
in the French Nation

As royal power strengthened, the nobility left its lands. This was the principal cause of the change of behavior that took place in the nation. They abandoned the simple behavior of the earliest times for the vanities of the cities; the women left wool aside[81] and scorned all occupations that were not pleasures.

The disorder advanced only imperceptibly. It began under Francis I[82] and continued under Henry II;[83] the luxury and sumptuousness of the Italians

---

81 I.e., spinning wool.   82 Francis I (1494–1547), king of France from 1515.
83 Henry II (1519–1559), king of France from 1547.

increased it under the regencies of Queen Catherine.[84] Under Henry III[85] a vice which is unfortunately known in all save barbaric nations manifested itself at court.[86] But corruption and independence continued in a sex that sometimes derives advantage even from scorn. Never was marriage more violated than under Henry IV.[87] The devoutness of Louis XIII[88] halted the evil where it was; the reserved gallantry of Anne of Austria[89] still left it at that point; the youth of Louis XIV[90] increased it; the austerity of his old age suspended it; its dikes were broken with his death.

Daughters no longer paid attention to the traditions of their mothers. The women who formerly had come only gradually to a certain freedom obtained it all at once from the first days of marriage. Women and the idle youth stayed up late every night, and often a husband began the day when his wife was finishing hers. Vices were no longer recognized as such; they were sensitive only to being laughed at, and what was laughable included a troublesome modesty or a timid virtue.

Each supper party hid some new convention, but the secret was kept only as long as it took to negotiate it. With women of rank, the perils could no longer be avoided. In this continual change, taste was fatigued and finally lost out to the pursuit of pleasures.

The education of children was no longer included among the mothers' concerns; the wife lived with total indifference to what the husband was up to; all family relationships were neglected; all respect was done away with: no more courtesy calls; all conversations became shameless; everything one dared to do was avowed and the only thing considered impolite was failure to dare, to intend, or to perform.

A woman's virtue was an utter loss for her; it was even sometimes like a sort of persecuted religion.

All this was not the last degree of dissoluteness. They cheated in their gambling, as in their loves, and added to what dishonors their sex all that can abase ours.

---

84 Henry II's wife, Catherine de' Medici (1519–1589).

85 Henry III (1551–1589), third son of Henry II and Catherine de' Medici and king of France from 1574; he succeeded to the throne upon the death of his brother Charles IX.

86 Montesquieu also comments on Henry III's homosexuality in *Reflections on Certain Princes and Certain Events in their Lives* (1731–1733).

87 An allusion to his reputation for philandering.

88 Louis XIII (1601–1643), king of France from 1610.

89 Wife of Louis XIII and daughter of King Philip III of Spain, she served as regent of Louis XIV prior to his attaining personal rule in 1660.

90 Louis XIV (1638–1715), king of France from 1643.

Pensées 1273

On Ranks

Another change is taking place now, which is the degradation of ranks. There is a certain cast of mind which is the support of all dignities and all powers. When an office has had some authority and has lost it, you still revere it after that loss until some small circumstance causes you to notice your error: then you are angry with yourself and want to demolish in a single day what you fear you have respected too long.

As soon as Louis XIV was dead, jealousy of ranks appeared. The common people added to what royal authority had already done.[91] They were willing to abase themselves before the prince's minister, but not to concede anything to the officer of the crown, and they regarded with indignation any subordination that was not servitude.

The great, surprised, got respect from no one; all distinction became burdensome, and instead of the honor attached to it, there was only mockery to expect.

The upper but untitled nobility,[92] which contributed the most to this abasement, thought to gain a great deal, but by bringing titled persons back down to themselves, they also brought up to the same level a multitude of people who would never have expected it. Everybody was a Montmorency;[93] everybody was a Châtillon.[94]

Pensées 1274

On Jesting

Every man who jests wants to appear clever; he even wants to be more so than the person he makes fun of. The proof is that if the latter responds, he is disconcerted.

On that basis, there is no line so thin as what separates a jester by profession from a fool or an impertinent.

Yet there are certain rules one must observe when jesting which, far from making the person who jests repugnant, can make him quite amiable.

---

91 Very likely a reference to the withdrawal of provincial authority from the nobility and its replacement by the authority of intendants.

92 I.e., those below the rank of marquis; "titles" in this context means those of the rank of duke, count, and marquis.

93 A distinguished noble family, prominent since the tenth century, from the city of Montmorency, a few miles northwest of Paris.

94 A distinguished noble family, prominent since the ninth century, from the province of Champagne in northeast France.

Only certain flaws can be touched upon, which one is not displeased to possess, or which are compensated for by greater virtues.

One must extend one's jesting equally to everyone to make it plain that it is only the result of our levity and not of a concerted design to attack someone in particular.

We must not engage in prolonged jesting and repeat it every day, for it will be assumed we hold a man in contempt by the very fact that we have continually preferred him as the focus of our jabs.

Finally, the goal must be to bring laughter to the person we are teasing, and not to a third party.

We should not deny ourselves jesting, for it often enlivens conversation; but we should also not stoop to indulging in it excessively and be like the target everyone shoots at.

Pensées 1275
Gallantry

Failure to treat women decently has always been the most certain sign of the corruption of morals.

Gallantry requires a good deal of wit, as does preparing for women conversations which they can sustain.

The nations which have most abused that sex are those which have most spared it the trouble of defending itself.

They are exposed to affronts which they cannot parry.

Pensées 1276

With respect to the exalted in past ages you had only to protect freedom; today it is difficult to combine the familiarity that is so prevalent with the respect that we must distinguish from that familiarity.

Pensées 1277
On Conversations

The pitfalls into which we habitually fall in conversations are apparent to almost everyone. I will just say that we ought to keep three things in mind:

The first, that we are addressing people who, just like us, have some vanity, and that theirs suffers to the degree that ours is satisfied.

The second, that there are few truths important enough to make it worth mortifying someone and reproaching him for not knowing them.

And finally, that every man who takes over every conversation is a fool, or a man who would be happy to be one.

Pensées 1278

A Courageous Act Performed in Our Time

A northern king[95] having struck an officer of his troops with his walking stick, the man in despair withdrew without a word; a half-hour later he returned with a pistol, pointed it at the king, and suddenly turned it on himself. What a lesson!

Pensées 1279

On Fortune

We should not discourage this goal; we should only discourage most of the means.

Let us suppose there was on earth a land so felicitous that ranks, positions, and pardons were granted only for virtue, intrigues and shady means were unknown; and there was born a devious man who, to make his fortune, set about making use of maneuvers that seem quite innocent to us: would not this man be regarded by all sensible people as a disturber of the public happiness and as the most dangerous man this land could have produced?

Indeed, how satisfying it would be to people of good will to need only to be deserving and be relieved of the bother of acquiring.

The reason why persons of merit more rarely amass a fortune than those who have little is that they are less concerned about it. Persons of merit attain consideration independently of fortune; they are loved and esteemed: thus they do not regard wealth as something as significant as do those who can obtain esteem only in a certain post and by dint of honors and possessions.

Pensées 1280

On Business

The true manner of succeeding in your business is to contribute also to the business of those with whom you contract so that you can act in concert for the good of the cause.

In short, the terms should be made as simple as one can and much good will be brought to bear; in that way we encourage honest men to deal with us, which is the greatest advantage of civil life.

We owe it to the memory of our forefathers to preserve as much as we can the houses they have owned and cherished, for one can judge, by the care they have taken of them and their expenses in building and adorning them, the great likelihood that their intention was to have them pass on to their posterity.

---

95 Frederick William I (1688–1740), king of Prussia and Elector of Brandenburg from 1713.

Now there is nothing that should be more sacred for children than this spirit of their fathers, and we can believe, at least for our own satisfaction even if it is not true, that they take part from above in the business here below.

On Consideration and Reputation

(1725)

De la considération et de la réputation, text by Sheila Mason (*OC* viii, 449–455). After publishing *Persian Letters* (1721), Montesquieu spent more time in Paris and was welcomed into numerous elegant and intellectual circles. Influencing his writing during the 1720s was a cadre of literati gathering weekly at the apartments of Anne Thérèse de Marguenat de Courcelles, marquise de Lambert (1647–1733). Discussions there influenced him to compose this work, read to the Academy of Bordeaux by Jean de Sarrau de Vésis on 25 August 1725, and first published in *Deux opuscules de Montesquieu* (Bordeaux and Paris, 1891). As Montesquieu explains in *Pensées* 1655, Madame de Lambert borrowed substantially from his essay in writing her own composition on the same subject, published in 1748. Since 1957, the manuscript of *On Consideration and Reputation* has been part of the Montesquieu collection at the municipal library of Bordeaux (MS 2101).

* * *

A gentleman who is well considered in society could not be in a happier state. At every moment he enjoys the deference of everyone around him. He finds signs of public esteem in all the trifles that occur, in the slightest words and in the slightest gestures, and his soul is delightfully maintained in that satisfaction that makes one feel satisfactions, and that pleasure that brightens even pleasures.

Consideration contributes much more to our happiness than birth, wealth, positions, and honors. I know no sadder role in the world than that of a great lord without merit, who is always treated with formally respectful expressions, rather than with the naïve and subtle gestures that suggest consideration.

Although civility seems to exist to put everyone's merit on the same level for the sake of peace, still men cannot, nor even wish to, disguise themselves so completely as not to signal large differences between those to whom their civility needs to concede nothing and those to whom it must concede everything. It is a simple matter to perceive this sort of imposture; the game is so patent, instances recur so often that it is rare that many are taken in.

The reason why so few persons attain consideration is the excessive desire everyone has to obtain it; it is not sufficient for us to distinguish ourselves in the course of our lives; we also want to distinguish ourselves at every moment, and, so to speak, in detail. But that is what real qualities – probity, good faith, modesty – do not provide. They only make for general merit, but we must have distinction in the present moment. That is why we so often utter a witticism that will dishonor us tomorrow, why to succeed in one society we undermine ourselves in four, and why we are constantly copying eccentrics whom we disdain.

Moreover, in our desire for consideration, we do not evaluate but rather just count the votes: to impress three fools, we have the brashness to offend an intelligent man, but that intelligent man will do us more harm later than any good the three others will do us. We run after the white tickets and miss the black ones.[96]

We place more value on men with respect to their qualities of mind than with respect to those of their heart, and perhaps we are not so wrong. Aside from the fact that the heart is more hidden, it is to be feared that the important differences are in the mind and small ones in the heart. It seems that the judgments of the heart depend more on the overall economy of the machine, which is ultimately the same thing,[97] and that the mind depends more on a particular construction which is different in every subject.[98]

Feelings all come down to the esteem and love we have for ourselves, whereas our thoughts are infinitely varied.

There is one thing that, most unfortunately, costs us more consideration than vices do, and that is ridicule. A certain clumsy demeanor dishonors a woman much more than an obvious affair. As vices are generally shared, we have agreed to let these pass, but since each foolish trait is singular, it is treated mercilessly.

Reputation contributes less to our happiness than consideration. For when a famous man has once accepted the notion that some strangers greatly esteem him, he has reached his pinnacle of happiness; that feeling is only renewed on occasion.

We attain consideration from those with whom we associate and reputation from those we do not know; but the great difference is that consideration is the result of a whole lifetime, whereas it often takes only a single blunder to give us a reputation.

There is nothing so difficult as keeping up one's reputation, and here is the reason: he who praises someone ordinarily does so only to manifest the

96 Lottery terms: black tickets win a prize.   97 I.e., the same for all human beings.
98 Cf. Part One of *Essay on the Causes that Can Affect Minds and Characters* (1736–1738).

subtlety of his discernment; in praising a man, you take pride in having made him praiseworthy and perceived his merit, which had escaped others' eyes; you wish to add something distinctive, but as you add nothing to a man whose reputation is made, and you speak of him only along with everyone else, you would rather give preference to a man little known. Whence so many reputations made and lost and whence this eternal contradiction in men's judgments.

Brilliant reputations are the most at risk, for there is no merit in perceiving them; it appears much more ingenious to be capable of demolishing them. The dazzle of Prince Eugene[99] raised by three-quarters the merit of another of the emperor's generals;[100] the dazzle of Monsieur le Prince[101] contributed greatly to the glory of Monsieur de Turenne,[102] and we can say that the conquest of the world was detrimental to Alexander when people compared him to Caesar.

Men's pride is almost the sole cause of all moral effects; we lose patience in searching for moral causes because we always find pride in our path and always have to repeat the same thing.

That pride that enters into all our judgments provides a certain compensation for all things in this world and avenges many men for the blows of fortune.

A man is of distinguished nobility: if he has no property, we will leave him his nobility; we will even be happy to restore it; but if his fortune gives rise to envy we will examine his birth with envious eyes; not only will we question the fanciful, we will also deny him some of what is real. If two men bear the same name, you may be sure that the courtier will be the pretender and the provincial one authentic.

It is not that it is impossible for a man to maintain his reputation, either because envy does not always succeed, or because certain means which prudence supplies sustain it against envy.

It takes but one great day to acquire a reputation, and chance can provide that day; but to maintain it one must put himself on the line at every moment.

Sometimes this is achieved by modesty; at other times one maintains oneself by audacity. Often envy rises up against an audacious man, and often it is angered to see a modest man covered in glory.

---

99 Prince Eugene of Savoy (1663–1736), famed general of the Holy Roman Empire. Montesquieu met him in Vienna in 1728, early in his European travels.

100 Guido Wald Rüdiger, count of Starhemberg (1657–1737), cousin of Ernst Rüdiger von Starhemberg (1638–1701).

101 Louis II de Bourbon, prince of Condé (1621–1686), known as "the Great Condé."

102 Henri de La Tour d'Auvergne, Viscount of Turenne (1611–1675), victor in numerous battles during the Thirty Years' War and the War of Devolution against Holland. After originally supporting the Fronde, he took the Royal side in 1651 and defeated the rebellious army of Condé.

Yet the best of all the means that can be employed to preserve one's reputation is modesty, which should prevent men from regretting their favor by making them see that it is not being used against them. There is a means of preserving one's reputation that consoles even for not having preserved it, and that is virtue.

And it is a great advantage to seek it in the exercise of those deeds that are good because they confer it on us and are also good if they do not.

Of all the virtues, that which contributes the most to giving us a firm reputation is loving our fellow citizens: the populace, who always believe we have little love and great disdain for them, are never ungrateful for the love we grant them. In republics, where every citizen shares power, the popular spirit makes it abhorrent, but in monarchies, where ambition can be pursued only through obedience, and where with respect to power the favor of the people grants nothing if it does not grant everything, it gives a sure reputation because it cannot be suspected of any but virtuous motives.

What betrays most people is that they do not sustain their character. This means that they have none that is fixed, which is the worst of all characters. A man who has acquired a reputation as a man who is true, and who becomes an artful courtier, loses his reputation as a man who is true, and does not obtain that of an artful courtier.

When a man has distinguished himself by some notable deed, honors can lift him higher still, but he will demean himself if he seems to seek them too much. He should be pleased with himself and think that the proper and natural effect of homages is to save from anonymity those who are not fortunate enough to have distinguished themselves by their personal merit.[103]

I ask everyone, who even thinks today that the famous coadjutor became a cardinal. . .[104]

If chance has led us to an unmerited reputation, we must rejoice in secret and laugh to ourselves at the expense of the people and ourselves.

I seem to remember that Gracián[105] said more or less that if merit is greater than reputation, it must be displayed, because merit is to be manifested; if reputation is superior to merit, one should be very reserved, for fear of demonstrating only reputation.

---

103 Cf. *Pensées* 1320, where Montesquieu mocks the scientist Jean-Jacques Dortous de Mairan (1678–1771) for his obsession with honors.

104 Jean François de Gondi, coadjutor of Paris in 1643, named Cardinal de Retz in 1651.

105 Baltasar Gracián y Morales (1601–1658), Jesuit priest and author of *L'Homme de cour* (*Oráculo manual y arte de prudencia* [1647], Paris, 1684; *Catalogue* 2388) and *L'Homme universel* (*El Discreto*, Paris, 1723; *Catalogue* 2389).

Nothing is more likely to demolish or sustain a great reputation than favor because it subjects a man who has appeared in full daylight to even greater exposure. But what merit is not required to enjoy before the eyes of the whole world something for which so many have dishonored themselves without managing to obtain it?

It is difficult to acquire great wealth without losing public esteem unless one has first acquired so many honors and so much glory that the wealth came, in a manner of speaking, all by itself, like an accessory which is almost inseparable from them. Then you enjoy your wealth like a negligible prize of virtue. Who has ever been offended by the vast possessions of Prince Eugene? They are no more envied than the gold we see in the temples of the gods.

The reason why envy is more aroused by wealth than by honors is that it is an easier target. Everyone knows precisely that a cordon bleu is a cordon bleu,[106] and nothing more, but they do not know whether a man who is seen acquiring a million has not acquired four.

Nothing preserves and sets reputation better than misfortune; there are no virtues that people do not attribute to someone they pity or mourn.

"Marius returned from Africa," says Florus[107] elegantly, "greater after his misfortunes, for his imprisonment, his flight, and his exile had cast a sort of holy horror on his reputation: *carcer, catenæ, fuga, exitiave horrificaverant dignitatem.*"

History preserves with much more care the memory of great catastrophes than of happy and tranquil reigns; even fable has always marked its heroes by some setbacks. Man is only exalted in prosperity, but he is great in adversity.

But as most men do not occupy a high enough station to be gravely offended by fortune, they have retreat, which often has to their benefit the effect of misfortune.

A great man of our century retired at just the right time: it was just after a great feat, and he managed to give that virtuous deed a motive more virtuous still.[108]

But the world is an arena in which it is difficult to begin well and finish well, and the experience we lack for the former often harms us for the latter.

Moreover, innumerable people have deprived themselves by their past life of the resource of a graceful retreat; it would only be seen now as the despair

---

106 The blue sash designating the Ordre du Saint-Esprit, the loftiest honorific order of the realm, established by king Henry III in 1578.

107 Publius Annius Florus, African provincial and second-century CE historian of Rome who composed an *Epitome of Roman History* (*Catalogue* 2834, 2836) based mainly on Livy.

108 Possibly a reference to Philip of Orléans, regent of France between 1715 and 1723 who for a time nursed the ambition of replacing Philip V (1683–1746), grandson of Louis XIV, as king of Spain.

of a man overwhelmed by the memory of his dissoluteness or his misfortunes, which has nothing noble in itself.

Something really necessary for sustaining one's reputation is a good understanding of the ethos of one's time. There have been mistakes made by illustrious persons which made it quite clear that they did not know what their contemporaries were like and that they knew as little of the French as of the Japanese. If. . .

In every century there are certain dominant prejudices in which vanity is mixed with politics or superstition, and these prejudices are always embraced by people who want to acquire some reputation by paths easier than that of virtue. I would have much to say about our times, but I will speak only of those that have come before. When Luther and Calvin were publishing their reform measures, it was stylish to be Lutheran or Calvinist, and those who wished to pass for intelligent were impelled to follow the party that distinguished them from the ignorant theologian and the superstitious people. Since entire nations have decided in favor of one church or the other, there have always been opinions which those who want to have some reputation have particularly feigned.

Discourse on the Equity that Must Determine Judgments and the Execution of Laws

(1725)

Discours sur l'équité qui doit régler les jugements et l'exécution des lois, text by Sheila Mason (*OC* VIII, 475–487). Montesquieu read the text of this *Discourse* to the parlement of Bordeaux on 12 November 1725. In September 1717 charges had been brought against two counselors (*conseillers*) of the parlement, one serving the *Chambre des Enquêtes* and the other the *Chambre des Requêtes*, for financial fraud, and this scandal had brought about the renewal of an earlier practice of opening annual sessions of the parlement with a moral discourse regarding the need for magistrates and court officials to be just in all their rulings and also in all their personal conduct. There are several copies extant. In the version used in the *OC* edition which we are following, the word "pause" is written several times in the margins, suggesting that this is the text Montesquieu read to the parlement. During the French Revolution this manuscript was transferred from the Academy of Bordeaux to the municipal library (MS 828/XL, no. 13). It was first published in Geneva and Paris in 1772 with the title: *Discours prononcé par M. le Président de Montesquieu, à la rentrée du parlement de Bordeaux, le jour de la St Martin 1725;* a summary was published that same year in the *Mercure de France.*

* * *

May he among us who has made laws slaves to the iniquity of his judgments perish at once; may he find in all places the presence of an avenging god and the powers of heaven angered; may a fire come out of the earth and devour his house; may his posterity be forever brought low; may he seek his bread and never find it; may he be a frightening example of heaven's justice as he has been of the earth's. Such is approximately, my friends, the way a great emperor used to speak,[109] and these words, so sad and so fearsome, are full of consolation for you: you may all say now to this people assembled, with the confidence of a judge of Israel: "If I have committed some injustice, if I have oppressed one of you, if I have received presents from any among you, may he raise his voice, may he speak against us in the Lord's sight: *loquimini de me coram domino et contemnam illud hodie.*"[110]

I shall therefore not evoke those great corruptions which in all times have been the precursors of change or the fall of states; of intentional acts of injustice, of systematic malice, of those lives stamped with crimes, where days of iniquity have always followed days of iniquity; of magistracies exercised in the midst of the reproaches, weeping, tears, and fears of all the fellow citizens against such judges: against men so dreadful it would take a bolt of lightning; shame and remorse have no effect.

Thus, supposing a magistrate possesses his essential virtue, which is justice, a quality without which he is but a monster in society, and with which he can be a very poor citizen, I shall speak only of the accessories that can make this justice more or less abound. It must be enlightened; it must be prompt; let it not be too austere, and finally let it be universal.

At the beginning of our monarchy, our fathers, poor and rather shepherds than farmers, soldiers rather than citizens, had few interests to regulate; a few laws on the division of booty, pasturing rights or theft of livestock regulated the whole republic.[111] Anyone was able to serve as magistrate among a people whose ways followed from the simplicity of

109 According to *OC* VIII, 475, note 2, Montesquieu alludes here to an edict of Constantine in 331 which he could have read at least partially in a compendium in his library (*Catalogue* 167).
110 Paraphrase of 1 Samuel (1 Kings) 12:3. In the time of Montesquieu, the Bible was always quoted in the Latin Vulgate, which was the official text of the Church. It has certain disparities of reference with respect to Protestant Bibles, for instance here, where its I–IV Kings became I–II Samuel and I–II Kings.
111 Cf. *SL* XVIII, 13.

nature, and to whom ignorance and their crudeness furnished means as ready as they were unjust for ending disputes, such as drawing lots and trial by water or fire and single combat.

But since we have abandoned our savage ways; since, as conquerors of the Gauls, we have adopted their public order; since the military code has given way to the civil code; above all since the laws of fiefs have ceased to be the only laws, and the nobility the only institution of the state, and by this last change trade and agriculture have been encouraged; since the wealth of individuals and their avarice have grown; since great interests have had to be sorted out, and interests almost always hidden; since good faith has reserved to itself only a handful of matters of little importance, whereas trickery and deceit have withdrawn into contracts, our codes have expanded;[112] we have had to combine foreign with national laws; respect for religion has further added canonical laws, and magistracies have fallen to only the most enlightened of citizens.

Judges found themselves surrounded by pitfalls and surprises, and truth left in their minds the same wariness as error.

The obscurity of substance gave rise to form; the scoundrels who hoped they could hide their malice made a sort of art of it; whole professions were established, some to obscure, others to prolong lawsuits; and the judge had less difficulty defending himself from the bad faith of the plaintiff than from the artifice of those to whom he entrusted his interests.

At that point it was no longer enough for the magistrate to examine the purity of his intentions; it was no longer enough for him to be able to say to God: *Proba me deus et scito cor meum*,[113] he had to examine his mind, his knowledge, and his talents.

He was required to draw on his studies, to bear his whole life long the weight of unstinting application, and see whether his application could give his mind the measure of knowledge and the degree of insight which his position demanded.

We read in the relations of certain travelers that there are mines where men work who have never seen the light of day: they are a quite natural image of those people whose mind, weighted down by the organs, is incapable of receiving any degree of perspicacity.

---

112 Cf. *SL* XVIII and XXXI correlating complexity of law to stages of economic development.
113 "Search me, O God, and know my heart" (Psalms 139 [138]:23), King James translation.

Such an incapacity requires a just man to withdraw from the magistracy; a lesser incapacity requires a just man to overcome it with sweat and midnight oil.[114]

Further, justice must be prompt. Often the injustice is not in the verdict but in the delays; often the examination process has done more harm than a negative decision.[115]

In the present setup, launching lawsuits is an occupation; one carries that reputation one's whole life; it passes on to posterity and goes from one scion to the next, to the end of a wretched family.

To this sorry reputation poverty always seems attached; the strictest justice never spares one more than a share of adversity; and such is the state of things that the formalities introduced to preserve the public order are today the scourge of private citizens.[116]

The industry of the courthouse has become, like commerce and agriculture, a source of fortunes; tax collection has found a good harvest there and rivaled the mania for lawsuits for the ruin of the unhappy litigant.

It used to be that men of good will brought unjust men before our tribunals; today it is the unjust men who summon men of good will to them; the depository has had the gall to deny what he is holding in the hope that timid good faith would soon weary of suing him for it, and the oppressor has made it clear to his victim that it was not prudent for him to continue trying to make him pay for his violence.

We have seen – oh unhappy times![117] – iniquitous men threatening to take to court those whose money they were stealing, and advancing as the reason

114 Montesquieu had already decided to withdraw from the parlement at the time he delivered his *Discourse*. Among other considerations, he found the procedures of the court complex and difficult to master; see the autobiographical *Pensées* 213 where he remarks: "As for my profession as president [. . .] I had a good understanding of the questions in themselves; but as for the procedure, I was in the dark. I had nevertheless applied myself to it; but what disappointed me the most about it is that I could see in animals, so to speak, the very talent that eluded me."

115 The longer cases remained before the court, the higher the fees earned by the judges and other court officials.

116 Cf. *SL* XXIX, 1: "The formalities of justice are necessary to liberty; but their number could be so great that it would clash with the goal of the very laws that would have established them: disputes would have no end; the possession of property would remain uncertain; one party would be given the property of the other without examination, or both would be ruined by dint of examination." See also *SL* VI, 2, where Montesquieu contends that although the formalities of justice are sometimes frustrating to litigants owing to expenses, delays, and uncertain outcomes, they are "the price which each citizen pays for his freedom." In despotisms there are no such formalities, and trials are swiftly dispatched to the detriment of pleaders seeking justice.

117 A rhetorical flourish that echoes the exclamation "*O tempora, o mores*" ("Oh, what times! oh, what behavior!") in Cicero's orations against Catiline.

for their harassments the hard times and the inevitable ruin of those who might try to make them cease.

But were the status of plaintiffs not ruinous, its uncertainty would suffice to make us want to put an end to it. Their situation is always unfortunate since they lack any security, whether in terms of their holdings, their honor, or their life.

This same consideration should inspire great affability in a magistrate, since he is always dealing with unfortunate persons; people must always find him attentive to their slightest concerns, like milestones which travelers find along the highways, on which they rest their burdens.

Yet we have seen judges who, refusing all deference to plaintiffs so as to preserve their neutrality (or so they said), lapsed into strictness that made them more surely abandon it.

But who, with exception of the stoics, was ever able to say that this general affection for humankind which is the virtue of man considered as such, is a virtue foreign to the character of the judge; if it is power that must harden the heart, see how paternal authority hardens the heart of fathers, and model your magistracy on the first of all magistracies.[118]

But independently of humanity, decency and affability become a part of justice to a refined people, and a judge who lacks any for his clients is already beginning to fail in rendering to each his due.

Thus, by our standards, a judge must conduct himself in such a manner toward his litigants that he appears to them as reserved rather than grave, and displays to them the probity of the Catos without manifesting their severity and austerity.[119]

I confess that there are occasions when there is no good soul who does not feel indignant; the practice which introduced solicitations seems purposely made to test the patience of judges who have any courage and probity. Such is the corruption of men's hearts that it seems the usual thing is always to assume it is in the hearts of others.

To you who employ all the most foolproof ways you can imagine to seduce us; who look for all our weaknesses the better to win us over; who put into play flattery, pandering, the charm of our friends, the sway

118 Cf. *SL* v, 7, where Montesquieu praises paternal authority as fostering good morals, and *PL* 76, where Usbek laments that the French, while taking much that was "worthless" from Roman law, did not follow the Roman practice of awarding fathers broad authority over their children – a more effective restraint on behavior than even the laws themselves.

119 Cato the Elder (234–149 BCE) and his great-grandson Marcus Porcius Cato Uticensis (85–46 BCE), both known for their gravitas and austere morals.

of the great, the influence of a cherished spouse, sometimes even an influence you believe more powerful because you take it to be criminal; who, selecting all our passions, set upon our heart in the least defended spot: may you forever fail in all your designs, and only be confounded in your ventures.

We will not incur God's reproach to sinners in the holy books: "Thou hast made me to serve with thy sins";[120] we shall resist your boldest solicitations, and we shall make you feel the corruption of your heart and the righteousness of ours.

Justice must be universal. A judge must not be like Cato the Elder, who was the most just of Romans in his tribunal and not in his family.[121] Justice in us must be an overall conduct; let us be just in all places, just in every respect, toward all persons, on all occasions.

Those who are just only in cases where their profession requires it, who pretend to be equitable in others' affairs when they are not incorruptible in what interests them directly, who have not put equity into the smallest events of their lives, run the risk of soon losing that very justice which they dispense from their tribunal.

Judges of this sort are like the monstrous deities that fable had invented, who indeed brought some order to the universe, but who, saddled with crimes and imperfections, disrupted their own laws and plunged nature back into all the disorders which the fable had banished from it.

May the role of the private man therefore not prejudice that of the public man; for into what turmoil does a judge not plunge his litigants when they see he has the same passions as those persons he is called upon to correct, and find his conduct as reprehensible as the conduct which elicited their complaints.

If he loved justice, they will say, would he refuse it to the persons who are linked to him by such gentle, strong, and sacred bonds; to whom he must cling by so many reasons for esteem, love, or gratitude, and who have perhaps placed all their happiness in his hands?

The judgments we dispense from the tribunal can rarely determine our probity; it is in the disputes that particularly concern us that our heart unfolds and reveals itself: that is how people judge us; that is how they fear us or place hope in us.

If our conduct is condemned, if it is suspect, we become subject to a sort of public accusation, and the right to judge which we exercise is held by those who are obliged to bear it as among their calamities.

---

120 [...] *verumtamen servire me fecisti in peccatis tuis* (Isaiah 43:24).
121 According to Plutarch (*Life of Cato*, IV–V), Cato the Elder did not treat his slaves well.

It is time, my friends, to bring up this young prince who is the heir to the justice of his ancestors as he is to their crown.[122]

History knows no prince whose days even at a mature age and in the prime of his government have been as precious to Europe as those of this monarch's childhood;[123] heaven had attached such great destinies to the course of his innocent life that he seemed to be the pupil and the king of all nations; the men of the remotest climes regarded his life as their own; in the jealousies of the various interests all peoples were living in a common fear; we, the faithful subjects, we Frenchmen who are praised as loving our king single-heartedly, we scarcely had any advantage, in that regard, over the allied nations, over rival nations, over enemy nations.

Such a present from heaven, so great by what has taken place, so great in the present time, is in addition an illustrious promise for the future. Born for the felicity of humankind, could it be his subjects alone whom he would not make happy, and could he like the sun give life to all that is distant and burn all that approaches it?

We have just seen a great princess put an end to the mourning all about her;[124] she appeared, and peoples all over, solely attentive in these sorts of events to their own interests, saw only the virtues and charms which heaven has showered on her; the young monarch yielded to his heart; virtue is our assurance for the future of the tender love which charms and graces have spawned.

Be, O great king, the happiest of kings; we who love you bless heaven for initiating the happiness of the monarchy with that of the royal family; whatever felicity you enjoy, you have no more than what your peoples have a thousand times desired for you. We besought heaven every day, and it has granted us everything. But again we beseech heaven that your youth may be cited to all the kings who will come after you; that you at a mature age may find nothing in it to regret, and in the great engagements into which you enter, may you always be aware of what the first of mortals owes to the world.

May you ever cultivate in peace virtues which are not less royal than the military ones, and never forget that heaven, in bringing you into the world,

122 Louis XV was only five when he inherited the crown in 1715; the regency of Philip, Duke of Orléans ended in 1723 when Louis XIII turned thirteen. "Justice" refers here to the institutional apparatus which dispenses justice.
123 Montesquieu here alludes to the formation of the Quadruple Alliance in 1718 with England, Austria, and Savoy, joined by Spain in 1720.
124 Maria Leszczyńska, whose father Stanislas Leszczyńska (1677–1766) was deposed as king of Poland in 1709, causing him to relocate his family to Alsace; the "mourning" refers to the family's long exile. Maria married Louis XV in August 1725.

has already given you all the greatness you need, and that like the vast ocean, you have nothing to acquire.

May the prince in whom you have placed your principal trust,[125] who finds your glory only where he finds your justice; that prince, inflexible like the laws themselves, who decrees forever what he has once decided; that prince who embraces the rules and knows no exceptions; who is always consequential, and sees the end as well as the beginning of his projects; who is able to reduce courtiers to demands that are just, to tell the difference between their services and their affectations, and teach them that they are not more yours than your other subjects. May he be long beside your throne and share with you there the burdens of monarchy.

Barristers,[126] the court is pleased to confirm to you that it is cognizant of your integrity. The complaints against your honor have not yet reached so high;[127] do know, however, that to be pure it is insufficient for your ministry to be disinterested; you have zeal for clients, and that we praise, but zeal becomes criminal when it makes you forget what you owe to your adversaries.

I realize that the laws of a just defense often oblige you to reveal matters which shame had buried; but that is an evil we tolerate only when it is absolutely necessary. Learn from us this maxim and always remember it:

Never tell the truth
At the cost of your virtue.

What a sorry talent is the ability to tear men apart! The sallies of some wits are perhaps the greatest thorns of our ministry; and what makes the populace laugh, far from attracting our applause, always makes us weep over the unfortunate beings who are being dishonored.[128]

Must shame follow all those who approach this sacred tribunal? Do we fear, alas, lest the mercy of justice be too pure? What worse can we do for the adversaries? We make them anguish even over their successes, and to them, to use here words of Scripture, we make *the fruits of justice bitter as absinth.*[129]

---

125 Louis Henri, Duke of Bourbon (1692–1740), first minister of France from 1723 until 1726.
126 Montesquieu distinguishes between those who are magistrates, and thus presumably in all cases neutral, and barristers who practice before the court as advocates.
127 I.e., for final adjudication.
128 Cf. Montesquieu's strictures, in his *In Praise of Sincerity* (c. 1717), on taking mockery too far.
129 "ye have turned judgment into gall, and the fruit of righteousness into hemlock" (Amos 6:12, King James version).

And in good faith, what do you want us to reply when they come to us and say: "We have come before you and have been covered in embarrassment and ignominy. You have seen our wounds and been unwilling to soothe them with oil; you wanted to repair the harm we have suffered far from you: they did us more real harm before your very eyes, and you have said nothing. You whom we looked upon as gods of the earth where you sat in your tribunal have been silent as statues of wood and stone. You say you are preserving our possessions for us, and our honor is a thousand times dearer to us than our possessions; you say that you are making our lives secure, and our honor is more priceless to us than our lives. If you have not the strength to halt the insinuations of an impetuous orator, point us at least to some tribunal more just than yours. Who even knows whether you have not shared the pitiless pleasure they have just given to our adversaries, whether you have not enjoyed our despair, and whether what we admonish you for as a weakness is not something we should rather be admonishing as a crime?" Barristers, we would never have the strength to bear such cruel admonitions, and it would never be said that you would be quicker thus to fail in the first of duties than we would be to rebuke you.

Prosecutors,[130] you must tremble every day of your lives over your ministry; nay, you must make even us tremble. You can at every moment close our eyes to truth and open them to glimmers and appearances; you can tie our hands, elude or abuse the most just of provisions, constantly present justice to your clients and make them embrace only its shadow, make them anticipate the end and constantly defer it; make them walk in a labyrinth of errors: then, all the more dangerous the more skilled you were, you would have part of the hatred poured on us. What would be sad about your profession you would shed on ours, and we would soon become the greatest of criminals after those who were most to blame.

But why do you not ennoble your profession with the virtue that becomes them all? How delighted we would be if you strived to become more just than we; with what pleasure we would pardon you such emulation, and how low would our dignities seem to us beside a virtue that would seem to us so dear.

---

130 Prosecutors (*procureurs*) were employed by the parlements of France to develop the facts in particular cases. In criminal cases they could recommend conviction with a specific penalty, acquittal, continuation of factual inquiry, or, in capital cases, torture to obtain confession. During his years of service from 1716 to 1727 as one of the nine *présidents à mortier* of the Bordeaux parlement, Montesquieu was assigned to the *Chambre de la Tournelle*, the criminal law division of the court.

When several among you have merited the esteem of the court, we have rejoiced at the commendations we have given them; it seemed to us we were going to walk in more secure paths; we imagined we had ourselves attained a new level of justice. We said, "We will not have to defend ourselves against their tricks. They are going to work with us on today's agenda, and perhaps we will see a time when the people will be delivered from every burden." Prosecutors, your duties are so akin to ours that we who are in a position to correct you beg you to observe them; we speak to you not as judges; we even overlook the fact that we are your magistrates: we entreat you to leave us our probity, not to take from us the respect of the people, and not to prevent us from being their fathers.

Dialogue between Xanthippus and Xenocrates

(1727)

Dialogue de Xantipe et de Xenocrate, text by Sheila Mason (*OC* VIII, 575–580). The manuscript of this dialogue was among those sent to England in 1818; it must also have been (though it is not specifically named) among those returned to La Brède in 1828 (see "A General Note on the Texts"). Subsequently it was sold, first in 1919 and again in 1957; the final purchaser was the Houghton Library at Harvard University (MS Fr 267). It is that manuscript which has served as our base text, as in *OC* VIII. The dialogue was first published in *Mélanges inédits* (1892).

* * *

When I left Africa, I embarked on the vessel which the Carthaginians had given to Xanthippus[131] to return to Greece, and I was delighted to find myself with a man whose virtue was respected throughout the world.

Xanthippus was modest, he was very simply attired, and in our ship it was at first difficult to discern which of us had destroyed the armies of the Romans and restored liberty and domination to Carthage.

---

131 Xanthippus was a Spartan mercenary recruited by the Carthaginians when they were losing the First Punic War. He blamed their earlier defeats on poor decision-making and designed battle formations to maximize Carthage's superiority in cavalry and ability to use elephants to lead the infantry charge. The result was the complete rout of Roman forces under the command of Regulus in a battle waged near Tunis in 255 BCE. After this victory, Xanthippus was sent back to Greece, according to Montesquieu's account, in a leaky boat designed to sink.

He was affable without descending into an unseemly familiarity, and the respect one had for him was not of the same kind as the respect one reserves for the great, which is less the effect of love and admiration than of timidity and fear.

I remained silent for a long time but finally spoke up. "Xanthippus," I said, "a free man is allowed to speak to a Greek. It was not for you alone that the gods made you virtuous; from whom might I learn to better myself, if it is not from a man such as you?"

We began to talk. Never have words made more of an impression on me than his. I felt my heart warming; virtue seemed to me more beautiful. Ever attentive and ever stirred, I felt a god was speaking to me and communicating with me.

One day, when we were discussing the great things he had done in Africa, he said: "I carried out what every Lacedæmonian would have attempted, like me, what our old men had taught us and what we will teach others. I halted the initiatives of an enemy who was asking for something beyond glory and who wanted to be unjust because he was successful.[132] I could not understand why the Romans did not want to forgive Carthage, as we have forgiven Athens,[133] and why they do not sense that vanquished peoples are no longer enemies."[134]

"Never was seen so rapid a change," I replied. "You were living as a private citizen in Carthage; you saw your fellow citizens discouraged by the number of their defeats; you restored hope in them; you took command and did things that before you had never been seen."

"Xenocrates," he said, "I merely did my duty."

"Duty," I said, "did not bind you to the Carthaginians."

"It binds me," he replied, "to all humans. Is not each Lacedæmonian born a protector of the common liberty? And that is the first thing that Lycurgus[135] taught us; if he had thought only of his city, I do not believe he would have subjected it to such severe discipline; but he wanted to form extraordinary men who would watch over the interests of all humans. I saw the

---

132 Prior to the intervention of Xanthippus, Regulus had won a great victory over Carthage in 256 BCE, after which he offered peace terms so unjust that they had little choice but to decline them. For Montesquieu's criticisms of Rome's ruthless negotiating tactics with defeated enemies, see *Romans*, chapters IV and VI.

133 At the end of the Peloponnesian war (431–404 BCE), Corinth and Thebes wanted Athens to be destroyed, but Sparta refused to be party to this plan.

134 In *SL* X, 2, 3 Montesquieu developed the argument that just wars are waged only for self-defense and that the rights of conquerors do not include destroying their enemies.

135 Lycurgus was the legendary founder of the Spartan political, economic, and social system, whose life was first chronicled by Herodotus in the fifth century BCE.

Carthaginians about to fall under a foreign yoke. Carthage," I said, "has a Lacedæmonian within its walls. It must not be a subject; may Lacedæmon be pleased to learn that the citizens she degraded have still preserved the noble ambition of becoming worthy of her, and that if I was not able to contribute to her happiness, I have at least contributed to her glory."

"There is," I said, "one thing that will surprise everyone. It is that you have not found asylum in a city that you have liberated."

"It is because I have saved her that I leave her today. One cannot be free and have his liberator at every moment before him. Is it just for a single man to trouble an immense people? I leave laws in Carthage for which I have fought and do not wish by my persistent presence to lessen the gift I have made to it."

"I admit," I said, "that if you had kept the command of the armies, you could have become suspect; but you gave it up at once and disappeared into the mass of citizens."

"I was," he said, "known by the soldiers and loved by them. Ye gods, how a Lacedæmonian must blush to be a tyrant, he before whom all peoples must be free! What would my enemies say, or rather what would my family say, if they knew I allowed myself to do in Carthage what I was accused of in Lacedæmon? No, Xenocrates, I must someday render an account to my fatherland even for my exile and show what use I made of its punishments and its wrath. Let those exiled from Athens go raise the Greeks and barbarians against her; let them, arms in hand, demand the return of rights one can only merit by one's virtues. I pity a mother who has such cruel children, and who, having seen them submissive only in that tender age when one fears everything, has obtained something from their weakness and nothing from their love.

For me, Xenocrates, I have never ceased for a moment to be a citizen of Sparta. I have been in foreign lands what I would have been within her walls, always a child of Lycurgus, in other words an enemy of tyranny. I flee from all places where I could be suspected of that."

"Xanthippus," I replied, "I know all the greatness of your soul, but there is not a single Greek who is not indignant, on your account, at the ingratitude of the Carthaginians. Is it possible that after receiving so much, they have granted you not a single honor nor a single benefit?"

"And what benefit, good gods," he responded, "could a barbarian people offer a Lacedæmonian? Is it silver or gold? Gold which does not bedazzle the children of Sparta, gold which our prostitutes would blush to wear; gold which is not even envied by our slaves? Lycurgus has forbidden its use; our fathers who adopted his laws abandoned it without regret, and we claim no virtue for doing without it."

"Xanthippus," I said, "your replies would humiliate me if they did not strike my heart with an intense desire to be like you. But as I am only a man, allow my fondness for you to encourage me to speak to you a moment more. You are exiled from Lacedæmon, and you are leaving Carthage. Where will you go?"

"Xenocrates," he said, "since the day I last saw Sparta, all places are the same to me. Lacedæmon, by striking us from her citizen rolls, leaves us with what she was giving us, namely virtue. Let the exiled of Lampsacus[136] and Sybaris[137] weep: they lose everything, deprived of a fatherland which alone can bear their lethargy and refuses them the delights she had promised them. But I have lost only what I can have in every country."

"Xanthippus," I said to him, "you heroes compensate for everything with the thought of the universal admiration you command. The memory of one's great accomplishments soothes much bitterness; victories are companions that are always consoling. It is very wrong to pity men who after their fall are still so far above all others, and whom we call unfortunate when they are covered in glory."

"Xenocrates," he replied, "I do not know the sort of happiness that relates only to the man who enjoys it; glory separates us from other men but virtue reunites us with them, and in so doing constitutes our true happiness. Our laws that obstruct all the passions especially constrain those of heroes; among us, honor is not an imaginary being invented to serve humans' greatest errors, which is obtained by chance, preserved without design, lost inadvertently, and follows sometimes crime and sometimes virtue. Exact obedience to the laws is honor among us; otherwise birth, genius, talents, and brilliant acts can make a citizen more famous only by making him more infamous; and if our king Agesilaus,[138] the day of his return from Asia, had not come to join in with his citizens at a frugal repast, the last of the Lacedæmonians would have blushed at his victories. As for me, Xenocrates, I am not proudest of those achievements that were most renowned through the world. I am content with myself because I have never had more than the wealth, the

---

136 Lampsacus was a prosperous wine-producing city on the Asiatic shore of the Hellespont whose inhabitants worshipped Priapus, a god of procreation and fertility.
137 Sybaris was a southern Italian town known for the extreme hedonism of its inhabitants.
138 Agesilaus II (445–359 BCE), the Spartan king who liberated the Greek cities of Anatolia from Persian rule but was called back to Sparta in 395 to deal with local problems.

ambition, and the delights that Lycurgus allowed me. If I am content with myself, it is because I have borne without difficulty the preferences that have been given to my rivals, because I have always loved the laws even when they have done me present harm and my enemies have most abused them; because I have so governed my conduct that I have appeared before each citizen as I would have appeared before my magistrates. So if, with all that, the Lacedæmonians have exiled me, I pray to the gods every day not to be angrier than I am and to pay less attention to a few criminal citizens than to the fatherland, which is innocent. And what reassures me is that a nation which has laws like ours must be pleasing to the gods."

While we were talking, the vessel cracked open and we discovered the Carthaginians' deceit. Xanthippus said nothing for a moment, and then he cried, "Why must I live if my life is a burden to the two greatest peoples on earth? Let us die, Xenocrates," he said to me, "death only brings us closer to the gods." But the immortal gods did not allow such a great crime to be consummated: we were near the shore; a fisherman's bark came to us; we boarded it, and our vessel sank.

Lysimachus

(1751)

Lisimaque, text by Catherine Volpilhac-Auger (*OC* ix, 419–422). Montesquieu was inspired to write this essay by his reading of Justin, the second-century CE Roman historian (*Catalogue* 2845, 2846) who excerpted the work of Gnaeus Pompeius Trogus, a first-century CE historian and contemporary of Livy. Lysimachus (c. 361–281 BCE) was a Macedonian general and bodyguard of Alexander. As one of his successors (*diadochoi*), rewarded for his loyalty and bravery, he subsequently ruled Thrace. Montesquieu composed this piece of historical fiction in response to an invitation from the just formed Academy of Science and Literature of Nancy. It was read at the Academy on 8 May 1751 and published in late December 1754 or early January 1755 in the Academy's *Mémoires* and also in the December 1754 edition of the *Mercure de France*. A manuscript obtained by Laurent de La Beaumelle remains in his family archives.[139] Our base text is the *Mercure* version as in *OC* ix, which includes corrections apparently made by Montesquieu prior to printing.

139 See *OC* ix, 412–413 and Claude Lauriol, *Études sur La Beaumelle* (Paris: Champion, 2008), pp. 276–278 and 282–287.

* * *

When Alexander[140] had destroyed the Persian empire, he wanted people to believe he was the son of Jupiter. The Macedonians were indignant to see this prince blush at having Philip as his father. Their discontent grew when they saw him adopting the ways, the clothing, and the manners of the Persians, and they all regretted having done so much for a man who was beginning to disdain them. But in the army they murmured and did not speak.

A philosopher named Callisthenes[141] had followed the king on his expedition. One day when he greeted him in the Greek manner, Alexander said to him: "How is it that you do not bow down before me?"[142] "Sire," said Callisthenes, "you are the master of two nations: one, a slave nation before you subjected it,[143] is no less so since you conquered it; the other,[144] free before it helped you win so many victories, is still free since you won them. I am a Greek, sire, and that is a name you have raised so high that you no longer can abase it without demeaning yourself."

Alexander the Great's vices were extreme like his virtues. He was fearsome in his anger, which made him cruel: he had Callisthenes' feet, nose, and ears cut off, ordered he be put in an iron cage, and had him carried in that state in the army's retinue.

I loved Callisthenes, and I had always spent time listening to him when my occupations left me a few hours of leisure; and if I have some love for virtue, I owe it to the impressions which his homilies made on my heart. I went to see him. "I salute you," I said, "illustrious unfortunate, whom I see in an iron cage, the way we pen wild beasts, for being the only man in the army."

"Lysimachus," he said to me, "when I am in a situation that requires strength and courage, I feel somehow in my place. In truth, if the gods had put me on earth only to live an easy and sensuous life, I would think it was for nothing that they had given me a great and immortal soul. To enjoy sensate pleasures is something all men are easily capable of doing, and if the gods

140 Alexander III of Macedon (356–323 BCE), known to history as Alexander the Great.
141 Callisthenes of Olynthus (c. 360–327 BCE), great-nephew of Aristotle and historian of Alexander's Asian expedition. In addition to his *Deeds of Alexander*, he wrote a history of Greece. Both works were widely consulted in antiquity; neither is extant.
142 In the summer of 327, Alexander proclaimed himself divine (the son of Zeus) and insisted his entourage prostrate themselves before him in the Persian manner (*proskynesis*). Callisthenes, who refused, was soon after arrested for alleged complicity in a plot to kill Alexander. Some classical sources report that he was imprisoned in an iron cage, tortured, and executed (Strabo 11.11.4; Arrian, *Anabasis*, 4173). Plutarch records that Callisthenes died of obesity and pediculosis after long imprisonment (*Life of Alexander* VII, LV).
143 Persia. 144 Greece.

have made us for nothing but that, their creation is more perfect than they intended, and they have achieved more than they attempted. It is not," he added, "that I am insensitive; you make me see only too well that I am not. When you came to me, I immediately felt some pleasure at seeing you perform an act of courage, but in the name of the gods, may it be for the last time. Let me bear my misfortunes, and do not have the cruelty of adding your own to them."

"Callisthenes," I said, "I shall see you every day. If the king saw you abandoned by men of virtue, he would have no more remorse and would begin to believe it was your fault. How I hope that he will not enjoy the pleasure of seeing that the fear of his punishments makes me abandon a friend!"

One day Callisthenes said to me: "The immortal gods have consoled me, and since that time I feel in myself something divine that has kept me from awareness of my miseries: I have seen the great Jupiter in a vision; you were beside him, you had a scepter in your hand and a royal headband on your brow. He pointed to you and said: 'He will make you happy.' It was my emotion that awakened me: I was extending my hands toward heaven and straining to say: 'Great Jupiter, if Lysimachus is to reign, may he reign with justice.' Lysimachus, you shall reign: have confidence in a man who must be agreeable to the gods, since he suffers for virtue."

Meanwhile, Alexander having learned that I respected the wretchedness of Callisthenes, that I visited him and dared to pity him, exploded again in wrath: "Go fight the lions," he said, "you fool who so enjoy the company of ferocious beasts!" They put off my punishment so more people could be there to watch.

The day just before it, I wrote these words to Callisthenes: "I am going to die; all the ideas you had given me of my future greatness have vanished from my mind. Would that I could have allayed the miseries of a man such as you. . ." Prexachus, who was in my confidence, brought me this reply.

"Lysimachus, if it is the gods' intention that you reign, Alexander cannot take your life; for men do not stand against the will of the gods."

This letter encouraged me and, reflecting that the most and least fortunate of men are equally surrounded by the divine hand, I determined to conduct myself, not by my expectations, but by my courage, and to defend to the end a life which contained such great promise.

I was led into the arena. A great crowd had gathered to witness my courage or my consternation. They released a fierce lion upon me. I had folded my mantle around my arm; I held that arm out to him: he tried to devour it; I seized his tongue, ripped it from his mouth, and cast it at my feet.

Alexander naturally approved acts of courage. He admired my resolution, and that was the moment when his great soul reappeared. He sent for me, and extending his hand, said to me: "Lysimachus, I restore to you my friendship; restore yours to me. My anger only made you accomplish a feat which the life of Alexander cannot boast." I accepted the king's pardon, I worshiped the decrees of the gods, and I awaited their promises but neither sought nor fled them.

Alexander died,[145] and all the nations were without a master. The king's sons were in their childhood, and his brother Arrhidaeus[146] was not yet beyond it. Olympias[147] had only the boldness of weak souls, and everything that was cruel seemed courageous to her. Roxana, Eurydice, and Stateira[148] were lost in grief. Everyone in the palace was able to mourn, and no one to reign. So Alexander's captains eyed the throne, but the ambition of each was contained by the ambition of all. We divided up the empire, and each of us considered his share the recompense for his labors. The lots made me king of Asia, and, now that I can do anything, I need Callisthenes' lessons more than ever. His joy informs me that I have done some good deed, and his sighs tell me I have some harm to make right. I find him between myself and the gods; I find him between my people and me. I am the king of a people that loves me: fathers hope my life, like their children's, will be long; children fear losing me, as they fear losing their father; my subjects are happy, and I am as well.[149]

---

145 Alexander died unexpectedly at the age of thirty-two in 323 BCE.

146 Philip III Arrhidaeus (c. 359–317 BCE), half-brother of Alexander, who after serving as one of his generals became king of Macedonia following his death.

147 Olympias (c. 375–316 BCE), Alexander's mother.

148 Roxanna was Alexander's first wife; Eurydice II (d. 317 BCE) was the wife of Arrhidaeus; Stateira II, daughter of Stateira I and Darius III of Persia, was another of Alexander's wives.

149 Montesquieu later wrote a different ending, which he placed in *Pensées* 2161: "The laws were silenced, necessity spoke, and we obeyed. My subjects are happy, but not I. The state is tranquil and my house is still distressed; my empire prospers, and I have troubles only within my palace. Who knows what misfortunes might have befallen me if Callisthenes had not ceaselessly calmed my soul. The strange condition of kings: they have none but great passions; their strength is only for taking action, and they are too weak to defend themselves. O Callisthenes! You make me fear remorse, when I only barely fear crimes; I quake at the horrors from which you have saved me."

Statecraft

Letters from Xenocrates to Pheres

(1724)

Lettres de Xenocrate à Phérès, text by Sheila Mason (*OC* VIII, 299–305). The sole manuscript of this text, now owned by the Bibliothèque Nationale, was among the papers sent from Bordeaux to England in 1818 and apparently returned in 1828 (see "A General Note on the Texts"). It was first published in *Mélanges inédits*, which is the text used here and in the *OC* edition.

* * *

First Letter

You wish me to tell you, Pheres, about the prince who reigns in Sicyon.[1] I shall tell you what I know about him.

Alcmenes[2] was born with a superior genius, and yet undergoes the influence of any other genius.

He has few flaws issuing from a bad temperament; his mind has a lot to do with them, and his heart very little.

He has a certain strange taste that leads him to show himself worse than he is; the character of his mind, with respect to vices, is to seek to appear to have a few, as a sign of freedom and independence.

He has a supreme disdain for men; he believes in talents, and he does not believe in virtues.

---

1 Sicyon, a small territory between Corinth and Achaea, governed in the sixth century BCE by tyrants who ruled with moderation and justice.
2 Alcmenes (c. 740–c. 700 BCE) was the ninth king of Sparta, but here he is an allegorical stand-in for Philip, Duke of Orléans (1674–1723), regent of France from 1715.

As a result, he is wholly unaware of the infinite distance that exists between the honest and the wicked man, and all the different degrees between these two extremes.

With him, the advantage of virtue is that it does no harm.

No man has been more aware than he of the foolishness of persons, nor often more oblivious to the foolishness of things.

Made for society, he was bound to be his nation's idol, whether as a private man or as its master.

Instead of the constraint that reigned in Sicyon, Alcmenes instilled a certain ease of command and obedience such that whatever disadvantages people experienced, they still preferred to obey him.

The words he has so admirably spoken are always rejoinders, as if he had denied himself all the charming things that do not spring from the occasion and which he was not obliged to say.

He scoffs at the work of politicians; his retorts are his principles: he guesses what they are contemplating and captures in an instant everything they have pondered.

He has an indifference for events appropriate only to those whom heaven has not brought forth to determine events.[3]

He has a firm heart and a timid mind, but that timidity comes as much from his reluctance to do harm as from any weakness of soul.

He is fortunate to live at a time when obedience, so to speak, anticipates the command; for had he reigned in troubled times, the disposition of his mind was such that he would never have been daring enough and would have undertaken too much.

Not that he does not sometimes launch bold thrusts, but it takes much doing to try his clemency: then he surprises those who have offended him and those who feared seeing him offended with impunity.[4]

Alcmenes likes to forgive; you would say he finds peace in the soul of his enemies; clemency is so natural to him that he almost believes it is always up

3 Referring to the regent in *Pensées* 1656, Montesquieu cites Vergil's *Georgics*, ii, 491–492: *Atque metus omnes [omnis] et inexorabile fatum, subjecit pedibus, strepitumque Acherontis avari* ("[Blessed be he] who has cast underfoot all dread and inexorable destiny, and the wails of hungry Acheron").

4 As regent, Philip faced a revolt in Brittany against royal taxes, an exploding budget deficit, controversy over enforcement of the papal bull *Unigenitus*, the Cellemare conspiracy, a rebellious Paris Parlement, and scathing verses claiming he was planning to poison the young Louis XV and was guilty of an incestuous relation with his daughter, the duchesse de Berry (J. H. Shennan, *Philippe Duke of Orléans, regent of France, 1715–1723*, London: Thames and Hudson, 1979, pp. 135–138).

to him to feel it and to others to receive it. He is incapable of vengeance. If vengeance is difficult, he has no desire for it, and as soon as it is easy he says he has no motivation for it. Indeed, in vengeance he felt constrained, and that is when he would complain about his power.

With that sublime spirit that makes for great virtues and great crimes, Alcmenes could be an appalling man if his heart did not offset his lack of principles. But the heart so dominates him that he is unable either to refuse or to punish; falling rarely into difficulties by doing wrong, he constantly plunges into them by doing good.

He has the active tension of ambition rather than its vast desires.

Leaving men in peace, but constantly troubling their fortunes, as others ruin by impulse, he ruins people by testing them or seeking to enrich them. One gets angry with him, yet it is impossible to hate him.

Alcmenes is very capable of making mistakes; no one senses them more quickly or corrects them better. He does not use his intelligence to justify himself, but to do better, and after wandering from reason he often comes back to it, so those mistakes turn out to be fortunate, and we see the harm perish and the good reborn.

What prevents him from succeeding as well in the government inside the kingdom is that he constantly wants to go from good to best, and that he is always more struck by what is wrong than by the disadvantage involved in rectifying it.

He corrects things he should put up with, as if the people who think so slowly could change their minds in an instant and regard as abuses things which time, examples, and even reason have made them see as laws.

Sometimes abuses are the result of necessity; sometimes by letting up on a law we have made it into what the legislator should have made it, and the people who have executed have shown themselves wiser than the legislator who prescribed. In short, there are many things that it would have been good never to have created, and that it would have been desirable not to have destroyed.

I do believe that Alcmenes fears the immortal gods, but he sometimes lacks a certain respect for their ministers. When it comes to administration, his principle is that heaven has no less made religion for men than men for religion.[5]

---

5 Louis de Rouvroy, Duke of Saint-Simon (1675–1755) said Philip regarded religion "as a political invention" serving "to create fear in ordinary minds and keep peoples in submission" (*Mémoires*, Paris: Pléiade, 1985, v, p. 243).

Second Letter

Alcmenes has turned away few women, but there are very few who can boast that he has had any esteem for them.

He loved in his early years; he found a tender heart, and pleasures reserved for those who love. Later he ran from one object to another; he exhausted the sources of his passions: he tired his senses to give him back what he had lost, but was left with nothing but the letdown of pleasures.

He brought some charms to debauchery; but whatever they say, debauchery is insusceptible to refinement, and if Alcmenes ever ceased to be lovable, it was in the moments he reserved for joy, where he wanted to be pleased, and wanted to please.

Soon his mistresses were no more than witnesses to a life not free but licentious. But Alcmenes may lose his reason, and never his private thoughts.[6]

Third Letter

The gods, angry at Sicyon, sent a dream one night to Alcmenes, making him believe he was master of all the treasures on earth. This dream was the cause of public misery.[7]

Meanwhile, Themis removed her blindfold and saw that temples to Plutus[8] were going up all over Sicyon. "Mortals," she cried, "beware the god you are serving!" But she was herself driven from her temple; she ceased to speak and no longer gave her oracles.[9] In one night all of Plutus' altars were overturned; his priests fled,[10] and all who had believed in him were delivered up as prey to the four Titans.[11]

Apollo, angry at Alcmenes, aimed a thousand poisoned darts at him. Covered by a sort of shield, he laughed at this god's impotence; the darts

---

6 According to Saint-Simon, neither the regent's mistresses nor cronies who drank with him ever learned anything even slightly important regarding government and business (*ibid.*, p. 825).

7 The regent readily accepted the financial schemes devised by John Law, who served briefly in 1720 as Controller General of the Finances. Law's "System" at first generated vast sums of speculative wealth for investors in the Mississippi Company, followed by bankruptcy on 25 May 1720.

8 The Greek god of wealth.

9 Themis, wife of Zeus, here represents the Paris Parlement, exiled to Pontoise from July to December 1720 for resisting Law's program.

10 From March 1720 on, the value of the bank notes at the center of Law's system declined precipitously, causing Law to flee to Venice in December.

11 Possible allusion to the financial council of four ministers which was restored following the bankruptcy of Law's system.

that reached him were blunted and fell to the ground. "Insolent god," he said, "I shall not appease thee with presents, I shall not anger thee with my resentment; thou canst only be conjured by contempt."

A man of obscure birth was received into Alcmenes' house. At first he regarded him with scorn, and then, without passing through consideration, he obtained his trust. Proud of sharing his secrets, he made bold demands and was granted them. Soon Alcmenes, weary of command, placed the sovereign authority in his hands.[12] The ambition of this favorite son of fortune grew by a surfeit of luck, but a goddess in whom he had never really believed sent him a disease that dispelled all his plans.[13]

Fourth Letter

The king who reigned so long in Sicyon[14] had conquered the states of a neighboring prince, leaving him nothing but his capital.[15] He sent Alcmenes to besiege him; a reinforcement arrives, and the Sicyonians let it through. Alcmenes withdraws, abandons all the conquests. They could have been preserved, but everyone defends Alcmenes' honor. They agree that he had not lacked resolve and that it was not he who had conducted himself improperly.[16]

In unsuccessful operations a general is charged with all the mistakes of the army and of the court; here the court and the army take all the blame in order to absolve the general.

The late king had placed a prince of his house on a neighboring throne.[17] He had sent a great army to maintain him; he gave command of it to Alcmenes. In this whole army Alcmenes lacked success. He

12 Guillaume Dubois (1656–1723), principal minister of the regent from 1715.

13 Venus: some attributed the death of Dubois on 10 August 1723 to venereal disease: "This illness was in appearance the consequence and effect of chronic v. . .," i.e., *vérole* or syphilis (Edmond Barbier, *Chronique de la régence et du règne de Louis XV*, Paris: Charpentier, 1858, I, p. 296).

14 Louis XIV (1638–1715) was king of France from 1643, the first eight years under the regency of his mother, Anne of Austria (1601–1666).

15 By 1705 France was in control of most of northern Italy and parts of Savoy due to victories in the War of the Spanish Succession (1701–1714).

16 In 1706 Louis XIV dispatched the Duke of Orléans to Turin as the titular head of the French armies in Italy, with Marshal Ferdinand de Marsin (1656–1706) as his advisor. Prospects for victory dimmed when Prince Eugene of Savoy intervened to assist the defending forces of Victor Amadeus, Duke of Savoy. Orléans favored a bold attack, but Marsin rejected that plan; the French defeat was therefore blamed on Marsin, who was mortally wounded in the fray. Orléans was warmly received by Louis XIV on his return to France, and a year later became commander of the French army in Spain.

17 In 1700 Louis XIV succeeded in making his grandson Philip (1683–1743), Duke of Anjou, king Philip V of Spain, thereby starting the War of the Spanish Succession.

arrived three days after the victory;[18] he felt his misfortune and felt nothing else. He made it plain that the victory had been won on his watch; it was his glory to envy no one else's. He had not conquered but knew how to take advantage of the victory. Such was the magic of the love people had for him. No one was content with his own glory unless he could behold that of Alcmenes.

Fifth Letter

Alcmenes has just died.[19] That prince who never ceased planning for the future was constantly truncating his life and shortening his days.

He was stricken with a deadly illness at a time when he had none of his family with him; everyone came running, but they found him bathed in his blood and in the sorriest condition in the world.

Every Sicyonian believed that Alcmenes had in his treasuries everything he had lost. He was found to have neither gold nor silver: the vices of petty souls were not the vices of Alcmenes.

The monarch[20] who reigns today in Sicyon is a young prince who makes every Sicyonian hope for happy days. He has a delightful physiognomy, the best disposition in the world; he likes to do good, to correct evil, and finally truth pleases him.

Heaven did a great thing when it placed a prince in such a high rank that all the others have their eyes on him, that he is their example and their model, that he can, so to speak, give the tone to humankind and govern all of them by his behavior, as another governs his subjects by his laws.

For my part, I hope that, as the immortal gods sometimes elect instruments to be the scourge of the nations they wish to punish, it will turn out that they have brought this one into the world to show their love for men and that they have wished to give him as a recompense to the virtuous and justify their providence thereby.

May he give his subjects not only riches and abundance, but also the calm of the spirit that can be enjoyed only under good princes, the security of one's state, and that inner peace that is always due to honor and virtue.

18 The French armies in Spain won a substantial victory in 1707 at Almanza, but the acclaim went to Orléans's deputy, the Duke of Berwick, since Orléans himself was in Madrid on business when the fighting broke out.
19 The Duke of Orléans died at Versailles on 2 December 1723 in the embrace of his latest mistress, the duchesse de Falari.
20 Louis XV (1710–1774), king of France from 1715.

May we never see those sad reigns where innocence is no more tranquil than crime, and where everyone also of himself suffers the injustice visited on one of his fellow citizens.

On Politics

(1725)

De la politique, text by Sheila Mason (*OC* VIII, 511–522), first published in *Mélanges inédits*, originally formed the final two chapters of Montesquieu's *Treatise on Duties*. The manuscript remained in the archives at the Château de La Brède until 1818 when it was sent with other papers to England (see "A General Note on the Texts") and returned to La Brède in 1828. It is now owned by the National Assembly (MS 1638). For other texts Montesquieu had intended to include in his *Treatise on Duties*, see *Pensées* 220 and 1252–1280.

* * *

There is no point in attacking politics[21] directly by dwelling on how repug- nant it is to morality, reason, and justice: these sorts of discourse persuade everyone and influence no one. Politics will continue to exist as long as there are passions independent of the yoke of the laws. I believe it is better to adopt an indirect approach and try to make the powerful lose some of their taste for it by demonstrating how little utility it has for them. I shall further discredit politics by showing that those who have used it to acquire the greatest reputation have flagrantly abused the spirit of the people.

Most effects occur via such circuitous paths or depend on causes so imperceptible and remote that they defy prediction.[22]

Moreover, we can posit as a general maxim that every revolution that is foreseen will never happen, for if a great politician does not deal with people as clever as he is, neither is he dealing with imbeciles who see calamities about to befall them and do nothing to avert them.

Everyone will acknowledge this to be true, and if each of us will recollect past events, we will find that, in our own experience, almost all the things that were predicted have failed to take place.

---

21 *La politique* had the pejorative connotation of duplicity used to defeat one's enemies at home, or more usually abroad. Montesquieu criticizes "great politicians" (*grands politiques*) employing devious and deceptive tactics when simpler and more moral acts would have produced equally good or even better results.

22 See what I have put in *Romans*. (M)

But if on the other hand we refer to history, we will discover momentous unforeseen events everywhere we look.

When Henry VIII had destroyed in his realms the religion that recognizes a visible head,[23] he thought he had merely thrown off a yoke that weighed particularly heavily on England. Everyone thought he had increased his power by becoming head of his own church, as well as dispenser of the spoils of the old one.[24] But not so. Once minds that had formerly been constrained found themselves free, they plunged into fanaticism and frenzy. Soon they no longer respected authority and even resented the laws. A trace of the old attitude remained under Henry VIII's three children,[25] but James I[26] found only a ghost of royalty, Charles I[27] was sent to the scaffold, and I remain silent on all the misfortunes that have followed.[28]

Who could have told the Huguenots, who came with an army to lead Henry IV[29] to the throne, that their sect would be worn down by his son[30] and utterly destroyed by his grandson?[31] Their total ruin was tied to accidents they could not foresee.

Who could have told the great Gustavus[32] that he was destined for such great things? This prince who had nothing in his favor except his courage, king of a distant, impoverished nation that, emerging from slavery to the Danes, had no reputation in Europe, offered himself like a soldier of fortune to all princes, and his offers of alliance were always

---

23 I.e., by means of the English Reformation that severed ties between the Church of Rome and a newly independent Church of England.

24 Henry dissolved the convents and monasteries of England in order to sell their lands and properties. The purchasers became a new landed gentry, which was at first loyal to the crown, but in the seventeenth century supported the Parliament against Charles I.

25 Edward VI (1547–1553), Mary (1553–1558), and Elizabeth (1558–1603).

26 James I's reign (1603–1625) was marked by such extreme conflict with Parliament that between 1614 and 1621 he ruled without convening that body.

27 Charles I (1600–1649), king from 1625, was executed by vote of Parliament in 1649, following a lengthy civil war.

28 I.e., the republican experiment of the Commonwealth (1649–1653) and Protectorate (1653–1660). See *SL* iii, 3 for Montesquieu's criticisms of this period of English history.

29 Henry IV (1553–1610), king of France from 1589. His Edict of Nantes (1598) granted limited civil liberties to Calvinists in France.

30 Louis XIII (1610–1643), king of France from 1610, annexed the Protestant province of Béarn, provoking armed resistance by Huguenots, which was put down by Louis and his chief minister, Cardinal de Richelieu, in 1627. The Treaty of Alais (1629) terminated the rights of Protestants to arm strongholds.

31 Louis XIV (1643–1715), king from 1643, revoked the Edict of Nantes in 1685, thereby outlawing Protestantism in France except in Alsace, where Lutheranism was protected by the treaties of Westphalia (1648).

32 Gustavus Adolphus II (1594–1632), king of Sweden from 1611.

met with contempt.[33] No one neglected him more than Cardinal Richelieu himself until, finally, chance, urgency, and despair forced him to accept it.[34] Gustavus descended into Germany with four thousand men and the whole face of Europe was transformed.[35]

What politics could have saved Heraclius[36] and the last Persian kings[37] from the misfortunes that fate had in store for them? Natural rivals on account of their might, these rulers thought only of deceiving one another and gaining a relative advantage. Mohammed, residing in an obscure city which these kings had perhaps never heard of, takes it into his head to preach. He gathers some people together, his system catches on, and in the space of four years his successors destroy all of Heraclius' armies,[38] overthrow the Persian throne, invade every part of the world, and devour nearly the whole earth.

I confess I do not see where subtlety that is so highly praised leads princes; and if I must cite examples, I do not see what advantage the four great politicians of recent times, Louis XI,[39] Sforza,[40] Sixtus V,[41] and

---

33 At first the Lutheran princes of Germany were reluctant to ally with a Swedish king whose prospects seemed dim and whose goals were thought to include placing the lands around the Baltic Sea under Swedish control.

34 Actually, by 1630 France was eager for an alliance with Sweden, but the final bargain with Richelieu, embodied in the Treaty of Bärwalde (1631), benefited Sweden more than France. Richelieu agreed to pay the Swedes a million livres per year to maintain an army of 36,000 in Germany to oppose the Habsburgs.

35 Gustavus deployed roughly 30,000 men and 6,000 cavalry in Germany. His victory at Breitenfeld in 1631 reversed Catholic gains made between 1618 and 1629 and prevented the Habsburgs from creating a politically unified empire.

36 Heraclius (575–641 CE), facing as Eastern Roman Emperor what seemed a sure defeat by the Persians, nonetheless won a victory at Nineveh in 627, only to encounter an even more serious threat from the Muslims, since Mohammed had unified all the tribes of the Arabian Peninsula.

37 The last three kings of the Sassanid empire of Persia were Khosrow II, Kavadh II, and Yazdegerd III.

38 Although Mohammed died in 632, his armies defeated the forces of Heraclius in 636 CE, resulting in the loss of the Levant and Egypt to the Muslims.

39 Louis XI (1423–1483), king of France from 1461, became known as "Louis the Cunning" or "Louis the Universal Spider" for his intrigues, plots, and conspiracies along with ceaseless diplomatic negotiations. See also *Pensées* 1302 and *Reflections on Certain Princes*.

40 Ludovico Sforza (1452–1508) successfully plotted to make himself Duke of Milan in 1494 but in spite of treacherous diplomacy involving making and breaking alliances he was captured by Louis XII of France in 1500 and imprisoned for the last eight years of his life.

41 Sixtus V (1520–1590), pope from 1585, pursued an unrealistic foreign policy, renewing the excommunication of queen Elizabeth of England, supporting Spain's unsuccessful armada attack on England in 1588, and excommunicating Henry of Navarre of France while imposing burdensome taxes on the people of the papal states. Although he improved papal finances, he died loathed by his political subjects. For more on Sixtus, see *Reflections on the Character of Certain Princes*.

Philip II,[42] derived from their cunning. I see Louis XI ready to abandon his kingdom to seek refuge in Italy. I see him a prisoner of the Duke of Burgundy, forced to go and destroy his own allies,[43] and later, fail to gain the Burgundian succession as a result of a blunder whose consequences could never be undone.[44] I see the Duke of Milan die in prison,[45] Sixtus lose England,[46] and Philip the Netherlands,[47] both by mistakes which less gifted men would not have committed. Finally, I see the latter fail, in like manner, to destroy the French monarchy in spite of very favorable circumstances.[48] Did not Louis XIV wear Europe down as much as all the other great politicians who are on everyone's lips?[49]

Prudence actually amounts to very little. In most situations, deliberation is useless because, except where major disadvantages are immediately obvious, all the courses of action one might adopt are equally good.

Remember what we have seen during the minority of a great European prince.[50] One could say that there has never been a more unusual government and that from the first day to the last France was in the grip of

42 Philip II (1527–1598), son of Charles V and king of Spain from 1556, failed in his goals of ending the rebellion from Spanish rule in the Netherlands and conquering England by sending the Spanish Armada there in 1588.

43 Louis XI fell into a trap set by his intransigent vassal Charles Martin, Duke of Burgundy and became his prisoner, whereupon the Duke forced him to command French troops to sack and burn Liège where forces of Louis were planning to strike back at the Duke.

44 After the Duke of Burgundy was killed by Swiss forces in 1476, his sole heir was his daughter Mary who prevented the Duchy of Burgundy from reverting to the French crown as a male fief of the kingdom by marrying Maximilian I of Austria, Holy Roman Emperor and grandfather of Charles V. Her marriage greatly contributed to the Bourbon–Habsburg rivalry.

45 I.e., Ludovico Sforza.   46 For pope Sixtus V, see pp. 190–191.

47 I.e., Philip II of Spain. In his *Reflections on the Character of Certain Princes* Montesquieu attributed the loss of the northern provinces to Philip's personal shortcomings rather than to difficulties no monarch could have overcome. He judged him much inferior to the Roman emperor Tiberius, with whom he compared him. His main drawback was inflexibility, a plodding nature, and a lack of prudence. He compounded his problems by attempting to rule his vast empire from afar. See pp. 189–190.

48 Philip II, son-in-law of king Henry II of France (1547–1559), was one of several possible claimants to the French throne when king Henry III of France (1551–1589) was assassinated. The Catholic Guise faction initially favored Philip over Henry of Navarre, who was Protestant; but in 1590, and again in 1592, Philip unwisely sent Spanish troops under the command of Alexander Farnese to France; this alarmed even some of his supporters and contributed to the Estates General's decision in 1593 to confer the French crown on Henry of Navarre, who converted to Catholicism and became king Henry IV.

49 Louis XIV (1610–1715), king from 1643, kept France at war for twenty-eight of the fifty-four years of his personal rule, which began in 1661.

50 I.e., Louis XV (1710–1774), king of France from 1715. Since he was only five years old when his great-grandfather Louis XIV died in 1715, the Paris Parlement declared Philip Duke of Orléans regent in defiance of contrary provisions in Louis XIV's will.

extraordinary events;[51] that someone who had done the opposite of what was done, who for every resolution taken had chosen the contrary resolution, would all the same have finished his regency quite as felicitously as this one ended; that if fifty other princes in turn had taken up the government and conducted themselves each in his own way, they would also have completed this regency successfully; and that attitudes,[52] circumstances, situations, and respective interests were arranged in such a way that the end result would have been the same, whatever cause or power was at work.

In all societies, which are only groupings of minds, a common character, that collective soul,[53] takes on a manner of thinking which is the effect of a chain of infinite causes that multiply and combine over the course of centuries. Once the tone is set and takes root, it alone governs, and all that the sovereigns, magistrates, and peoples are able to do or contrive, whether it seems to go against that tone or follow it, is always in relation to it, and it dominates even to total destruction.

The spirit of obedience is generally widespread here. Thus princes are able to be less than elsewhere. This spirit governs for them and whatever they do the end result is always the same, whether their actions are bad, equivocal, or good.

Such was the tone under Charles I[54] that, however he acted, his power was sure to be diminished. Prudence was of no value against such agitation and widespread delirium.[55]

If this king had not offended his subjects in one way, he would have offended them in another; it was fated by the order of causes that he would be in the wrong.

If a given tone is lost or disappears, it is always the result of unusual circumstances that one cannot foresee. They depend on such remote causes that it would seem any other cause could just as well have been in play, or else it is a minor effect hidden under a great cause, which produces other major, readily apparent effects, while holding this one in abeyance to ferment, sometimes three centuries later.

---

51 I.e., the fierce battles over the bull *Unigenitus* issued by pope Clement XI in 1713, banning Jansenist theology in France; the Cellamare conspiracy of 1718, hatched in Spain and designed to make Philip V of Spain the regent of France; and the swirl of events set in motion by John Law's abortive scheme to cure France's debts by creating the Mississippi Company, the result of which was intense speculation in shares of that company and ruin for many investors when the bubble burst in 1720.

52 *Esprits.*   53 *Âme universelle.*   54 Charles I (1600–1649), king of England from 1625.

55 *Ivresse.*

One can easily conclude from all we have just said that a straightforward and natural course of action can achieve the ends of government just as well as a more devious one.

Rarely do great politicians understand men. Since they have subtle and artful viewpoints, they assume that all other men likewise have them, but it is far from the case that men are subtle; on the contrary, they almost always act out of whim or passion, or else they act simply to act so it will not be said that they are not acting.

One thing about great politicians is that their reputation hurts them. No one wants to deal with them for the simple reason that they excel in their art; thus they are deprived of all the conventions that mutual trust can lead to.

In the negotiations which France initiated after Louis XIV's minority to persuade several princes to oppose the emperor if he were to violate the treaties of Westphalia,[56] our ambassadors were under orders to deal, preferably, with the Dukes of Brunswick and to grant them more concessions than the others because of their reputation for the utmost integrity. One good thing about a swindler is that he is constantly praising candor since he wants everyone else to deal honestly with a knave like him.

Moreover, great politicians see too many things, and often it would be better to see too few than too many. They write too many clauses into the treaties they make, torturing their imagination in order to foresee every eventuality. They think that by piling on articles they will anticipate every dispute and every tension, which is absolutely ridiculous, for the more you multiply the conventions, the more you multiply opportunities for disputes.

You foresee something that could happen but will not; with this in mind, you put a clause in your treaty; one party will wish to reject it, the other party will not since it hopes to profit from the advantage it sees in it. Such a circumstance was the cause of the tension that prevailed between France and Sweden at the beginning of the reign of Louis XIV.

We see too that politicians whose affliction is wanting to be forever negotiating are not being shrewd even if they have concluded one treaty after the other, for since conditions are reciprocal, a needless treaty is always burdensome.

It is very easy for those who have made a name for themselves in diplomacy to mislead the people. Since we imagine their heads must be full of nothing but treaties, deliberations, and plans, we credit them with all

56 I.e., the treaty that ended the Thirty Years' War and greatly altered the map of Europe.

ordinary events. What, you say, this man has the whole Quadruple Alliance[57] in his head, and he jests and curses like me! How admirable!

I have often heard Cardinal de Richelieu praised[58] for the following transaction. Wishing to transmit two million livres to Germany, he fetches a German to Paris, sends the two million to the home of one of his own men, ordering him to turn it over without a receipt to an unnamed person of a certain dress and appearance. How can one fail to see in this a ridiculous affectation? How much simpler it would have been to send a valid bill of exchange without encumbering this German with such a large sum which could have exposed him to all kinds of dangers; or if Richelieu wished to deliver the money in Paris, why did he not just deliver it himself?

That minister, who paid for comedies so he could pass for a good poet,[59] and tried to steal every kind of merit, constantly fretted about how to usurp further esteem. Here is another bit of worthless bravado!

Having allowed a trusted person to remain in his office while he left to accompany someone else, the cardinal remembered that he could have read some important papers that were on his table. He immediately wrote a letter which he gave to the man to take to the governor of the Bastille, which ordered the governor to hold him for a month, after which time the matter would be no longer secret. This was done, and when the month was up, the prisoner was released and generously compensated. Pure bravado, planned and carried out complacently and even without much judgment. First of all, one does not admit several persons to an office where there are papers of such importance; prudent men write papers of that kind in code; in short, there were a thousand, less showy ways to repair this crude error: but he wanted to make waves and to be a great minister at any price.

If you read Cardinal Mazarin's letters[60] relevant to his negotiations with Don Louis de Haro,[61] you will see a great charlatan. You would think Don

---

57 The Quadruple Alliance was formed in 1718 by Britain, France, the Netherlands, and Austria to counter Spanish aggression in Sardinia and Savoy.

58 See *L'Art de régner*, by Father Lemoyne. (M) (Pierre Le Moyne, *De l'art de régner* ("On the Art of Ruling"), Paris, 1665, III, vii, 5, pp. 489–490.)

59 For performance at his own theater in his Parisian home, Le Palais Cardinal (today's Palais Royal), Richelieu commissioned plays from Jean Chapelain (1595–1674), François Boisrobert (1589–1662), Pierre Corneille (1606–1684), and Jean Desmarets (1595–1676) and did not refute the inference that he had supplied the plots for several of these plays.

60 Mazarin, *Lettres* (Amsterdam, 1693; *Catalogue* 2294). Cardinal Jules Mazarin (1602–1661) succeeded Richelieu as the chief minister of France when Richelieu died in 1642.

61 Luis Méndez de Haro, who in 1643 replaced his uncle, the Duke d'Olivarès, as chief advisor to Philip IV of Spain (1605–1665). His diplomacy resulted in very unfavorable terms for Spain in the Treaty of the Pyrenees (1659) with France.

Louis de Haro had no common sense and that the cardinal was negotiating with a monkey.

It is reported that when Louvois was planning an expedition into Flanders, he sent an intendant a packet with instructions not to open it until he was ordered to do so. The purpose was to give marching orders to troops that were widely dispersed, and the packet contained instructions for the execution of the operation by all the individuals under this intendant's command, so the intendant would only have to sign and his clerks would not reveal his secret. This is pathetic. Did not having the package lying around for a fortnight jeopardize his secret? What purpose did this serve other than to arouse curiosity? Besides, were not the minister's secretaries as likely as those of the intendant to be untrustworthy? Could the intendant's secretaries have divulged the secret of the expedition in the two hours it would have taken them to write out the orders? Taking useless precautions often shows less acumen than not taking enough.

I have heard people praise a minister[62] so vain that he preferred dictating carelessly to three secretaries rather than carefully to only one.

The same minister was so busy that he granted audience at one, two, or three in the morning. These things do not impress me. I know that the Grand Vizier,[63] who runs the political, civil, and military government of an empire 1,200 leagues wide, has spare time.

I have seen individuals pass for great men[64] because they were able to tell a young courtier where he had supped the evening before; and anyone could have found out as well as they did, if by that he would have made himself look important: all it required was a tipsy footman.[65]

In our time we have had another minister[66] who never had a single paper on his desk and who never read one. If he had succeeded in his major projects, he would have been thought of as a genius who ran the government as if by magic.

As for the merit which ministers think is theirs for keeping affairs of state secret, how could they betray it? They cannot speak without appearing conspicuously foolish. Who would be foolish enough to ask them questions? How could they be foolish enough to respond? Their vanity gives them an aura of mystery that preserves their secrets.

---

62 D'Argenson. (M) Marc René de Voyer d'Argenson (1652–1721), president of the Regency Council of Finance.
63 The Grand Vizier served as chief minister to the Sultan of the Ottoman empire.
64 Le Blanc. (M) Claude Le Blanc (1669–1728), Secretary of State for War from 1716 to 1723.
65 An allusion to the practice of tipping footmen for information on their masters.
66 Law. (M) I.e., the French economic minister John Law (1671–1729).

Thucydides said that men of middling ability were best suited to governing.[67] One should start with that.

It was the invention of the postal service that produced politics.

On Princes

The least warlike princes have been the most cunning.[68] I hold that we have lost something with princes no longer taking part in war. As a result of that, another talent has taken shape and has been put to use by each prince eager to stand out in his state. It is subtle politics[69] that consists of deceiving one another, experience having shown us that those rulers who have spent most of their time in their chambers have been the most devious because they have made their personal merit consist of subtle politics rather than openness and courage.

I find in our history two actions of particular probity: the return by Louis the Young,[70] in repudiating Eleanor, of her Duchy of Guyenne; and the return by St. Louis[71] on his own initiative of that same Duchy to England once he was convinced that he was holding it unjustly.

Although they deserve undying fame, these two actions have received very little praise.

If we have heartily praised the act of Regulus,[72] we could scarcely praise that of Francis I.[73]

... of Charles V having yielded ...

We are poor judges of things. As much politics is often employed to obtain a small benefice as to obtain the Papacy: there are as many causes that contribute and as many obstacles to be anticipated and broken through.

---

67 *History of the Peloponnesian War*, III, 37. Montesquieu signaled the importance he attached to Thucydides' observation by writing on the back of the page: "It is necessary to begin with this."

68 *Les plus politiques.*   69 *Une politique raffinée.*

70 Louis VII (1120–1180), king of France from 1137, had his marriage to Eleanor of Aquitaine annulled.

71 Louis XI (1214–1270), king of France from 1226, who signed the Treaty of Paris with Henry III of England in 1259, confirming Aquitaine as English territory, and awarding Anjou, Normandy, Poitou, Maine, and Touraine to France.

72 Marcus Atilius Regulus (c. 307–250 BCE), the Roman consul and general who, according to legend, was taken prisoner by the Carthaginians in 255 and allowed to return to Rome to negotiate peace in return for promising to return to Carthage. Once home, he advised against peace and then returned to Carthage, where he was tortured to death.

73 Francis I (1494–1547), king of France from 1515, who, after being imprisoned in Madrid after losing the Battle of Pavia to Charles V in 1525, welched on his promise in the Treaty of Madrid to declare Burgundy independent of France in return for his being set free to return to France. Cf. *Pensées* 225.

I have seen two ministers[74] at the same time make their names known throughout all Europe only to fall three months later. There is nothing easier than for a man occupying certain positions to astonish us by means of a grand scheme. But there is something false about that. It is not the means that should be brilliant but the outcome. True politics is achieving it by means unseen.

Reflections on Universal Monarchy in Europe

(1734)

Réflexions sur la monarchie universelle en Europe, text by Françoise Weil (*OC* II, 339–364). Montesquieu's original plan was to include this essay in the first edition of *Romans* (1734). Fearing the reaction of Louis XV's censors to his negative comments regarding France, however, he withdrew it from publication. No manuscript is extant; the *OC* text, which this translation follows, reproduces the text of the single printed copy of 1734 now owned by the municipal library of Bordeaux (MS 2511). It was first published in *Deux opuscules de Montesquieu* (Bordeaux and Paris: G. Gounouilhou, 1891).

* * *

I

It is legitimate to ask whether, given the present state of Europe, it might happen that one nation could acquire a lasting superiority over the others, as the Romans did.

I believe that such a thing has become all but impossible, for the following reasons.

New discoveries in war have equalized the strength of all individuals and consequently of all nations.

---

74 John Law and Giulio Alberoni. The Italian Giulio Alberoni (1664–1752) rose to substantial power and influence in the Spain of Philip V (1683–1746), becoming a duke and member of the king's council prior to appointment as cardinal by pope Clement XI in 1717. Alberoni strongly supported Spanish attempts to regain lost territory in Italy, which led to the formation, in 1718, of the Quadruple Alliance against Spain between Britain, France, the Netherlands, and the Austrians. This in turn prompted Alberoni to attempt to splinter the Anglo-French Alliance by devising the Cellamare conspiracy. After France had easily quashed that conspiracy and then invaded Spain, as did England, Alberoni was dismissed from office in 1719 and expelled from Spain.

The law of nations has changed, and because of today's laws war is conducted in such a way that it ruins first and foremost those who have the greatest advantages.

Formerly, it was the practice to destroy the cities one had taken; the lands were sold, and much worse, all the inhabitants. The sacking of a city provided pay for an army and a successful campaign enriched a conqueror. Now that such barbarities are rightly regarded with horror, states ruin themselves capturing strongholds that surrender, which one maintains, and which more often than not are abandoned.

Romans in their triumphs[75] carried to Rome all the wealth of the conquered nations. Today, victories confer only sterile laurels.

When a monarch sends an army into an enemy country, he sends with it a portion of his treasury to support it. He enriches the country he has begun to conquer and very often enables it to drive him out.

Luxury has increased and given our armies needs which they ought not to have. Nothing aided Holland more in sustaining the great wars she has waged than the commerce she has been able to conduct in provisioning her armies, those of her allies and even those of her enemies.

Today war is waged with so many men that a people constantly at war would inevitably exhaust itself.

In the past, princes sought armies in order to lead them to fight in another country. Now we seek countries where we can lead armies to fight.

II

Moreover, there are specific reasons why prosperity can nowhere be permanent in Europe and why there must be continual fluctuation in the power that, in the other three parts of the world, is more or less fixed.

At present, Europe conducts all the commerce and shipping of the whole world. Now, depending on the smaller or larger role a state takes in this shipping or commerce, its power must increase or diminish. But since it is in the nature of such things to change continually and to depend on a plethora of chance factors, especially on the wisdom of each government, it happens that a state which appears to be victorious abroad is ruining itself at home, while states that remain neutral are increasing their strength, or conquered nations are regaining theirs. And decline begins especially at the time of the

---

75 Triumphs were authorized at the discretion of the senate in recognition of military victories involving at least 5,000 enemy casualties. The victorious commander entered Rome in a chariot drawn by four horses, wearing a purple toga embroidered in gold and a laurel crown.

greatest successes that cannot be achieved or maintained except by violent means.

It is characteristic of powers based on commerce and industry that they are limited by their very prosperity. A large amount of gold and silver in a state, which causes everything to become more expensive, results in artisans being paid more for the luxuries they produce, and other nations can sell their goods at a lower price.

In former times, a poor nation might be in an advantageous position. Here is why.

Since cities used only their own citizens in their wars, the armies of rich cities were made up of men ruined by ease, idleness, and pleasures. Consequently, they were often destroyed by the armies of their neighbors who, being accustomed to a hard and demanding life, were more fit for war and for the military exercises of those times. But things are different now that soldiers, who are the basest part of every nation, are all equal with respect to luxury, military exercises no longer demand the same strength and skill as before, and it is easier to produce disciplined troops.

Often a poor people would become formidable to all the others because it was warlike, and because emerging from nowhere, it appeared suddenly at full strength to confront a nation whose strength lay only in the respect in which it was held. But now that all civilized nations are, so to speak, members of one great republic, it is wealth that creates power, there being no nation today that enjoys advantages that a richer one cannot almost always obtain.

But with wealth continually fluctuating, so, too, does power. And whatever success a conquering state may attain, there is always a certain reaction that reduces it to its former condition.

III

If we review history, we will see that it is not wars that for four hundred years have produced the great changes in Europe, but marriages, rights of succession, treaties and edicts; in short it is by civil transactions that Europe changes and has changed.

IV

Many have noted that fewer lives are lost in battle now than in the past, which is to say that wars are less decisive.

I shall offer one very extraordinary reason, which is that the infantry no longer carry any defensive weapons. In the past they had such cumbersome ones that when their army was defeated, they would immediately abandon them so they could flee;[76] that is why we read in the history books about armies fleeing and not armies retreating.

In combat, the lightly armed were delivered to slaughter by the heavily armed; in defeat, the heavily armed were exterminated by the lightly armed.

V

Plans which require considerable time to be carried out hardly ever succeed. Changes of fortune, the inconstancy of minds, the diversity of passions, constant changes in circumstances, and differences in motives give rise to all kinds of obstacles.

Monarchies in particular suffer the disadvantage of being governed sometimes with the public good in mind and sometimes in light of private interests and follow by turns the interests of favorites, ministers, and kings.

Now conquests take more time today than in the past and have become proportionately more difficult.

VI

It is clear that the situation here is more stable than in ancient times. The Spanish monarchy in the wars of Philip III[77] against France was unsuccessful in twenty-five campaigns, but Spain lost only a small piece of a remote province. The least populous people in Europe[78] at that time sustained a war against her for fifty years with neither side having the advantage, and in our own times we have seen a monarch, weakened by the cruelest possible wounds he could receive at Höchstädt, Turin, Ramillies, Barcelona, Oudenarde, and Lille,[79] shore up the continual prosperity of his enemies without his greatness being significantly diminished.

There is no parallel in antiquity to a frontier like the one Louis XIV carved out along the Flemish border where he placed three lines of fortifications to protect the most exposed part of his territories.[80]

---

76 See the whole history of Livy. (M)   77 Philip III (1578–1621), king of Spain from 1598.
78 I.e., the people of the Netherlands, who revolted against Spanish rule in 1566 and waged intermittent war with Spain until a truce was arranged in 1609. The independence of the Dutch republic was formally recognized in the treaties of Westphalia that ended the Thirty Years' War in 1648.
79 Louis XIV's armies sustained those severe defeats during the War of the Spanish Succession (1701–1714).
80 The so-called "belt of iron" was designed by Sébastian Le Prestre de Vauban (1653–1707), appointed General Commissioner of Fortifications by Louis XIV in 1688. Montesquieu owned Vauban's *Testament politique* (*Catalogue* 2442).

VII

Nowadays we are constantly imitating one another. If Prince Maurice[81] learns the art of siege, we quickly master it too. Does Coëhorn[82] change his approach? We change ours. If some people makes use of a new weapon, all the other nations are suddenly trying it. Does a state increase the size of its army, or impose a new tax? It is a warning to the others to do the same. Finally, when Louis XIV borrows from his subjects, the English and the Dutch borrow from theirs.

In Persia, it took a very long time for the court to learn that Tissaphernes[83] had rebelled. Polybius tells us that kings did not know whether the government of Rome was aristocratic or popular; and when Rome ruled the world, Pharnaces,[84] who offered his daughter to Caesar, did not know whether the Romans could have barbarians as wives or if they could have more than one.

VIII

Large empires have always been characteristic of Asia; in Europe they have never been sustainable. This is because the Asia that we know has larger plains and is divided into larger units by its mountains and seas. And since Asia is more southerly, the rivers are less swollen and thus form smaller barriers.[85]

A large empire necessarily supposes despotic authority in the one who governs; decisions must be made promptly to compensate for the distances over which they must be conveyed; fear must prevent negligence[86] on the part of the distant governor or magistrate; law must originate from a single person so that it will constantly change like the unexpected events that always multiply in a state in proportion to its size.[87]

Were that not the case,[88] such monarchies would be dismembered and the different peoples, weary of a rule they would consider alien, would begin to live under their own laws.

---

81 Prince Maurice of Nassau (1567–1625), stadtholder of Holland from 1585.
82 Menno van Coëhorn (1641–1704), known as "the Vauban of Holland" as a result of his brilliance at constructing fortifications.
83 Tissaphernes (445–395 BCE) was a Persian satrap executed for treason for treating with both sides in the Peloponnesian war.
84 Pharnaces II (c. 97–47 BCE) was the son of Mithridates VI Eupator (135–63) of Pontus. During the civil war between Caesar and Pompey he sought independence for his kingdom of Bosphorus, but was defeated by Caesar at Zera in 47 BCE.
85 There is less snow on the mountains there. (M)
86 In a vast empire there must be large armies always distant, often not completely known to the Prince. (M)
87 Included in the *Laws*. (M): see *SL* VIII, 19.
88 The example of the Spanish monarchy does not contradict what I am saying for the states of Italy and Flanders were governed by their laws and were rewarded for their

Power will therefore always be despotic in Asia because if servitude were not extreme, partition would at once result, which the nature of the country cannot allow.

In Europe natural divisions form several medium-sized states in which the rule of law is not incompatible with the preservation of the state; on the contrary such lawful rule is so conducive to preservation that without it the state sinks into decline and becomes inferior to all the others.

That is what forms, from age to age and perpetually through the centuries a spirit of liberty that makes it difficult to subjugate and subject any part to a foreign power except by laws and the benefits of commerce.

In Asia, on the contrary, there prevails a spirit of servitude that has always been there, and in all the histories of that region it is impossible to find a single action that indicates a free soul.[89]

IX

Since the destruction of the Romans in the West, there have been several occasions when Europe seemed destined to revert to control by a single hand.

X

After the French had subjugated several previously existing barbarian nations, Charlemagne founded[90] a large empire, but that action itself divided Europe up again into an endless number of sovereign units.

When the barbarians established themselves, each leader founded a kingdom, that is, a large independent fief, which had power over several others.[91] The conqueror's army was governed on the plan of the government of their country, and the conquered country on the plan of the government of their army.

The reason why they established this sort of government is that they knew of no other, and if by chance a Gothic or Germanic prince of that

---

dependency by the immense sums that the Spanish expended there, and the Indies are held fast by a particular kind of chain. (M)

89 Cf. *SL* xvii, 6.

90 This Prince subjugated part of the Empire, but he was stopped in Spain, in Italy, in the North; a portion of his own states were never completely subdued; having no sea forces, he did not extend his conquest to islands. (M) Charlemagne (742–814), king of the Franks from 768 and of the Lombards from 774, crowned Emperor of the Romans on Christmas Day 800 by pope Leo III.

91 In 843, following a three-year civil war, the Carolingian empire, ruled between 814 and 840 by Charlemagne's only surviving son, Louis the Pious (778–840), was divided into three parts by the Treaty of Verdun, each of Louis's sons (Lothair, Pepin, and Louis) receiving a portion.

day had taken it into his head to talk of arbitrary power, or supreme authority, or unlimited power, his whole army would have mocked him.[92]

Now, for the reasons we have mentioned a great empire where the prince did not have absolute authority would necessarily become divided, either because the provincial governors did not obey, or because, in order to make them better obey, it was necessary to divide the empire into several kingdoms.[93]

Such is the origin of the kingdoms of France, Italy, Germania, and Aquitaine, and of all the territorial divisions that took place in those times.

When titles and fiefs were established in perpetuity, it was impossible for the great princes to enlarge their territory through their vassals, who would come to their aid only to defend themselves and would conquer only to divide up the spoils.

XI

The Normans, having made themselves masters of the sea, penetrated inland along the river estuaries, and although they did not conquer Europe, they almost destroyed it.[94]

They were given the finest province of western France; their duke William conquered England,[95] which became the center of power of the Norman kings, and of the proud Plantagenets who followed them.

The kings of England were soon the most powerful princes of those times; they held the finest provinces in France, and their victories promised them the imminent conquest of all the others.

We must not judge the strength of the different countries of Europe in the past by what they presently possess. It was not actually the size and wealth of a kingdom which determined its power but the size of the prince's domain. The kings of England, who enjoyed very large revenues, accomplished very great things, while the kings of France, who had greater vassals, were for a long time more harassed than helped by them.

When armies made a conquest, the lands were shared between them and the overlords,[96] but the more time elapsed since the conquest, the more they had been able to despoil the kings by usurpations, gifts, and indemnities; and since the Normans were the last conquerors, king William, who retained his

---

92 Cf. *Pensées* 699.   93 Cf. *SL* VIII, 17.   94 Cf. *SL* XXXI, 10.

95 William the Conqueror (1027–1087), Duke of Normandy, was crowned king of England in Westminster Abbey on Christmas Day 1066.

96 *Chefs*.

former domain along with what he received from the new division, was the richest prince in Europe.[97]

But when we in France realized that it was more a question of wearing down the English than of conquering them, when we gave ourselves time to profit from their internal divisions, when we began to doubt the value of battles, to understand that our infantry was weak and that we would have to fight hard, we changed our fortunes as well as our tactics; and since we were always near and they always distant, they were soon confined to their island, and realizing the futility of their former ambitions they thought only of enjoying the prosperity they could always have had, but had not yet known.

XII

There was a time when it would not have been impossible for the popes to become the sole monarchs of Europe.

I avow that it was a miracle of circumstances that allowed the pontiffs, who were not even sovereigns of their city, suddenly to acquire secular as well as spiritual power and drive from Italy the Emperors both Eastern and Western.

In order to become masters of Rome they made her free, taking advantage of the war that some Eastern Emperors were waging against icons to free her from allegiance to them.[98]

Charlemagne, who had taken Lombardy, to which the Eastern Emperors had pretensions, gave sovereignty over some lands to the popes, natural enemies of those Emperors, to create a barrier against them.

It was also fortunate that the seat of the Western Empire was transferred to the Germanic kingdom and that the kingdom of Italy remained joined to it. The Emperors were soon regarded as foreigners in Italy, and the popes were able to take up that country's defense against the invasion of foreigners.

Other circumstances conspired to extend the power of the Papacy in all directions: the dread of excommunications, the weakness of the great princes, the proliferation of small ones, and the need Europe often had of being united under a single leader.

In the court there was less ignorance than anywhere else, and as their judgments were equitable, they attracted everyone to their court, like

---

97 His revenues rose to 1061 pounds sterling per day. Oderici Vitalis, Book 1. (M) Oderic Vitalis (1075–c. 1142), *Gesta Normannorum ducum* ("Deeds of the Norman Dukes").

98 In 730 the Eastern Roman Emperor Leo III (717–741) decreed that all religious icons be destroyed, and this policy alienated Western Christians, including pope Gregory III (731–741), who decreed that anyone destroying icons would be excommunicated.

Dejoces,[99] of whom we hear it said that he obtained sovereignty and empire over the Medes on account of the justice of his rule.

But the length of the schisms,[100] during which the Papacy seemed to be struggling with itself and was continually degraded by various rivals, whose only aim was staying in power, contained it where it could be limited.

XIII

Judging by the accounts[101] of certain monks who were sent by pope Innocent IV[102] in the mid-thirteenth century to the sons of Genghis Khan,[103] it was feared in those times[104] that Europe would be conquered by the Tatars. Those peoples, after conquering the Orient, had invaded Russia, Hungary, and Poland, where they had wreaked havoc.

One law of Genghis Khan ordered them to conquer the whole world. They always kept five large armies in readiness, and they engaged in sustained military expeditions of twenty-five or thirty years' duration. Sometimes they held out against a stronghold for ten or twelve years, and if they ran short of food, they eliminated some of their own men in order to feed those who remained. They always sent an advance guard of troops to kill all the men they encountered. The peoples who resisted them were put to death, and those who capitulated were enslaved. They separated out the artisans to use for their military engineering, and they made the rest into a militia that they exposed to every danger. They employed every known ruse to rid themselves of the princes and nobility of the countries they wished to subdue. In short, their system was quite well designed: they never pardoned deserters or soldiers who indulged in pillage before the enemy was totally defeated, and contrary to the usual custom of the time, their leaders concentrated on every

99 Dejoces was a priest and village judge who, according to Herodotus, was elected the first king of the Medes in the late eighth or early seventh century BCE.

100 A schism between Eastern and Western churches erupted in 1054 over the source of the Holy Spirit and whether leavened bread should be used in the eucharist. During the Great Schism (1378–1417), two popes, Gregory XII and Benedict XIII, were elected, and then a third; it ended when Martin V was elected pope at the Council of Constance in 1417.

101 See the relation of brother Jean du Plan Carpin, and the history of Genghis Khan by Pétis de la Croix. (M) I.e., Giovanni da Pian del Carpine, *Relation des voyages en Tartarie* (Paris, 1634), and François Pétis de la Croix's *Vie de Genghis Khan* ("Life of Genghis Khan") (1710).

102 Innocent IV, pope from 1243 to 1254, sent a message in 1245 via Pian del Carpine to the emperor of the Tatars imploring him to convert to Christianity and cease threatening Europe.

103 Genghis Khan (1162–1227), founder of the Mongol empire.

104 All the more so because Europe was divided into an infinite number of sovereign parts. (M)

detail of the action and never took part in the fighting. They had good defensive and offensive weapons, and they had the same speed, the same lightness, the same talent for ravaging a country and for escaping the armies that were defending it, as the present-day European Tatars have. In short, they were fearsome in an age when there were few regular armies.

But since Europe was covered with castles and fortified cities, the Tatars failed to make any significant progress; and having quarreled among themselves they were about to be exterminated[105] by the Russians. Mahomet II[106] gave them the Crimea where they were confined to ravaging their neighbors, which they still do.

XIV

After conquering the East, the Turks threatened the West, but fortunately, instead of continuing their thrust through southern Europe, where they could have imperiled it, they attacked from the north, which for them was unconquerable.

All the histories show that it is very difficult for southern nations to conquer northern ones, as especially shown by the Romans, always busy combatting them and pushing them beyond the Danube and the Rhine.[107]

The first enemy of southern nations in the north is the climate; horses cannot survive it and men, overwhelmed by suffering, can no longer envisage glorious endeavors and are preoccupied only by their own self-preservation.

Besides these general reasons, there are particular ones which prevent the Turks from being able to make conquests in the north; they drink only water, and they have customs and fasts which prevent them from holding out for long and which a cold climate cannot support.

Thus the Arabs conquered only the countries of the south.

XV

As the government of the Goths gradually became weaker, either from the inevitable corruption of all governments, or from the establishment of well-trained armies, sovereign authority imperceptibly replaced feudal authority in Europe; then, more independent princes kept all they acquired either by conquest, by thievery, or by marriage. France had the good fortune to inherit

---

105 I am speaking of those who had subjugated Capchak. (M)
106 Sultan Mahomet Fateh II (1432–1481), who conquered Constantinople in 1453.
107 Cf. *Pensées* 545.

large fiefs. Castile and Aragon united their kingdoms,[108] and the House of Austria[109] used the empire to confiscate very large provinces for its benefit.

The fortune of this house became prodigious. Charles V succeeded to Burgundy, Castile, and Aragon. He attained empire, and by a new form of greatness the known world expanded and a New World came into being under his rule.[110]

But France, which everywhere separated Charles V's territories, and which, being in the middle of Europe, was its heart not to say its head, was the center around which rallied all the princes who wanted to defend their dying liberty.

Francis I,[111] who did not have the numerous provinces which the crown has since acquired, and who was the victim of a misfortune which cost him everything, even his personal liberty,[112] nevertheless continued to be Charles's perpetual rival, and although by his own decree the laws had put limits on his power, he was not thereby weakened because arbitrary power indeed induces people to make greater, but less enduring, efforts.

XVI[113]

What most intimidated Europe was a new kind of strength that seemed to accrue to the House of Austria. She imported such a prodigious quantity of gold and silver from the newly discovered world that the amounts previously possessed seemed minute in comparison.

But what no one could have foreseen is that poverty caused her to fail almost everywhere. Philip II,[114] who succeeded Charles V, had to declare himself bankrupt, as everyone knows, and there has scarcely ever been any prince who has had to put up with more complaints, insolence, and insubordination from his chronically ill-paid troops.

From then on, the Spanish monarchy was in a continual state of decline, the reason for which was that there was an inherent physical

---

108 By the marriage in 1469 of Ferdinand II of Aragon and Isabella of Castile.

109 I.e., the Habsburgs, Holy Roman Emperors from 1438 to 1740.

110 Charles V (1500–1558), grandson of Ferdinand and Isabella, was elected Holy Roman Emperor in 1519 and inherited rule over Spain and the Spanish empire, including the Netherlands, Austria, the Duchy of Burgundy, and South American territories. See also *SL* xxi, 21.

111 Francis I (1494–1547), king of France from 1515.

112 The armies of Charles V captured Francis at Pavia in Italy in 1525 and imprisoned him in Madrid. He was able to secure his release only by signing the Treaty of Madrid ceding significant French territory to Charles.

113 Much of the content of Article xvi is also present in *Considerations on the Wealth of Spain*; see also *SL* xxi, 22.

114 Philip II (1527–1598), king of Spain from 1556.

defect in the nature of its riches, which made them futile, and which increased by the day.

Everyone knows that gold and silver are only a fictional or symbolic wealth. Since these signs are very durable and are little eroded by use, as befits their nature, the more common they become, the more they fall in value, because they represent fewer things.

The misfortune of the Spanish was that, because they conquered Mexico and Peru, they left aside their natural wealth in order to obtain this symbolic wealth that loses its value. At the time of the conquest, gold and silver were very rare in Europe, and Spain, suddenly the possessor of a very great quantity of these metals, developed ambitions that she had never had before. The riches that were found in the conquered countries, however, were not proportional to those of her mines. The Indians hid some of it; moreover, since these peoples made use of gold and silver only to enhance the magnificence of the temples of the gods and the palaces of kings, they did not seek precious metals with the same lust that we do. Finally, they did not know the technique of extracting metal from all the mines, but only from those where the separation is made by fire, not knowing the use of mercury and perhaps unfamiliar with mercury itself.

Meanwhile, there was soon double the quantity of silver in Europe, which was evident in that the price of everything on the market was just about doubled.

The Spanish scoured the mines, hollowed out the mountains, and invented machines to extract water, crush the ore and extract the metal; and since they cared nothing for the lives of the Indians, they forced them to work pitilessly; silver soon doubled again in Europe, and the profit was again lower by half for Spain, which each year had only the same quantity of a metal that had become less precious by half.

In twice the time silver doubled again, and the profit again shrank by half.

It even shrank by more than half. Here is why.

To extract the gold from the mines, process it as needed, and ship it to Europe, required a given outlay. I will assume it was as 1 to 64; when the silver had once doubled, and consequently was half as precious, the expense was as 2 to 64. Thus the fleets that bore the same quantity of gold to Spain bore something which in reality was worth one-half less, and cost one-half more.

If we follow the matter from one doubling to the next, we will find the progression of the cause of the powerlessness of the wealth of Spain.

The mines of the Indies have been worked for about two hundred years. I will assume that the quantity of silver presently in the commercial world, compared to the quantity there was before the discovery, is 32 to 1; in other words, it has doubled five times. In two hundred years, the same quantity again will be, compared to what there was before the discovery, as 64 is to 1; in other words, it will again double. Now at present fifty[115] hundredweight of gold ore yield four, five, or six ounces of gold, and when there are only two, the miner recovers only his costs. In two hundred years, when there are only four ounces, the miner will again recover only his costs. Thus there will be little profit to be made on gold.

Were one to discover mines so rich that they yield more profit, the richer they are, the sooner the profit will cease.

It will perhaps be argued that the mines of Germany and Hungary, the revenues of which little exceed the costs, are still very useful in that, being situated in the countries themselves, they employ several thousand men who consume agricultural surplus and are thus a kind of national manufactory.

The difference is that working the mines of Germany and Hungary stimulates agriculture, whereas working those run by the Spanish destroys it.

The Indies and Spain are two powers under a single master but the Indies are the principal one, and Spain is only the accessory. It is in vain that politics tries to reinstate the principal one as the accessory: the Indies still draw Spain to themselves.

Of fifty million in merchandise that goes every year to the Indies, Spain furnishes only two and a half million; the Indies are thus doing a trade of fifty million, and Spain two and a half million.

Wealth that is an accidental tribute and owes nothing to a nation's industry, to the number of its inhabitants, or to its agriculture, is a bad kind of wealth. The king of Spain, who receives large sums from his customs house in Cadiz, is in this respect just a very rich individual in a very poor state.

Everything takes place between foreigners and him with his subjects playing hardly any role at all and is independent of his kingdom's good or ill fortune.

And if a few provinces in Castile gave him a sum like that of the customs house in Cadiz, his power would be much greater; his wealth could only result from the country's wealth; these provinces would drive all the others, and all together they would be in a better position to sustain their respective burdens.

The king of Spain has only a great treasury, but he would have a great people.

---

115 See the Voyages of Frézier. (M) Amédée François Frézier, *Relation du voyage de la mer du Sud* ("Relation of the voyage to the Southern Sea") (Paris, 1714) (*Catalogue* 2742).

XVII

The enemies of a great prince[116] who reigned in our day have accused him a thousand times, based rather on their fears than on their reasoning, of having fashioned and implemented the project of universal monarchy. If he had succeeded in that, nothing would have been more fatal to Europe, to his former subjects, to himself, and to his family. Heaven, which knows what is truly advantageous, better served him through his defeats than it would have done through victories, and instead of making him the sole king of Europe, favored him more by making him the most powerful king of all.[117]

Even if he had won the famous battle where he received his first setback,[118] far from the project being completed, it would barely have begun;[119] he would have had to stretch his forces and his frontiers even further. Germany, which was hardly taking part in the war except by supplying mercenaries, would have entered the fray on its own; the North would have risen up; all the neutral powers would have taken sides, and his allies could have perceived their interests differently.

The character of the French is such that when they are in a foreign country, they think only of what they have left behind; when they leave France on a military expedition, they see glory as the ultimate good and, when they are abroad, they see it as an obstacle to their returning home; they become hated abroad as a result of their good qualities, because these qualities are always accompanied by scorn; they can brave danger and wounds, but they cannot face losing their pleasures; they know how to achieve military success but not how to profit from it; when they are defeated, they abandon everything rather than losing only what they have to lose; they always do very well half of what is necessary, and they sometimes do the other half very badly; they are incorrigibly light-hearted and forget they have lost a battle as soon as they have extolled the general. In short they would never have pursued the conquest of Europe to its end, because if such an enterprise fails in one place, it will fail everywhere, or if it fails at one time, it will fail forever.

XVIII

Europe has become just one nation composed of many; France and England need the opulence of Poland and Muscovy, just as each of their provinces

116 Louis XIV.   117 Cf. *SL* IX, 7.
118 Höchstädt (1704), known in England as the Battle of Blenheim.   119 Cf. *Pensées* 562.

needs the others;[120] and a state that imagines it increases its power by ruining its neighbor, as a rule, weakens itself along with them.

XIX[121]

The true strength of a prince does not lie in his ability to conquer, but in the difficulty of attacking him and, if I dare put it this way, in the immutability of his position; but the enlargement of monarchies only serves to make them reveal new sides by which they may be taken. Look, for instance, at the neighbors Muscovy has just given herself: Persia, China,[122] and Japan. She has made herself the boundary of these empires whereas she used to be happily separated from them by vast open spaces. And so it has occurred since these new conquests that the ordinary revenues[123] of the state have no longer been able to sustain it.

XX[124]

If a state is to be at full strength, its size must be such that there is a relation between the speed with which some undertaking can be launched against it and the haste it can summon to repel it. Since the invader may initially appear anywhere, the defender must likewise be able to position itself anywhere, and consequently the state must be of moderate extent so that it will be commensurate to the degree of speed nature has given men for moving from one place to another.

France and Spain are exactly the requisite size. Their forces interact so well that they quickly move to where they are needed; the armies join their forces and move swiftly from one border to another and they fear none of the things that require more than a few days to carry out.

France by wonderful good fortune has her capital closer to certain frontiers than to others, exactly in proportion to their vulnerability, and the prince is better able to maintain vigilance over each part of the country to the extent it is most exposed.

XXI[125]

But when a vast state, such as Persia, is attacked, it takes several months for the scattered troops to assemble, and a forced march such as would be workable over a week's time would be unthinkable. If the army that is on the border is defeated, it is inevitably dispersed because its redoubts are not close at hand; the

---

120 Cf. *Pensées* 318.　121 Cf. *SL* IX, 6.　122 She had already made China her neighbor. (M)
123 Among other taxes, one has just been established for one-eighth of all the empire's assets. (M)
124 Cf. *SL* IX, 6.　125 Cf. *SL* IX, 6.

conquering army, finding no resistance, advances in long days' marches, shows up before the capital and lays siege to it, almost before the governors of the provinces can be alerted to send relief. Those who judge the revolution imminent hasten it by failing to obey, for men who are loyal only because punishment is at hand are no longer loyal when it is distant; they work to advance their own private interests; the empire dissolves, the capital is taken, and the conqueror fights with the governors for control of the provinces.

XXII

China also is a vast country and like her is densely populated; if the rice harvest fails, gangs of three, four, or five bandits form in many places in different provinces in order to pillage. Most of them are exterminated in short order; others gain adherents and are still destroyed. But, with such a large number of provinces so distant from one another, it can happen that some gang will achieve success, survive, gain strength, turn into a proper army, and make straight for the capital where its leader claims the throne.[126]

XXIII

In Louis XIV's last war,[127] when our armies and those of our enemies were in Spain, far from their own country, some things nearly occurred which are almost unheard of in Europe, namely that the two generals in concert were on the point of out-maneuvering all the monarchs of Europe and stunning them by their sheer audacity and the singularity of their undertakings.[128]

XXIV

If great conquests are so difficult, so useless, so futile, and so dangerous, how should one speak of this malady of our times which makes every state maintain an inordinate number[129] of troops? The disease worsens and necessarily becomes contagious since, as soon as one state increases what it calls its strength, the others immediately increase theirs, so that nothing is gained thereby except the common ruin. Each monarch keeps in a state of readiness all the armies he might need if his peoples were threatened with

126 Cf. *SL* VIII, 21.   127 The War of the Spanish Succession (1701–1714).

128 The French general, Louis Joseph de Bourbon, Duke of Vendôme (1654–1712), nearly came to an agreement with the Austrian general Guido Wald Rüdiger, count of Starhemberg (1657–1737), named Supreme Commander of the Austrians in Spain in 1708, to restore Philip V to the throne of Spain, later achieved in the Treaty of Utrecht (1713).

129 We are in a very different situation from that of the Romans who were disarming others to the extent that they were arming themselves. (M)

extermination, and we call peace[130] this straining of all against all. Thus Europe is ruined to such an extent that if three private individuals were in the same situation as the three wealthiest powers in this part of the world, they would have nothing to live on. We are poor with the wealth and trade of the whole world, and soon, by dint of having so many soldiers, we will have nothing but soldiers and will be like the Tatars.[131]

The great princes, not satisfied with buying the troops of the less powerful ones, seek to purchase alliances wherever they can; in other words they almost always squander their money.

The result of such a situation is that taxes are constantly being increased, and what rules out all future remedies is that states no longer rely on their revenues, but wage war with their capital. It is not unheard of for states to mortgage themselves even in times of peace, employing emergency measures that ruin them, measures so extreme that even the most prodigal son would scarcely be able to imagine them for himself.

XXV

Oriental monarchs are remarkable in that they raise nowadays only the same taxes as the founder of their monarchy used to raise. They make their peoples pay only what their fathers have told their children they themselves have paid. Since they enjoy a great surplus, many of them issue[132] edicts only to exempt one province of their empire each year from paying taxes. Their will is usually manifested through acts of generosity, but in Europe the princes' edicts are usually considered grievous even before we have seen them because they always refer to their needs and never to our own.

Oriental monarchs[133] are rich because their expenditures never increase, and they never increase because they never do anything new, or if they do, they prepare their plans well in advance: admirable slow planning that leads to prompt execution. Thus the pain passes quickly, and the benefit remains for a long time. They believe they have done quite well by preserving what was done before; they spend on projects whose end is in sight, and nothing on projects just begun. In

---

130 It is true that it is this condition of exertion which principally maintains the equilibrium because it exhausts the great powers. (M)

131 All it will take to get there is to put enough emphasis on the newly invented militias and take them to the same excess as we have the standing armies. (M)

132 That is the custom of the emperors of China. (M)

133 It is not my purpose in all this to praise the government of Asian peoples, but their climate; I even concede that they go to the opposite extreme, which is an unpardonable lack of concern. (M)

brief, those who govern the state do not torment it because they do not torment themselves.

It is clear from what I have just said that I am not talking about any particular European government; these remarks are applicable to all.

Iliacos intra muros peccatur et extra.[134]

Reflections on the Character of Certain Princes and on Certain Events in their Lives

(c. 1731–1733)

Réflexions sur le caractère de quelques princes et sur quelques événements de leur vie, text by Sheila Mason (*OC* IX, 51–65). The complete text of this treatise was first published in *Mélanges inédits* (1892). The manuscript, in Montesquieu's hand, was last sold at auction in Paris in 1957. Its whereabouts is now unknown. Section II of the treatise comparing Tiberius and Louis was published in the journal *La Gironde* in 1833 and then in the Ravenel edition of Montesquieu's *Œuvres complètes* (Paris, 1834).

* * *

I

It would be difficult to find in history two princes more alike than Charles XII, king of Sweden,[135] and Charles the last Duke of Burgundy.[136] They had the same courage, the same abilities, the same ambition, the same boldness, the same achievements, the same misfortunes, and the same end. They made themselves famous at an age when other princes are immersed in pleasures. Charles XII attempted to dethrone King Augustus,[137] just as Charles of Burgundy wished to diminish Louis XI,[138] and at the height of their glory the first lost his army in the siege of Poltava,[139] and the second lost his at Morat.[140]

---

134 "There are mistakes within the walls of Ilion and without" (Horace, *Epistles*, I, 2, 16).
135 Charles XII (1682–1718), king from 1697.
136 Charles Martin (1433–1477), known as Charles the Bold, was Duke of Burgundy from 1466.
137 Augustus II (1670–1733), Polish king dethroned by Charles XII in 1704 and restored in 1709 by Peter the Great of Russia.
138 Louis XI (1423–1483), king of France from 1461.
139 Charles XII's defeat at Poltava in 1709 by the combined forces of Denmark, Norway, Saxony, Poland, Lithuania, and Russia, ended the Great Northern War and presaged the collapse of the Swedish empire.
140 At the Battle of Morat on 22 June 1476, Charles the Bold, facing Swiss and Lorraine forces, lost a third of his army and ceased to pose a threat to Louis XI.

These princes were also similar in that they continually rebelled against their destiny; they became less wise when they became less fortunate. They did not lack prudence when it was useful to them, but they lost it entirely when it became essential.

They are alike in that the more they experienced new defeats, the more they sought out new enemies; they continued to undertake new things after a defeat as they would after a victory. In most cases when princes are killed on the battlefield, it is a result of chance; the conduct of these two was such that for them death became a necessity.

Reading the lives of these two princes, one is more deeply affected by the misfortunes of the Duke of Burgundy. The reason is that he is an original character, whereas Charles XII is a poor copy of Alexander.[141]

II

Tiberius[142] and Louis XI chose self-exile before attaining supreme power.[143] They were both brave in battle but indecisive in private life. They gloried in the art of dissimulation. They established arbitrary power.[144] They spent their lives in turmoil and remorse and their last years isolated, silent, and generally hated.

But looking closely at these two princes, one realizes at once how superior one was to the other. Tiberius sought to govern men; Louis sought only to deceive them. Tiberius only allowed his vices to show to the extent he could do so without danger; Louis was never master of his. Tiberius knew how to feign virtue when he needed to appear virtuous; Louis discredited himself from the first day of his reign.

In short, Louis was cunning; Tiberius had depth. Anyone could, with some acumen, counter Louis's artifices; the Roman was able to cloud everyone's judgment and eluded discovery when he was beginning to be found out.

---

141 Alexander III of Macedonia (356–323 BCE), known as Alexander the Great.
142 Tiberius Claudius Nero (42 BCE–37 CE), Roman emperor from 14 CE.
143 In 6 BCE Tiberius withdrew to Rhodes, uncertain whether his father-in-law, Augustus Caesar (63 BCE–14 CE), would name him as his successor. In 1445 Louis XI of France (1423–1483) went into exile in Dauphiné following a failed conspiracy against his father, king Charles VII (1403–1461).
144 For Tiberius as tyrant, see *Romans*, chapter 14; for Louis XI's tyranny, see *Pensées* 373 and 1302. Montesquieu owned three copies of Philip of Commines's *Memoirs* chronicling the reign of Louis XI (*Catalogue* 2920–2922); he composed a history of Louis XI that one of his secretaries mistakenly destroyed in 1739 or 1740: see Henri Barckhausen, "L'Histoire de Louis XI," *Revue Philomathique de Bordeaux et du Sud-Ouest* (1897–1898), 569–578.

Louis, whose art consisted only of false endearment and trifling flatteries, won over men through their own weakness, the Roman by means of his superior genius and an invincible force that captured them.

Louis was skilled at compensating for his acts of imprudence, and the Roman committed none.

When he could, Tiberius always left things as they were; Louis changed everything with a restlessness and insouciance bordering on folly.

III

Philip II[145] also seems to me to have been much inferior to Tiberius. He came to public life armed with forbearance, resolve, philosophy, and ambition. His desires were boundless as if he worshiped Fortune, and he showed moderation in setbacks as if he scorned her. But his faults and good qualities were mingled in such a way that he could scarcely achieve much,[146] and it is as a result of such different mixtures, sometimes well-matched and sometimes not, that some who seem born to achieve great things do not, while others, who seem destined to mediocrity, achieve great things.

Philip knew no other ties than those of empire and obedience. Ever a king and never a man, ever on his throne or in his council chambers, his dissimulation, which he was unable to hide, was of little use to him, but his relentlessness was a liability. For since it prevented him from seeking compromises, he displayed the same cast of mind in all the events in his life and never yielded to circumstances.

Mistakes became permanent because of his inflexibility. Always taking justice to excess, he never allowed crime to be expiated. He pursued punishment as others seek repentance, never moved by tears, yielding to pleas, or cowed by despair.

He was plodding, and not prudent; he was a master of dissimulation who had no understanding of events; he had the appearance of wisdom itself, with a misapprehension that infected all his resolutions.

His plan of taking the Inquisition to the Low Countries[147] and establishing Spanish government there, shows that he understood neither the Flemish, nor free peoples, nor even men. These provinces, which were so far from

---

145 Son of Charles V (1500–1558), king of Spain from 1556 until 1598.

146 As the result of a revolt that began in 1566, Philip lost most of the Netherlands. Later, he suffered defeat in sending the Spanish Armada against England (1588) and failed in his attempt to have his daughter, Isabella Clara Eugenia, progeny of his marriage in 1559 to Elisabeth of Valois, crowned queen of France.

147 Charles V had already set up a kind of Inquisition there. (M)

Spain and so unlike her, and which had such a wide choice of political masters, could be preserved only by the power of the laws.[148]

He engaged in many great enterprises, but he never knew how to position himself to bring them to fruition. From his council chambers he viewed Europe, his provinces, and his armies and always misperceived them, spending his whole life calculating from afar and summarily events that the slightest circumstance could cause to miscarry.[149]

He obtained no advantage from the French civil wars. He wasted his fortune on them, and in the confusion of that monarchy he chose of all schemes the one which met with the most obstacles,[150] which was most opposed to the spirit of the nation, and which rallied all hearts to the legitimate prince.

Unaware of the true measure of his power, he attacked France, England, and the Low Countries simultaneously. But he overcame neither Henry IV's courage, nor Elizabeth's prudence, nor the desperation of the rebellious provinces.

Thus he deserved no praise either as a peace-loving prince or as a warrior prince. He weakened his armies and left to his children the same territory, but not the same monarchy.

IV

Paul III[151] and Sixtus V[152] were both great men, but just as art is inferior to nature, so is Sixtus inferior to Paul III. One sees throughout the life of the first a certain effortlessness; one finds affectation in all the actions of the other.

Sixtus V took more pains to appear a great man than genuinely to be one, and he positioned himself less in the world than in the theater of the world.

To correct the common opinion of his low birth, he tried to impress with his loftiness. In this respect he was more like Boniface VIII[153] than like any of his predecessors. And as if Fortune, which could have done so much for him

---

148 Cf. *SL* viii, 18.

149 Philip departed the Netherlands in 1559 and remained for the rest of his life in Spain, ruling his vast empire by means of dispatches sent from his small office inside his sprawling palace in Madrid.

150 Of giving the crown to the Infanta and marrying her to a French prince. (M) See *Pensées* 617 for criticism of this plan.

151 Cardinal Alessandro Farnese (1468–1549) was elected pope Paul III in 1534. He approved the new Jesuit order in 1540, convened the Council of Trent in 1545, reestablished the Inquisition, and encouraged Francis I, king of France, to combine forces with Charles V, Holy Roman Emperor, to suppress Protestantism in France.

152 Cardinal Felix Peretti (1521–1590) was elected pope Sixtus V in 1585. He was one of the sternest and most bellicose popes of the Catholic Reformation. He reduced the dominant power of nobles in the Papal States and vigorously prosecuted adultery, prostitution, theft, and also more minor moral transgressions.

153 Cardinal Benedetto Caetani (1235–1303), elected pope Boniface VIII in 1294. His authority was challenged by all the monarchs in Europe, especially Philip IV (1268–1314) of

by giving him much less, had still not done enough, he was ambitious in the loftiest place in the Church, and he dared to manifest arrogance in his dealings with the Spanish.[154]

Whatever may have been said about his extreme harshness toward others, it can be excused insofar as it was always based on a strict sense of justice. Moreover, he was the first to destroy the temporal power of the Papacy by opening the door to loans,[155] which was bound to have disastrous consequences in a government which, though not hereditary, is nevertheless monarchical.

Paul III, who had natural but incisive intelligence, a resourceful genius, sound ideas and a great understanding of men, was the restorer of the Papacy, which he maintained but, we can say, just barely. In his dealings he displayed neither vanity, nor ill temper, nor prejudice, nor bias; he took advantage of every event, and everything that could be favorable to him remained so.

Nor did this decrepit old man have the defects natural to his years: he was neither slow, timid, suspicious, nor irresolute; and while he was cautious, he was no less wise.

He found himself in an intractable situation. There was as yet no wall separating Catholics and Protestants; and so the latter, skillfully adopting the language of the former and asking only for a council and the reform of certain abuses,[156] made it seem that it was solely the interests of Rome that were causing divisions among men.

Lutheranism was especially damaging in that the common people, seeing more or less the same form of worship, believed they had hardly changed at all and scarcely felt the infinite distance between one religion and the other; thus a ruler who styled himself a Catholic or one who styled himself a Protestant was quickly followed by his subjects; and as there were Protestants everywhere, everyone was constantly on the brink of seeing moderate princes abandon Rome for the sake of peace, and rapacious princes get their hands on the Church's wealth.

France, after he issued the bull *Unam sanctam* declaring the supremacy of spiritual over temporal power.

154 See also *Pensées* 179 and 623 for other appraisals of the actions of Sixtus as pope based on a French translation of Gregorio Leti's *Sixte Quint pape* (Paris, 1699; *Catalogue* 265).

155 Sixtus's sale of church offices and loaning money at interest were discussed in Leti, *Sixte Quint*, pp. 218, 221.

156 The requested meeting became the Augsburg Diet (1530), which adopted the Augsburg Confession, largely written by Philip Melanchthon, asserting that Lutherans "dissent in no article of faith from the Catholic Church" while nonetheless condemning several of its institutional aspects.

Moreover, Charles V's only well-known quality was great ambition, and it was certain that he would never protect religion until it was in his interest to do so.

But the Papal States were causing further problems, for while Charles supported the spiritual authority, he was always ready to invade the temporal.[157]

It was necessary to enlist Francis I[158] in the defense of the pope against Charles, and Charles in the defense of the Church against the Protestants. In short, Paul III was constantly obliged to change his tactics with princes who were constantly changing, and to abandon all his former plans at a time when all the states of Europe had acquired new interests.

He elevated all the worthy men he could find to positions of power and made them participate in the common defense.

He agreed to a Council[159] that his predecessors had so feared, so often promised and so often refused; and without being disturbed by what had happened at Constance[160] and Basel,[161] he saw that he confronted different circumstances; that his quarrel was that of the whole clergy; that, at a time when the general spirit was for corrections, he had to anticipate lay assemblies and thereby preserve the right to decide on dogma and introduce reforms.

He considered that since most rulers had lost their respect for the Papacy, that is to say for an authority that is defended only by respect, he needed to make himself someone to contend with by establishing an army and in that way facilitate negotiations.

He paid close attention to the different effects of the general ferment in Europe, benefited from some and made light of others, and was always the first to sense what could harm or help him.

When Charles V had taken the ill-advised step of settling the religious disputes himself,[162] the pope, who knew that in these sorts of affairs there can

---

157 In May 1527 Charles's troops, having defeated the combined forces of France, Milan, Venice, Florence, and the Papacy, sacked Rome, murdering thousands and taking pope Clement VII (1478–1534) prisoner.

158 Francis I (1494–1547), king of France from 1515.

159 Paul's predecessor, pope Clement VII (1523–1534), fearing conciliarism, opposed calling a general council of the Church. Paul convened a council in Trent, which met three times between 1545 and 1563 and clarified Catholic doctrine while also announcing clerical reforms.

160 The Council of Constance (1414–1418) issued the decree *Haec sancta synodus* asserting the superiority of general Church councils to popes.

161 The Council of Basel (1431) condemned Jan Hus for heresy and reaffirmed the conciliar decree issued by the Council of Constance.

162 Charles convened a diet at Augsburg in 1548 which allowed clerical marriage and communion in both kinds (bread and wine), confirmed transubstantiation, and rejected justification by faith alone. Protestant princes rejected it as too Catholic, and Catholic princes resented Charles's interference in their affairs.

be no conciliation and that all the parties are extreme, could only mock the ineptitude of this prince, who was about to attract the enmity of Protestants and Catholics, and he was never more in control of religious matters than when the Emperor thought he was going to keep him out of them.

Charles, whose business was intertwined with that of the whole world of his time, often failed him, and he never showed resentment; that could indeed alter his interests, but never his conduct.

Finally, he died after raising up the pontificate and making for his family, in such difficult times, one of the greatest establishments any pope has ever managed to build.[163]

V

The Duke of Mayenne[164] and Cromwell[165] seem to have found themselves in the same circumstances, but politics would have the first become king, and not the second.

The execution of Charles[166] had been an attack on royalty; the murder of Henry[167] was an attack only on the king. The goal of the English faction was to abolish the title; the goal of the French faction was to secure it for a Catholic family. Had he assumed the kingship, Cromwell would have destroyed the spirit of his faction; the Duke of Mayenne, by taking the crown, would have reinforced the spirit of his own.

The Duke of Mayenne made irreparable mistakes. He placed the interim crown on the head of the elderly Cardinal de Bourbon,[168] and in doing so he rallied the loyalty of the nation to the house of its kings. He soon had the Sixteen[169] hanged for their excesses and thereby destroyed the last vestiges of the spirit which stirred his party. Cromwell indeed killed with his own hand some of his followers who refused to obey him, but he avoided punishing

163 The duchies of Parma and Piacenza. (M)
164 Charles of Lorraine (1554–1611), leader of the Catholic League after the murder in 1588 of his two brothers.
165 Oliver Cromwell (1599–1658), leader of the Parliamentary forces during the English Civil War and Lord Protector of England from 1653. In *Pensées* 372 Montesquieu terms Cromwell a "tyrant" who established a military government in England.
166 Charles I (1600–1649), king of England from 1625.
167 Henry III (1551–1589), king of France from 1574.
168 Cardinal Charles de Bourbon (1523–1590).
169 The Sixteen were the municipal governors of Paris representing the sixteen quarters of Paris. They were ultra Catholics and supported making the daughter of Philip II of Spain queen of France. Initially, Mayenne favored that plan, but he changed his mind and supported Henry of Navarre's claim to the throne.

them for their fury against the opposing party. He sometimes used violent means to make his men go from one folly to another; but the Duke of Mayenne used them to impose some moderation on his party, that is, to cause its undoing.

Although two more different souls cannot be found than Cromwell and Caesar, yet it cannot be said that the Englishman was inferior in genius to the Roman.

Great men have a way to achieve their goals; Cromwell got there any way he could. The chain linking other men's designs can, with proper insight, be discovered, but this was not possible with him. He went from one contradiction to the next, but he was always going forward, like those pilots whom almost any wind ushers to port. He governed the English as if he was the only one who possessed a soul. He took no one into his confidence; he fooled everyone, and such was the success of his designs that even his accomplices were horrified by them.

The last crime that propelled him, like those celebrated in fables, seemed at first to horrify everything in Nature.[170] But he coolly took over the government, spread horror everywhere, made hatred give way to respect, and compelled even the proudest monarchs to reward the offense and become his allies.[171]

VI

Henry III, king of France, and Charles I, king of England, were weak and superstitious princes, always awkward in their personal dealings, full of bias in their animosities and their friendships, equally prepared to undertake and to concede anything, always timid or bold at the wrong moment, taking some care that their courtiers should love them, none to make themselves pleasing to their subjects.

There are circumstances where men of the least ability can govern well enough; there are others where the greatest minds are taken aback; the art of ruling is sometimes the easiest art in the world, and sometimes the most difficult.

In a prospering monarchy, a prince can afford to be despised since the strength of the government abets the weakness of the one who governs. But when a state is declining, only respect for the person of the prince can abet the

---

170 I.e., the execution of Charles I in 1649.
171 Sweden and France signed treaties with England in 1654 and 1657.

weakness of the laws, and in that case his imperfections and vices are the true scourges of the state.[172]

The hatred felt for the person of Charles turned in time into contempt. Contrariwise, contempt for the person of Henry gradually turned into hatred. And this is quite remarkable, because neither ruler had enough great qualities to deserve being hated.

Charles's private life was admirable, and the most austere critic could have found no grounds in him for reproach. Henry had vices which even a private citizen, who can hope to keep them secret, could not possess without shame.[173]

But Charles was by nature so incompetent to govern that there is no one like him in all the histories, not even Henry III's.

Some foolish acts are such that even a more foolish one would be preferable.

Louis XIII is an example of this: one degree less of weakness would have made this prince the plaything of events because he would have governed by himself; one degree more of weakness rendered him more powerful than all his predecessors because he continued to be dominated by a minister whose powerful genius devoured Europe.[174] It is true that he attained no more glory than the Tatar emperor who conquered China at the age of six.[175]

Henry III encountered a France long torn by civil wars. Charles provoked them in England: he forced the English to quarrel with him over everything, as it were; and if several circumstances that he could not have wished for had not positioned him to wage war,[176] an extraordinary spectacle would have resulted: a great monarch struck down in an instant by civil power alone without any conspiracy against him, without bloodshed, and without battle.

---

172 Cf. *Pensées* 955.
173 Henry III (ruled 1574–1589), reputedly homosexual, surrounded himself with effeminate favorites (*les mignons*); he wore rouge and also kid gloves to bed to keep his hands white. For other mentions of Henry III's sexuality, see *Pensées* 614, 1272, and 1340.
174 Cardinal Richelieu (1585–1642).
175 Xun-Chi (Shunzu; 1638–1661) who became Chinese emperor at the age of five in 1644. Montesquieu's source was P. Martino Martini, *Histoire de la guerre des Tartares* [. . .] *depuis quarante ans* (Lyon, 1667) (*Catalogue* 3155).
176 After an Irish uprising in October 1641, Oliver St John introduced a militia bill in the House of Commons authorizing the raising of armed forces. Since the bill gave Parliament rather than the king power to appoint land and sea commanders, Charles refused to sign it, and the Long Parliament issued it in March 1642 as an ordinance. This conflict over military appointments produced, on 15 July 1642, the first casualty of what became the Civil War.

VII

Since Henry III was the victim of his vices, I will say a bit more about this prince and about the sort of spirit that prevailed in his court and the state of his nation at the time.

He was weakened by the two factors most able to doom men: lethargy[177] and superstition.

A vice which is unfortunately unknown only in barbarous nations was carried at his court to the point of rampant licentiousness.

The ladies, who had played such an important role in the courts of Francis I and Henry II,[178] and in the different regencies of queen Catherine,[179] did not fail to decry this reign; and since they set the tone and were all-powerful in a party of which the young and the devout were the soul, they outwitted him in ways one would not have expected from their sex and did even more than the preachers to excite the League.[180]

The king, furious enough to hate them, did his best to discredit them. He revealed their amorous intrigues, and, worse still, certain hidden lapses that modesty hides even after one has lost it. Informed by his minions of all these details, he thought of nothing but this sort of talk, which is fine only when it is of no import and which one never excuses even for people with time to waste.

As the Queen of Navarre[181] had made withering jokes about the debauchery of the court, the king had held back nothing having to do with her liaisons, and each thus found endless opportunities for taking revenge.[182]

The duchesse de Montpensier,[183] outraged by the revelation of a secret, personally instructed Jacques Clément[184] on how to carry out his detestable parricide.[185] It was even believed that she gained his consent through her favors.[186]

---

177 *Mollesse*, here a euphemism for homosexuality.
178 Francis I (1494–1547), king from 1515; Henry II (1519–1559), king from 1547.
179 Catherine de' Medici (1519–1589), wife of Henry II.
180 The Catholic League was formed by Henry I, of Guise (1550–1588) in 1576.
181 Margaret of Valois (1553–1615), sister of king Henry III and wife of Henry of Navarre.
182 Montesquieu's source is Agrippa d'Aubigné's *Histoire universelle*, 2nd ed., 1616 (*Catalogue* 2905).
183 Catherine de Lorraine (1552–1596), daughter of Henry II and Catherine de' Medici. She reputedly despised Henry III because he and his minions made fun of her limp. In *SL* xii, 28, Montesquieu makes this a prime example of how dangerous it is for kings to insult their subjects.
184 Jacques Clément, a Dominican lay brother, assassinated Henry III in August 1589.
185 This term included regicide, for which no specific word existed at the time.
186 Pierre Bayle included this allegation in his article "Henry III" in his *Historical and Critical Dictionary* (1697) (*Catalogue* 2453).

The king's favorites kept him, so to speak, in a seraglio, and would allow him no escape either from his lethargy or from their ambition.

They continually got him to place new taxes on the people, which they at once appropriated; and as they were not bound to him out of either honor or duty, but by pleasures, they cared little if they made him contemptible to the people for his vices or detestable for his extravagances.

When a prince oppresses his subjects, he must at least make them imagine some benefit which they find attractive, and not afflict them to the point where they notice they are being deprived of necessities for his sensual pleasures. What determined the people of Rome to abandon Nero, in the end, was that, during a time of famine, they learned that three vessels had arrived from Alexandria laden with dirt for the wrestlers.[187]

Since Henry's favorites shied away from business dealings and regarded any money earmarked for war or for running the state as something taken from them, they often inappropriately chose the path of commutations and pardons. Insolent while they were favored and timid at the end, they troubled the royal majesty after having raised him to the heavens, abusing power either to exaggerate it or to degrade it beyond measure.

It would be hard to say whether the Queen Mother did more harm to the Catholics, the Huguenots, the kingdom, or her children who would be kings.[188]

During her several regencies she had merely been shrewd. Full of the little tricks which the heart and the mind of a woman so easily contrive, she had brought all the intrigues of the bedchamber into the council chamber, and the intrigues of her court ladies were the principal tools of her politics.

In the end she succeeded in discrediting sovereignty itself by causing people to see the words, the deeds, and the favors of our kings as traps in which only fools allowed themselves to be caught.

Although she had courage of a sort, she thought only of diminishing the king's: she always showed distrust for him and degraded his authority so that he would relinquish it into her hands.

The king, whose debaucheries were public knowledge, had the weakness of believing he could atone for them by outward show, but his devotion was becoming suspect as it became more public, and his religion was still being judged by his behavior.

---

187 See Suetonious, *Life of Nero*, 45. The Chevalier de Jaucourt, in his *Encyclopédie* article on wrestling ("Lutte," ix, p. 758), explains that wrestlers, to counter the slippery effect of oil rubbed on the skin, would roll in the dirt or cover each other with fine sand.

188 Catherine de' Medici's three sons, Francis II, Charles IX, and Henry III, all became king. Montesquieu criticizes her conduct in *Pensées* 615, 621, and 622.

The whole nation had contracted a certain zealous spirit which no longer distinguished Catholic from Protestant by religious practices. For if they had, what king would have appeared more Catholic than Henry III? But people regarded anyone who was ready to shed Protestant blood as a Catholic, and anyone who was prepared to shed Catholic blood as a Protestant.

Meanwhile, the advancement of the Guises[189] was so rapid that the need the king would have for the Huguenot party was already being felt; but the slightest concession was a blot of heresy.

The king did not prevent the Estates General from declaring that war had to be waged against the heretics; but as soon as they had done so, that resolution became the nation's unanimous inclination, and as the king was not leading that war, the opportunity was presented to form a league and to resort to an authority other than the laws.[190]

The weakness of the court at once created the impression that the religion was being threatened. As a result, the fearful people placed their confidence in the Guises; conversely, the strength of the Guises increased the weakness of the court.

In most civil wars, some traces of the former tone can subsist. It can be that order is disrupted without being utterly eradicated. People can fight for or against the government while adhering to the government's principles. But when people take up arms because they believe their religion is threatened, then everything is in disarray; everybody becomes a person of importance since each person has an equal interest in the matter and is, so to speak, a principal.

At that point all minds are given to excess; the interests of the state are sacrificed to the fortunes of each person's idea; the only bonds remaining in society are those of hatred and common rage; the weakest seize power to place at their head the most treacherous men who step forward; every extravagance is given a hearing, and hypocrisy takes the place of morals, virtues, and laws.[191]

The power of the king of Spain and the leniency of the other states for heretics had persuaded the monks that it was important to the Catholic religion for that prince to have the Catholic empire; thus, they were all on his side. The popes, who feared having a master if power became concentrated, were less Catholic than the monks, who are in the front ranks, who never have anything

---

189 The Guise family was based in Lorraine. The first to be made a duke was Claude de Lorraine (1496–1550), rewarded for his valor after suffering multiple wounds in the Battle of Marignano (1515).

190 The Catholic League gained strength after Henry III's youngest brother, Francis of Valois, Duke of Alençon, died without an heir, leaving the Protestant Henry of Navarre in the best position to claim the succession.

191 See if I can include fanaticism. (M)

in their heads but two or three theological principles with which they ever advance without ever fearing more than one thing at a time.[192]

The great qualities of the Duke of Guise[193] were ultimately undoing the king. History gives us no example of an outsider brought to power by the people's adulation; this one could use the hatred of the French for the French princes and lords.[194]

The king, wishing to display his zeal for the Catholic religion, allowed his subjects to form a league to protect it, and, as if the State were not itself a league, he gave it his approval, instead of viewing all parties from a kingly perspective.

There was in the national spirit an impotent fury for destroying each other, but the Catholics, in waging war, were serving the Huguenots, who thus became established, and who, by extracting edicts, were putting the law on their side.[195]

When a new religion arises in a state and, having parried the first blows struck against it and strengthened by its defeats, has reached a point where it can sustain itself by its own power, it is impolitic to attack it. There is no reason to fear it will spread further since proselytes are made only when the questions are undecided and everyone still imagines they are in the same religion. But once a schism has occurred, once the labels are given and accepted, and everyone has made his choice, proselytes are rare. At that moment it is therefore in the interest of the dominant religion to let the other one cool peaceably, to dispute power and not details of worship, and in short, to make artisans and ploughmen of its enemies rather than soldiers.[196]

The king was in a bind: he was unable to persuade his Catholic subjects that he was a Catholic and he was personally responsible, in the mind of his Protestant subjects, for a principal role in the Saint Bartholomew's Day business;[197] and if we

192 For Montesquieu's views on the theological, political, and economic problems caused by monks when they gain power, see *Pensées* 80 and 902; *Romans*, chapter 22; and *SL* XIV, 7 and XXV, 6.

193 Henry I, third Duke of Guise (1550–1588), founder of the Catholic League.

194 Add here that Calvinism was more contrary to kings than Lutheranism in that the former claimed to be more in keeping with what Jesus had said, and the latter with what the Apostles had done. (M) Cf. *SL* XXIV, 5.

195 The Protestants extracted pacification edicts from the crown, including the Edict of Boulogne and the Peace of La Rochelle signed in July 1573 by king Charles IX (1550–1574) of France, which permitted Protestant worship in private residences in La Rochelle, Montauban, and Nîmes.

196 The Protestant body was demoralized in France by the Edict of Nantes. It was favors that destroyed it, and not swords. (M)

197 The St. Bartholomew's Day Massacre of Protestants in August 1572 was planned by Henry III and his mother, Catherine de' Medici.

carefully note the evil deeds that preceded it, the fury with which it was carried out, and the insolent way it was sustained, we must admit that nothing was more capable of ruining a prince's reputation for all time.

It was in these circumstances that the assassinations of the Duke of Guise,[198] of his brother the cardinal,[199] and of the archbishop of Lyon petrified his friends and enraged his enemies.

It is as impossible to approve what he did as the way in which he did it, and whatever his situation was then, we must for the honor of virtue and for the sake of humankind deplore this act or refrain from judging it.

Sixtus V called the cardinals together: "My brothers," he said, "the king of France has had a cardinal put to death, as if God were not in heaven and as if we were not on earth." He excommunicated the king. This was a fatal proscription for, given the circumstances, it put his life in continual danger!

Memorandum on the Silence to Impose on the Constitution

(1754)

Mémoire sur le silence à imposer sur la Constitution, text by Pierre Rétat (*OC* IX, 529–535). "Constitution," which can refer to any papal bull, was particularly applied at the time to *Unigenitus*, a bull issued by pope Clement XI at the behest of Louis XIV on 8 September 1713. It condemned 101 propositions in Pasquier Quesnel's *Nouveaux Testament en français avec des réflexions morales sur le Nouveau Testament* ("New Testament in French with moral reflections on the New Testament," 1692)[200] and threatened with excommunication any Catholic who read, discussed, or even contemplated them. The manuscript, mainly in Montesquieu's hand, was preserved at La Brède prior to its first sale in 1939 along with other Montesquieu papers. A second sale in 1957 enabled the municipal library of Bordeaux to acquire it (MS 2103). It was first published in *Mélanges inédits* (1892). The highly

---

198 King Henry III (1551–1589) ordered the assassination of Henry I, Duke of Guise (1550–1588), founder of the Catholic League, on 23 December 1588 while he was in Blois to attend a meeting of the Estates General.

199 Cardinal Louis II of Lorraine (1555–1588), brother of Henry I, was also in Blois, and was assassinated a day later.

200 They allegedly reflected the teachings of the Flemish theologian Cornelius Jansen (1585–1638), bishop of Ypres, whose *Augustinus* (1640) asserted that efficacious, irresistible grace is freely given by God and cannot be earned.

indeterminate state of the manuscript led the *OC* editor to follow the 1892 edition, which is consequently our base text as well.

* * *

The author of this memorandum is taking part in the current disputes only because he is distressed by them. The origin of this dilemma and the dilemma itself arise from the fact that, recently, they[201] have confused outward toleration[202] with inner toleration;[203] indeed they have always confused the two, even though they are two quite distinct ideas, so distinct that they do not even depend on the same principles. This long-standing, erroneous confusion has put kings, ministers, magistrates, and the clergy too, into unspeakably awkward situations and labyrinths from which it is presently almost impossible to escape.

What does Your Majesty fear? Do you not have a true desire that all should live together in peace in your kingdom? Is this not a vital question as far as religion is concerned since it is undoubtedly true that a state where half the people have a complete loathing for the other half is in a situation where all of them are farther from salvation than they would be in a different state? It is true that one cannot be saved without faith, but one is even less likely to be saved without charity because, given human ignorance, it is sometimes easy to be mistaken about faith and impossible to be mistaken about charity.

There is more to it. In taking the line I am suggesting His Majesty takes on no responsibility and defers everything to the pope.

Otherwise His Majesty's reign will be very difficult. The other interests of the state will all be subordinated to this one,[204] and were the only harm done the constant attention that Your Majesty and your ministers are obliged to give to it, Your Majesty will only be doing what all the princes of Europe do, which is to impose strict silence on these matters.

Monsieur de M.[205] has attained an age that does not leave hope for a long life. It is felt that sovereign care is needed to select someone with a cool temperament and good judgment. There may be a thousand reasons why a

---

201 An earlier draft shows that by "they" Montesquieu meant "princes and ministers."

202 *Tolérance extérieure.*

203 *Tolérance intérieure.* Cf. *SL* xxv, 9: "I am talking here as a political writer and not as a theologian; and even for theologians, there is a great difference between tolerating a religion and approving it."

204 Cf. *Pensées* 543.

205 Jean François Boyer (1675–1755), bishop of Mirepoix (1730–1736), had the task of allocating ecclesiastical benefices beginning in 1743.

member of the laity would be better: Monsieur Milain, and it was during his ministry, this side of things was well administered.[206]

Everybody knows that the Catholic religion in no way countenances inner toleration; it does not allow any sect within its fold since, according to its principles, it alone promises salvation, and it cannot tolerate any sect where anyone could believe that salvation is not to be found.

Inner toleration would seem to imply a kind of approbation, and how could the Catholic religion approve something which, according to its principles, necessarily precludes salvation?

Outward toleration derives from a different principle so that the prince who has established outward toleration in his country and the Catholic subjects who live in a state under the laws of outward toleration cannot for that reason be suspected of, nor suspect themselves, of adopting this inner toleration disapproved[207] by the Catholic religion.

When a Catholic prince says that he neither has nor wants to adopt inner toleration, this is as if he were saying: "I am unable, internally, to approve any sect within my provinces because only the Catholic religion saves, and if I believed otherwise, I would not be a Catholic." When he approves outward toleration, it is as if he were to say: "I am ordained by God to maintain peace in my provinces, to prevent assassinations, murders and pillaging in order to ensure that my subjects do not exterminate each other and that they lead tranquil lives. Therefore in certain circumstances my laws must necessarily be such that they do not thwart this purpose. My conscience tells me not to approve inwardly those who do not think as I do, but my conscience also tells me that there are instances where it is my duty to tolerate them outwardly.

"It is not always in conformity with the theological principle to which I adhere that my laws must be made; now, there are occasions where they must be made in conformity with the principles of political laws on which all governments are based."

The salvation of the state is the supreme law. Thus, although our kings up until the Revocation of the Edict of Nantes[208] had granted external toleration toward the Huguenots, it cannot be said that they were not very good Catholics or that they adopted inner toleration of the Huguenots. Nor can

206 Milain served under the regent. The awkward wording of this paragraph provides evidence of the unfinished state of this text.
207 The manuscript has "approved" rather than "disapproved," but as previous editors have noted, only "disapproved" fits the context.
208 The Edict of Nantes (1598), issued by Henry IV, had granted Protestants a measure of toleration. It was revoked in 1685 by Louis XIV.

it be said that the Catholic princes of Germany stopped being Catholics when, by the treaties of Westphalia, they instituted outward toleration among Catholics, Calvinists, and Lutherans.[209]

Nor can it be said that Spain and Portugal are more Catholic than Italy and France because Spain and Portugal do not practice outward toleration of the Jews and the laws of Italy and France grant them such toleration, for Italy and France grant no greater inner toleration for the Jews than do Spain and Portugal.

No one on earth can deny this important distinction unless it is their wish that princes cease to be princes and that princes were not established by God to maintain peace between their subjects and do everything that can contribute to the welfare of the state and to its preservation.

Once these principles have been laid down, the main problems of the current disputes largely fall away since it follows that in the current disputes it will never happen that the prince can be obliged, in conscience, to establish penal laws against anyone from either of the two sides; if he always can and even sometimes must accord outward toleration to the sects in his provinces without involving his conscience, there is all the more reason why he will be able to grant it to the two current adversarial sides since it cannot be said that either of them is cut off from the Catholic Church unless one wishes to argue that the rage which animates them both separates them from it.[210]

It is definitely the case in this instance that the prince must never let himself be affected by whatever sophism may be argued to him about a certain apparent interest of religion; for what is involved is not the interest of religion but the interest of the disputes carried on over religion.

It is also obvious that the prince is not obliged, in conscience, to strive to understand things that theologians dispute. This is so true that, provided one believes in a few short articles contained in the catechism, the comprehension of which is inaccessible to our understanding, there is no man in the whole kingdom who, in this situation, is not as good a Catholic as all the theologians put together.

It is not difficult to be persuaded that it is impossible to arrive at peace through mutual agreement among theologians since, if such an agreement

---

209 In the treaties of Westphalia ending the Thirty Years' War, all parties agreed to honor the Peace of Augsburg of 1555 allowing each prince to determine what kind of Christianity would be practiced in his state and stipulating that Christians living in principalities where the established church was not their own should be allowed private worship "in perfect freedom of conscience" and be permitted "to have their children educated either at foreign schools or at home by private tutors."

210 Jansenists and Jesuits were part of the same Catholic Church in France; Jansenists were never in league with Protestants.

could have been reached through that means, the troubles and the indefatigable efforts which the ministers have sustained on that subject for forty years would certainly have procured it.

Once the Constitution had been received in France, it was natural to believe that peace would have followed from that and the weapons on both sides should have fallen from their hands. But it was the wretched destiny of this country that the two sides should set about examining how the Constitution had been received and how it should be understood[211] by both Church and state. Such a method could only prolong the dispute in perpetuity because even if one point were decided, the parties could always quarrel about another point, on and on to infinity.

The author of this memorandum admits that he has not carefully followed everything that has happened on both sides in this dispute because so many personal interests have been involved. These disputes have been the source of so many fortunes. So many men have gained status from them who in other circumstances would have had no standing either in the state or the Church. So many men have even introduced, with the best of intentions, their personal prejudices. And in short so many things have occurred but so little progress has been made that it would have been prudent to just ignore what has passed before our eyes and let brains overheat without sharing the fervor.

All one can say is that the king has wise and no doubt well-intentioned ministers in his council, and that this council should be his Council of Conscience, and that the clergy, however respectable they may be by their estate and their personage, should have no influence in the matter because, if they understand worldly matters, they are not in a position to govern his conscience, and if they do not, they are even less in a position to direct his business.

One of the means that could perhaps be used would be this. Given that the Constitution has been received in France, the king issues a declaration stating that since the Constitution has been received[212] and by all the subjects of the kingdom, all the disputes should have ceased; that it is forbidden to discuss the interpretation of the Constitution or to stir up any dispute concerning it until the pope has seen fit to interpret it himself and that all should refrain from asking him to do so for fear of reopening disputes. The punishment will be to be treated as a disturber of the public order.

---

211 *Qualifiée.*
212 The Parlement had been forced by Royal Letters Patent to register the bull in 1714. Conflict ensued over whether the bull was a "rule of faith" binding on all Catholics in France or a papal recommendation requiring approval by a general Church Council.

Such a declaration will necessarily tone down the disputes, not by suppressing them but by suspending them and by moving their resolution forward to a time when, minds having cooled and hearts having felt different passions, no one will care any longer whether they are decided.[213]

Secondly, everything will come down to matters necessarily pertaining to policing outward behavior. Will a dying person say that he does not accept the Constitution? Then the law will declare him a disturber of public order. Will a parish priest ask a dying person whether he accepts the Constitution? Then he will be declared a disturber of public order, and sometimes even both of them will.

Whatever solution is adopted, it must be considered permanent, and care must be taken to do nothing that can give one of the two sides an opportunity to renew the disputes.

This declaration will have the desired effect provided that distribution of benefices is placed in impartial hands; provided that no benefice is given, under any circumstances, to any who have acted immoderately, and provided they be granted only to those who have conducted themselves with wisdom and composure.

It will be noted, in this connection, that the benefices which are allocated by the king are better placed in the hands of the nobility than of people from the lower order and better placed in the hands of enlightened persons than of ignorant ecclesiastics because everyone likes to distinguish himself, and those who do not have a certain merit find that it is easier to distinguish themselves by zeal than by enlightenment and knowledge.

---

213 Louis XV issued a "declaration of silence" on 2 September 1754 which briefly suspended the disputes. Pope Benedict XIV's issuance of the encyclical *Ex Omnibus* in October 1756, however, prompted Louis to exempt French bishops from the ban of silence in a declaration signed on 10 December 1756, and this action renewed the bitter conflicts between bishops seeking to enforce *Unigenitus* and parlementary magistrates attempting to uphold the rights of Jansenists to receive the sacraments.

Economics and Fiscal Policy

Memorandum on the Debts of State

(1715)

Mémoire sur les dettes de l'État, text by Jean Ehrard (*OC* VIII, 55–64). There are two manuscripts of this memorandum. The first, in a secretary's hand, remained in Montesquieu's library at his château in La Brède prior to its first sale in Paris in 1939 and was later purchased in 1957 by the municipal library of Bordeaux (manuscript B, MS 2104). The second, an autograph manuscript (P) was discovered in the Bibliothèque Nationale in Paris in 1909 as part of a collection containing 303 *mémoires* providing advice to Philip, Duke of Orléans, regent under Louis XV, for addressing France's debt crisis. It was published in a German review in 1910 and is the base text presented here. Bracketed paragraphs contain the text of manuscript B.[1]

* * *

Memorandum Concerning the Means of Liquidating the Debts of State[2]

Your Royal Highness[3] is uniquely occupied with the care of relieving the state.

It is in a most sorry situation. The taxes we are levying are so high that it is impossible to impose new ones, and yet if we had a war, the king would scarcely be able to count on the twenty millions required for interest payments in order to sustain it. Thus one easily understands that your

---

1 See *OC* VIII, 46 for publication details for each draft.
2 Neither this title nor the shorter version above is in Montesquieu's hand in the manuscript; both are in current usage.
3 Philip, Duke of Orléans, regent of France from 1715 until 1723 during the minority of Louis XV.

Royal Highness cannot think of lowering taxes until he has freed the state from part of those debts.

I can imagine two means of retiring most of them. The first is the path of reduction,[4] the second that of redemption.[5]

[Your Royal Highness, who is working so effectively to repair the harm that was done by others, has given permission for any private individual to send him proposals which they judge to be the most suitable for the welfare of the kingdom.

The proposed tax on financiers would avenge the state rather than helping it. What happened during the reign of the late king and his predecessors concerning this problem is proof that such remedies can suspend the tears of the people for a short while, but not their misfortunes.[6]

The whole question is reducible to two points: how to relieve the king of his debts and how to relieve his subjects of the major part of the taxes they pay. There are two means of achieving these two goals, both of them simple: reduction and redemption.]

The reduction must be equitable and proportional. It would require issuing a decree obligating each individual to declare what portion of his assets he holds in royal debt,[7] whether it is, for example, one-quarter, one-third, or one-half, and a tariff would need to be established in approximately the following manner.

Those who have three-fourths of their assets in royal debt would endure a reduction of one-fourth of their declared royal debt.

Those who have two-thirds would lose a third.

One half would be subtracted from those who have only half of their assets on the king.

---

4 I.e., reductions in the crown's payments of debt obligations of various sorts, including annuities owed to royal bond purchasers (*rentiers*), interest on state notes (*billets d'État*), pension payments (*pensions*), wages (*gages*) paid to venal officers as interest on the sums they had paid to purchase their offices, and salaries (*appointements*) paid to those in the king's employ.

5 *Rachat*. Redemption was the payment of a large lump sum to the crown in return for exemption from a particular tax. The king benefited in the near term, but only at the cost of reduced future tax revenues from the Church, magistrates, a province, a municipality, or some corporation or guild.

6 Montesquieu refers here to using a *chambre de justice* to levy fines against individuals allegedly abusing their powers in administering the crown's multi-layered network of finances. The regent convened a *chambre* on 17 March 1716; 4,410 individuals were sentenced to restitutions and fines totaling 219.5 million livres, but the government collected less than half that amount. (Paul Harsin, *Les Doctrines monétaires et financières en France du XVIᵉ au XVIIIᵉ siècle*, Paris, 1929, p. 135).

7 *Effets royaux*.

Two-thirds would be subtracted from those who have only one-third, and three-fourths from those who have only a fourth.

Those who have more than three-quarters of their assets on the king would lose only a fifth.

Any who made a false declaration would lose their debt and be required to pay a fine.

Everything would be subject to this reduction: annuities, state notes, wages, salaries, pensions.

One could, by this means, abolish several taxes, and as a result everyone would conserve real assets and only lose assets that exist only notionally. What is lost on one side would be gained on the other. It is not the king who pays the annuities. It is in reality the subjects who pay them to themselves.

The justice of all this appears self-evident. It is in the interest of those who have only a fourth of their assets in the king's hands to lose three-fourths of it, and for the king to credit his accounts in the transaction, because the three-quarters of their assets that will be left over will more than compensate them for this loss. But it is also in the interest of those who have three-quarters of their assets on the king for the reduction to be only one-quarter because if it were more, they would be absolutely ruined, one-fourth of their remaining assets not being sufficient to compensate them.

[No one will lose, if everyone loses proportionally. And what a source of pride for Your Royal Highness to be able to say, on the last day of the Regency, that he has repaired the parlous condition of state finances without having ruined a single family.

Once the state's burden is eased by this reduction, the revenue from taxation will greatly exceed state expenditures. And if this happens just once, one can have high hopes for the Ministry whose purpose is achieving savings and economies.

It will be easy to find new ways to continue to free up the king more and more.

In 1714 the late king reduced all contracts on the city hall to four percent,[8] and, during your Regency, the same thing was done in the case of all other royal contracts, whatever their nature.

These measures were very sensible, and all that was lacking was that they should have been applied more widely.

---

8 I.e., reduced the interest rate paid to holders of the crown's annuities (*rentes sur l'Hôtel de ville*).

The clergy is burdened with many debts; the provincial assemblies, the towns, and the urban municipalities are no less burdened.

These debts are really royal debts since they were contracted only on the king's behalf. The king was, so to speak, the borrower who raised money, backed by the clergy, the estates, the towns, and the guilds.

Hence it is necessary to reduce to four percent all the annuities paid out by the clergy, the estates, the towns, and the urban municipalities while obliging them at the same time to pay, in the name of and instead of the king, the annuities on the city hall in proportion to the relief they obtain from the reduction of their own interest payments.

No injustice would be done to these creditors since their situation would be no worse than bondholders of the king.

Moreover they would be in a better situation than the landed proprietors, whose income is often swallowed up by the *taille*,[9] and by the very considerable excise duties[10] levied on certain goods.

Their situation would be even better than that of those who have placed their money in commercial ventures and who have suffered so many bankruptcies.[11]

And even if the only advantage gained from this new reduction were to relieve the towns of several burdensome taxes which were established to pay the large number of debts with which they were saddled, this would still be a big step forward.]

Once the king had reduced his debts in this way, he could easily retire them completely by means of redemption.[12] Royal debt is declining in value by fifty percent, but as it would be difficult to cure this problem, one must seek to draw a real advantage from it for the state.

If the king had money, he would acquit himself very advantageously since with a hundred million he could eliminate two hundred million worth of contracts.

The people would lose half of their assets almost without feeling the loss, which it would attribute to the harshness of the times and not to that of the ministry.

---

9 The *taille* was a direct tax from which the nobility were for the most part exempt. The *taille réelle* was annexed to land, and if nobles bought such taxed land, they had to pay it; the *taille personnelle* was levied on individuals.

10 *Droits d'aides*.

11 The intendant at Bordeaux had begun to complain of the alarming rate of bankruptcies beginning in 1684; by 1715 the situation was dire: in one two-month period no fewer than twenty-two bankruptcies were declared in Bordeaux, though some were no doubt fraudulent (Wallace Scoville, *The Persecution of Huguenots and French Economic Development, 1680–1720*, Berkeley: University of California Press, 1960, p. 198).

12 I.e., by buying back, at a reduced price owing to their declining value, annuities on which the crown was obligated to make interest payments.

It would be necessary, then, to seek out someone who could retire the royal debts on behalf of the king and thus free up the finances.[13]

It seems to me that if the king had the people redeem the most onerous taxes and received royal debt as payment, he would procure an infinite advantage for them.

The king would lose nothing in this. If he raised less, he would pay less, and the result would be the same with respect to his current revenue. But on the other hand he would gain considerably because in a war he would have resources, whereas now he has none since it is impossible for him, given the current state of things, ever to impose new taxes.

For the people this would be enormously advantageous. Suppose, for example, that the salt taxes bring the king ten million every year. We can affirm without exaggeration that the raising of these ten million costs the people five. In addition to that, the tax farmer needs to earn one million. I am not taking into account the injury the people suffer when they are unable to give salt to their animals to prevent them from dying. But here you have at least sixteen million which the king raises in order to pay ten million in annuities on the city hall, for he makes no other use of that revenue.

Suppose now that the king orders that the provinces and the towns redeem the salt taxes, allowing them to make their payments in royal debt, and allowing them to borrow a sum sufficient to acquire royal debt in order to make their payment. With one hundred million that they will borrow, [supposing that the contract establishes five percent interest,] which they could do by committing themselves for five million in interest, they would acquire two hundred million worth of royal debt and relieve the king of ten million in annuities. And they would really relieve themselves of eleven million since instead of sixteen million they would pay only five.

To pay the annuities on the Paris city hall, the government has been obliged to charge exorbitant duties on all the goods entering and exiting.[14] Suppose that all these duties amount to four million, more or less, which is used to pay four million in annuities. Now suppose that the king reduces all these duties to one-quarter. One can say without fear of exaggeration that since consumption would double, the product of one-quarter of these taxes would also double, and would yield two million although it formerly yielded only one.

13 I.e., someone like Samuel Bernard who had loaned the king very large sums of money between 1701 and 1715.
14 These Paris duties were called *octrois* and were set at a very high rate.

Suppose now that an Assembly of Notables[15] is convened in Paris, which borrows forty million, of which those two million would be the interest. With these forty million they could buy paper[16] at a fifty percent discount and retire four million in annuities on the city hall. The annuities would therefore be paid and the people acquitted of three-quarters of the taxes, not including the fact that Paris would get out of the frightful poverty it is in. The revenues would increase through the consumption of goods[17] and the expenses of the middle class would diminish; and as for the artisans, at the present daily wage rate, two days' work per week would be enough to feed them. Thus we would soon see Paris flourish anew and forget about the large losses it has sustained.

In order to properly restore the urban municipalities which are no longer anything but a shadow, [as shown by the fact that no man of honor these days wishes to undertake municipal duties so much have they been degraded. Alternatively, it would be necessary to reestablish the estates in all the provinces] or what would be even better, establish estates in all the provinces, the king's authority would not be weakened, for it is no less great in the *pays d'états* than in the *pays de généralités*.

The province of Artois pays more proportionally than the others, but everyone lives happily and contentedly, and the same can be said of all the other provinces with estates.[18]

The provincial estates ought not to arouse suspicion on the part of the government, because they never deal with general matters.[19]

The king neither has nor can any longer have any credit, but the estates would have some, and would find it easy to borrow. In this system it would be necessary to maintain [state notes[20]] royal debt at a fifty percent discount, which would be easy, for the value could be made to fall or rise as the

---

15 Historically, French kings had convened Assemblies of Notables to approve policies which the Parlement of Paris was sure to oppose. Since their members were selected by the king, such bodies were usually compliant.

16 I.e., government debt paper.   17 I.e., higher consumption level.

18 France was divided into *pays d'états*, where provincial estates continued to meet, and *pays d'élection*, where such assemblies had been extinguished. Montesquieu favored decentralizing administration by reestablishing estates and reducing the influence of the king's agents, i.e., the intendants.

19 They were purely advisory bodies whose business was mainly restricted to local administration and the floating of loans on behalf of the crown.

20 Faced with the extraordinary costs of the War of the Spanish Succession (1701–1714), Louis XIV issued short-term interest-bearing notes called *billets d'état*. Unlike the lifetime and perpetual annuities sold by the crown at varying rates of interest and terms of amortization, the *billets d'état* were not secured against specific forms of revenue such as the *gabelles* (salt taxes) or the *aides* (customs duties).

commercial exchange of such debt was hampered or facilitated. The king would convert as many contracts as necessary into state notes to maintain royal debt constantly at a fifty percent discount.

Ceasing to pay the interest on said notes would bring about the same effect.

That would entail no prejudice to the state. All subjects together would earn what a portion of them loses.

It would be desirable for Your Royal Highness to be able to abolish the *dixième*[21] and the *capitation*.[22] He knows how onerous these taxes are to the public and harmful to the nobility. The French nation that cherishes Your Royal Highness flatters herself that she will soon have him to thank for the suppression of all these innovations.

But if the disorder of the finances does not permit him to do anything so substantial, we venture that it would be better to have every individual redeem the *dixième* rather than continuing it.

In payment, the state would accept all sorts of debt whatever their nature.

It would be a sort of tax that would extend to everyone.

It would be just, because each individual must contribute to the payment of the state's debts.

The collection of these sums would be easy for the king, who would not ask for any money.

The subjects would willingly pay in royal debt which they do not value highly and which they have in abundance.

The king is disadvantaged to pay the interest on a contract as if it were good[23] when he is losing fifty percent.

We could exempt from the redemption those for whom the *dixième* does not exceed a modest sum, for example ten or twenty livres.

The *dixième* and the *capitation* imposed on those subject to the *taille* is, properly speaking, nothing but an increase in their *taille*, which was already too high to be paid easily. Thus the king would not lose much from the *taillables*,[24] who would not be in a position to redeem them.

Magistrates would easily pay this redemption. The king would make a deduction from their wages and wage increases.

---

21 The *dixième*, levied from 1710 to 1718, was a ten percent tax on the self-assessed gross income of all Frenchmen, though the clergy, several cities, and five provinces purchased an exemption or made a lump sum payment in return for the right to farm the tax.

22 The *capitation* was a progressive tax on incomes ranging from 2,000 livres on members of the royal family to 1 livre on the poorest individuals.

23 I.e., worth its full value.   24 Those subject to payment of the *taille*.

Many military men would pay through the reduction in their pensions and the salaries of their positions and governments. Everything that would free up the state would be accepted.

The bourgeois of the towns would gladly pay with debt paper on which they would make a profit of fifty percent. [Your Royal Highness would be able to put into practice the idea he has of diminishing the power of the intendants, who have ridden roughshod over the provinces.] Finally, in the provinces everyone would seek to rid themselves of the extortion they believe they suffer from intendants who tax arbitrarily.

If we had the *dixième* redeemed, we would necessarily have to retire the *capitation*, which has been redeemed in large part under the reign of the late king, for it would be contrary to good sense to make subjects redeem the *dixième* while making them pay the *capitation* which they had already redeemed.

There are some errors of calculation in this dissertation because I have not taken account of the reduction of the annuities to four percent.[25]

I had previously written a memorandum on reducing the annuities issued by the clergy, the estates, and urban municipalities. It must be duly noted that that dissertation and this one are in a way incompatible, and can hardly both be acted upon.[26]

What I have said with regard to the establishment of new estates in the provinces will at first seem singular and extraordinary, but if one examines this project a thousand advantages will be found in it, not the least of which will be to make your regency unshakeable, for everyone will have an interest in supporting your work.

Considerations on the Wealth of Spain

(c. 1727)

Considérations sur les richesses de l'Espagne, text by Pierre Rétat (*OC* VIII, 611–623). Two manuscript versions of this essay are extant. The first is autograph, and the second is partially autograph and partially in the hand of abbé Bottereau-Duval, secretary to Montesquieu from 1718 to 1731 or 1732. It is the second draft that is translated here. Both were preserved at La Brède prior

---

25 Montesquieu had referenced this rate reduction in draft B, but that discussion was not incorporated in draft P.

26 I.e., because in draft P Montesquieu recommends that the crown buy back outstanding annuities on the city hall (*rentes sur l'Hôtel de ville*). The capital sums required to achieve this goal were to be generated by the sale of annuities by the clergy, the provincial estates, and urban municipalities.

to being sent to Joachim Lainé for transmission to Charles Louis de Montesquieu in England (see "A General Note on the Texts"), and both were among those papers returned from England to La Brède in 1828; however, unlike others in that collection, they were then sent back to Lainé in Paris. After his death, they passed through numerous hands, eventually becoming the property of the Fondation Martin Bodmer in Geneva in May 1964.

* * *

Article 1[27]

The galleons and the fleet[28] from the Indies[29] bring to Cadiz[30] about thirty-five million piasters' worth of gold and silver, and as they only depart twice every four years, by these two means seventeen to eighteen million piasters arrive every year in Europe.

I think that what enters fraudulently and what is smuggled in by boat and other indirect means easily comes to half this sum, that the value of close to eighteen to twenty million German florins enters via Portugal, and that two to three millions are extracted from the mines of Europe, which makes about forty million piasters.

I firmly believe that by the trading conducted by subjects of the king of Morocco in Timbuktu, by that conducted by Egyptians in Abyssinia, and by that which most nations of Europe conduct on the coasts of Africa, the value of four to five million piasters in gold and silver is readily drawn every year from that part of the world.

With regard to the East Indies, there are gold mines in China, in Japan, in Siam, Pegu, Azem, Tripara, Camboya, Cochinchina, Sumatra, and Macassar. And while there are silver mines only in Japan, they are very rich and abundant.

Note further that there is such a quantity of gold in the East Indies that although the nations of Europe are constantly taking silver there to conduct

27 The first draft was entitled "Concerning the Principal Cause of the Decline of Spain" and had the following opening paragraph: "Several explanations have been advanced for the decline of Spain. There is, however, one explanation which as far as I know nobody has noticed and which is nevertheless the most important."

28 The destination of the galleons was Peru and the South American colonies, and the destination of the fleet was New Spain, i.e., Mexico.

29 I.e., the West Indies, which included Spanish and Portuguese colonies in much of Central and northern South America, including portions of Mexico.

30 Cadiz was the home port of the Spanish treasure fleet. Christopher Columbus embarked from there on his second and fourth voyages.

their trade, having very few goods to send them, and although the silver mines of Japan are very abundant, there is still only ten to twelve times as much silver as gold in the East Indies whereas in Europe there is fourteen and a half times as much silver as gold.

And it cannot be said that there is scarcely any gold in the East Indies because none is brought to Europe; the reason for this is that it is more profitable to transport it to the Indies from the Indies, from places where there are mines to those where there are none.

Until about three hundred years ago we knew of even fewer countries than the Romans did. If we had more knowledge of certain countries than they, we knew less of certain others. Aside from the fact that Africa, America, and a large part of Asia were unknown, almost every people of that region of the world of that day was separated from all others by its ferocity, its poverty, and its fear. There were hardly any artisans anywhere, only farm workers and men of war.

The arts had been destroyed in Asia and Africa by the conquests of the Mohammedans; they had been destroyed in Europe by the barbarians who had taken it over. We still have in Hungary and Poland a good idea of the Europe of those earlier times.

In several parts of the earth, the use of gold and silver was unknown; in others it did not pass from one nation to another, and everywhere mines were neglected or unknown, or badly mined as a result of the deficiency or ignorance of the workers.

Now that the globe is almost all one nation in which every people knows what it possesses in excess and what it lacks and seeks to acquire the means of obtaining, gold and silver are mined all over the world. These metals are transported everywhere; every people transmits them, and there is not a single nation whose capital in gold and silver does not increase every year, although more quickly and abundantly in some nations than in others.

The consumption which different workers make of these metals in various manufactures cannot extend terribly far especially as a large part of the matter subsists after the fabrication, artistry returning it to its original state.

Article 2

Spain derives little advantage from the large quantity of gold and silver that she receives every year from the Indies. At first the profit was considerable, but it destroyed itself on account of the inherent flaw of the thing itself. I shall now explain my thought.

Every nation that trades in Europe has its own finished goods or agricultural products,[31] which it exchanges for the finished goods or agricultural products of other countries.

There are two types of goods: some have a natural use and are consumed by that usage, like grain, wine, and fabrics; others have a fictitious use, like gold and silver.

Of all the goods a state can have, those of only fictitious or representative value are those that enrich it the least, for these signs of wealth being very durable, and being little consumed or destroyed, as suits their nature as signs, it happens that the more these sorts of wealth increase, the more they lose their value because they represent fewer things.[32]

The Spanish, after conquering Mexico and Peru, abandoned sources of natural wealth for fictitious wealth, and the sight of quick profit made them complete dupes.

At the time of the conquest of the New World, gold and silver were very rare in Europe, for two reasons: first, because the ravages of the nations of the North, the pillaging and burning of towns, had destroyed or scattered almost all the gold of the Romans; second, because these barbaric peoples having no manufactures, all the silver was traded away for the goods of Asia; and although the Venetians subsequently did a great deal of trading in the Orient, that could not bring it back because the Orientals traded us their products without having much need of ours.

Spain, sitting on a very large quantity of gold and silver, astonished all her neighbors and conceived hopes she had never had.[33] The wealth she found in the conquered countries was not proportionate, however, to that of their mines, because the Indians hid a part of it; because making use of gold and silver only to augment the grandeur of the temples of the gods and the palaces of kings, they did not seek them with the same avarice we display;[34] because they did not

---

31 *Marchandises ou denrées.*
32 Jean Bodin had discussed the inflationary effect of the influx of precious metals from the Spanish colonies in his *Réponse [. . .] de M. de Malestroict [. . .]* (1568) printed in the 1593 Lyon edition of *Les six livres de la république* (*Catalogue* 2372). In the concluding sentence of the first draft of this essay, Montesquieu wrote: "At the time of Bodin the proportion between gold and silver was twelve to one" (Lyon edition, p. 466).
33 Samuel Pufendorf, in his *Introduction à l'histoire des principaux États tels qu'ils sont aujourd'hui dans l'Europe* ("Introduction to the history of the principal states as they are today in Europe"), 1687, I, p. 96 (*Catalogue* 2709), asserted that it was Spain's wealth in gold that had caused her to "conceive the design of universal Monarchy in Europe."
34 Garcilaso de la Vega, in his *Le commentaire royal des Incas* ("The royal commentary of the Incas"), trans. J. Gaudouin, Paris, 1633, p. 526 (*Catalogue* 3174) explained that the Indians used gold and silver only for decoration and regarded it as having little value since it could not be consumed.

possess the secret of extracting these metals from every mine, but only from those where the separation is done by fire, being unfamiliar with how to use mercury, and perhaps not being acquainted with mercury itself.[35]

Silver nevertheless quickly doubled in Europe, which became apparent in the doubling of the price of everything that could be bought.

The Spanish scoured the mines, excavated the mountains, and invented machines for drawing water, breaking up the ore, and separating it. And as they had little regard for the lives of the Indians, they made them work mercilessly.[36] Silver soon doubled again in Europe, and the profit always again declined by half for Spain, which every year received from the Indies only the same quantity of a metal which had become less precious by half.

In twice the time, silver again doubled and the profit again diminished by half.

It diminished by even more than half; here is how.

To extract gold from the mines, to give it the necessary preparations, and to transport it to Europe, a certain expenditure was required; I estimate it at one to sixty-four. When silver had doubled once and was consequently less precious by half, the expense was as two to sixty-four, or one to thirty-two. Thus, the fleets which brought the same quantity of gold to Spain were bringing something that was really worth one-half less and cost one-half more.

If we follow the matter from doubling to doubling, we shall easily find the progression of the poverty of Spain.

The mines of the Indies have been worked for about two hundred years. Let us suppose that the quantity of gold and silver presently in the commercial world, compared to what there was before the discovery, is thirty-two to one, which is to say that it has doubled five times. In two hundred more years that same quantity will be sixty-four to one, which is to say it will again double. At present fifty quintals of gold ore yield four, five, or six ounces of gold; when it is only two, the miner only recovers his costs.[37] In two hundred more years, when the yield will be only four ounces, the miner will again scarcely recover more than his expenses. There will therefore be little or no profit to be drawn from gold.

---

35 The use of mercury to extract gold and silver from rock and sediment was introduced in 1557 by the Spaniard Bartolomé de Medina and resulted in substantially increased yields, but there were dangers associated with mercury's use.

36 Cf. *Pensées* 207.

37 A marginal note in the first draft reveals that Montesquieu's source was Amédée François Frézier, *Relation du voyage de la mer du sud aux côtes du Chili et du Pérou et de Brésil* ("Relation of the voyage to the Southern Sea along the coasts of Chile, Peru, and Brazil"), Paris, 1714 (*Catalogue* 2742).

Same reasoning for silver except that the work in silver mines is somewhat more advantageous than that in gold mines.

Inevitably, then, working the mines will decline, as it did in the mines of Egypt, Attica, the Pyrenees, and Germany.

Now if we discover some mines so rich that they yield more profit, the richer they are, the sooner the profit will end.[38]

The Spanish have thus based their fortune on the worst commodity in the world because it is little consumed by use. As a result of its limited use for manufacturing and the avarice of those who possess it, almost none of it perishes.

Article 3

While the Spaniards commanded the gold and silver of the Indies, the English and Dutch inadvertently discovered the means of lowering the value of these metals: they established banks and companies,[39] and through new fictions they so multiplied the signs of commodities that gold and silver only partially fulfilled that function.

Thus public credit took the place of mines and diminished the profit which the Spaniards drew from theirs.

Article 4

Philip II was the first of the Spanish kings who was fooled by the falseness of his wealth, and what he would never have suspected was the destitution that made him fail almost everywhere. Finally, he was obliged to declare the famous bankruptcy that everyone knows about, and there has scarcely ever been a prince who has suffered more than he from the murmurs, insolence, and rebellion of his continually ill-paid troops.[40]

Article 5

The East Indian trade, which is almost all carried on with Spanish silver, has always relieved her of a part of her merchandise which is too abundant in Europe. For it is in her interest that the gold and silver that come from her be rare in Europe so that they will be worth more and represent more merchandise.

---

38 The first draft included the statement: "In Brazil the Portuguese have found gold mines so rich that they will necessarily cut into Spanish profits as well as their own."
39 The Bank of Amsterdam was established in 1609 and the Bank of England in 1694.
40 Philip II first declared bankruptcy in 1557. Unpaid Spanish troops stationed in the Netherlands mutinied in Brussels in 1577 and looted Antwerp.

Thus the ordinances she has made to forbid the use of gold and silver for gilding resemble those that the states of Holland would make if they forbade the consumption of cinnamon.[41]

And this trade which seemed to have nothing to do with Spain, this trade which she has always viewed with jealousy, is as advantageous to her as to any other nation, since it is conducted solely with her merchandise.

For it is in the interest of Spain that there not be too great a quantity of gold and silver coming from her in Europe so they will be more valuable.

On this basis one can judge the most recent ordinances from the Spanish Council which forbid the use of gold and silver for gilding and other super-fluities, a decree similar in result to what the states of Holland would do if they forbade the consumption of cinnamon.

Article 6

Besides the intrinsic flaw in the traffic in gold and silver extracted from mines, there are other particular reasons that caused Spain to gamble on America with very little advantage for herself.

Because of the vast extent of that country, she can hardly withdraw much from it, the strength of her large body being entirely employed in supporting it and defending it against the whole world's ambition.[42]

Moreover, the great distance puts it, so to speak, outside the sphere of her power; the Indies and Spain are properly two powers under a single master, but the Indies are the principal power and Spain only the accessory; it is useless for the ministers to employ statecraft[43] to try to restore the principal power as accessory: the Indies still draw Spain to them.[44]

It is only the Indies that profit from trade in the metals found in her mines. It is very favorable to them, since for their gold and their silver they receive the same value in European goods.

Of fifty million in merchandise that goes every year to the Indies, Spain furnishes only two and a half million.[45] The Indies therefore transact fifty million in trade while Spain does only two and a half million.

---

41 A flawed reflection because Spain undoubtedly prohibits only gilded objects produced by foreign manufacture. (M)

42 Spanish ships transporting gold were continually preyed upon, particularly by the Dutch and the English.

43 *La politique.*   44 Cf. *SL* XXI, 22.

45 See Pufendorf, *Introduction à l'histoire des principaux États*, I, p. 160 for how greatly France, England, and Holland surpassed Spain in producing goods shipped by the Spanish to the Indies. The Spanish, he observed, bore the expense of keeping the cow alive while foreign

Thus, however real the power of the Indies, it is imaginary for Spain. It is a great, useless warehouse in her hands, more useful to a commercial power which could equally sell and buy. But the profit that would be made in the Indies would accrue solely to the Indies and never to that power.

Besides, such a power to which the Indies would be accessory could never have at home all the different sorts of merchandise and agricultural products required for those vast regions, and even if its industry so intended, the climate would refuse it. And even if she were in a position to make all the shipments by herself, that would not enable her to do so, for how could she prevent shipments from other nations to such a vast expanse of coasts, given that even a small volume of a country's merchandise will always make smuggling profitable?

Presently the commerce of the Indies is not Spain's but Europe's as a whole, and it is in the interest of all nations to prevent smuggling and not engage in it. But if some nation undertook that trade alone, all the others would immediately call on their strength or their skill against her.

Article 7

The principal nations that have mined gold and silver are the Egyptians, the Athenians, the Macedonians, and the Carthaginians, and while their mines were much less rich than those of the Spanish, they nevertheless derived more advantage from them because they were not in the same circumstances. Those mines were located within their states; the gold and silver they extracted from them were a commodity of their country,[46] and along with the commodities similar to what other countries had, they also had gold and silver specific to them.

There was also an interior trade in Egypt, Attica, and Macedonia; the man who worked in the mines received the products of his country in return for silver, and the other citizens received silver for their merchandise.

And since silver was more plentiful in these states than in the neighboring states, the commodities of these countries were more expensive, work better paid, industry more encouraged, neighboring peoples more motivated to come live there, and the needs of the state and of individuals more easily satisfied.[47]

---

nations drank the milk. Spain received a commission for transporting foreign-made goods, but this was not nearly as lucrative as producing its own goods for sale would have been.

46 Manufacture as in Hungary. (M)

47 The first draft included the following paragraph: "Thus I have seen in Hungary that, although the gold, silver, and copper mines only break even, they are nevertheless very useful because, being situated in a country with abundant stocks of grain and wine, they provide work for ten thousand men who consume a portion of this grain and wine

The Carthaginians also worked the mines of Spain, but although those mines were far from Carthage, they were nevertheless within their sphere of power. Obliged to wage continual war in Spain, they used the gold of the Iberians to subjugate the Iberians, not to mention that since they were almost the only traders in the West, they trafficked in that commodity, as in all the others.[48]

Article 8

The principal source of the king of Spain's revenues is the money that comes into Cadiz (1) through the duty of one-fifth on silver and one-twentieth on gold; (2) through its duty of six percent on the gold and silver of individuals that comes in through Cadiz; (3) from the different rights of passage he charges the ships that embark from Spain, reach the Indies, and return to Cadiz; (4) finally, from the duties he levies in Cadiz on foreign merchandise going to the Indies or on merchandise from the Indies returning for their profit.[49] All this takes place between foreigners and the Spanish king almost without the Spanish having any part in it and is independent of the good or ill fortune of Spain so that in this regard the king is merely a very rich individual in the state.[50]

I think that if some provinces of Castile, through their inhabitants' farming and population, gave to the king of Spain an approximately equivalent sum, his power would be infinitely greater; the taxes would be the result of the country's wealth; these provinces would stimulate all the others. They would all be in a better position, collectively, to bear the respective burdens.

The prince would derive from this all the things necessary for war: soldiers to wage it, useful commodities for the execution of his designs, and extraordinary resources for his needs. He would find enterprising negotiators, industrious workers, powerful cities, a people ever present to defend him.

---

and bring three or four tracts of land to life. Operation of the Hungarian mines enhances agriculture; operation of the Spanish mines destroys it."

48 The first draft included the statement: "I believe the Spanish are not in such a favorable situation, for two reasons: one, because the countries where their mines are located are too vast; the other, because these mines are too distant from the center of their power."

49 In universal monarchy. (M)

50 The first draft included the following lines: "This opulence is only a part of the connection that wealth must bear to the riches of private individuals, but even if he obtains it from Spain, this levy could only be a result and a consequence of the opulence of the whole State. ¶It is not enough to have water. Its source must be good. It must be able to increase, and it must spread abundance everywhere."

The prince's wealth must not come to him directly and by fortuitous means. It should be the result of tax revenues that result from the prosperity of the subjects. It is a terrible disadvantage for a prince to be deprived at home of the things that can render great designs successful and have to rely on foreign silver to get them.[51]

Article 9

I cannot often enough repeat that we have a very false idea of the power of gold and silver to which we attribute, despite ourselves, a real virtue; this manner of thinking comes principally from our seeing that the most powerful states possess much gold and silver, but the reason for this is that their good public order[52] and the good quality and cultivation of their lands necessarily attract it; and we make these metals a cause of the power of these states whereas they are just a sign of it.

Moreover, most of the states of Europe being caught up in debt and crushed by prevailing exchange values, gold and silver, being the most useful instruments enabling them to fulfill their obligations, have become more than ever by chance the necessary support of their power.

But if we will only pay attention to what has always happened in the world, we will see that most states that have been conquered or destroyed were not lacking in either gold or silver, and that the weakest were those where there was a greater quantity.[53]

These are the reflections I have made on the nature of Spanish commerce. I have often heard people deplore the blindness of Francis I's council, which refused Christopher Columbus, who first approached France to make her mistress of all the treasures of the Indies. In truth, one sometimes does very wise things for foolish reasons, and the present condition of Spain should console us.[54]

---

51 Antoine de Montchrestien, in his *Traité de l'économie politique*, 1615, ed. F. Billacois (Geneva: Droz, 1999), pp. 375–376, had stressed the importance of France's "five inexhaustible sources of natural wealth," which were wheat, wine, salt, wool, and cloth: these, he said, were the "true mines" of France.

52 *Bonne police.*

53 Montesquieu later realized that, although this assertion was valid for former ages, there was now a direct connection between wealth and power. Thus he added the following marginal note: "False reflection; I have set forth the reason for the difference in the universal monarchy" (i.e., his *Reflections on Universal Monarchy*).

54 The first draft included the following: "There is no state more favored by natural endowments than France. Her principal foodstuffs are consumed and renewed mostly every year. Always there is a new-found abundance for her new needs. And this cannot be said of the gold and silver of Spain, the lead and tin of England and Germany, and the copper and brass of the North. ¶We would face the same fate as Spain were we to

Let us leave it to another nation to travel afar to turn horrid mountains inside out; let us leave this work of the slave to her; let her sacrifice the life and health of a good share of her subjects while consoling herself in her contempt for them; let her destroy herself in Europe and vainly extend herself elsewhere; let her be like the man who almost perished in misery as a result of asking the gods to turn everything he touched into gold. For our part, we enjoy our land and our sun. Our wealth will be more lasting because our ever-present new needs will always be met by our continually renewed abundance.

renounce these true commodities in order to embrace false ones, not to mention the fact that the work of mines is the work of slaves, that it would consume many men and create little wealth. ¶And France draws more profit from the small island of Martinique, from her portion of Santo Domingo, and from the settlement she had before the peace at Newfoundland, than Spain has drawn from the vast continent of America. Here is my proof: ¶Foreigners send, each year, as part of the commerce with the colonies in America, fifty million in merchandise from their countries, at the price they sell it; that is the English six or seven millions, the people of Hamburg four, the Flemish six, the Dutch ten, the Genoese eleven to twelve, the French thirteen or fourteen."

VII

Defense of The Spirit of Law *(1750)*

Défense de l'Esprit des lois, text by Catherine Volpilhac-Auger (*OC* VII, 71–117). Montesquieu composed this work to rebut stinging attacks in the 9 October and 16 October 1749 numbers of the clandestine Jansenist journal *Nouvelles ecclésiastiques, ou Mémoires pour servir à l'histoire de la Constitution Unigenitus,* published twice monthly in Paris and surrounding towns. The author of these attacks is now thought to have been the abbé Jean-Baptiste Gaultier (1685–1755), rather than the abbé Jacques Fontaine de La Roche (1688–1761), the journal's editor (*OC* VII, 18). The base text for the *OC* edition is the second edition bearing the false imprint Geneva: Barrillot & Fils and published, with a tacit permission, by Huart in Paris. The manuscript of the *Defense* is no longer extant.

* * *

Part One

This Defense has been divided into three parts. In the first we have answered the general objections that have been made to the Author of *The Spirit of Law.* In the second, we answer to particular objections. The third contains reflections on the manner in which it has been criticized. The public will learn how things are and be able to judge.

I

Although *The Spirit of Law* is purely a work of politics and jurisprudence, its Author has often had occasion to bring up the Christian religion; he has done so in such a manner as to make one sense its full grandeur, and while it has not been his purpose to try to make people believe in it, he has sought to make it cherished.

Yet in two periodical broadsides which appeared one after the other,[1] he has been accused of the most terrible things. It is no less a question

---

1 One on 9 October 1749, the other on the 16th of the same month. (M)

than whether he is a Spinozist and a deist;[2] and although these two accusations are in themselves contradictory, he is endlessly taken from one to the other. Being incompatible, both cannot make him more guilty than one alone, but together can make him more despicable.

So he is a Spinozist, he who from the first paragraph of his book distinguished the material world from spiritual intelligences.

So he is a Spinozist, he who in the second paragraph attacked atheism. *Those who have said that a blind fate has produced all the effects that we see in the world have uttered a great absurdity; for what greater absurdity is there than a blind fate that has produced intelligent beings?*[3]

So he is a Spinozist, he who went on with these words: *God has a relationship with the universe as creator and as preserver;*[4] *the laws by which he created are those by which he preserves; he acts according to those rules because he knows them; he knows them because he made them; he made them, because they have a relationship with his wisdom and might.*

So he is a Spinozist, he who added: *As we see that the world,*[5] *formed by the movement of matter, and lacking intelligence, ever subsists, etc.*

So he is a Spinozist, he who showed[6] against Hobbes and Spinoza *that the relations of justice and equity were prior to all positive laws.*

So he is a Spinozist, he who said at the beginning of the second chapter: *That law which, by imprinting within us the idea of a creator, urges us toward him, is the first of natural laws in importance.*

So he is a Spinozist, he who with all his power refuted Bayle's paradox[7] that it is better to be an atheist than an idolator? A paradox from which atheists would draw the most dangerous consequences.[8]

---

2 For what being a Spinozist or a deist was thought to imply, see Introduction, pp. 21–22.

3 Montesquieu italicizes quotations from *The Spirit of Law*. Only some of these italicized segments, however, are direct quotations; others are paraphrases. Where Montesquieu did not employ a note to cite the Book and chapter number from which a quotation or paraphrase is drawn, we have added a note to convey that information.

4 Book I, chapter I. (M)   5 Book I, chapter I. (M)   6 Book I, chapter I. (M)

7 In *Pensées diverses écrites à un docteur de Sorbonne sur l'occasion de la comète qui parut au mois de décembre 1680* ("Various thoughts written to a doctor of the Sorbonne on the occasion of the comet that appeared in the month of December 1680," 1682; *Catalogue* 1521), Pierre Bayle (1647–1706) claimed it is less dangerous to be an atheist than an idolator, and that a society of atheists would be more successful than a society of idolators. In Book XXIV, chapter 2 of *The Spirit of Law*, entitled "Bayle's Paradox," Montesquieu argued the contrary proposition that even false religions can restrain passions and moderate conduct, which he deemed particularly important in curbing wrongful conduct of princes. See also *Pensées* 478, 1266, 1946, and 1993 for additional reflections by Montesquieu on ways to refute Bayle's paradox.

8 Several objections were raised, on religious grounds, to Alexander Pope's *Essay on Man*, in *Epistles to a Friend* (London, 1733). In addition to placing God in the great chain of

What does one say after such explicit assertions? And natural equity demands that the degree of proof be proportional to the importance of the accusation.

FIRST OBJECTION

The Author stumbles at his very first step: the laws in the broadest sense, he says, are the necessary relations which derive from the nature of things. The laws, relations! Is that conceivable? ... Yet the Author has not changed the ordinary definition of laws without design. What then is his purpose? It is this: according to the new system, there is, among all beings that form what Pope calls the Great Whole, such a necessary linkage that the least disorder would communicate the disarray to the throne of the primal Being. That is what leads Pope to say that things could not have been different from what they are, and that everything is right as it is. That given, the meaning of this language is extended: that laws are the necessary relations that derive from the nature of things, to which it is added that in this sense all beings have their laws: the deity has its laws, the material world has its laws, the intelligences superior to man have their laws, the beasts have their laws, and man has his laws.

RESPONSE

Darkness itself is not more obscure than this. The Critic has heard it said that Spinoza assumed a blind and necessary principle that governed the universe; he needs no more than that: the minute he finds the word *necessary*, it will be Spinozism. The Author has said that the laws were a necessary relation. This is therefore Spinozism, because it entails necessity; and what is surprising is that, to this critic, the Author turns out to be a Spinozist because of this paragraph, although this paragraph expressly combats dangerous systems. The Author had in mind to attack the system of Hobbes, a frightening system that made all virtues and vices depend on the establishment of laws that men made for themselves; and wanting to prove that men are all born in a state of war, and that the first natural law is the war of all against all, overturns both all religion and all morality, like Spinoza. On that basis, the Author has first established that there were

being, which subjected the deity to disorders in the chain below, Pope was accused of being a follower of natural religion, which elevated reason above faith. Also judged objectionable were Pope's contentions that God had no choice but to create the world in the way that he did and that "One truth is clear: whatever is, is right" (*Essay on Man*, Epistle I, v. 294). These assertions were judged equivalent to Spinozist fatalism.

laws of justice and equity before the establishment of positive laws; he has proven that all beings have laws; that even before their creation they had possible laws; that God himself had laws, in other words the laws he had made for himself. He has shown[9] that it was not true that men were born into a state of war; he has made it clear that the state of war had begun only after the establishment of societies. On that he has provided clear principles; but it still results from this that the Author has attacked Hobbes's errors and the consequences of Spinoza's, and that it has come about that he has been so little understood that the objections he formulates against Spinozism have been taken as the opinions of Spinoza. Before entering a dispute, one should first become informed of the state of the question and know at least whether the person you attack is a friend or an enemy.

SECOND OBJECTION

The Critic continues: *Upon which the Author quotes Plutarch, who says that the law is the queen of all mortals and immortals.*[10] *But is it from a pagan, etc.*

RESPONSE

It is true that the Author quotes Plutarch, who says that law is the queen of all mortals and immortals.

THIRD OBJECTION

The Author has said that *creation, which seems to be an arbitrary act, supposes rules as invariable as the fatality of the atheists.*[11] From these terms the Critic concludes that the Author admits the fatality of the atheists.

RESPONSE

A moment earlier the Author has destroyed that fatality with these words: *Those who have said that a blind fatality governs the universe have uttered a great absurdity; for what greater absurdity than a blind fatality that has produced intelligent beings?* Moreover, in the censured passage the Author can be made to speak only on his own subject; he is not speaking of causes, and he does not compare the causes; rather he is speaking of effects, and comparing effects. The whole paragraph, and the ones that precede and follow it, make it clear that the only subject here is the rules of motion, which the Author says have been established by God; those rules are

9 In Book I, chapter I. (M)   10 Book I, chapter I, footnote I.   11 Book I, chapter I.

invariable, and all of physics says so along with him; they are invariable because God wished them to be invariable, and because he wished to preserve the world. He says neither more nor less than this.

I repeat that the Critic never understands the meaning of an assertion and focuses only on the words. When the Author has said that the creation which appeared to be an arbitrary act presupposed rules as invariable as the fatality of the atheists, it was not possible to understand him to be saying that the creation was a necessary act like the fatality of the atheists, for he has already attacked that fatality. Besides, the two members of a comparison must relate to each other; thus the sentence must necessarily mean that creation, which it first seems must produce variable rules of motion, has rules as invariable as the fatality of the atheists: the Critic once more has seen, and sees, words alone.

II

Therefore there is no Spinozism in *The Spirit of Law*. Let us pass on to another accusation and see whether it is true that the Author does not recognize revealed religion. The Author, at the end of the first chapter, speaking of the man who is a finite intelligence, subject to ignorance and error, has said: *Such a being could at every moment forget his creator; God has recalled him to himself by the laws of religion.*

He has said in the first chapter of Book xxiv: *I shall examine the various religions of the world only with respect to the good derived from them in the civil state, whether I speak of the one that has its root in heaven, or of those that have theirs on earth.*

It will take very little fairness to see that I have never pretended to make the interests of religion yield to political ones, but to unite them; now to unite them, one must know them. The Christian religion, which commands men to love one other, no doubt wants every people to have the best political and the best civil laws, because they are, besides themselves, the greatest good which men can give and receive.

And in the second chapter of the same book: *A prince who loves religion and fears it is a lion who submits to the hand that strokes it, or to the voice that soothes it; one who fears religion and hates it is like the savage beasts who bite the chain that keeps them from leaping on passers-by. One who has no religion at all is that fearsome animal that feels his freedom only when he tears and devours.*

In the third chapter of the same Book: *While Mohammedan princes are constantly imposing or suffering death, the religion of the Christians makes princes less tentative, and consequently less cruel. The prince relies on his subjects, and the* subjects on the prince. How marvelous it is: the Christian religion, which seems to have no other end than felicity in the afterlife, also provides for our happiness in this one.

In the fourth chapter of the same Book: *Concerning the character of the Christian religion and that of the Mohommedan religion, one must, without further examination, embrace the one and reject the other.* Pray continue.

In the sixth chapter: *Mr. Bayle, after maligning all religions, stigmatizes the Christian religion: he dares to suggest that true Christians would not form a state capable of lasting. Why not? They would be citizens infinitely enlightened about their duties, and would have very great zeal for fulfilling them; they would be quite conscious of the rights of natural defense. The more they believed they owed to religion, the more they would think they owed to their homeland. The principles of Christianity, deeply engraved in their hearts, would be infinitely more powerful than the false honor of monarchies, the human virtues of republics, and the servile fear of despotic states.*

It is surprising that this great man was unable to distinguish the orders for the establishment of Christianity from Christianity itself and that he can be accused of mistaking the spirit of his own religion. When the legislator, instead of giving laws, has given words of counsel, it is because he has seen that his counsels, should they be commanded like laws, would be contrary to the spirit of his laws.

In the tenth chapter: *If I could for a moment cease to think that I am a Christian, I would have to list the destruction of the school of Zeno*[12] *among the misfortunes of humankind, etc. Leave aside revealed truths for a moment; seek in all of nature, and you will find no nobler object than the Antonines,*[13] *etc.*

And in the thirteenth chapter: *The pagan religion, which forbade only a few gross crimes, which checked the hand and left the heart alone, could have crimes that were inexpiable; but a religion that veils all the passions, which is not more vigilant for acts than for desires and thoughts, which keeps us attached not by a few chains but by innumerable threads, which leaves human justice behind and commences another justice made to lead constantly from repentance to love and from love to repentance, which places between judge and criminal a great mediator, and between the just and the mediator a great judge: such a religion ought not to have inexpiable crimes. But although it gives fears and hopes to all, it makes it plain enough that if*

---

12 Zeno of Citium, in Cyprus (c. 334–c. 262 BCE), founder of the Stoic school of philosophy.

13 There were four Antonine emperors: Antoninus Pius (reigned from 138 to 161 CE); Marcus Aurelius (reigned from 161 to 180); Lucius Verus (co-reigned with Marcus Aurelius from 161 to 169); and Commodus (co-reigned with Marcus Aurelius from 177 to 180).

there is no crime which by its nature is inexpiable, a whole life can be; that it would be very dangerous to besiege mercy with more crimes and more expiations; that uneasy over old debts, never settled with the Lord, we must fear contracting new ones, filling the cup and attaining the limit where paternal patience fails.

In chapter nineteen, at the end, the Author, after pointing out the abuses of various pagan religions with respect to the state of souls in the next life, says: *It is not enough that a religion establish a doctrine, it must also direct it; that is what the Christian religion has done admirably with respect to the doctrines of which we speak: it has us hope for a state we believe in, not a state that we feel or know; everything, including the resurrection of the body, leads us to spiritual thoughts.*

And in chapter twenty-six, at the end: *It follows from this that it is almost always appropriate for a religion to have specific doctrines and a generalized ritual. In the laws that relate to the practices of observance, few details are needed: for example, mortifications and not a particular mortification. Christianity is full of good sense: abstinence is a divine institution, but a particular abstinence is a matter of public policy, and can be changed.*

In the last chapter, Book xxv: *But it does not result from all this that a religion imported from a very distant country, one wholly different in climate, laws, behaviors, and manners, has all the success that its holiness ought to promise.*

And in chapter 3 of Book xxiv: *It is the Christian religion that, despite the greatness of the empire and the vice of the climate, has prevented despotism from establishing itself in Ethiopia, and carried to the center of Africa the ethos of Europe and her laws, etc. Not far from there we see Mohammedanism requiring the children of the king of Sennar*[14] *to be locked up: at his death the council sends them to be slaughtered in favor of the one who mounts the throne.*

Let us think of the continual massacres of Greek and Roman kings and chiefs, and on the other hand the destruction of peoples and cities by those same chiefs: Timor Beg[15] *and Genghis Khan, who ravaged Asia; and we shall see that we owe to Christianity both a certain political law in government and a certain law of nations in war, for which humankind cannot be too grateful. Pray read the entire chapter.*

---

14 The nominally Islamic kingdom of Sennar was founded in 1504 on territory that is now Sudan, northwestern Eritrea, and western Ethiopia. Montesquieu's source for the slaughter (see note 1 of *SL* xxiv, chapter 3), was Charles Jacques Poncet's account of his travels in Ethiopia incorporated in volume iv of J.-B. du Halde's multivolume *Lettres édifiantes et curieuses, écrites des mission étrangères* ("Edifying and curious letters of some missionaries of the Society of Jesus from foreign missions," 1702–1776).

15 Shuja-ud-din Timur (1336–1405), known historically as Timur or Tamerlane, was the founder of the Timurid empire in central Asia. His goal was to recreate the Mongol empire of Genghis Khan (c. 1162–1227).

In chapter 8 of Book xxiv: *In a country which has the misfortune of having a religion that did not come from God, it is still necessary for it to accord with morality, because religion, even if false, is the best assurance men can have of the probity of other men.*

These are explicit passages: one sees therein a writer who not only believes the Christian religion, but loves it. What do they say to prove the contrary? And we warn again that the proofs must be proportional to the accusation. This accusation is not frivolous, nor must the evidence be; and as these proofs are given in a rather extraordinary form, consisting always in half proofs and half calumny, and being more or less immersed in the development of a most vague discourse, I shall set out to find them.

FIRST OBJECTION

The Author has praised the Stoics,[16] who assumed a blind fatality, a necessary chain of events, etc.; and that is the foundation of natural religion.

RESPONSE

I shall suppose for a moment that this bad way of reasoning is good: did the Author praise the Stoics' physics and metaphysics? He has praised their morality; he has said that some peoples have drawn great benefit from it. He did say that and has said nothing more. I am wrong, he did say more. For from the first page of the book he has attacked this fatality of the Stoics; therefore he did not praise it when he praised the Stoics.

SECOND OBJECTION

The Author has praised Bayle,[17] calling him a great man.[18]

RESPONSE

Let us again suppose for a moment that in general this manner of reasoning is good, still at least in this case it is not. It is true that the Author has called Bayle a great man, but he has censured his opinions; if he has censured them, he does not agree with them. And since he has attacked his opinions, he does not call him a great man on account of his opinions. Everyone knows that Bayle had a great mind, which he abused; but he did have it, that mind which he abused. The Author has refuted his sophisms and pities his errors. I do not approve people overturning the laws of their country, but I would have

16 Page 165 of the second sheet of 16 October 1749. (M)
17 Page 165 of the second sheet. (M)   18 Book xxiv, chapter 6.

difficulty believing that Caesar and Cromwell were petty minds; I do not approve conquerors, but I can hardly be persuaded that Alexander and Gengis Khan were geniuses of a common sort. It would not have taken the Author much imagination to say that Bayle was an abominable man;[19] but it would appear he does not like to spout calumnies, either because he owes this disposition to nature, or because he has received it from his education. I have reason to believe that if he took up the pen he would not cast any insults, even at those who have tried to inflict on him one of the greatest harms a man can do to another man by trying to make him odious to all who do not know him and suspect to all those who do.

Besides, I have noticed that the declamations of irate men make little impression except on others who are themselves irate. Most readers are moderate persons. One is not likely to take up a book except when unperturbed; reasonable people like to reason. Had the Author hurled a thousand calumnies at Bayle, the consequence would have been neither that Bayle had reasoned well, nor that Bayle had reasoned ill; all that one could have concluded from it would have been that the Author knows how to cast insults.

THIRD OBJECTION

This one is taken from the fact that the Author has made no mention of original sin in his first chapter.[20]

RESPONSE

I ask any reasonable man whether this chapter is a treatise on theology. If the Author had spoken of original sin, he could just as well have been accused of failure to mention redemption, and thus from article to article *ad infinitum*.

FOURTH OBJECTION

This one is taken from the fact that M. Domat began his work differently from the Author, and brought up revelation from the start.[21]

RESPONSE

It is true that M. Domat began his work differently from the Author, and brought up revelation from the start.

---

19 See Introduction, p. 21.   20 Sheet of 9 October 1749, p. 162. (M)
21 Jean Domat (1625–1696), *Les lois civiles dans leur ordre naturel* ("Civil laws in their natural order"), 3 vols. (1689) and a fourth volume (1697), *Droit publique* ("Public law") asserting that our "duties and functions" are prescribed by God who is "the only natural sovereign over men" and the source of all "legitimate" "power and authority."

FIFTH OBJECTION

The Author has followed the system of Pope's poem.

RESPONSE

In the entire book there is not a word about Pope's system.

SIXTH OBJECTION

The Author says that the law that prescribes man's duties toward God is the most important, but he denies that it is the first one: he pretends that the first law of nature is peace, that men first were afraid of one other, etc., that children know that the first law is to love God, and the second is to love one's neighbor.

RESPONSE

Here are the Author's words: *That law[22] which, by imprinting within us the idea of a creator, urges us toward him, is the first of the natural laws in importance, though not in the order of those laws. Man in the state of nature would possess rather the faculty of knowing rather than any knowledge. It is obvious that his first notions would not be speculative ones. He would attend to the preservation of his being before inquiring into its origin. Such a man would at first be aware only of his weakness; he would be extremely timid: and if on that point we needed evidence, wild men have been found in the forests who quake at everything and flee everything.* The Author therefore has said that the law which, by imprinting within us the idea of the creator, draws us toward him, was the first of the natural laws. He was not prohibited, any more than the philosophers and writers on natural law, from considering man under various aspects; it was permissible for him to imagine a man as fallen from the sky, left to himself and without education, before the establishment of societies. Well! The Author has said that the first, most important, and consequently the capital natural law would be for him, as for all men, to be drawn to his creator; it was also permissible for the Author to examine what would be the first impression made on that man, and to see in what order those impressions would be received in his brain; and he believed he would have feelings before he would reflect; that the first one in order of time would be fear, then the need to nourish himself, etc. The Author has said that the law which, imprinting in us the idea of the creator, draws us toward him, is the first of natural laws; the Critic says that the first natural law is to love God. They are separated only by calumnies.

22 Book i, chapter 2. (M)

SEVENTH OBJECTION

This one is taken from the first chapter of the first Book, where the Author, after saying *that man was a limited being,* has added: *Such a being could at every moment forget his creator; God has called him back to himself through the laws of religion.* Now what is this religion of which the Author speaks? He is no doubt speaking of natural religion; he therefore believes only in natural religion.

RESPONSE

I shall again suppose for a moment that this manner of reasoning is good, and that from the fact that the Author was speaking there only of natural religion, one can conclude that he believes only in natural religion, and excludes revealed religion. I say that in this passage he was speaking of revealed religion, and not natural religion, for if he had addressed natural religion, he would be an idiot; it would be as if he were saying: such a being could easily forget his creator, in other words natural religion; God has called him back to himself with the laws of natural religion. Thus, God would have given him natural religion in order to perfect natural religion in him. Thus, in preparation for maligning the Author, one first strips his words of the clearest meaning in the world to give them the most absurd meaning in the world; and to defeat him more easily, one deprives him of common sense.

EIGHTH OBJECTION

The Author has said,[23] speaking of man: *Such a being could at every moment forget his creator; God has called him back to himself through the laws of religion; such a being could at every moment forget himself; philosophers have informed him through the laws of morality; made to live in society, he could forget others; legislators have returned him to his duties through political and civil laws.* Therefore, says the Critic,[24] according to the Author the government of the world is shared by God, philosophers, and legislators, etc. Where did philosophers learn the laws of morality? Where did legislators see what must be prescribed to govern societies with equity?

RESPONSE

And this response is very easy. They got it in revelation, if they were fortunate enough for that; or else in that law which, by imprinting in us the idea of the creator, draws us toward him. Has the Author of *The Spirit of*

---

23 In Book I, chapter I. (M)   24 Page 162 of the sheet of 9 October 1749. (M)

Law spoken like Vergil? Caesar shares the empire with Jupiter.[25] Has God, who governs the universe, not given to certain men more understanding and to others more power? You would think the Author has said that because God wanted men to govern other men, he no longer wanted them to obey him, and that he has stood down from the sway he held over them, etc. That is what those are reduced to who, having much weakness for reasoning, have great strength for declaiming.

NINTH OBJECTION

The Critic continues: *Let us again note that the Author who finds that God cannot govern free beings as well as others, because, being free, they must act on their own* (I note in passing that the Author does not use the expression that God cannot), *remedies this disorder only with laws that can indeed show man what he must do, but do not enable him to do it. Thus, in the Author's system, God creates beings whose disorder he cannot prevent nor remedy. . . . How blind, not to see that God does what he wishes, even with those who do not do what he wishes!*

RESPONSE

The Critic has already reproached the Author with failure to mention original sin; he catches him again in the act: he has not mentioned grace. It is a sad thing to have to deal with a man who censures every paragraph in a book and has only one prevailing thought. It's the tale of that village curate to whom astronomers show the moon in a telescope, and who sees nothing but his steeple.

The Author of *The Spirit of Law* believed he should first offer some notion of general laws and the law of nature and of nations; this subject was immense, and he treated it in two chapters: he was obliged to omit many things that belonged to his subject, all the more reason for omitting those which had no relevance to it.

TENTH OBJECTION

The Author has said that murder of oneself[26] in England was the effect of an illness, and that it could not be punished because one does not punish the effects of dementia. A disciple of natural religion does not forget that England is the cradle of his sect; he suppresses all the crimes he perceives.

---

25 A casual line from Vergil repeated by Aelius Donatus (fourth century) in his *Life of Vergil*.

26 *Homicide de soi-même*; the word *suicide* does not appear in a French dictionary until 1762.

RESPONSE

The Author does not know whether England is the cradle of natural religion, but he knows that England is not his own cradle because he spoke of a physical effect that is seen in England. He does not think of religion like the English any more than an Englishman who might speak of a physical effect that occurred in France would think about religion like the French. The Author of *The Spirit of Law* is not at all a disciple of natural religion, but he wishes his Critic were a disciple of natural logic.

I think I have already made the Critic drop the terrifying weapons he has used; now I shall give a notion of his opening statement, which is such that I fear it will appear I speak of it here with derision.

First he says, and these are his words, that *the book on the Spirit of Law is one of those irregular productions. . . that have so powerfully multiplied only since the advent of the bull Unigenitus.* But is attributing the advent of *The Spirit of Law* to the advent of the Constitution *Unigenitus* not meant to provoke laughter? The bull *Unigenitus* is not the occasional cause of the book on the Spirit of Law; but the bull *Unigenitus* and the book on the Spirit of Law have been the occasional causes that have made the Critic engage in such puerile reasoning. The Critic continues: *The Author says that he has repeatedly begun and abandoned his work. . . Yet when he cast his first productions into the fire, he was nearer the truth than when he began to be pleased with his work.* What does he know about it? He adds: *If the Author had wished to follow a beaten path, his book would have cost him less labor.* Again, what does he know about it? Next he pronounces this oracle: *It does not require much astuteness to perceive that the book on the Spirit of Law is based on the system of natural religion.* [. . .] *We have shown that in the letters against the poem of Pope entitled "Essay on Man" the system of natural religion enters into that of Spinoza;*[27] *that is enough to inspire in a Christian a horror of the new book which we announce.* I reply that not only is it enough, but it would even be far too much; but I have just proven that the Author's system is not that of natural religion; and while conceding to him that the system of natural religion enters into that of Spinoza, the Author's system would not enter into that of Spinoza, since it is not that of natural religion.

So he wants to inspire horror before he has proven that horror is called for.

---

27 Jean-Baptiste Gaultier, the author of the attack Montesquieu is addressing in the *Defense* (see Introduction, p. 19), was also the author of *Le Poème de Pope intitulé "Essay sur l'homme" convaincu d'impiété* ("Pope's poem *An Essay on Man* convicted of impiety," 1746). Ever on the watch for irreligion, Gaultier also was to publish, in 1751, *Les Lettres persanes convaincus d'impiété* ("The *Persian Letters* convicted of impiety").

Here are the two formulas of reasoning distributed throughout these two writings to which I am responding: the Author of *The Spirit of Law* is a disciple of natural religion; therefore what he says must be explained here by the principles of natural religion; now if what he says here is based on principles of natural religion, he is a disciple of natural religion.

The other formula is this: the Author of *The Spirit of Law* is a disciple of natural religion; therefore what he says in his book in favor of revelation is there only to hide the fact that he is a disciple of natural religion: now if he hides in this way, he is a disciple of natural religion.

Before finishing this Part One, I would be tempted to voice an objection to the man who has voiced so many; he has so startled us with the words *adherent of natural religion* that I, who am defending the Author, hardly dare pronounce that term; I will however summon my courage. Would his two pieces not require more explanation than the man I am defending? Is it advisable for someone, when speaking of natural and revealed religion, perpetually to adhere to one side and make us lose sight of the other? Is it advisable never to distinguish between those who recognize only natural religion and those who recognize both natural religion and revelation? Is it advisable to be alarmed every time the Author considers man in the state of natural religion, and explains something on the principles of natural religion? Is it advisable to conflate natural religion with atheism? Have I not always heard that we were all imbued with a natural religion? Have I not heard that Christianity was the perfection of natural religion? Have I not heard that natural religion was used to prove revelation against the deists? And that the same natural religion was used to prove the existence of God against the atheists? He says that the Stoics were adherents of natural religion; and I for my part say to him that they were atheists,[28] since they believed that a blind fatality governed the universe, and that it is with natural religion that one combats the Stoics. He says that the system of natural religion enters into that of Spinoza,[29] and I for my part say to him that they are contradictory, and it is by means of natural religion that one destroys the system of Spinoza. I say to him that confounding natural religion with atheism conflates the proof with the thing you are trying to

---

28 See page 165 of the broadsides of 9 October 1749. *The Stoics accepted only one god, but that god was nothing other than the soul of the world; they held that all beings, beginning with the first, were necessarily linked to each other: a fatal necessity enveloped all. They denied the immortality of the soul, and saw ultimate happiness as consisting in living in conformity with nature: that is the essence of the system of natural religion.* (M)

29 See page 161 of the first sheet of 9 October 1749, at the bottom of the first column. (M)

prove, and the objection to error with error itself; it takes away the powerful weapons we have against that error. God forbid I should impute any evil
design to the Critic, nor call attention to what could be drawn from his
principles. Although he exhibits little indulgence, we would have some for
him. I say only that metaphysical ideas are extremely confused in his head;
that he lacks the faculty of discrimination; that he could by no means make
good judgments because, among the various things one must see, he never
sees but one; and even this I say not to make reproach to him, but to
counter his own reproaches.

Part Two
General Argument

I have absolved the book on the Spirit of Law of two general reproaches
which had been brought against it; there are still some particular charges to
which I must respond. But to shed more light on what I have said and on
what I shall say in what follows, I am going to explain what gave rise to, or
served as pretext for, those invectives.

The most sensible persons of various countries in Europe, the most
enlightened men and the wisest, have regarded the book on the Spirit of
Law as a useful work; they have found that its morality is pure and its
principles just; that it was proper for the instruction of good men; that its
Author destroyed pernicious opinions; and that he encouraged good ones.

On the other hand, here is a man who speaks of it as a dangerous book; he
has made it the subject of the most outlandish invectives. I must explain
this.

Far from having understood the particular passages he criticized in this book,
he was not even clear on the material it treated; thus, declaiming into the void
and attacking the wind, he has not criticized the Author's book. But how could
a man have so badly missed the subject and the purpose of a work he had before
his eyes? Those who have some understanding will see at first glance that the
object of this work is the laws, customs, and various ways of all the peoples of
the earth. One can say that its subject is immense since it embraces all the
institutions that are received among men; since the Author distinguishes these
institutions, examines those that are best suited to society and to each society,
seeks their origin, discovers their physical and moral causes, examines those
which have a degree of goodness in themselves and those that have none; since
of two pernicious practices he asks which is the more and which less so; since he
discusses those that can have good effects in a certain respect and ill ones in
another. He has believed his research useful because good sense consists largely

of knowing the nuances of things. Now in such an extensive subject it has been necessary to deal with religion, for, there being on the earth one true religion and countless false ones, a religion sent from heaven and countless others that were spawned on earth, he could look at all the false religions only as human institutions. He therefore had to examine them like all other human institutions, and as for the Christian religion, he had only to worship it as being a divine institution. It was not this religion he was to discuss, because by its nature it is not subject to any scrutiny; and so, when he has spoken of it, he has never done so in order to bring it into the compass of his work, but to pay it the tribute of respect and love it is owed by every Christian, and so that in the comparisons he might make of it with other religions, he could make it triumph over them all. What I am saying can be seen in the work; but the Author has particularly explained it at the beginning of Book xxiv, which is the first of the two Books he has written on religion. He begins it as follows: *As we can judge among shadows which are the least dark, and among chasms which are the least deep, so we can seek among false religions those which are the most consistent with the welfare of society; those which, though they have not the effect of leading men to the felicities of the afterlife, can contribute the most to their happiness in this one.*

I shall therefore examine the various religions of the world only with respect to the good derived from them in the civil state, whether I speak of the one that has its root in heaven, or of those that have theirs on earth.

The Author therefore, regarding human religions only as human institutions, had to speak of them, because they entered necessarily into his design; he did not go looking for them, rather they came looking for him. And as for the Christian religion, he has spoken of it only occasionally because, by its nature not being susceptible to modification, mitigation, or correction, it did not enter into the design he had in mind.

What has he done to give ample play to declamations and to open the widest door to invectives? The Author has been considered as if, following the example of M. Abbadie,[30] he had set out to write a treatise on the Christian religion; he has been attacked as if his two Books on religion were two treatises on Christian theology; he has been reproached as if, speaking of a religion that is not Christian, he needed to examine it according to the principles and dogmas of the Christian religion; he has been judged as if he

---

30 Jacques Abbadie (1765–1727), author of *Traité de la vérité de la religion chrétienne* ("Treatise on the truth of the Christian religion," Rotterdam, 1684) and a companion *Traité de la divinité de Notre Seigneur Jésus-Christ* ("Treatise on the divinity of Our Lord Jesus Christ," 1689) and *L'Art de se connaitre soi-même* ("The art of knowing oneself," 1692).

had undertaken in his two Books to establish for Christians, and to preach to Mohammedans and idolaters, the dogmas of the Christian religion. Every time he has spoken of religion in general, every time he used the word religion, it was asserted that it means the Christian religion; every time he has compared the religious practices of some random nations and has said they were more suited to the political government of that country than some other practice, the Critic has said: So you approve them and abandon the Christian faith. When he has spoken of some people that has not embraced Christianity, or which preceded the coming of Jesus Christ, the Critic has said: So you do not recognize Christian morality; when he has examined as a political writer any practice whatever, he has been told: It was such-and-such dogma of Christian theology you should have put there: you call yourself a jurisconsult, and I will make you into a theologian despite yourself. Indeed you give us some lovely things on the Christian religion, but you say them only to hide, for I know your heart and read your thoughts. It is true that I do not understand your book; it does not matter whether I have well or poorly discerned the purpose for which it has been written; but I know all your thoughts thoroughly. I do not know a single word of what you say, but I understand very well what you do not say. Let us now explore the matter.

ON RELIGIOUS COUNSEL

The Author, in the Book on religion, has refuted Bayle's error; here are his words:[31] *Mr. Bayle, after maligning all religions, stigmatizes the Christian religion: he dares to suggest that true Christians would not form a state capable of lasting. Why not? They would be citizens infinitely enlightened about their duties, and who have very great zeal for fulfilling them. They would be quite conscious of the rights of natural defense; the more they believed they owed to religion, the more they would think they owed to their homeland. The principles of Christianity, deeply engraved in the heart, would be infinitely more powerful than that false honor of monarchies, the human virtues of republics, and that servile fear of despotic states.*

It is surprising that this great man was unable to distinguish the orders for the establishment of Christianity from Christianity itself, and that one can impute to him misjudgment of the spirit of his own religion. When the legislator, instead of giving laws, has given counsel, it is because he has seen that his words of counsel, were they commands like laws, would be contrary to the spirit of his laws. What

31 Book xxiv, chapter 6. (M)

has he done to deprive the Author of the glory of thus having attacked Bayle's error? He takes the following chapter,[32] which has nothing to do with Bayle: *Human laws, it says there, made to speak to the mind must give precepts and not counsel; religion, made to speak to the heart, should give much counsel and few precepts.* And from that he concludes that the Author regards all the precepts of the Gospel as words of counsel. He could also say that the person who made this criticism himself regards all the words of counsel in the Gospel as precepts: but that is not his manner of reasoning, and even less his manner of behaving. Let us get to the fact; we must expand a bit what the Author has abbreviated. M. Bayle had maintained that a society of Christians could not survive, and he based that on the Gospel's command to turn the other cheek when we are slapped; to renounce the world; to withdraw into the deserts, etc. The Author has said that Bayle took for precepts what were no more than words of counsel, and for general rules what were merely particular rules; in that, the Author has defended religion. What then happens? He hears it posited as the first article of his belief that all the books of the Gospel contain only words of counsel.

ON POLYGAMY

Other passages also furnished convenient subjects for declamations. Polygamy was an excellent example: the Author wrote a chapter expressly to condemn it, and here it is:

On Polygamy in Itself[33]

To consider polygamy in general, independently of the circumstances which can make it somewhat acceptable, it is not useful to the human race, nor to either of the two sexes, whether to the one that abuses or to the one that is abused. Neither is it useful to children, and one of its great drawbacks is that the father and mother cannot have the same affection for their children: a father cannot love twenty children as a mother loves two. It is much worse when a woman has multiple husbands, for then paternal love hangs only on this opinion: that a father may believe, if he wishes, or that the others may believe, that certain children are his.

A plurality of wives – who would have thought it? – leads to that love which nature disowns; for one degradation always brings another with it, etc.

Moreover, the possession of many wives does not always preclude desires for another's wife; lust is like avarice, which gets thirstier from the acquisition of treasures.

---

32 This is chapter 7 of Book xxiv. (M)   33 Book xvi, chapter 6.

In the time of Justinian,[34] several philosophers constrained by Christianity withdrew to Persia with Khosrow.[35] What struck them the most, says Agathias,[36] was that polygamy was permitted to men who did not even abstain from adultery.[37]

The Author has therefore established that polygamy is by its nature and in itself a bad thing. This chapter should have been the starting point, and yet it is about this chapter that nothing has been said. The Author has moreover philosophically examined in what countries, in what climates, and in what circumstances it has fewer bad effects. He has compared climates to other climates and countries to other countries, and he has found that there are countries where it had fewer ill effects than in others, because according to the accounts of them, the number of men and women not being equal in all countries, it is clear that if there are countries where there are many more women than men, polygamy, bad in itself, is less so than in others. The Author discussed this in chapter 4 of the same Book. But since the title of that chapter bore the words: *That the law on polygamy is a matter of calculation*, this title was seized upon; yet as the title of a chapter relates to the chapter itself, and can say neither more nor less than that chapter, let us look at it:

According to the calculations being made in various places in Europe, more boys are born there than girls; on the contrary, the reports from Asia tell us that many more girls are born there than boys. The law of a single wife in Europe and the one that allows several in Asia therefore have a certain relationship to the climate.

In the cold climates of Asia, as in Europe, more boys are born than girls; this, say the lamas, is the reason for the law there which there allows a woman to have more than one husband.

But I have difficulty believing there are many countries where the disproportion is great enough to require the introduction of the law of multiple wives or the law of multiple husbands. That just means that the plurality of women or even the plurality of men is more in conformity with nature in certain countries than in others.

---

34 Justinian I (c. 482–565) was the Eastern Roman Emperor from 527 to 565 who took steps to restore imperial power in portions of the former Western Roman Empire by conquering the Vandals in North Africa and the Ostrogoths in Dalmatia, Sicily, Italy, and Rome. He arranged for the codification of Roman law, known collectively as the *Corpus juris civilis* and consisting of the *Codex Justinianeus*, the *Digesta* or *Pandectae*, the *Institutiones*, and the *Novellae*.

35 Khosrow I was King of Kings of Iran from 531 to 579 and head of the Sasanian Empire, which he fashioned by means of successful wars against the Hephthalites in the east, the Aksumites in the south, and the Byzantine empire in the west.

36 Agathias (c. 536–c. 582) was a Byzantine historian, lawyer, and poet during the latter portion of the reign of Justinian. His *De imperio et rebus gestis Justiani* ("On the reign and acts of Justinian"; *Catalogue* 2808) continues the work of Procopius (c. 500–after 565).

37 *SL* xvi, 6.

I admit that if it were true, as the relation tells us, that in Bantam there are ten women for every man, that would be a most particular case of polygamy. In all this I am not justifying the customs but giving the reasons for them.

Let us return to the title: polygamy is a matter of calculation. Yes, it is, when one wants to know whether it is more or less pernicious in certain climates, in certain countries, and in certain circumstances than in others. It is not a matter of calculation when one must decide whether it is good or bad in itself.

It is not a matter of calculation when one reasons about its nature; it can be a matter of calculation when one combines its effects; finally, it is never a matter of calculation when one examines the ends of marriage, and even less so when one examines marriage as it was established by Jesus Christ.

I shall add here that chance has served the Author very well. He doubtless did not foresee that one explicit chapter would be overlooked so as to give an equivocal meaning to another one, and he is fortunate to have ended that other one with these words: *In all this I am not justifying the customs, but giving the reasons for them.*

The Author has just said that he did not see that there could be climates in which the number of women could so far exceed that of men, or the number of men that of women, that any country would engage in polygamy; and he has added:[38] *That only means that the plurality of women and even the plurality of men is more in keeping with nature in certain countries than in others.* The Critic has seized on the words *is more in keeping with nature* in order to make the Author say that he approves of polygamy. But if I said I prefer fever over scurvy, would that mean that I like fever, or merely that I find scurvy more unpleasant than fever?

Here is word for word a most extraordinary objection:

The polygamy[39] of a woman who has multiple husbands is a monstrous disorder that has been allowed in no instance, and which the Author in no way distinguishes from the polygamy of a man who has multiple wives. This language in a disciple of natural religion requires no commentary.

I beg the reader to pay attention to the linkage of the Critic's ideas: according to him, it follows from the Author's being a disciple of natural religion that he has not mentioned what he had no reason for mentioning; or else it follows, according to him, that the Author has not mentioned what he

---

38 Chapter 4, Book xvi. (M)   39 Page 164 of the sheet of 9 October 1749. (M)

had no reason to mention because he is a disciple of natural religion. These two arguments are of the same sort, and in both the consequences are found in the premises. The ordinary manner is to criticize what has been written, and here the Critic fantasizes over what has not been written.

I say all this supposing with the Critic that the Author would not have distinguished the polygamy of a woman who has multiple husbands from one where a husband had multiple wives. But if the Author has distinguished between them, what will he say? If the Author has made it plain that in the former case the abuses were greater, what will he say? I beg the reader to reread chapter 6 of Book XVI; I have cited it above. The Critic has maligned him because he had kept his peace about that matter; it only remains to malign him for not keeping it.

But here is something I cannot understand. The Critic has written in the second of his broadsides, page 166: *The Author has told us above that religion ought to allow polygamy in warm countries and not in cold countries.* But the Author has nowhere said that. It is no longer a matter of poor reasoning between the Critic and him; it is a matter of fact. And as the Author has nowhere said that religion ought to allow polygamy in warm countries and not in cold countries, if the charge is false, as it is, and grave, as it is, I beg the Critic to judge himself: this is not the only place where the Author has had to cry out. On page 163 at the end of the first sheet, it is said: *Chapter IV bears as its title that the law of polygamy is a matter of calculation, in other words that in places where more boys than girls are born, as in Europe, one should marry but one woman; in those where more girls are born than boys, polygamy should be introduced.* Thus, when the Author explains some customs, or gives the reasons for some practices, they are turned into maxims, and what is even sadder, into religious maxims. And as he has discussed innumerable customs and practices in every country in the world, one can with a similar method blame him for the errors and even the abominations of all creation. The Critic says at the end of the second broadside that God has given him some zeal; well, I reply to him that it was not God who gave him that one.

CLIMATE

What the Author had to say about climate is again a matter very suited to rhetoric, but all effects of every sort have causes, and climate and other causes produce an infinite number of effects. If the Author had said the contrary, he would have looked like a numbskull; the whole question comes down to knowing whether in countries distant from each other and whether under different climates there are national characters of mind.[40] Now that there are differences is established by the near unanimity of the books that have been written; and as the character of mind greatly influences the disposition of the heart, it cannot still be doubted that there are certain qualities of the heart that are more frequent in one country than in another; and we have as additional proof an infinite number of writers from all over and from all times. As these things are human, the Author has spoken of them in a human manner; he could well have added many questions that are raised in schools over human virtues and Christian virtues, but it is not with these questions that one makes books of physics, politics, and jurisprudence. In a word, this physics of climate can produce various dispositions of mind, and these dispositions can influence human actions: does this clash with the might of him who created, or the merits of him who redeemed?

If the Author has inquired into what the magistrates in various countries could do to conduct their nation in the most suitable manner and the one most in conformity with its character, what harm has he done thereby?

The same reasoning would apply with respect to various local religious practices: the Author did not need to consider them either good or bad; he has merely said that there were climates where certain religious practices were easier to accept, in other words were easier to practice, by the people in those climates than by peoples in another. It is needless to offer examples of this: there are a hundred thousand.

I am quite aware that religion is independent in itself of whatever physical effect, that the one that is good in one country is good in another, and that it cannot be bad in one country without being bad in all. But I say that as it is practiced by and for men, there are places where any religion whatever lends itself better to being practiced either in whole or in part in certain countries than in others, and in certain circumstances than in others; anyone who says the contrary will be renouncing good sense.

The Author has observed that the climate of the Indies produced a certain gentleness of behavior; but, says the Critic, the women there burn themselves when their husbands die. This objection is wanting in philosophy. Is the Critic unaware of the contradictions of the human mind, and how it is able to separate things that are most united and unite those that are the most separated? See on this subject the Author's reflections in Book xiv, chapter 3.

40 *Caractères d'esprit.*

TOLERATION

All that the Author has said about toleration relates to this proposition in Book xxv, chapter 9: *We are being political and not theological here, and even for theologians there is a big difference between tolerating a religion and approving of it.*

When the laws of a state have thought it best to allow multiple religions, they must also oblige them to tolerate each other. One is invited to read the rest of the chapter.

There was much outcry because the Author added to Book xxv, chapter 10: *Here is the fundamental principle of political laws where religion is concerned: when one is free to decide whether to allow a new religion into a state or not to allow it, one should not establish it; when it is established there, one must tolerate it.*

The objection is made to the Author that he will warn idolatrous princes to shut the Christian religion out of their states; indeed that is a secret which he went and whispered in the ear of the king of Cochinchina. As this argument has supplied material for many declamations, I will make two replies. The first is that the Author specifically excepted the Christian religion in his book. He has said, in Book xxiv, at the end of chapter 1: *The Christian religion, which commands men to love one another, no doubt wills that every people should have the best political laws and the best civil laws because they are, next to itself, the greatest good that men can give and receive.* Therefore if the Christian religion is the primary good and the political and civil laws the second, there are no political and civil laws in a state that can or should prevent the introduction of the Christian religion.

My second reply is that the religion of heaven does not establish itself by the same means as the religions of earth: read the history of the Church and you will see the wonders of the Christian religion. When she has resolved to enter a country, she is able to make the gates open up to her. Every means is appropriate for that. Sometimes God wants to work through a few sinners, sometimes he will take an emperor on the throne and make his head bow under the yoke of the Gospel. Does the Christian religion hide in underground places? Wait a moment, and you will see the imperial majesty speak for her. She crosses, when she so wishes, the seas, rivers, and mountains; it is not the obstacles here below that prevent her from going. Put resistance into minds and she will find a way to overcome that resistance; establish customs, mould traditions, publish edicts, make laws: she will triumph over the climate, the laws that result from it, and the legislators who have made them.

God, following decrees unknown to us, extends or restrains the limits of his religion.

I have heard it said it is as if you were to tell the kings of the East that they must not allow the Christian religion in. To speak in this way is to be very charnal:[41] was it then Herod who was to be the Messiah? It seems that Jesus Christ is being regarded as a king who, wanting to conquer a neighboring state, hides his practices and intelligence. Let us do ourselves justice: is the way in which we behave in human affairs pure enough to think of using it for the conversion of peoples?

ON CELIBACY

We have come to the matter of celibacy. Everything the Author has said about it relates to this proposition which is found in Book xxv, chapter 4. Here it is:

I shall not address here the consequences of the law of celibacy. It is obvious that it could become harmful to the degree that the body of the clergy was too extensive and that consequently the body of the laity would not be extensive enough. It is clear that the Author is speaking here only of the greatest or smallest extension that ought to be given to celibacy with respect to the greater or lesser number of those who are to embrace it, and as the Author has said in another place,[42] this law of perfection cannot be made for all men. We know moreover that the law of celibacy such as we have it is only a disciplinary law; the nature of celibacy itself or its degree of goodness has never been an issue in *The Spirit of Law*, and it is in no way a matter that should enter into a book on political and civil laws. The Critic never wants the Author to treat his subject; he constantly wants him to treat his own, and because he is always a theologian, he does not want anyone to be a juriconsult, even in a book of law. Yet we shall see shortly that he shares the theologians' opinion on celibacy; in other words, he has recognized its goodness. He makes it known that in Book xxiii, which treats the relationship which the laws have with the number of inhabitants, the Author has offered a theory of what the political and civil laws of various peoples have done in that regard. He has made it known, by examining the histories of various peoples of the earth, that there have been circumstances where those laws were more necessary than in others, peoples who have had greater need of them, and certain times when those peoples have had even greater need of them. And as he has thought that the Romans were the wisest people on earth, and who to repair their losses had the greatest need of such laws, he has collected with great care the laws they had

41 As opposed to spiritual.   42 Cf. *SL* xxiii, 21.

made with regard to it; he has delineated precisely the circumstances in which they were made, and in which other circumstances they had been revoked. There is no theology in all this, and none is needed for all this. Nevertheless he has judged it appropriate to insert some. Here are his words:[43] *God forbid that I should speak here against the celibacy which religion has adopted, but who could keep silent against that celibacy formed by libertinism, where the two sexes, corrupting themselves through the natural sentiments themselves, flee a union that would make them better in order to live in those that make them ever worse?*

It is a rule drawn from nature that the more the number of marriages that could take place diminishes, the more corrupted are those that do marry; the fewer married persons there are, the less fidelity there is in marriages, as the more thieves there are, the more thefts.

The Author has therefore not disapproved of celibacy that is motivated by religion; no one could complain that he rose up against the celibacy introduced by libertinism, that he disapproved that an infinite number of wealthy and sensual people should be inclined to flee the yoke of marriage for the convenience of their debauchery, or that they revel in delights and sensuality for themselves and leave the pains to the wretched: no one, I say, could complain about those things. But the Critic, after quoting what the Author has said, pronounces these words: *Here we perceive all the malignity of the Author who wants to impugn the Christian religion for disorders which it detests.* There is no point in accusing the Critic of not wanting to understand the Author; I will simply say that he did not understand him, and that he makes him say against religion what he has said against libertinism. He must be very annoyed at that.

A PARTICULAR ERROR OF THE CRITIC'S

One would think that the Critic has sworn never to be current on the question, and not to understand a single one of the passages he attacks; the whole second chapter of Book xxv turns on the more or less powerful motives that attach men to the preservation of their religion: the Critic discovers in his imagination another chapter of which the subject is motives that oblige men to move from one religion to another. The first subject entails a passive state, the second an action state; and applying to one subject what the Author has said on another gives him license to talk nonsense.

The Author has said in the second paragraph of chapter 2 of Book xxv: *We are extremely prone to idolatry, and yet we are not strongly attached to idolatrous*

43 Book xxiii, end of chapter 21. (M)

religions; we are not at all prone to spiritual thoughts, and yet we are very attached to the religions that have us worship a spiritual being. This is explained by the satisfaction we find in ourselves for being intelligent enough to have chosen a religion that raises the deity from the humiliation where the others had placed it. The Author had written this paragraph only to explain why the Mohammedans and the Jews, who do not have the same graces[44] we have, are as invincibly attached to their religion as we know them to be by experience. The Critic understands it differently: *It is pride,* he says, *that is credited with*[45] *making men pass from idolatry to the unity of one God.* But it is not a question here nor in the entire chapter of any passage from one religion to another; and if a Christian feels satisfaction at the thought of glory and the sight of the greatness of God, and that is styled pride, it is a very good pride.

MARRIAGE

Here is another objection that is not common. The Author wrote two chapters[46] in Book xxiii, one with the title: *Of men and animals, with respect to the multiplication of their species,* and the other: *On marriages.* In the first, he has said these words: *The females of animals have fairly constant fertility. But in the human species, the manner of thinking, the character, the passions, the fancies, the caprice, the idea of preserving one's beauty, the ungainliness of pregnancy, and the nuisance of an overlarge family, disrupt propagation in a thousand ways;* and in the other he has said: *The father's natural obligation to feed his children brought about the institution of marriage, which designates who must fulfill that obligation.*

Upon which the Critic says: *A Christian would relate the institution of marriage to God himself, who gave a companion to Adam, and united the first man with the first woman by an indissoluble bond before they had children to feed, but the Author avoids anything having to do with revelation.* The Author will reply that he is a Christian, but not an imbecile; that he worships these truths, but does not want to broadcast at random all the truths he believes. The emperor Justinian was a Christian, and his compiler was also. Well, in their books of law which we teach the young in our schools, they define marriage[47] as the union of man and woman who form their own lifetime society. It has never entered anyone's head to reproach them for failing to mention revelation.

---

44 In the theological sense.   45 Page 166 of the second sheet. (M)   46 Chapters 1 and 2.
47 Maris et fœminæ conjunctio individuam vitæ societatem continens. (M)

USURY

We have come to the usury business. I fear that the reader may be tired of hearing me say that the Critic is never up to snuff and never gets the meaning of the passages he censures. He says on the subject of maritime usury: *The Author sees nothing wrong with maritime usury: these are his terms.* In truth this work *The Spirit of Law* has a terrible interpreter. The Author has treated maritime usury in chapter 20 of Book xxii: he has therefore said in that chapter that the maritime usury was just. Let us see.

On Maritime Usury

The high rates of maritime usuries are based on two things: the peril of the sea, which makes a person risk lending his money only in order to acquire much more, and the facility which commerce offers the borrower to close large and numerous deals in short order; whereas other usuries,[48] being based on neither of these two reasons, are either forbidden by legislators or reduced to fair limits, which makes more sense.

I ask any sensible man whether the Author has just decided that maritime usury is just, or whether he has simply said that the high rates of maritime usury were less repugnant to natural equity than the high rates of other usuries. The Critic knows only positive and absolute qualities; he does not understand the terms *more or less.* If you told him that a mulatto is less black than a Negro, that would mean according to him that he is white as snow; if you told him that he is blacker than a European, he would again believe what is meant is that he is black as coal. But let us continue.

In Book xxii of *The Spirit of Law* there are four chapters on usury. In the first two, which are the nineteenth and the one you have just read, the Author examines usury[49] in the way it can relate to the commerce of the different nations and to the world's various governments. Those two chapters are concerned with nothing but that; the two following are written only to explain the variations in usury among the Romans. But now the Author is made to be a casuist, canonist, and theologian, solely for the reason that the man who criticizes is a casuist, canonist, and theologian, or two of the three, or one of the three, or perhaps at bottom none of the three. The Author knows that in looking at lending for interest in its relation to the Christian religion, the matter has endless distinctions and limitations; he knows that the jurisconsults and several tribunals are not always in

---

48 *Usures de terre*, i.e., land-based contracts, or every form of lending not involving shipping.
49 Usury or interest meant the same thing to the Romans. (M)

agreement with the casuists and canonists, that some allow certain limitations to the general principle of never requiring interest, and that others allow larger exceptions. Had all these questions pertained to his subject, which is not the case, how could he have dealt with them? One is hard-pressed to know what one has carefully studied; even less does one know what one has never studied in one's life; but the very chapters that are being used against him prove sufficiently that he is but a historian and jurisconsult. Let us read chapter 19.[50]

Money is the sign of values. It is clear that whoever needs this sign must hire it, as he does all the things he may need. The whole difference is that other things can be either hired or purchased, whereas money, which is the price of things, can be hired but not purchased.[51]

It is, to be sure, a worthy deed to lend one's money to someone else without interest, but clearly it can only be a counsel of religion and not a civil law.

For commerce to work well, money must have a price, but that price must be moderate. If it is too high, the trader, who sees that it would cost him more in interest than he could gain in his commerce, undertakes nothing; if money has no price, no one lends any, and again the trader undertakes nothing.

I am wrong to say that no one lends any. The business of society must in any case go forward; usury comes into play, but with the disorders that people have experienced in all times.

Mohammed's law conflates usury with lending at interest. In Mohammedan countries, usury increases in proportion to the severity of the prohibition; the lender indemnifies himself for the risk of the infraction.

In eastern countries, most men have nothing that is secure; there is almost no relation between the present possession of a sum and the expectation of getting it back once it has been loaned: usury thus increases in proportion to the risk of insolvency.

Next come the chapter *On maritime usury,* which I have related above, and chapter 21 which treats *On lending by contract, and on usury among the Romans,* which follows: *Besides lending for commerce, there is another kind of lending done by civil contract which results in interest or usury.*

With the people of Rome increasing their power by the day, the magistrates sought to flatter them, and get the laws most agreeable to them enacted. The people withdrew capital, lowered interest, forbade the taking of interest, and removed corporal constraints; and finally the abolition of debts was agitated every time a tribune wanted to make himself popular.

---

50 Book xxii. (M)
51 This discussion does not include cases where gold and silver are considered as merchandise.

These continual changes, either by laws or by plebiscites, naturalized usury in Rome, for the creditors, seeing in the people their debtor, their legislature, and their judge, no longer had confidence in contracts. The people, like a debtor with reduced credit, could tempt lenders without huge profits, all the more since, although laws only came from time to time, the complaints of the people were continual and always intimidated the creditors. The result was that all honest means of lending and borrowing were abolished in Rome, and horrendous usury, repeatedly struck down[52] and repeatedly reborn, became established.

Cicero tells us that in his time lending in Rome was at thirty-four percent and at forty-eight percent in the provinces.[53] Again, this was the unfortunate consequence of the laws having been insufficiently restrained. Extreme laws for good purposes foment extreme harm; it was necessary to pay for the loan of the money and for the danger imposed by the law's penalties. Clearly, the Author has dealt with lending at interest only in its relation to various peoples' trade, or with the Romans' civil laws; and that is so true that he has distinguished in the second paragraph of chapter xix what the legislators of religion have established from those of the political legislators. If he had spoken there specifically of the Christian religion, having another subject to treat, he would have used different terms, and he would have had the Christian religion command what it commands and counsel what it counsels; like the theologians he would have distinguished the various cases; he would have formulated all the limitations that the principles of the Christian religion leave to that general law, sometimes established among the Romans and always among the Mohammedans: *One must never in any case or any circumstance receive interest for money.* That was not the subject the Author was to treat; rather this one: that general, unlimited, indistinct, and unrestricted prohibition is ruining commerce for the Mohammedans, and very nearly wrecked the republic for the Romans. Whence it follows that because the Christians do not live under those rigid terms, their commerce is not destroyed, and one does not see in their states those frightful usuries that are required among the Mohammedans and were in the past extorted among the Romans.

The Author has used chapters 21 and 22[54] to examine what were the laws among the Romans on the subject of lending by contract in the different times of their republic; his Critic momentarily leaves the benches of theology and turns toward erudition. We shall see that he is again mistaken in his

---

52 Tacitus, *Annals*, vi.   53 *Letters to Atticus*, Book v, letter xxi.   54 Book xxii. (M)

erudition, and that he is not even current on the questions he treats. Let us read chapter 22.[55]

Tacitus says that the law of the Twelve Tables set interest at one percent per annum. Obviously he was wrong, and had taken for the law of the Twelve Tables a different law which I shall now discuss. If the law of the Twelve Tables had so determined, why, in the disputes that arose between creditors and debtors, would they not have invoked its Authority? We find no vestige of this law on lending at interest, and anyone who is at all versed in Roman history will see that such a law could not have been the work of the decemvirs. And a little later the Author adds: In the Roman year 398, the tribunes Duellius and Menenius[56] put through a law that reduced interest to one percent per annum.[57] It is this law that Tacitus[58] confuses with the law of the Twelve Tables, and it is the first one enacted among the Romans to set the interest rate, etc. Now let us see.

The Author has said that Tacitus was mistaken in saying that the Law of the Twelve Tables had fixed usury among the Romans. He has said that Tacitus took for the Law of the Twelve Tables a law that was made by the tribunes Duellius and Menenius about 95 years after the Law of the Twelve Tables, and that that law was the first to fix the rate of usury in Rome. What does one say to him? Tacitus was not mistaken; he spoke of usury at one percent per month, and not about usury at one percent per year. But what is at issue here is not the rate of usury, but the question of whether the Law of the Twelve Tables made any disposition whatever concerning usury. The Author says that Tacitus was mistaken because he said that the decem-virs in the Law of the Twelve Tables had made a regulation to fix the rate of usury: and at that point the Critic says that Tacitus was not mistaken because he spoke of usury at one percent per month, and not at one percent per year. I was therefore right in saying that the Critic does not know the state of the question.

But there remains another question, which is whether any law mentioned by Tacitus fixed usury at one percent per year, as the Author has said, or at one percent per month, as the Critic says. Prudence would have dictated that he not undertake a dispute with the Author on Roman laws without knowing the Roman laws; that he not deny him a fact he did not know, and which he did not even know how to clarify for himself. The question was what Tacitus

55 Book XXII. (M)
56 In *SL* XXII, 22, he gives the Roman year 398 (356 BCE). Marcus Duellius is named by Livy in the fifth century BCE; Marcus Menenius served several times as tribune between 410 and 384 BCE.
57 *Unciaria usura.* Livy 7.   58 *Annals*, Book VI.

had meant by the words *Unciarium fœnus*:[59] he had only to open the dictionaries; he would have found in that of Calvinus or Kahl[60] that *unciaria*[61] was one percent per year, and not one percent per month. Had he wished to consult the scholars, he would have found the same thing in Saumaise.[62]

Testis mearum centimanus Gias Sententiarum.[63]

If he had gone back to the sources, he would have found clear texts on that matter in the lawbooks;[64] he would not have confused all the ideas, he would have distinguished the times and occasions when *unciaria* meant one percent per month from the times and occasions when it meant one percent per year; and he would not have taken one twelfth of the *centesimo* for the *centesimo*.

When there was no law on the rate of usury among the Romans, the usual thing was that the usurers took twelve ounces of copper out of a hundred ounces which they lent, which is to say twelve percent per year; and as one *as*[65] was worth twelve ounces of copper, the usurers withheld every year one *as* from every hundred ounces. And as usury often had to be counted out by the month, the usury for six months was called *semis* or half an *as*, the usury for four months was called *triens* or one-third of an *as*, the usury for three months was called *quadrans* or a quarter of an *as*, and finally the usury for one month was called *unciaria* or the twelfth of an *as*. And so, as they took one ounce each month for a hundred ounces they had loaned, this *unciaria* usury, or one percent per month, or twelve percent per annum, was called

59 Nam primo duodecim tabulis sanctum, ne quis unciario fœnore amplius exerceret. *Anales, Liv. 6.* (M)
60 Usurarum species ex assis partibus denominantur: quod ut intelligatur, illud scire oportet, sortem omnem ad centenarium numerum revocari; summam autem usuram esse, cum pars sortis centesima singulis mensibus persolvitur. Et quoniam ista ratione summa hæc usura duodecim aureos annuos in centenos efficit, duodenarius numerus Jurisconsultos movit, ut assem hunc usurarium appellarent. Quemadmodum [autem] hic as, non ex menstrua, sed ex annua pensione æstimandus est; similiter omnes ejus partes ex anni ratione intelligendæ sunt: ut si unus in centenos annuatim pendatur, unciaria usura; si bini, sextans; si terni, quadrans; si quaterni, triens; si quini, quinqunx [quincunx]; si seni, semis; si septeni, septunx; si octoni, bes; si novem, dodrans; si deni, dextrans; si undeni, deunx; si duodeni, as. *Lexicon Joannis Calvini, alias Kahl*, Coloniæ Allobrogum, anno 1622, apud Petrum Balduinum, *in verbo* Usura, p. 960. (M)
61 One part in twelve.
62 De modo usurarum, Lugduni Batavorum, ex officina Elseviriorum, anno 1639, p. 269, 270, and 271; *and above all these words:* Unde verius sit unciarium fœnus eorum, vel uncias usuras, ut eas quoque appellatas infra ostendam, non unciam dare menstruam in centum, sed annuam. (M) The author is Claude Saumaise (1588–1653), *Catalogue*, 978.
63 Horace, *Odes.* (M) (III, 4, vv. 69–70.)
64 Argumentum Legis 47, § Præfectus Legionis, *ff.* de administ. et periculo tutoris. (M)
65 A Roman coin, based on its weight: "the Roman *as* is the same thing as the Roman pound, and was made up of twelve ounces" (*Trévoux*).

centesimal usury. The Critic was aware of this meaning of centesimal usury and applied it very poorly.

It can be seen that all this was only a sort of method, or formula or rule between the debtor and the creditor to count their usuries, in the supposition that usury was at twelve percent per annum, which was the commonest practice; and if someone had loaned at eighteen percent per year, the same method would have been used, by increasing by one-third[66] the usury of each month, so that the *unciaria* would have been one ounce and a half per month.

When the Romans made laws on usury, they made no use of this method, which had served and still served debtors and creditors for the division of time and the convenience of payment of their usuries. The legislator had a public regulation to make; the issue was not to divide the usury by months: he had to fix and did fix usury by the year. They continued to use the terms taken from the division of the *as*, without applying to them the same ideas: thus *unciaria* meant one percent per year, *ex quadrante* usury meant three percent per year, *ex triente* usury four percent per year, *semis* usury six percent per year. And if *unciaria* usury had meant one percent per month, the laws that fixed them *ex quadrante*, *ex triente*, and *ex semise* would have fixed usury at three percent, four percent, or six percent per month, which would have been absurd, because the laws made to repress usury would have been more cruel than the usurers.

The Critic has therefore confused two kinds of things. But it helps me here to transcribe his own words, so the reader will be quite convinced that the intrepidity with which he speaks should fool no one. Here they are:[67] *Tacitus was not mistaken, he speaks of interest at one percent per month, and the Author has imagined that he speaks of one percent per year. Nothing is so well known as the centesimo that was paid to the usurer every month. Should a man who writes two quarto volumes on the laws be unaware of that?*

Whether this man was unaware or not of the centesimo is a quite indifferent matter. But he was not unaware of it, since he has dealt with it in three places. But how has he dealt with it? And where has he done so?[68] I could well defy the Critic to guess because he would not find the same terms and expressions that he knows.

The present purpose is not to determine whether the Author of *The Spirit of Law* has been short on erudition or not, but to defend his altars.[69] Yet it was

---

66 In fact 1½ oz. would represent an increase of ½.
67 Broadside of 9 October 1749, page 164. (M)
68 The third and last note, chapter 22, Book xxii, and the text of the third note. (M)
69 *Pro Aris.* (M) From the Latin idea of fighting *pro aris et focis*, for the altar and the home foyer.

necessary to let the public see that the Critic, adopting such a decisive tone over things he knows nothing about, and of which he has so little doubt that he does not even open a dictionary to reassure himself, knowing nothing and accusing others of failing to know even his own errors, deserves no more confidence in his other accusations. Cannot one believe that the arrogance and pride of tone which he adopts throughout does not in any way prevent his being wrong? That when he gets worked up, that does not mean he is not wrong? That when he anathematizes with his words *impious* and *adherent of natural religion*, one can still believe he is wrong? That one should beware receiving the impressions that the activity of his mind and the impetuosity of his style could give? That it is well to separate, in his two writings, his calumnies from his reasons and then set aside the reasons that are false, after which there would be nothing left?

The Author, in the chapters on lending at interest and usury among the Romans, treating this subject, no doubt the most important in their history, this subject that was so dependent on the constitution that it was a thousand times almost overthrown by it, speaking of the laws they made out of despair, of those where they followed their prudence, of regulations that were only temporary, of those they made for all time, says toward the end of chapter 22: *In the Roman year 398, the tribunes Duellius and Menenius put through a law that reduced interest to one percent per annum. [. . .] Ten years later, this usury was reduced to half that; later it was completely suppressed . . .*

This law had the same fate as all laws where the legislator took things too far: innumerable means were found to evade it. It took many others to confirm, correct, and temper it. Sometimes they left laws aside to follow the practices, sometimes they left practices aside to follow the laws. But in this case practice easily prevailed. When a man borrows, he finds an obstacle in the very law that is made in his favor; that law will be opposed both by the person it helps and by the person it condemns. Prætor Sempronius Asellus, having allowed debtors to act in accordance with the laws, was killed by the creditors for wanting to revive the memory of a rigidity that could no longer be maintained.

Under Sulla, Lucius Valerius Flaccus made a law allowing interest at three percent per annum. This law was the most equitable and moderate of those the Romans enacted on this subject, but Paterculus disapproved of it. But if this law was necessary to the republic, if it was useful to all individuals, and if it provided a transfer of wealth between the debtor and the borrower, it was not unjust.

He who pays later, says Ulpian, pays less: that decides the question of whether interest is legitimate, that is to say, whether the creditor can sell time, and the debtor buy it.

Here is how the Critic reasons on this last passage which relates solely to the law of Flaccus and the Romans' political arrangements. The Author, he says, while summarizing everything he has said about usury, maintains that a creditor was permitted to sell time. One would say, to hear the Critic, that the Author has just written a treatise on theology or canon law, and then summarizes that treatise on theology and canon law, whereas it is clear that he speaks only of the Romans' political arrangements, the law of Flaccus, and the opinion of Paterculus, in such a way that this law of Flaccus, the opinion of Paterculus, the reflection of Ulpian, and that of the Author are mutually dependent and cannot be separated.

I should have many more things to say, but I would rather refer back to the broadsides themselves. *Believe me, my dear Pisons, they resemble a work which, like the dreams of a sick man, reveals nothing but vain phantoms.*[70]

Part Three
We have seen in parts one and two that all that results from so many bitter criticisms comes to this, that the Author of *The Spirit of Law* did not write his work following the plan and the views of his critics; and that if his critics had written a work on the same subject, they would have put into it a very large number of things they know. It further results that they are theologians, and that the Author is a jurisconsult; that they believe themselves to be fit for his profession, and he does not feel fit to exercise theirs. Finally, there results from it that instead of attacking him so sharply, they would have done better to take cognizance themselves of the value of the things he has said in favor of religion, which he has equally respected and defended. It remains for me to make a few observations.

This manner of reasoning is not good which, invoked against any good book whatever, can make it appear as bad as any bad book, and which, practiced against any bad book whatever, can make it appear as good as any good book.

This manner of reasoning is not good which to the things in question recalls others which are not relevant, and which confounds the various sciences and the ideas of each science.[71]

One should not argue over a work written about a science with reasons that could weaken the science itself.

70 Credite, Pisones, isti tabulæ fore librum / Persimilem, cujus, velut ægri somnia, vanæ / Fingentur species. Horace, *De arte poetica* [vv. 6–8]. (M)
71 Implicitly, *science* here includes theology, which used to claim the title of the highest kind of knowledge.

When one criticizes a work, and an important work, one should try to procure a particular familiarity with the science which it treats and read carefully the approved authors who have already written on that science, so as to see whether the author has strayed from the accepted and ordinary manner of treating it.

When an author explains himself with his words, or with his writings, which are their image, it is unreasonable to diverge from the outward signs of his thoughts in order to seek his thoughts, because he is the only one who knows his thoughts. It is much worse when his thoughts are good, and bad ones are attributed to him.

When one writes against an author and becomes angry with him, the objections must be proven by the facts, and not the facts by the objections.

When one can see that an author's intention is generally good, one will more rarely be mistaken if in certain places that one believes equivocal one judges the general intention rather than attributing to him a specific bad intention.

In books written for amusement, three or four pages give an idea of the style and qualities of the work; in well-reasoned books you grasp nothing if you do not grasp the entire chain.

As it is very difficult to write a good work, and very easy to criticize it because the author has had all the gorges to defend, and the critic has only one of them to attack, the latter must not be wrong, and if it happened that he was continually wrong, he would be inexcusable.

Moreover, since criticism can be considered as showing off one's superiority over others, and its usual effect is to yield delicious moments for human pride, those who indulge in it always deserve fair treatment, but rarely indulgence.

And since of all kinds of writing, criticism is the one in which it is most difficult to show a good disposition, you must take care not to exacerbate the lamentable reality by the bitterness of the words.

When you write on important matters, it is not enough to be guided by your zeal; you must also be guided by your understanding; and if heaven has not granted us great talents, we can compensate by self-awareness, and by care, work, and reflection.

This art of finding in a thing that naturally has a good meaning all the bad meanings that a mind that reasons awry can give them is not useful to men; those who practice it are like crows that flee living bodies and fly in all directions in search of cadavers.

Such a manner of criticizing produces two great disadvantages: the first is that it spoils readers' minds with a mixture of the true and the false, good and evil; they become accustomed to seeking a bad meaning in things which naturally have a very good one; for this reason it is easy for them to pass into that frame of mind, to seek a good meaning in things that naturally have a bad one. You cause them to lose the faculty of sound reasoning only to precipitate them into the subtleties of bad logic. The second is that making good books suspect by that kind of reasoning leaves you no other weapons for attacking bad writings, leaving the public with no rule for distinguishing them. If Spinozists and deists are treated like those who are not, what will be said of those who are?

Although we should be able to assume that those who write against us on matters that are of interest to all men are led to do so out of Christian charity, nonetheless, as it is the nature of that virtue never to be hidden, as it shows itself in us despite ourselves, and as it shines and dazzles in every direction, if it occurred that in two pieces written against the same person one after the other,[72] no trace could be found of that charity, that it appeared in no sentence, in no turn, no word, no expression, he who had written such works would have just reason to fear it was not Christian charity that impelled to do so.

And as the purely human virtues are the effect in us of what is called a good temperament, if it were impossible to discover in them any vestige of that good temperament, the public could conclude that those writings would not even be the effect of human virtues.

People always perceive acts as more sincere than motives, and it is easier for them to believe that the act of uttering atrocious insults is an evil than to persuade themselves that the motive that has caused them to be said is good.

When a man belongs to an order that makes religion respected, and which religion causes to be respected,[73] and he attacks before worldly people another man who lives in the world, it is essential for him to maintain by his manner of acting the superiority of his estate. The world is very corrupt, but certain passions there are greatly restrained; there are preferred ones that prevent others from appearing. Consider worldly people as a group: nothing is so cautious. It is pride that dares not utter its secrets, and which in the deference it has for the other passions estranges itself only to return.

---

72 An allusion to the two successive articles attacking *The Spirit of Law* that had appeared in *Nouvelles ecclésiastiques*.

73 Montesquieu is not referring *per se* to Jansenism, which is not an order, but may be assuming the author is an Oratorian, as that order was often allied with the Jansenists.

Christianity gives us the habit of restraining that pride; the world gives us the habit of hiding it. With our paltry virtue, what would become of us if our entire soul were set free, and if we were not so attentive to the slightest words, the slightest signs, the slightest gestures?[74] Now when men of respected standing manifest anger that worldly people would not dare disclose, the latter begin to believe themselves better than they really are, which is a very great evil.

We worldly people are so weak that we are most deserving of being humored. Thus, when we are made to see all the outer signs of violent passions, what are we to think of what lies within? Can one hope that we, with our usual temerity for judging, should not judge?

One might have noted in disputes and conversations what happens to persons whose minds are severe and contentious: as they do not do battle in order to aid each other, but to cast each other down, they wander farther from the truth, not in proportion to the loftiness or pettiness of their minds, but to the greater or lesser oddity or inflexibility of their character. The reverse happens to those on whom nature or education has bestowed gentleness: as their disputes are mutual assistance, as they work toward the same object, think differently only to succeed in thinking alike, they find truth in proportion to their understanding: that is the reward of a good temperament.

When a man writes about religious matters, he must so rely on the piety of his readers that he says things contrary to good sense because in order to gain credit with those who have more piety than understanding, he loses credit with those who have more understanding than piety.

And as religion largely defends itself, it loses more when it is poorly defended than when it is not defended at all.

If it should happen that a man after losing his readers attacked someone of some reputation and thus found the means of being read, one could perhaps suspect that under the pretext of sacrificing that victim to religion he was sacrificing it to his vanity.

The means of criticizing we are discussing is the thing in the world that is most capable of limiting the breadth and diminishing, if I may use that term, the total of national[75] genius. Theology has its boundaries and its formulas because, the truths it teaches being known, men must remain within them,

---

74 Cf. *SL* IV, 2: the world is the "school of what is called honor [. . .] that universal master who must guide us wherever we go." See also *On Consideration and Reputation*.

75 The original says *natural*, but the correction is indicated in the notebook compiled by Montesquieu's Irish secretary Florence Fitzpatrick.

and must be prevented from straying from them. It is there that genius must not soar; we circumscribe it, so to speak, within an enclosure. But it is a mockery to want to place that same enclosure around those who deal with the human sciences. The principles of geometry are very exact; but if they were applied to matters of taste, reason itself would be made to rave. Nothing stifles doctrine like putting a doctoral robe on everything: those who always want to teach prevent many from learning; there is no genius that one does not shrink by enveloping it in a million vain scruples. If you have the best intentions in the world you will be forced to doubt them; you can no longer be intent on speaking rightly when you are constantly frightened by the fear of speaking badly, and when instead of following your thought you are focused only on terms that may escape the subtlety of the critics. They come put a hood on our head to tell us at every word: Be careful not to fall; you want to speak like yourself, I want you to speak like me. If you are about to soar, they grab you by the sleeve; if you have strength and life, they take it away by pinpricks; if you rise up a little, men come running with their rule or their gauge, raise their heads and yell at you to get down so they can measure you; if you are running your course, they will want you to look at all the stones that ants have placed in your path; there is neither science nor literature that can hold out against such pedantry. Our century has created academies, and they will want us to return to the schools of the dark ages.[76] Descartes is the one to reassure those who, with an infinitely lesser genius than himself, have intentions just as good. That great man was constantly accused of atheism, and now the best arguments brought against atheists are his own.

Moreover, we should regard criticisms as personal only in the cases where those who make them have intended them as such. It is quite permissible to criticize works that have been given to the public, because it would be ridiculous for those who have wished to enlighten others not to desire to be enlightened themselves. Those who warn us are the companions of our labors; if the critic and the author seek the truth, they have the same interest, for the truth is the possession of all men: they will be confederates, and not enemies.

It is with great pleasure that I lay down my pen. I would have continued to keep my peace if doing so had not persuaded numerous persons that I was reduced to that.

---

76 *Écoles des siècles ténébreux* alludes to scholastic disputes in the tradition of the Middle Ages. The structure of this *Defense* partly imitates the "Objection" and "Response" alternation of such quarrels.

Clarifications *on* The Spirit of Law

I

Several persons have made this objection. In the book on the Spirit of Law, it is honor or fear that is the principle of certain governments, not virtue; and virtue is only the principle of some others. Therefore Christian virtues are not required in most governments.[77]

Here is the reply: the Author placed this note in chapter 5 of Book III: *I am speaking here of political virtue, which is moral virtue in the sense that it tends in general toward the good, very little of the private moral virtues, and none at all of that virtue which relates to revealed truths.* There is another note in the following chapter that refers back to this one; and in chapters 2 and 3 of Book V the Author has defined his virtue as *love of country.* He defines love of country as *love of equality and frugality.* All of Book V rests on these principles. When a writer has defined a word in his work, when he has given, to use this expression, his dictionary, ought not his words to be understood with the meaning he has given them?

The word *virtue*, like most words in all languages, is taken to mean many things. Sometimes it designates Christian virtues, and sometimes pagan virtues; often a certain Christian virtue, or else a certain pagan virtue; at times strength, at times in some languages a certain aptitude for one or several arts. It is what precedes or follows that word that determines its meaning. Here the Author has gone farther, by repeating his definition several times. The objection has thus been made only because the work was read too rapidly.

II

The Author has said in Book II, chapter 3: *The best aristocracy is one where the portion of the people who have no share in power is so small and so poor that the dominant portion has no interest in oppressing them. Thus, when Antipater*[78] *decreed*[79] *in Athens that those who had less than two thousand drachmas would be excluded from the right of suffrage, he created the best possible aristocracy, because that cens*[80] *was so small that it excluded only a few, and no one of any standing in the*

---

77 This too was one of the criticisms stressed in the 9 October 1749 issue of *Nouvelles ecclésiastiques* (*OC* VII, 27–28).

78 Antipater (c. 400–319 BCE) was a Macedonian general who served under Philip II of Macedon and Alexander the Great; after Alexander's sudden death in 323 BCE he was at first given control of Athens and other parts of Greece and then, in 321, he became regent of Alexander's empire.

79 Diodorus, Book XVIII, p. 601, Rhodoman edition. (M)

80 In both Latin and French, this word has had various meanings: quota, capitation, poll tax, rent, census, or civic registry.

city. Aristocratic families should therefore belong to the populace insofar as possible. The closer an aristocracy comes to democracy, the more perfect it will be; and it will become progressively less perfect the closer it comes to monarchy.

In a letter inserted in the *Journal de Trévoux* for the month of April 1749,[81] objection was made to the Author's own citation: we have, it says, before our eyes the cited passage, and we find that there were only nine thousand persons who had the *cens* prescribed by Antipater; that there were twenty-two thousand who did not: whence we conclude that the Author applies his quotations wrongly, since in that republic of Antipater's the smaller number were in the *cens*, and the larger number were not.

Response

It would have been desirable for the person who made this criticism to have paid better attention to what the Author said, and to what Diodorus said.

There were not twenty-two thousand persons who did not have the *cens* in the republic of Antipater: the twenty-two thousand persons of whom Diodorus speaks were relegated to and established in Thrace; and there remained to form that republic but the nine thousand citizens who had the *cens*, and those of the plebs who did not want to leave for Thrace. The reader may consult Diodorus.

Secondly, had twenty-two thousand persons remained in Athens who did not have the *cens*, the objection would not be more accurate. The words *large* and *small* are relative. Nine thousand sovereigns in a state are an immense number, and twenty-two thousand subjects in the same state make up an infinitely small number.

---

81 Montesquieu is referring to a "Letter to P[ère] B[erthier] J[ésuite] on the Book entitled *The Spirit of Law*" (*OC* VII, 7) published in the April 1749 issue of the *Mémoires de Trévoux*. This letter, reputedly written by one Father Plesse of Brittany, was quite complimentary regarding Montesquieu's "erudition" and "singular knowledge of history, ancient and modern," and of "the jurisprudence of the Greek and Romans and the Asiatics and Europeans," but its author wished to point out what he wrongly supposed was an error Montesquieu had made in his use of information reported by Diodorus of Sicily in his *Universal History* (*Catalogue* 2671), written between 60 and 30 BCE and now only partially extant.

Montesquieu Chronology

1689	Birth of Charles Louis de Secondat (18 January) at the Château de La Brède, near Bordeaux.
1700–1705	Studies at the Oratorian school in Juilly. Attains a strong foundation in Latin.
1705–1708	Study of law in Bordeaux. Attains a strong foundation in Roman law.
1709–1713	In Paris to complement his knowledge of legal practice. Frequents learned and mundane societies.
1713	Returns to Bordeaux after death of his father, Jacques de Secondat (15 November).
1714	At age twenty-five, enters as counselor in the Bordeaux parlement.
1715	Marries the Protestant Jeanne de Lartigue in Bordeaux (30 April). *Memorandum on the Debts of State.*
1716	Birth of son, Jean-Baptiste de Secondat (10 February). Inherits (24 April) from his uncle Jean-Baptiste de Montesquieu the title of baron de Montesquieu and office of *président à mortier* (one of nine mortared judges) in the Bordeaux parlement. Elected member of the Bordeaux academy (3 April), where he reads *Dissertation on Roman Politics in Religion* (18 June).
1717	Birth of daughter Marie de Montesquieu (22 January). *Discourse on Cicero.*
1717–1720	Composes various academic papers, especially on scientific subjects.
1721	*Persian Letters* published anonymously in Amsterdam.
1724	*Dialogue between Sulla and Eucrates; Letters from Xenocrates to Pheres.*
1725	Anonymous publication of *The Temple of Gnidus*, a mildly erotic prose poem. *On Consideration and Reputation; Discourse on Equity; On the Motives that Should Encourage Us toward the Sciences; Treatise on Duties.*
1726	Sells his parlementary office to achieve freedom to study and travel.
1727	Birth of daughter Denise de Montesquieu (22 January). *Considerations on the Wealth of Spain.*
1728	Election to Académie Française.
1728–1729	Travels in Austria, Hungary, Italy, Germany, and Holland. Composes *Voyage from Gratz to The Hague*; begins an eighteen-month stay in England; only *Notes on England* survives.
1731–1733	In Bordeaux and La Brède. *Reflections on the Character of Certain Princes.*

1734–1738	*Considerations on the Causes of the Greatness of the Romans and their Decline* published anonymously. *Reflections on Universal Monarchy in Europe.* Begins work on what will be *The Spirit of Law. Essay on the Causes that Can Affect Minds and Characters.*
1748	*The Spirit of Law* published anonymously in Geneva; other editions soon follow.
1749	*The Spirit of Law* attacked in *Nouvelles ecclésiastiques* (9 and 16 October).
1750	*Defense of The Spirit of Law* published bearing the false imprint Geneva: Barrillot & Fils.
1751	*The Spirit of Law* placed on Papal Index of Prohibited Books (29 November).
1754	*Memorandum on the Silence to Impose on the Constitution.*
1755	Montesquieu dies in Paris (10 February).

Bibliographical Note

Life of Montesquieu

The only biography based on up-to-date documentation is Catherine Volpilhac-Auger, *Montesquieu* (Paris: Gallimard, 2017). See also Pierre Barrière, *Un grand provincial: Charles Louis de Secondat baron de La Brède et de Montesquieu* (Bordeaux: Delmas, 1946); Robert Shackleton, *Montesquieu: A Critical Biography* (Oxford: Oxford University Press, 1961); Jean Starobinski, *Montesquieu* (Paris: Seuil, [1953] 1994); Louis Desgraves, *Montesquieu* (Paris: Mazarine, 1986); Louis Desgraves, *Montesquieu: l'œuvre et la vie* (Bordeaux: L'Esprit du Temps, 1994); Louis Desgraves, *Chronologie critique de la vie et des œuvres de Montesquieu* (Paris: Champion, 1998).

Uses of Science

For background, consult Christian Licoppe, *La Formation de la pratique scientifique: le discours de l'expérience en France et en Angleterre (1630–1820)* (Paris: La Decouverte, 1996); Laurence Brocklin and Colin Jones, *The Medical World of Early Modern France* (Oxford: Clarendon Press, 1997); Denis de Casabianca, *Montesquieu: de l'étude des sciences à "L'Esprit des lois"* (Paris: Champion, 2008). For Montesquieu's scientific endeavors, see Jean Torlais, "Montesquieu homme de sciences," *Actes du Congrès Montesquieu réuni à Bordeaux du 23 au 26 mai 1955 pour commémorer le deuxième centenaire de la mort de Montesquieu* (Bordeaux: Delmas, 1956), pp. 349–352; Gérard Milhaud, "Le regard scientifique de Montesquieu," *Europe* 574 (1977), 31–41; Alberto Postigliola, "Montesquieu entre Descartes et Newton," in Catherine Volpilhac-Auger (ed.), *Montesquieu: les années de formation (1689–1720)* (Naples: Liguori, and Oxford: Voltaire Foundation, 1999), pp. 91–108; Lorenzo Bianchi, "Montesquieu naturaliste," in *ibid.*, pp. 109–124. For Montesquieu's views on the usefulness of science, see Sheila Mason, Introduction to *Discours sur les motifs qui doivent nous encourager aux sciences*, OC VIII, 491–493, and Diana J. Schaub, "Montesquieu's Popular Science," *The New Atlantis* 20 (2008), 37–46.

For Montesquieu's views on the effects of physical and moral causes on human behavior, see Pierre Rétat, Introduction to *Essai sur les causes qui peuvent affecter les esprits et les caractères*, OC IX, 205–217; Robert Shackleton, "The Evolution of Montesquieu's Theory of Climate," *Revue Internationale de Philosophie* 9 (1955), 317–329; Catherine Volpilhac-Auger, "La

Dissertation sur la différence des génies: essai de reconstitution," in *RM* IV (2000), pp. 227–237; Sharon Krause, "History and the Human Soul in Montesquieu," *History of Political Thought* 24(2) (2003), 235–261; Jean-Patrice Courtois, "Le Physique et le moral dans la théorie du climat chez Montesquieu," in Céline Spector and Thierry Hoquet (eds.), *Lectures de "L'Esprit des lois"* (Bordeaux: Presses Universitaires de Bordeaux, 2004), pp. 101–119; Paul A. Rahe, *Montesquieu and the Logic of Liberty: War, Religion, Commerce, Climate, Terrain, Technology, Uneasiness of Mind, the Spirit of Political Vigilance, and the Foundations of the Modern Republic* (New Haven: Yale University Press, 2009), pp. 150–169;Domenico Felice, *Montesquieu: An Introduction. A Universal Mind for a Universal Science of Political-Legal Studies* (Milan: Mimesis International, 2018); Céline Spector, "Soul," in *DM*; Denis de Casabianca, "Science," in *DM*.

The Romans

For Montesquieu's views on Roman history, see *Considerations on the Causes of the Greatness of the Romans and their Decline*, ed. and trans. David Lowenthal (Indianapolis: Hacket, [1965] 1999); Patrick Andrivet and Catherine Volpilhac-Auger, Introduction to *Considérations sur les causes de la grandeur des Romains et de leur décadence*, *OC* II, 3–86; Vanessa de Senarclens, *Montesquieu historien de Rome: un tournant pour la réflexion sur le statut de l'histoire au XVIIIe siècle* (Geneva: Droz, 2003); Jean Ehrard, "Rome que je hais," in *L'Esprit des mots: Montesquieu en lui-même et parmi les siens* (Geneva: Droz, 1998), pp. 55–65; Rahe, *Montesquieu and the Logic of Liberty*, pp. 27–42; Patrick Andrivet, *"Rome enfin que je hais … "? Une étude sur les différentes vues de Montesquieu concernant les anciens Romains* (Orléans: Paradigme, 2012).

On Roman religion, see Cicero, *On the Nature of the Gods*, trans. H. Rackham (Cambridge, MA: Harvard University Press, 1933); Ramsay MacMullen, *Paganism in the Roman Empire* (New Haven: Yale University Press, 1983); Mary Beard, John North, and Simon Price, *Religions of Rome*, 2 vols. (Cambridge: Cambridge University Press, 1998). For Montesquieu's views on Roman paganism, see Lorenzo Bianchi, "Nécessité de la religion et de la tolérance chez Montesquieu: la 'Dissertation sur la politique des Romains dans la religion'," in Edgar Mass and Alberto Postigliola (eds.), *Lectures de Montesquieu: Actes du Colloque de Wolfenbüttel (26–28 octobre 1989)* (Oxford: Voltaire Foundation, 1993), pp. 25–39; Salvatore Rotta, "Montesquieu et le paganisme ancien," in *ibid.*, pp. 151–175.

For Montesquieu's views on Cicero, see Pierre Rétat, Introduction to *Discours sur Cicéron*, in *OC* VIII, 119–124; Catherine Larrère, "Le stoïcism dans les œuvres de jeunesse de Montesquieu," in Volpilhac-Auger (ed.), *Montesquieu: les années de formation*, pp. 163–183; Patrick Andrivet, "Montesquieu et Cicéron: de l'enthousiasme à la sagesse," in Jean-Louis Jam (ed.), *Éclectisme et cohérences des Lumières: mélanges offerts à Jean Ehrard* (Paris: Nizet, 1992), pp. 25–34; Andrivet, "Cicero," in *DM*. For Montesquieu's views on other Roman authors, see Lawrence Levin, *The Political Doctrine of Montesquieu's "Esprit des lois": Its Classical Background* (Westport, CT: Greenwood Press, [1936] 1973);Catherine Volpilhac-Auger, *Tacite et Montesquieu* (Oxford: Voltaire Foundation, 1985); Volpilhac-Auger, "Latin Writers," in *DM*; Sheila Mason, "Montesquieu and Livy," in T. A. Dorey (ed.), *Livy* (London: Routledge & Kegan Paul, 1971), pp. 118–158.

Reflections on National Character

For Montesquieu on national character, see Roberto Romani, "All Montesquieu's Sons: The Place of *esprit général, caractère national*, and *mœurs* in French Political Philosophy, 1748–1789," *Studies on Voltaire and the Eighteenth Century* 362 (1998), 189–235. For French opinions on the English, see Gabriel Bonnot, *La Constitution britannique devant l'opinion française de Montesquieu à Bonaparte* (New York: Burt Franklin, [1931] 1971); Frances Acomb, *Anglophobia in France, 1763–1789: An Essay in the History of Constitutionalism and Nationalism* (Durham, NC: Duke University Press, 1950); Josephine Grieder, *Anglomania in France, 1740–1789: Fact, Fiction and Political Discourse* (Geneva: Droz, 1985).

For Montesquieu's views on England, see J. B. Sturges, *Montesquieu en Angleterre: le voyage de Montesquieu en Angleterre et l'influence des pensées et des mœurs anglaises sur la vie et les œuvres de Montesquieu* (Paris: Sirey, 1934); David Carrithers, "Montesquieu et l'étude comparé des constitutions: analyses des régimes anglais et français," in Louis Desgraves (ed.), *Actes du Colloque international tenu à Bordeaux du 3 au 6 décembre 1998* (Bordeaux: Académie de Bordeaux, 1999), pp. 243–253; Cecil P. Courtney, "L'Image de l'Angleterre dans *L'Esprit des lois*," in *ibid.*, pp. 243–253; Courtney, "Montesquieu and English Liberty," in David W. Carrithers, Michael Mosher, and Paul A. Rahe (eds.), *Montesquieu's Science of Politics: Essays on "The Spirit of Laws"* (Lanham, MD: Rowman and Littlefield, 2001), pp. 273–290; Ian Stewart, "Montesquieu in England: His 'Notes on England,' with Commentary and Translation Commentary," *Oxford University Comparative Literature Forum* 6 (2002) at ouclf.law.ox.ac.uk; Céline Spector, *Montesquieu et l'émergence de l'économie politique* (Paris: Honoré Champion, 2006), pp. 182–220; Ursula Haskins Gonthier, *Montesquieu and England: Enlightened Exchanges, 1689–1755* (London: Pickering & Chatto, 2010).

For Montesquieu's views on modern Romans, see Sheila Mason and Pierre Rétat, Introduction to *Réflexions sur les habitants de Rome, OC* IX, 69–76; Sheila Mason, "La Physiologie des mœurs selon Montesquieu, cadre académique et postérité médicale," in *Actes du Colloque international tenu à Bordeaux*, pp. 387–396.

Politics and Morality

For Montesquieu as moral philosopher, see Robert Shackleton, "La Genèse de *L'Esprit des lois*," *Revue d'Histoire Littéraire de la France* 52 (1952), 425–438; M. W. Rombout, *La Conception stoïcienne du bonheur chez Montesquieu et chez quelques-uns de ses contemporains* (Leiden: Universitaire Pers, 1958); Mark Waddicor, *Montesquieu and the Philosophy of Natural Law* (The Hague: Martinus Nijhoff, 1970); Corrado Rosso, *Montesquieu moraliste: des lois au bonheur*, trans. M. Régaldo (Paris: Ducros, 1971); Sheila Mason, *Montesquieu's Idea of Justice* (The Hague: Martinus Nijhoff, 1975); Dennis C. Rasmussen, *The Pragmatic Enlightenment: Recovering the Liberalism of Hume, Smith, Montesquieu, and Voltaire* (Cambridge: Cambridge University Press, 2013), pp. 58–69; Sheila Mason, Introduction to *Traité des devoirs, OC* VIII, 432–436; Domenico Felice, *Montesquieu: An Introduction*, pp. 47–62; Sheila Mason, Introduction to *De la considération et de la réputation, OC* VIII, 449–455; Mason, Introduction to *Traité des devoirs, OC* VIII, 432–436.

For Montesquieu on Hobbes, see Paul Dimhoff, "Cicéron, Hobbes, et Montesquieu," *Annales Universitatis Savariensis* (1952), 19–47; Simone Goyard-Fabre, *Montesquieu, adversaire de Hobbes* (Paris: Lettres Modernes, 1980); Michael Zuckert, "Natural Law, Natural Rights, and Classical Liberalism: On Montesquieu's Critique of Hobbes," *Social Philosophy and Policy* 16(1) (2001), 227–251; Vicki Sullivan, *Montesquieu and the Despotic Ideas of Europe: An Interpretation of "The Spirit of the Laws"* (Chicago: University of Chicago Press, 2017), pp. 13–21, 50–76; Felice, *Montesquieu: An Introduction*, pp. 95–106; Jean Terrel, "Hobbes," in *DM*.

For Montesquieu's views on justice, see Sheila Mason, Introduction to *Discours sur l'équité* in *OC* VIII, 463–474; Georges Boyer, "La Notion d'équité et son rôle dans la jurisprudence des Parlements," in *Mélanges d'histoire du droit occidental*, I (Paris: Sirey, 1962), pp. 210–235; Rebecca Kingston, *Montesquieu and the Parlement of Bordeaux* (Geneva: Droz, 1996), pp. 70–72; Louis Desgraves, "Montesquieu et la justice de son temps," in David W. Carrithers and Patrick Coleman (eds.), *Montesquieu and the Spirit of Modernity* (Oxford: Voltaire Foundation, 2002), pp. 205–211. For his views on the virtue displayed by the Spartan mercenary Xanthippus, see Sheila Mason, Introduction to *Dialogue de Xantippe et de Xenocrate, OC* VIII, 571–574. For background on Montesquieu's views on the career of Lysimachus, historian of Alexander the Great's Asian campaigns, see Catherine Volpilhac-Auger, Introduction to *Lysimache, OC* IX, 411–418.

Statecraft

For Montesquieu and Machiavelli, see André Bertière, "Montesquieu lecteur de Machiavel," in *Actes du Congrès Montesquieu réuni à Bordeaux*, pp. 141–158; Robert Shackleton, "Montesquieu and Machiavelli: A Reappraisal," *Comparative Literature Studies* 1 (1964), 1–13; Paul Carrese, "The Machiavellian Spirit of Montesquieu's Liberal Republic," in Paul Rahe (ed.), *Machiavelli's Liberal Republican Legacy* (Cambridge: Cambridge University Press, 2005), pp. 121–142; Vicki Sullivan, "Against the Despotism of a Republic: Montesquieu's Correction of Machiavelli in the Name of the Security of the Individual," *History of Political Thought* 27(2) (2006), 263–289; Nizar Ben Saad, *Machiavel en France des lumières à la révolution* (Paris: L'Harmattan, 2007); Paul Rahe, "Montesquieu's Anti-Machiavellian Machiavellianism," *History of European Ideas* 37(2) (2011), 128–136; Randal R. Hendrickson, "Montesquieu's (Anti-)Machiavellianism: Ordinary Acquisitiveness in *The Spirit of Laws*," *Journal of Politics* 85(2) (2013), 385–396; Sullivan, *Montesquieu and the Despotic Ideas of Europe*; Lorenzo Bianchi, "Machiavelli," in *DM*; Norbert Campagna, "Raison d'État," in *DM*.

For politics, morals, and economics in regency France, see Sheila Mason, Introduction to *Lettres de Xenocrate à Phérés, OC* VIII, 293–297; J. H. Shennan, *Philippe, Duke of Orléans, Regent of France, 1715–1723* (London: Thames and Hudson, 1979); Thomas E. Kaiser, "Money, Despotism, and Public Opinion in Early Eighteenth-Century France: John Law and the Debate on Royal Credit," *Journal of Modern History* 63 (1991), 1–28; Antoin E. Murphy, *John Law: Economic Theorist and Policy-Maker* (Oxford: Clarendon Press, 1997); Jean Ehrard, "La Régence," in *L'Esprit des mots*, pp. 109–120; Arnaud Orian, *La Politique du merveilleux: une autre histoire du Système de Law (1695–1795)* (Paris: Fayard, 2018).

For Montesquieu's views on the need for morality in politics, see Sheila Mason, Introduction to *De la politique, OC* VIII, 503–510; Sheila Mason and Catherine Volpilhac-Auger, Introduction to *Réflexions sur le caractère de quelque princes, OC* IX, 45–49;

David Carrithers, "Montesquieu's Philosophy of History,"*Journal of the History of Ideas* 47 (1986), 61–80. For his views on universal monarchy, see Catherine Larrère and Françoise Weil, Introduction to *Réflexions sur la monarchie universelle en Europe*, *OC* ii, 321–337; Michel Porret, Introduction to *Montesquieu: Réflexions sur la monarchie universelle en Europe* (Geneva: Droz, 2000), pp. 7–68; Paul A. Rahe, "The Book That Never Was: Montesquieu's *Considerations on the Romans* in Historical Context," *History of Political Thought* 26(1) (2005), 43–89; Michael Mosher, "Montesquieu on Empire and Enlightenment," in Sankar Muthu (ed.), *Empire and Modern Political Thought* (Cambridge: Cambridge University Press, 2010,), pp. 112–154; essays by Céline Spector, Michael Mosher, Catherine Larrère, Jean Terrel, and Pierre Briant in *RM* viii (2008).

For Montesquieu and Jansenism, see Catherine Maire and Pierre Rétat, Introduction to *Mémoire sur le silence à imposer sur la Constitution*, *OC* ix, 521–528; William Doyle, *Jansenism: Catholic Resistance to Authority from the Reformation to the French Revolution* (New York: St. Martin's Press, 2000); Jeffrey W. Merrick, *The Desacralization of the French Monarchy in the Eighteenth Century* (Baton Rouge: Louisiana State University Press, 1990); Dale K. Van Kley, *The Religious Origins of the French Revolution from Calvin to the Civil Constitution, 1560–1791* (New Haven: Yale University Press, 1996); Catherine Maire, *De la cause de Dieu à la cause de la Nation: le jansénisme au XVIIIe siècle* (Paris: Gallimard, 1998); Catherine Maire, "Jansenism," in *DM*; Maire, "*Unigenitus* (Constitution)," in *DM*.

Economics and Fiscal Policy

For background, see Marcel Marion, *Histoire financière de la France depuis 1715* (Paris: A. Rousseau, 1914), Catherine Larrère, *L'Invention de l'économie au XVIIIe siècle* (Paris: Presses Universitaires de France, 1992); Henry C. Clark, *Compass of Society: Commerce and Absolutism in Old Regime France* (Lanham, MD: Lexington Books, 2007); Guy Rowland, *The Financial Decline of a Great Power: War, Influence, and Money in Louis XIV's France* (Oxford: Oxford University Press, 2012). For Montesquieu on the French national debt, see Jean Ehrard, Introduction to *Mémoire concernant les moyens d'acquitter les dettes de l'État*, *OC* viii, 45–53; Ehrard, "À la découverte des finances publiques: le *Mémoire sur les dettes de l'État*," in Volpilhac-Auger (ed.), *Montesquieu: les années de formation*, pp. 487–500; David W. Carrithers, "Montesquieu and the Spirit of French Finance: An Analysis of his *Mémoire sur les dettes de l'État* (1715)," in *Montesquieu and the Spirit of Modernity*, pp. 159–190; Andrew Scott Bibby, *Montesquieu's Political Economy* (New York: Palgrave MacMillan, 2016), pp. 15–35.

For historical background on Spanish decline, see John H. Elliott, "The Decline of Spain," *Past & Present* 20 (November 1961), 52–75; Elliott, *Imperial Spain: 1469–1716* (London: Edward Arnold, 1963); Anthony Pagden, *Lords of All the World: Ideologies of Empire in Spain, Britain and France c. 1500–c. 1800* (New Haven: Yale University Press, 1995); John R. Fisher, *The Economic Aspects of Spanish Imperialism in America, 1492–1810* (Liverpool: Liverpool University Press, 1997). For Montesquieu's views on the decline of Spain, see Pierre Rétat, Introduction to *Considérations sur les richesses de l'Espagne*, *OC* viii, 583–594; Guillaume Barrera, "La Figure de l'Espagne dans l'œuvre de Montesquieu," in *Actes du Colloque international tenu a Bordeaux*, pp. 153–171; Barrera, "Spain," in *DM*.

Bibliographical Note

Defense of The Spirit of Law

For background on ecclesiastical censures of *The Spirit of Law*, see Pierre Rétat, Introduction to *Défense de l'Esprit des lois*, *OC* VII, xv–xxx, 41–63; Shackleton, *Montesquieu*, pp. 356–377; Charles Jacques Beyer, "Montesquieu et la censure religieuse de *L'Esprit des lois*," *Revue des Sciences Humaines* 70 (1953), 105–131; Andrew J. Lynch, "Montesquieu's Ecclesiastical Critics," *Journal of the History of Ideas* 38 (1977), 487–500; Claude Lauriol, "La Condamnation de *L'Esprit des lois* dans les archives de la Congrégation de l'Index," in Catherine Larrère (ed.), *Montesquieu, œuvre ouverte? (1748–1755)* (Naples: Liguori; Oxford: Voltaire Foundation, 2005), pp. 91–114. For Montesquieu's methodology in the *Defense*, see Catherine Larrère, "La Défense de *L'Esprit des lois* et les 'sciences humaines'," in *ibid.*, pp. 115–130.

For Montesquieu on religion, see Robert Shackleton, "La religion de Montesquieu," in *Actes du Congrès Montesquieu réuni à Bordeaux*, pp. 287–294; Marc Régaldo, *Montesquieu et la religion* (Bordeaux: Académie Montesquieu, 1998); Rebecca Kingston, "Montesquieu on Religion and on the Question of Toleration," in Carrithers *et al.*, *Montesquieu's Science of Politics*, pp. 375–408; Diana Schaub, "Of Believers and Barbarians: Montesquieu's Enlightened Toleration," in Alan Levine (ed.), *Early Modern Skepticism and the Origins of Toleration* (Lanham, MD: Lexington Books, 1999), pp. 115–147; Lorenzo Bianchi, "Histoire et nature: la religion dans *L'Esprit des lois*," in Michel Porret and Catherine Volpilhac-Auger (eds.), *Le Temps de Montesquieu: Actes du Colloque international de Genève (28–31 octobre 1998)* (Geneva: Droz, 2002), pp. 289–304; Keegan Callanan, "*Une infinité de biens*: Montesquieu on Religion and Free Government," *History of Political Thought* 35(4) (2014), 739–767; Callanan, *Montesquieu's Liberalism and the Problem of Universal Politics* (Cambridge: Cambridge University Press, 2018), pp. 175–204; Thomas Pangle, *The Theological Basis of Liberal Modernity in Montesquieu's "Spirit of the Laws"* (Chicago: University of Chicago Press, 2010).

For Montesquieu and Spinoza, see Paul Vernière, *Spinoza et la pensée française avant la Révolution*, 2 vols. (Paris: Presses Universitaires de France, 1954), II, pp. 447–465; Shackleton, *Montesquieu*, pp. 251–264; Sheila Mason, *Montesquieu's Idea of Justice* (The Hague: Martinus Nijhoff, 1975), pp. 246–253 and *passim*; Jonathan Israel, *Radical Enlightenment: Philosophy and the Making of Modernity, 1650–1750* (Oxford: Oxford University Press, 2001), pp.159–174 and *passim*. For Montesquieu and Bayle, see Robert Shackleton, "Bayle and Montesquieu," in Paul Dibon (ed.), *Pierre Bayle, le philosophe de Rotterdam* (Amsterdam: Elsevier, 1959), pp. 142–149; Robert C. Bartlett, "On the Politics of Faith and Reason: The Project of Enlightenment in Pierre Bayle and Montesquieu," *Journal of Politics* 63(1) (2001), 1–28; Lorenzo Bianchi, "'L'Auteur a loué Bayle, en l'appelant un grand homme': Bayle dans la *Défense de l'Esprit des lois*," in *Montesquieu œuvre ouverte?* pp. 103–130; Israel, *Radical Enlightenment*, pp. 331–341 and *passim*; Lorenzo Bianchi, "Atheism," in *DM*; Bianchi, "Bayle," in *DM*.

271

Index